The Balanced Company

The Balanced Company

A Theory of Corporate Integrity

MUEL KAPTEIN AND JOHAN WEMPE

OXFORD
UNIVERSITY PRESS

OXFORD
UNIVERSITY PRESS

Great Clarendon Street, Oxford OX2 6DP

Oxford University Press is a department of the University of Oxford.
It furthers the University's objective of excellence in research, scholarship,
and education by publishing worldwide in

Oxford New York

Auckland Bangkok Buenos Aires Cape Town Chennai
Dar es Salaam Delhi Hong Kong Istanbul Karachi Kolkata
Kuala Lumpur Madrid Melbourne Mexico City Mumbai Nairobi
São Paulo Shanghai Singapore Taipei Tokyo Toronto
with an associated company in Berlin

Oxford is a registered trade mark of Oxford University Press
in the UK and in certain other countries

Published in the United States
by Oxford University Press Inc., New York

British Library Cataloguing in Publication Data
Data available

Library of Congress Cataloging in Publication Data

Kaptein, Muel.
   The balanced company : a theory of corporate integrity / Muel Kaptein and
   Johan Wempe
      p. cm.
   Includes bibliographical references and index.
   1. Business ethics.   2. Integrity. I. Wempe, Johan Ferdinand Dietrich Bernardus, 1952–
   II. Title.
   HF5387 .K353   2002   174'.4—dc21   2002025042

ISBN 0–19–925550–4 (hbk.)
ISBN 0–19–925551–2 (pbk.)

1 3 5 7 9 10 8 6 4 2

Typeset by Newgen Imaging systems (P) Ltd, Chennai, India
Printed in Great Britain
on acid-free paper by
T.J. International Ltd., Padstow, Cornwall

ACKNOWLEDGEMENTS

We would like to extend our thanks to a number of people. Without the commentary we gratefully received from our colleagues, this book would have been significantly less balanced. We would like to thank professors Tom Donaldson, Thomas Dunfee, Eduard Kimman, Henk van Luijk, George Molenkamp, Rob van Tulder, Cees Veerman, Co van der Wal, and Philip Wallage. Gratitude is due also to Jan van Dalen, Juup Essers, Andre Nijhof, and three anonymous reviewers for their critical remarks. We thank Pursey Heugens and Hans van Oosterhout for their inspiring contributions to the classification of the contractual problems and principles in Chapter 6. Thanks also to Ben Wempe for his critical ideas on the application of the social contract concept to the corporate domain and to professor Theo van Willigenburg, for his insights on the integrity concept. In Chapter 3, we made use of the gripping account Edmond Offner shared with us of his ascent of Mount Everest. Shell (in the person of Tom Delfgaauw and Tim van Kooten) and KPN (in the person of Han ten Broeke and Otto Kuis) we thank for the opportunity to consult them and to write down our "common" experience. Thanks also to Chris Togliatti for his proofing work and to Friedl Marincowitz for editing the final manuscript. Finally, we would like to thank David Musson from Oxford University Press for his assistance and confidence in this book, and Jaap ten Wolde, senior partner at KPMG Ethics & Integrity Consulting, for sponsoring this project.

Muel Kaptein and Johan Wempe
www.ethicsmanagement.org

CONTENTS

LIST OF FIGURES

LIST OF TABLES

ABOUT THE AUTHORS

Dr Muel Kaptein and Dr Johan Wempe have been active as consultants in the field of corporate ethics, integrity, social responsibility, and compliance since the early 1990s. They assist profit and non-profit organizations in developing and implementing business codes by providing training sessions, conducting integrity audits, and setting up compliance processes. Muel Kaptein and Johan Wempe are respectively senior manager and partner at KPMG Ethics & Integrity, which they co-founded in 1995. Johan is co-developer of the ethics game "Cards on the Table." Muel has also developed "The Integrity Thermometer," which has since been used to review a large number of organizations. They have facilitated the development of business codes for many companies. In addition, they also assisted Shell in developing its very first sustainability report in 1998 and have been verifiers of subsequent reports. Both teach business ethics at Erasmus University, Rotterdam. Muel is director of Ethicon, the Center for Ethics Management at Erasmus University. Papers by the authors have appeared in the *Journal of Business Ethics, Business Ethics, Corporate Reputation Review, Journal of Corporate Citizenship*, and *European Management Journal*.

Invitation to Dialogue

Business ethics is fast becoming business as usual. With a few exceptions, all core US corporations have a business code of ethics and almost half of the top Western European corporations have a code of conduct. A code provides answers to fundamental questions. What do we stand for? What are our primary responsibilities? What values do we share? What is, and what is not done? More specifically, a code formulates corporate policy, for example with regard to the acceptance of gifts, the private use of corporate property, and the use of confidential information. Corporations employ an increasing number of measures to institutionalize their codes. They often utilize the code in performance appraisals, introduction programs for novices, and in contracts with suppliers. The appointment of an ethics officer is no longer uncommon and serves as a focal point for employees to share dilemmas and report irregularities. Since the mid-nineties, an increasing number of corporations publishes an annual ethics report to communicate to stakeholders the extent to which the code is implemented in practice. Information is disclosed, for example, about employee awareness of the code, the measures that are in place to prevent human rights violations, the promotion of fair business practices, and the steps that are taken to avoid internal discriminatory practices. An ethics report can also contain information about a company's environmental performance, labor standards, legal transgressions, and flawed products launched on the market.

THE BUSINESS CASE FOR ETHICS

The attention corporations are paying to ethics is driven by more than idealism and a sense of duty; it is often also motivated by enlightened self-interest. For instance, good corporate ethics keeps employees from vandalizing company property and minimizes legal fees in the event that an employee is found guilty of violating the law. It also wards off bad press if a corporation inflicts damage upon someone or something. In addition, sound corporate ethics can improve a corporation's public image, empower its stakeholders, and boost profits. Hence, the ethics of business is business. It would, however, be a misconception simply to equate business ethics with the optimization of corporate profits. The role of ethics is not merely instrumental. It is, after all, possible to conceive of situations where ethical decisions come at the cost of profits. A refusal to pay bribes to corrupt politicians, officials, or buyers, for example, can lead to forfeiting profitable assignments. Similarly, great sums of money may be involved in acquiring energy-efficient technology to protect the environment. It thus follows that ethics is not simply business in the sense of maximizing profits. Business ethics is legitimate in itself and appeals to corporations to conduct business in an ethical manner. This is not to suggest that good business is simply about maximizing stakeholder interests, either. To the extent that stakeholder interests offer important leads for making ethically sound decisions, good business practice does coincide with stakeholder interest maximization. Nevertheless, stakeholder interest maximization is not always synonymous with morally desirable decisions. Sometimes, it may be justified to give priority to one stakeholder group over stakeholder interest maximization. Take the example of a female candidate who stands out head and shoulders above other applicants for the position of new head of production. Should particularly male employees be averse to having a woman in a leadership position, a conflict arises between the ethical principles "appointment on the basis of merit" and "gender equality" and the sentiments expressed by her potential colleagues. If the female candidate is appointed on the basis of ethical convictions, total employee satisfaction may decrease and staff turnover could increase, leading to an overall decline in productivity of the department. Accordingly, ethical business sometimes demands respect for individual stakeholder rights irrespective of whether the greater sum of interests is satisfied. It is particularly in this field of tension between the corporate interest, the general interest, and the interests of individual stakeholders that the kind of ethics business stands for, becomes manifest. On the one hand, business ethics is about realizing the interests of stakeholders. On the other hand, it is about finding a balance when these interests cannot be simultaneously realized. For this reason, many business codes indicate what employees are strictly prohibited from doing, which stakeholder rights should always be protected, and which ambitions the corporation has with respect to different stakeholders. Many business codes also contain guidelines for resolving dilemmas. It is not only in the interest of corporations to achieve a balance in the face of conflicting demands—it is also an ethical responsibility. Therefore, the business of business is ethical business.

IN SEARCH OF SOUND THEORIES

Ethical business practice requires sound business ethical theories. The business community has no interest in quick fixes or impractical theories. On the contrary, it has a profound interest in theories that reflect an understanding of the role of business and in criteria that are formulated on this basis. Moreover, if business ethics theory seeks a productive and lasting place in business and academia, a solid theoretical foundation is essential. So, what business ethical theories exist and what is their quality?

At the dawn of the twenty-first century, a diverse range of themes and theories characterizes business ethical literature. Debate between the different theoretical perspectives and theoretical refinement is increasingly taking place and different streams of thought are gradually emerging. Some groups of business ethicists adopt general ethical approaches such as consequentialism, Kantian ethics, or virtue ethics and attempt to apply these to the corporate domain. Highly promising are those approaches that are developed specifically for corporations. These include the corporate social contract approach (Donaldson and Dunfee), a corporate virtue theory (Solomon), the organizational climate school of thought (which can be traced back to Victor and Cullen), and the corporate sustainability approach (Elkington). Since these "corporate-specific" approaches take the corporate context into account, their impact on business and organizational theory is much greater than that of the more general approaches.

As an academic discipline, business ethics is still in its infancy. As a field of research, it found its academic footing as recently as the outset of the 1980s. Its relative immaturity can also be explained by the composition of the academic business ethics community. Business ethics is essentially a hybrid of two disciplines: business administration and ethics. Although grounded in philosophical theory, it also has its roots in the applied sciences. An inherent risk for business ethics is that too much emphasis is placed on one of the two disciplines. The challenge for business ethics is to balance business and ethics. Developing ethical concepts and theories that are completely removed from reality is undesirable as they can easily be rejected as naive and unrealistic. The dominance of the practical perspective should, needless to say, also be avoided. Business ethical questions are often very fundamental and require thorough deliberation. To address the tension between either practice becoming the norm or the norm losing its effectiveness in practice, we need sound business ethical theories. Business ethics thereby fulfils both the role of plaintiff (in indicating what should be done or could have been done differently) and defender (in signaling what is being done properly, which can therefore be defended). Business ethics involves more than creating (generally high) expectations of corporations—it also places limits on what can reasonably be expected from corporations. A continuous cross-pollination between the spheres of philosophy/ethics, business administration, and actual business practice is therefore imperative for constructing fruitful business ethical theories.

In this book we seek to further explore and strengthen the intersection of these three spheres with a view to offering a sound theoretical foundation for the practice of business ethics. We believe that our academic background in business administration and philosophy/theology and our joint experience as part-time ethics and integrity consultants for a decade equip us well to make a meaningful contribution to the field of business ethics. We hope that others will respond to our work with as much enthusiasm as we have received and responded to theirs. This book is certainly not devoid of its own pretensions. We endeavor nothing less than setting down a body of corporate ethical criteria that is suitable for universal application. With this, we invite all to enter the discussion with one another and us. This brings us to the central message of this book.

THE MESSAGE OF THIS BOOK

We believe that all corporate ethical dilemmas can be related back to three fundamental fields of tension that are characteristic of the corporate domain. We use the metaphor of "hands" to capture their essence. First, there is the problem of dirty hands. When corporations have to choose between conflicting, though legitimate, expectations of stakeholders, it has to dirty its hands. That is, the corporation has to infringe upon one or more stakeholder interest. Second, a host of problems can arise as a result of the fact that corporations consist of a multitude of "hands." Where corporations consist of more than one actor, imperfect coordination can lead to responsibilities for the whole getting lost. Third, the problem of entangled hands refers to a situation where the individual interests of representatives of a corporation are at odds with organizational interests.

Organizations should not only acknowledge the existence of these three problems they should also resolve them and institutionalize their solutions. Our contribution is to develop ethical criteria that are relevant for such a balancing process. On the basis of the three general ethical theories, we draw a distinction between stakeholder benefits, behavioral principles, and organizational qualities. Stakeholder benefits refer to the stakeholder interests that the corporation strives towards (the ambitions of the corporation). Behavioral principles are guidelines for conduct. Ethical qualities are characteristics that the corporation should possess to stimulate employees to come to a careful resolution of dilemmas.

The notion of integrity takes up central-stage in this book. This is, on the one hand, because of the concept's flexibility, and, on the other, because it enables us to set down absolute requirements corporations should meet. Integrity is a concept that establishes a connection between the three general ethical theories. The integrity of a corporation is localized in efforts, conduct, and outcomes. Should dilemmas stand in the way of achieving optimal results, the integrity of the corporation (wholeness, integration) can remain intact on the condition that its input and actions meet a number of requirements. On the basis of inductive and deductive research, we present a set of principles and a set of qualities that

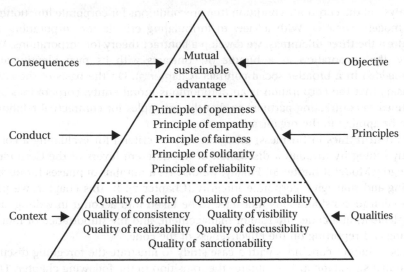

Fig. 0.1. The Corporate Integrity Model.

apply to the three fundamental dilemmas. Figure 0.1 depicts the Corporate Integrity Model that we develop and provide arguments for in this book.

The criteria we distill can be used for developing codes of practice, implementing ethics in an organization, and monitoring and auditing the ethics of corporations. While these criteria are universal and realistic, they also allow for a pluralistic approach.

STRUCTURE

This book engages with business and ethics in three parts. The first problematizes the field of business ethics, and the second provides the theoretical foundation for the ethics of business. The last part formulates practical applications based on the preceding analyses and arguments.

Part I (Business Ethics) describes the rise of business ethics in practice. General misconceptions about the field are discussed (Chapter 1) and a summary of common ethical theories is presented (Chapter 2). Part I concludes with a discussion of the concept of integrity.

Part II (Ethics of Business) commences with the question whether the notion of integrity is applicable to organizations and whether an organization can be viewed as an autonomous entity (Chapter 3). Following this, a description is given of the three fundamental moral dilemmas (Chapter 4) on the basis of an analysis of the corporate condition (the preconditions for corporate functioning in modern society). With a view to formulating criteria for corporations to address the three dilemmas, we develop a contract theory for corporations. We view the corporation as a bundle of contracts with its own identity and embedded in a broader social contract (Chapter 5). On the basis of the conclusion that the corporation is an autonomous moral entity, corporations are defined as contracting partners so that the principles for contractual relations can be applied to the organization.

Part III (Ethics in Business) advances various criteria for evaluating a company's integrity through a discussion of the different layers of the Corporate Integrity Model (Chapter 6). Finally, we discuss a number of phases for developing and managing corporate integrity (Chapter 7). In this chapter, we pay attention to considerations that have to be taken into account in writing and implementing a code, the role of management, and the importance of monitoring and reporting on the effectiveness of the code.

Each chapter concludes with a case study to illustrate the foregoing discussion that simultaneously facilitates the transition to the following chapter. The Shell case is used twice. In the introduction, we discuss Shell to illuminate a number of ethical questions corporations can be confronted with as regards their policy. In the final chapter, Shell's ethics management by means of a code of business principles and a sustainability report is discussed. The case of KPN Telecom is discussed in Chapter 1 to illustrate why a corporation should be concerned with ethics. In Chapter 6, the same case shows how the integrity criteria we develop can be incorporated in a code. In Chapter 2, the case of IHC Caland illustrates the inadequacy of applying general ethical theories to the corporate domain. Chapter 3 discusses the disaster of the *Herald of Free Enterprise* so as to illustrate the autonomy model of organizations. In Chapter 4, the three dilemmas are illustrated with reference to the issue of bribery and corruption. Chapter 5 discusses the near bankruptcy of Avebe to illustrate the contract theory of corporations. Questions for class discussions and guidelines for developing cases can be found at our website: www.ethicsmanagement.org

Shell

In October 1997, Tom Delfgaauw was appointed to lead the newly founded Social Accountability Team of Shell International. At the time, Shell was facing mounting public criticism due to its operations in Nigeria; a country plagued by widespread human rights violations. Shell's reputation had already taken a severe beating with the Brent Spar oil platform it sought to sink in the ocean with permission from the British authorities. Shell's own employees even seemed to have lost faith in the company. The Social Accountability Team was assigned with the task to lead Shell's transformation process.

For decades, Shell had to cope with a constant flow of public criticism. Up until this point, Shell's response remained defensive. The company continuously pointed out its good intentions and all the positive contributions it made. This attitude underwent a significant shift. The message that is being conveyed just a few years later is that the Shell of the future is one that will maintain a constant dialogue with civil society representatives. The Social Accountability Team supports this dialogue by publishing an annual report (since 1998) on how Shell goes about fulfilling the obligations formulated in the Shell Business Principles.

The company

The Royal Dutch/Shell Group was created in 1907 out of the merger between Koninklijke Olie and the Shell Transport and Trading Company. All activities of the two companies were merged. The original companies became two holding companies with ownership being split between Koninklijke Olie (60 per cent) and Shell Transport and Trading (40 per cent). Shell's operating units are now active in more than 130 countries. They are supported by five business organizations: Exploration and Production, Oil Products, Chemicals, Gas and Coal, and Renewables. The North American Shell Petroleum Inc. is subject to a different set of rules. Although it is controlled by the two holding companies, it owns Shell Oil Company USA that is responsible for all operations in North America. The Committee of Managing Directors (CMD) heads the Group and each operating company is run by a General Manager. In countries where multiple Shell companies are active, a Country Chairman represents them in the Group.

Issues

Shell has a great impact on the communities where it is active. This is due to the major strategic importance of oil, its great role in our daily lives, and the sheer size of the company. Its visible presence in virtually every country around the globe and its susceptibility to consumer campaigns makes Shell a prime target for activists. For years, the eyes of a whole range of social groupings have been focused on Shell. Some main issues include Shell's presence in the former Rhodesia and South Africa, its role in Nigeria, and the conflict with Greenpeace on whether to sink the defunct Brent Spar oil platform. At the end of the 1990s, Shell's possible participation in projects in Chad and Cameroon also received a lot of attention.

Southern Africa

At the end of the 1960s and the beginning of the 1970s, the former Rhodesia was locked in a fierce and bloody independence struggle. During this period the UN announced a boycott of its oil and oil products. At the time, Shell was accused of collaborating with efforts to evade the boycott—an allegation Shell always categorically denied.

Nevertheless, Southern Africa remained an albatross around Shell's neck, even after Rhodesia freed itself of white minority rule and the country was renamed

Zimbabwe. Shell's presence in South Africa during the Apartheid years was widely condemned by social groupings. The white minority government employed an extensive and severely oppressive state apparatus to enforce its Apartheid ideology. The protests against Shell turned nasty when people sabotaged gas stations and disrupted general stockholders' meetings. The UN also proclaimed an embargo on the supply of oil and oils products to South Africa. Economic pressure was viewed as the most effective measure to oust the government and bring an end to its abominable human rights abuses.

Critics perceived Shell's mere presence in the former Rhodesia and South Africa as support for the oppressive regimes. Their taxes contributed to the economy and thus provided sustenance to the ruling governments. Shell's response to this criticism was generally dismissive. According to Shell, it made use of opportunities during the 1980s to persuade the South African white minority government to reform the political system and even collaborated with the opposition behind the scenes. Shell was of the opinion that its presence was generally having a positive effect on South African society. Pulling out would not have brought the necessary change, as another company, possibly one with a less critical view of the government, could simply have taken its place.

Another issue concerned the fact that racial discrimination was institutionalized in the legal system. Operating in South Africa therefore meant being legally obliged to partake in discriminatory practices. In its defense, Shell maintained that it used all devices at its disposal (for example, a sound human resources policy) to avoid the segregation of blacks and whites on its premises. In some areas, it even transgressed the law. According to Shell, it also invested large sums of money in education and healthcare specifically aimed at the black population.

Another point of critique concerned the UN oil sanctions Shell allegedly obstructed. The Shipping Research Bureau, established by the Southern Africa Committee and the Christian Kairos Task Force, conducted meticulous investigations into the country's evasion of the boycott. The role that Shell played in this—one repeatedly cited—was emphatically denied by Shell. As the corporation stated in its brochure *Shell and South Africa*, "The reality is that not one single Shell company outside South Africa sells or supplies crude oil or oil products to South Africa. There is not one single Shell company that knowingly sells crude oil to third parties who are of the intention to sell such oil to South Africa—whether directly or indirectly." According to Shell International it was keeping to the UN sanctions like it was supposed to. Yet, Shell International refused to take any responsibility for Shell South Africa's actions in connection with the UN embargo. Criticism of Shell abated when general political reforms were signaled at the end of the 1980s and beginning of the 1990s. Democratic elections and the end of the Apartheid regime were in sight.

Nigeria

At the beginning of 1993, Shell in Nigeria was drawn into a conflict between the Ogoni people and the central Nigerian government. In a remote corner of Nigeria, the Ogonis, a people of about half a million (and just one of Nigeria's 250 ethnic groups) started a fierce battle against the oil Group.

Shell has been active in Nigeria since the late 1940s when Nigeria was still a British colony. The Nigerian government has a controlling interest in the company while Shell is responsible for its operations. The Shell Petroleum Development Company (SPDC) in Nigeria is one of Shell's largest operating companies: 350 million barrels of oil were produced in Nigeria in 1994; Shell's share accounts for an estimated 10 billion barrels. Over and above this, Nigerian oil is not only of an extremely high quality but it is also easy to extract.

The Ogonis occupy one of the richest oil regions in Nigeria. Their homeland lies exactly between two key oil cities, Port Harcourt and Warri, which is situated further inland. Shell has eight oil fields in this area and some 200 wells. A network of underground pipes largely links the reserves and during the extraction process, oil is burnt off at the surface. Not only does this procedure damage and pollute the environment, worn out pipes and sabotage of the pipe system cause leaks, also taking its toll on the natural environment.

The Ogoni people are poverty-stricken and subsist from farming and fishing. The leaking pipes have polluted their water and have rendered a substantial section of their land no longer fit for use. Moreover, the Ogonis see precious little of the proceeds from the oil that is extracted from the land they inhabit. Due to the sharp drop in oil prices, oil revenues declined dramatically. The government is dependent on oil for 80 per cent of its revenue and instead of curbing its own expenditure, it stopped allocating funds to its various ethnic groups. The Ogonis are one of the ethnic groups in Nigeria that do not receive a cent from the oil revenues, despite the fact that they literally live on top of the reserves and are subject to the dangers of Shell's operations there. In 1990, Ken Saro-Wiwa founded MOSOP, the Movement for the Survival of the Ogoni People. Saro-Wiwa succeeded in drawing a lot of international attention to the plight of the Ogoni people. According to Saro-Wiwa, Shell was the guilty party. Even though the Nigerian government has a controlling interest in Shell Nigeria, it was due to the revenue that Shell generated that the government could remain in power. Moreover, since Shell was responsible for all local operations, it was to blame for polluting the environment and refusing to compensate the Ogoni people. Shell interpreted the situation quite differently. In a company memo it stated that "The major emphasis of the activists now appears to lie on garnering international recognition for the problems of the oil-producing areas by using the press and pressure groups . . . This entails a risk for Shell." Shell made clear that it was aware of the environmental risks involved in leaking pipelines, oil spills, and flaring. According to Shell, concerted efforts were being made to minimize damage and compensation was offered for damage that did occur. Shell also maintained that it was cleaning up its environmental pollution. The incidence of sabotage posed a problem of a different nature. It was well known that the local population delib-erately damaged the pipelines to obtain compensation for damage to their land. During the course of 1993 the protests against Shell and the Nigerian govern-ment turned increasingly violent. The Nigerian government responded with force and gross human rights abuses. The situation for the company's employees was anything but safe, which resulted in Shell suspending operations in Ogoniland.

Ken Saro-Wiwa and eight other MOSOP leaders were arrested and sentenced to death for attempting to undermine the state. Shortly before the executions,

Shell appealed to the Nigerian president to pardon the nine prisoners. In November 1995, all nine were executed none the less. The public outrage was overwhelming and Shell also came under fire. The general perception was that Saro-Wiwa was arrested for protesting against Shell. Shell's request for amnesty came too late and was consequently regarded as lacking credibility.

The Brent Spar

Another incident that unleashed strong emotions was the Brent Spar affair. The Brent Spar was a floating oil storage and transfer installation that became redundant after years of service in oil extraction in the North Sea. After years of research and lengthy consultations with the UK government, it was decided to dispose of the platform in the Atlantic Ocean. Greenpeace found it unacceptable and launched a campaign in Western Europe to prevent Shell from executing its plan. According to Greenpeace, the Brent Spar harbored a "deadly chemical cocktail" of more than 100 tons of toxic sludge with oil residues and cadmium, lead, zinc, and PCB-containing fluids. They also claimed that the platform contained 30 tons of radioactive waste. To sink the Brent Spar would have spelt disaster for the environment the moment the construction began to corrode and leak. Greenpeace also claimed that compared to the potential costs of dismantling the installation, Shell was getting rid of the Brent Spar for a pittance. Shell dismissed all accusations, since to its knowledge, more than 90 per cent of the sludge consisted of sand; the remaining 10 per cent consisting of oil residues and negligibly small amounts of heavy metals. Moreover, the Brent Spar was to sink to a place so deep that no life was possible in its vicinity. The small levels of toxic materials that might escape would thus have had no effect on the environment whatsoever. According to Shell, all other methods for decommissioning the Brent Spar posed even greater risks. Bringing the colossus to shore for dismantling would have significantly increased the risk of an accident.

Demonstrations by Greenpeace intensified when the operation to tow the Brent Spar to its final resting-place was set in motion. Its efforts took on the guise of a major spectacle as members of Greenpeace boarded a tugboat and occupied the platform. With this gesture, Greenpeace appealed to the public to boycott Shell. The success of the campaign was so great that even German government officials publicly turned against Shell. At the very last moment, in June 1995, Shell decided not to sink the Brent Spar. Instead, the monster was towed to a Norwegian fjord. In the wake of extensive consultation with a variety of social interest groups, the Brent Spar was dismantled and part of it incorporated into a wharf as a kind of monument.

By that time, the grounds for Greenpeace's accusations of the Brent Spar's toxic content were being investigated. Various test results showed that Greenpeace was wrong. There was no evidence to substantiate their claims. For Shell, however, something seemed to have gone seriously wrong. Society at large appeared to have lost faith in Shell and the perception prevailed that the corporation was motivated solely by financial gain. People, it seems, are largely driven by sentiment. If the government requests citizens to act in an environmentally responsible manner by, for instance, separating domestic waste, a multinational company that considers dumping redundant materials in the ocean comes across as anything but trustworthy.

From defensiveness to dialogue

All the issues Shell was confronted with generated a considerable amount of conflict. Shell's response to critics' calls to account for its conduct was consistently defensive. The standard response seemed to consist of a denial of the facts and giving an account of its good intentions. After the Brent Spar debacle, it became clear that this approach was no longer effective. Shell spent more than 4 billion dollars a year on meeting environmental requirements. This included preparing reports on its environmental performance, conducting research, and consulting with the relevant authorities. It seemed that all an action group had to do to gain widespread public support was to make accusations, even if it lacked solid scientific evidence.

Something was so fundamentally amiss that despite the evidence in support of its original decision, Shell's damaged reputation could not be rectified. The public had lost faith in Shell to the extent that everything Shell said was regarded with mistrust. To change this, the public had to be convinced that Shell cared about more than financial gain. It was (and is) after all, also in Shell's interest to see to it that social issues are adequately dealt with. To rebuild the trust it had lost, Shell had to demonstrate that it takes the well-being of society seriously and therefore also the representatives of social interests.

The issues that fueled the heated public debate all share a number of common features. First, none of these issues is either black or white. Instead, there are a lot of gray areas that require taking all parties seriously and weighing up various stakeholder rights and interests. Each of the perspectives is valid to a greater or lesser extent. For instance, while it might not be desirable for Shell to get mixed up in local politics, it is unacceptable for it to stand by and watch while the government commits gross human rights violations. The difficult question is at what point the violation of human rights merits getting involved. Is it legitimate for a company to make political statements or to undertake political action?

What is also relevant is that these questions concern social issues in which Shell was just one of several role-players. Yet, Shell was considered to be the culprit and therefore the chief party responsible. The Nigerian government is corrupt and has a poor human rights record. The Nigerian people are unable to solve their problems alone but not even the international community has a solution at hand. What role could Shell play? The public demands good products at low prices. We also like going on vacation to far away places. And that requires fuel. Yet, when it comes to addressing environmental pollution and degradation, all eyes turn to major corporations like Shell. It should be clear that the answers to these questions will be more than just technical in nature. The problems are complex and so are the possible solutions. They have much to do with the actual choices consumers make along with the role that oil companies could play.

An important step in the direction of solving dilemmas of this nature is for a corporation to articulate its commitments clearly and work together with social factions that represent public interests. In this way, it may be possible to find solutions that have society's full support.

Issues

The problems Shell was confronted with and the ensuing transformation process it embarked upon evoke a number of ethical questions:

- Which actions qualify as corporate actions? If Shell South Africa defies the UN embargo and decides to uphold South African law instead, is Shell as a whole to blame? The Shell group has a minority interest in Shell Nigeria whereas the Nigerian government has the final say. Is Shell still responsible for local operations? Can the actions of Shell Nigeria be attributed to Shell? Shell has a minority interest in Chad, whereas Exxon is responsible for local operations. Are we justified in blaming Shell for whatever the joint venture undertakes in Chad?
- Shell's latitude depends on a great many role-players: stockholders, employees, partners, governments, the consumers, social factions, and public opinion. How far does Shell's responsibility reach? What is the nature of the moral responsibility resting on a corporation like Shell? Where does its responsibility begin and where does it end? Shell certainly cannot be held responsible for all of society's problems. It would therefore be useful to draw a distinction between demands that can and cannot be made of Shell. Expectations do not always imply like obligations.
- Should Shell develop a model for sharing responsibilities with social group-ings, it signals an acknowledgement of its role in finding a solution to social issues of which it is a part. In order to share the responsibility, reliable informa-tion is necessary for dialogue. How can a company objectively account for its social, environmental, and ethical performance? How far should one go in providing information? Is it financially viable for a company to make this information available?
- What is the source of the criteria for evaluating corporate performance? Is this something that can simply be drawn up with a selection of stakeholder representatives?
- Shell is unable to sit down at the round table with everyone. Which stake-holders should be invited? The selection of stakeholders is, after all, up to the company. And how frank can one be towards certain stakeholders during the dialogue?
- How do we deal with dilemmas? Dilemmas require making a choice in favor of some stakeholders over and above others. What is the best way to explain such choices and what criteria can we formulate for this purpose?
- What other instruments does Shell have at its disposal for clarifying its position and actions? Is a corporate code a valuable instrument? Would it be productive to annually report to stakeholders on the extent to which the code

is honored? What are the risks involved? What should such a code and the corresponding report look like? And what would be the most appropriate development process to this end?

These are some of the issues—which are more or less relevant to other companies as well—we shall be focusing on in this book. In Chapter 7, we discuss how Shell has dealt with the issues above.

BUSINESS ETHICS

1

Why Business Ethics?

A broad range of issues in the corporate domain contains an ethical dimension. Incidents that increasingly attract wide media coverage coupled with the search for a guilty party to blame for unethical behavior occur in all branches of industry, types of corporations, professions, and jobs. Similar affairs afflict governmental and other non-profit organizations.

In the economic sphere, we have examples such as the collapse of the Bank of Credit and Commerce International (BCCI) when it turned out that the bank had concealed enormous financial losses with a complex system of fraudulent transactions. We may also recall the Wall Street insider trading scandals during the 1980s that centered on Michael Milken and Drexel Burnham Lambert. Nor can anyone forget the demise of Barings Bank's independent existence after Nick Leeson gambled away millions of dollars in the derivatives trade. Then there was the undoing of the energy giant Enron in 2001 when it came to light that the company's profits were artificially inflated (through a complex network of partnership, for example) and that managers cashed in millions of dollars of stocks shortly before the company collapsed (such as chairman Ken Lay who sold stocks worth USD 37,683,887).

As to the environment, we can cite accidents such as the Exxon Valdez oil spill that polluted a large part of the Alaskan coast, where seabird deaths climbed from 28,000 to 580,000 in two years' time. In Europe, we had the fire at the Sandoz chemical plant in Basle that sent a toxic wave down the River Rhine, killing much of its wildlife. And in the Indian subcontinent, we witnessed the explosion at the Union Carbide plant in Bhopal that killed 3,800 people and injured up to half a million with its toxic emissions. And who can forget the 1986 nuclear power disaster in Chernobyl, which resulted in over 30 instantaneous deaths, 200 seriously injured radiation victims, and subsequently, according to estimates, some 5,000 cancer-related deaths.

Other incidents also had a high impact on society. These include the explosion of the Space Shuttle *Challenger*, where the entire crew perished before the eyes of millions of spectators and the shipping disasters of the *Herald of Free Enterprise* and the *Estonia*, where 193 and 852 people respectively lost their lives. During the 1990s, Nike faced fierce accusations of using child labor. Last, but not least, the case of the Swiss firm Nestlé's powdered milk also received wide coverage. Its use in developing countries by illiterate mothers who lacked access to clean water and sterilized bottles had disastrous consequences for millions of babies.

This chapter gives an exposition of what business ethics is all about. We start with a description of the integrity management approach, which advances an integrated and balanced perspective on business ethics. Then we discuss three historically ambiguous moral intuitions regarding the appropriateness of ethics within corporations. A discussion of significant social developments explains the need for ethics in the corporate context. Finally, we present our view on the academic role of business ethics by paying attention to the relativism–universalism debate in ethics. The KPN case at the end of the chapter gives an account of the factors that stimulated this corporation to embark on an ethics project and how it went about deciding which route to follow to improve its corporate ethics.

A BALANCED VIEW ON BUSINESS ETHICS

Table 1.1 provides an overview of the features of a one-sided view on business ethics, as opposed to a balanced view on business ethics.[1] These and other features of business ethics will be worked out in this book. In this section, we give a concise overview of the two approaches.

Whenever unethical business practices such as those described above are revealed the public is quick to pass harsh judgment. The response is usually one of widespread outrage and disbelief. Outsiders are unlikely to investigate the context within which these kinds of incidents occur. Instead, they tend to want to single out someone to blame. It is generally assumed that the corporation or the employees involved were conscious of their unacceptable or criminal behavior and that they simply hoped that the press or the public would not find them out. At first glance, these kinds of incidents seem to be a matter for criminal law: by catching the culprit, the transgression can be redressed. Following this line of thought, a stern hand and heavy sanctions seem to offer the most suitable reprisal. Sometimes, less-severe steps may be considered such as a re-education program for putting offenders back on the right track. Not only outsiders hold such views; even managers in organizations tend to downplay bad decisions or abuses as mere incidents. They are inclined to regard these incidents as an unfortunate coincidence (i.e. bad luck) or the inevitable result of employees with evil intentions.[2] Management often assumes that such incidents can be resolved by singling out a guilty party and taking the necessary steps to punish or bring the individual back on track. In extreme situations, management will simply fire the employee. Here, the notion prevails that discarding the proverbial "rotten apple" or "cutting out the bad spots" can remedy the situation. In keeping with this line of thinking, business ethics as a management and an academic discipline focuses solely on coming up with explanations

Table 1.1. Two views on business ethics

One-sided view on business ethics		Balanced view on business ethics
1. Focus on bad practices	→ → →	Good practices *too*
2. Focus on major sensational issues	→ → →	Minor daily issues at all corporate levels *too*
3. Focus on the ethics of people and individuals (apple theory)	→ → →	Crux of the context and circumstances (barrel theory) *too*
4. Reactive and defensive stance toward ethical issues	→ → →	Proactive *too*
5. Focus on compliance with the law	→ → →	Positively driven responsible conduct *too*
6. Focus on black and white situations	→ → →	Ethical dilemmas (gray situations) *too*
7. Focus on consequences	→ → →	On intentions and processes *too*
8. Ethics is seen as immutable or as a fact	→ → →	Can be improved (ethical behavior can be learned and structured) *too*
9. Focus on sanctions for transgressors	→ → →	Learning from transgressions *too*
10. Attention to ethics from the perspective of preventing discrediting incidents	→ → →	Attention from the perspective of aims, ambitions, and excellence *too*
11. Attention to ethics during good times (in a financial sense)	→ → →	Attention during bad times *too*
12. Subjective or relative ethical standards	→ → →	Inter-subjective and even universal standards *too*
13. Ethics as framework within which core business can be realized	→ → →	Core business *too*
14. Attention to ethics in reaction to incidents	→ → →	Systematic attention *too*
15. Attention to ethics by employees	→ → →	Especially by managers *too*

for types of behavior that are unacceptable, for imposing the right sanctions, and developing education and re-education programs for present and future business people.[3]

The question is whether these incidents can be ascribed to the evil intentions among a few employees. The "rotten-apple approach" set out above (i.e. paying attention only to those individuals who deliberately do wrong)[4] prevents us from gaining adequate insight into how these types of abuses occur and how they can subsequently be evaluated and managed. People inside and outside corporations are generally reluctant to pose moral questions at a contextual or organizational level. From this point of view, the framework in which the abuse took place does not warrant attention, since doing so would only take time and complicate matters further. Moreover, examining the context might lead to the conclusion that others can also be blamed for not correcting the problem or the wrongdoer in time.

The likelihood of an offence being repeated in the rotten-apple approach is great. A more balanced view on business ethics would also take the context of people's actions (known as the "barrel" or "context" approach) into consideration.[5] Besides being able to find a possible explanation for an employee's misconduct (and an answer to the question as to why rotten apples tend to come from the same place), it opens up an opportunity for management to guide and positively influence employee behavior. When misconduct occurs, it is insufficient to simply establish who was responsible, to what extent, and how big a price has to be paid. Such incidents also offer a learning opportunity: to determine how it happened and what improvements could be made to prevent its repetition. A balanced approach to business ethics takes both the individual and the context into account. For an effective approach to the ethics of business (from a practical/management and academic perspective), an overview of the whole picture is important.

Newspaper headlines and examples in books and articles on the ethics of business often report on the major ethical issues of particular companies or industries. Ethical questions, however, are not limited to sensational incidents. The workplace is also the scene of ethically questionable practices of a less sensational, yet more persistent and insidious, nature. These include discrimination, sexual harassment, pestering, the improper use of company equipment, the systematic use of working hours for private purposes, and conflicting sideline activities. Studies by the US Department of Commerce have shown that these forms of misconduct are not insignificant. Internal fraud in US companies amount to $40–$50 billion per year and US companies lose out on $36 billion in international business deals (since bribery is prohibited by law).[6] According to the International Labor Organization, 7.6 per cent of female professionals experience sexual harassment at work[7] and the National Council on Alcoholism and Drug Dependencies shows that US businesses lose $102 billion per year in productivity as a direct result of alcohol abuse.[8] Transparency International found that corruption leads to large welfare losses.[9] Table 1.2 below depicts a KPMG[10] study on the extent to which US citizens are aware of violations in their immediate work environment.

As already mentioned in the Shell case, and contrary to outsiders' first impressions, no situation is clear cut. If damage, loss, and suffering are the only factors taken into consideration, a company's actions can only be labeled unacceptable. Most situations, however, involve dimensions that render decision-making anything but simple or straightforward. If conflicting requirements or expectations are at play, it is impossible to satisfy each and every party. Failing to please everyone is thus unavoidable. This is very much the case if mass lay-offs are necessary to secure the continuity of the company. Marketing a product on time or at all does not always come with an absolute guarantee of product safety. The 100 per cent safe car and aircraft still have to be invented. Decisions to launch a product on the

Table 1.2. US workplace ethics violations

First hand knowledge of violations sometimes, often, or continually occurring over the past 12 months	% US employees
False/misleading promises to customers	22
Discrimination in job appointments, evaluations, promotions, etc.	22
Violation of employee rights to privacy	21
Violation of workplace health/safety rules	17
Sexual harassment	17
Carelessness with confidential/proprietary information	13
False/misleading information to public or media	10
Unfair competition (e.g. monopoly markets, disparaging competitors)	9
Activities posing a conflict of interest	9
Abuse of alcohol or drugs	8
Improper gifts/entertainment to influence others	7
Violation of environmental standards	7
Forgery of product quality/safety test results	6
Shipping product not meeting quality/safety standards	6
False/misleading information to investors or creditors	5
Forgery/improper manipulation of financials	5
Dishonesty/unfair treatment of current suppliers	5
Making false/misleading statements to regulators	5

market come down to weighing up the risks and possible damages against the benefits for the company and its customers. Even the private use of company equipment has a flip side. Why should an employee who, for example, makes regular business calls from home in the evening refrain from making personal calls from the office during the day? Is it not give and take for employees as well? The task of business ethics as a discipline is to help map out these gray areas and to unravel conflicting situations. Ethics concerns both the proper analysis of incidents in terms of underlying dilemmas and making them manageable.

Organizations easily feel overwhelmed by ethical dilemmas and—just as in the Greek myths—to see this as a test of fate. The value of business ethics as a discipline is not confined to addressing actual dilemmas or infringements. Many casebooks in the field of business ethics (to which the introduction of this chapter forms no exception) stimulate such thinking. What is more important is to determine whether and how infringements and dilemmas can be *prevented*. This is particularly relevant from a management perspective. When companies are called to account for their actions, more is at stake than simply showing that decisions regarding the dilemma were taken responsibly. It is just as important to show that a real effort was made to prevent the undesirable situation from arising. Business ethics thus focuses not only on evaluating the decisions that were made in the face of particular dilemmas. It also focuses on how the decision was made and whether any attempt was made to prevent the situation from arising in the first place.

Focusing purely on negative incidents fosters cynicism and mistrust and negates the positive contributions of business. Book titles like *Dirty Business*[11] and *Cannibals with Forks*[12] fuel this attitude. Business ethics is more than a crusade against everything that has gone awry in the corporate world. Taking this stance would be counter-productive in that it tends to bolster resistance from the business community and an even greater unwillingness to improve corporate ethics. The business ethicist is not an evangelist who keeps calling upon the business community to take the witness stand. Business ethics also illuminates the other side of business: doing the right thing right. This covers a wide spectrum, from putting preventative measures in place to realizing good things as well. It is not only motivated by opportunism but also by an inner drive to do good for the sake of goodness. Being responsible, unswerving, committed, and in harmony with stakeholders complements a prevention and repression approach. Preventing unethical practices (i.e. driven by compliance or risk-management factors) and stimulating ethical practices (i.e. driven by values or positive energy) are two dimensions of the field of business ethics.

Paying attention to ethics is important not only in times of misfortune or when abuse occurs. In good times, employees are usually less inclined to feel responsible for abuses. People also tend to regard damage as a result of carelessness and misconduct as unavoidable. However, apparently innocent habits can quickly degenerate into fraudulent practices or offenses that are more serious. Correcting an organization gone astray is always more difficult and also more costly than safeguarding its ethics in advance. Ethics is not a pursuit in times of financial prosperity alone—it is in troubled times especially that a corporation shows its true colors. Ethics is no luxury: it is the very fiber of a company. Instead of playing a marginal role, ethics is of strategic importance to an organization's future. It thus merits more than *ad hoc* attention and has to occupy the minds of management and employees continuously. Managing business ethics requires the systematic attention of management.

One of the oldest debates in ethics, which will be discussed in further detail later in this chapter, concerns the extent to which norms and values are subjective or objective, relative or absolute, particularistic or universalistic. Relativists believe that companies can define ethically correct behavior in any way they wish. Reducing ethics to a purely personal matter does not do justice to the fact that ethics is socially embedded. It also fails to appreciate the fundamental interests of people and groups that are affected by corporations' activities. As an academic discipline, business ethics is not only descriptive; it is also prescriptive in that it also articulates norms. The question that arises in this regard is to what extent universally applicable norms and values can be developed for corporations. Apart from giving an answer to which norms and values this could be (which will be returned to later), business ethics ultimately attempts to formulate norms and values that can be applied universally. Ethical debates are characterized by their participants' call for general consent. Whereas relevant stakeholders and local communities need to understand what companies are doing, companies need to acknowledge stakeholder and community expectations in order to have a constructive ethical debate.

Before we continue, we would like to pause to make an observation. This book argues for greater acceptance of the fact that in order to conduct their business, corporations often have no other choice but to dirty their hands. It is misguided to assume that all damage and suffering a company might inflict stem from bad intentions or vindictive motives. It is also unrealistic to (want to) classify companies as "moral saints" or "corporate angels."[13] Once we depart from such rigid thinking, we can morally evaluate individuals and organizations with greater understanding and compassion. Which is not to suggest that we should lower our moral expectations. This book offers an account of reasonable moral criteria for organizing corporate ethics and assessing corporate ethical performance. Companies can be expected to observe a set of universal moral criteria that goes beyond profit maximization. We therefore make a strong case for corporations to manage their ethics and set down a solid foundation on the basis of which corporations can be held accountable for their actions. This book is the outcome of a quest for reasonable and realistic ethical criteria for corporations. As a first step in that direction, we shall now examine the origins of the moral ambiguity with which corporations are regarded.

AMBIGUOUS MORAL INTUITIONS WITH RESPECT TO CORPORATIONS

The concept "business ethics" seems like a contradiction in terms. "The business of business is business" will be the likely response of both the traditionalist business person and the outside skeptic. Is it wise to burden people with responsibilities other than maximizing, or optimizing the profits of their companies? Is the risk of bankruptcy not too great if a company takes on too many responsibilities? Will we not run the risk of entrepreneurs starting to call the shots in politics?

Even people who think that corporations operate in an arena where ethical questions are not or are only minimally appropriate are extremely ambivalent about their feelings. Cases such as those discussed in the introduction to this chapter are standard fare for the press and they go beyond instances where local or international laws are actually broken. In the case of reorganizations, for example, mass lay-offs are perfectly legal, at least if proper procedures are followed. However, as soon as bad management is blamed for such a reorganization, people start thinking in terms of moral responsibility.[14]

The question of moral responsibility in the corporate domain cannot be reduced to obeying the law. Legislation often lags behind reality.[15] The rise of information technology, for example, has made it necessary to revise legislation in the area of personal privacy. Increasing internationalization has led to new international conventions such as those of the OECD and ICC. An increase in traffic accidents, for instance, has led to supplementary regulations and directives in the area of vehicle and road safety. Not all moral norms can also be translated into legislation. Such is the case when monitoring compliance is impossible.

The discussion about Shell's role in South Africa in the 1980s and Nigeria in the 1990s shows that even when a corporation's actions are legal, it does not necessarily follow that they will be accepted as moral. Shell was not criticized for violating laws. The corporation was criticized for its mere presence in these countries because it was seen as support for corrupt regimes with appalling human rights records. If we viewed the corporate world as a purely amoral arena, such criticism of Shell would have been most inappropriate. From this perspective, criticism should have been directed at the South African or Nigerian governments and not at a corporation operating within that framework.

That people find it unacceptable for corporations to hide behind laws or regimes shows that they do indeed have moral expectations of corporations. There are limits to the extent to which corporations can be held morally responsible. The proposition is often made that corporations should not meddle in politics. Corporations that do so assume more social responsibility than is good for them. ITT (International Telephone and Telegraph) was criticized at the beginning of the 1970s for allegedly having been involved in the *coup d'état* in Chile. It should be clear that if these allegations were true, the company did indeed overstep the bounds of its moral authority. It is with good reason that many corporate codes express the aim to abstain from all forms of party politics.

The commonly accepted intuitions towards and within the business world can, at the very least, be seen as ambivalent. We do hold corporations morally responsible. At the same time, we also realize that corporate responsibility is limited and special in nature. A corporation is not a being of flesh and blood but a social institution. The moral responsibility of a corporation is therefore not synonymous with that of a natural person.

The origins of moral ambiguity in the corporate domain

The ambivalence towards the moral responsibility of corporations can largely be traced back to classical and neoclassical economics. From this perspective, corporations function in a way that renders ethical questions in this domain barely appropriate or entirely inappropriate.

At least three factors have contributed to the amoral perception of business. First, the split between facts and values severed the connection between business and morality rendering it illogical to link morality with business. Second, the emphasis on functionality and efficiency, and the introduction of the specialization and scientific approach to business that is based on that emphasis, led to moral considerations within business falling into discredit. With this, moral considerations in the corporate domain came to be regarded as undesirable. A third significant factor is the notion of "equilibrium" that, partly thanks to Adam Smith, came to play a pivotal role in economic thought. The concept of balance reduces morality to a force that disrupts the economic order.

In this section, we shall examine and discuss these features of neoclassical economic thinking in more detail. We shall show that the arguments in favor of labeling the corporate context as amoral or perhaps as necessarily immoral are untenable. In support of the position that reflecting on corporate morality requires a unique frame of reference, the arguments point towards the special character of moral questions in the corporate context.

Is corporate morality logical?

The distinction between facts and values that originated in the seventeenth and eigthteenth centuries, is presumably the most fundamental obstacle to applying ethics to business. As this distinction was applied in areas such as the economic sciences, the idea came about that running a business can and should be carried out independently of morality. The focus in economics is on man as he is by nature—not on man as he could be.

In the twentieth century the distinction between facts and values received a new impulse. In his early work, the sociologist Max Weber argued for a value-free science. The positivists insisted that science should limit itself to the facts.[16] Ethics came to be seen as "pamphletology." It became, at any rate, a field which scientists (including economists) should best avoid. Modern Western society is largely a product of the logical and methodological distinction that was historically drawn between values and facts and between ethics and economics.

Is corporate morality desirable?

Contemporary Western thought is also marked by an ever-increasing emphasis on efficiency and functionality. This is partly a result of the distinction that was

---

Three historically ambiguous moral sentiments regarding business and ethics:
- corporate morality is illogical
- corporate morality is undesirable
- corporate morality is unnecessary

Fig. 1.1. Ambiguous moral sentiments.

made between facts and values and the concomitant stripping of science of values.

In his *Fable of the Bees*, a bestseller in its time, Mandeville (1705) analyzes the double morality of self-proclaimed Christian people. In his view, ethics in economics leads to grave social consequences. In the beehive, the story goes, the bees are one day seized by virtue and start leading sober lives. They avoid all pomp and circumstance and become thrifty, humble, and honest. The result is that the flourishing bee economy falls into malaise. Before this change, life is described as follows:

> Thus every part was full of vice,
> yet the whole mass a paradise;
> flatter'd in peace, and fear'd in wars,
> they were th'esteem of foreigners,
> and lavish of their wealth and lives,
> the balance of all other hives.
> Such were the blessings of that state;
> their crimes conspir'd to make them great.[17]

When the bees start to live virtuously, life in the beehive changes dramatically:

> As pride and luxury decrease,
> so by degrees they leave the seas.
> Nor merchants now, but companies
> remove whole manufactories.
> All arts and crafts neglected lie;
> content, the bane of industry,
> makes 'em admire their homely store,
> and neither seek nor covet more.[18]

The message Mandeville conveys with his fable is that prosperity and moral values are mutually exclusive. For Mandeville, a society that applies Christian virtues in practice is bound to lapse into decline.

Moral values are reserved for the personal arena that is the sanctuary of morality and religion. This emphasis on efficiency and functionality prompted the view that managing a corporation is a "science" that can be taught at universities and colleges. The central concern for the manager is the objective relationship between resources and targets. Targets are a given—they are not up for discussion. The owners of the corporation and other interested parties expect managers to keep the corporation going and to turn a profit on capital invested. In order to carry out this responsibility, the manager must anticipate consumer demands and use resources as efficiently and effectively as possible so as to reach the targets set by the stockholders and consumers. There is no room for moral considerations in this functional approach.

Is corporate morality necessary?

An egotistical standpoint is often advanced in discussions about the nature of corporations: corporations function purely on the basis of egotistical motives. The view is that corporations cannot but act in the corporate interest. Altruism and philanthropy are concepts that do not exist in an entrepreneur's vocabulary. Competition compels every corporation to ask the most competitive price possible.

The ethical-egoist argument holds that one cannot and may not expect business people to act on the basis of motives other than self-interest. Ethical egoism, however, falls short as a normative theory. The demand that people pursue their self-interest is ultimately self-defeating if we elevate the relentless pursuit of self-interest to the status of moral duty. The problem is this: if we want to accept egoism as an ethical theory, we must apply this criterion not only to our own actions or those of our own corporation, we must demand that everyone else (stakeholders and competitors included) acts accordingly. This claim to universal applicability implies that others must also let themselves be led by unbridled self-interest. If others also pursue only their interests, the possibility exists that they might do something that conflicts with my interests. Ethical egoism holds that in order for us to realize our interests optimally, we must persuade others to act altruistically in a way that clashes with *their* moral obligation to pursue their interests. Ethical egoism leads to inconsistencies and accordingly cannot be regarded as a fully fledged ethical theory. Adam Smith draws the conclusion that in the economic context, this dilemma is resolved by the mechanism that coordinates people who pursue their self-interest. According to Smith, the market mechanism functions as an "invisible hand": if everyone pursues his or her self-interest a "natural" harmony will arise by itself. With this he departs from ethical egoism. The ultimate criterion for the rightness or wrongness of an action is not self-interest, but the common interest. The position Adam Smith holds is therefore utilitarian.

The metaphor of the "invisible hand" is one of the most extraordinary ideas in the work of Adam Smith. Although the term is used only twice (once in each major work), it takes up a central role in his theory. In the *Theory of Moral Sentiments* and the *Wealth of Nations*, Smith expresses his wonder at how individuals' pursuit of their interests and aims come together to form a social order without it having been the conscious intention of any individual as such. For Smith, this social order is the result of a natural process of establishing order:

[E]very individual generally, indeed, neither intends to promote the public interest, nor knows how much he is promoting it ... he intends only his own gain, and he is in this, as in many other cases, led by an invisible hand to promote an end which was not part of his intention. Nor is it always the worse for society that it was no part of it. By pursuing his own interest he frequently promotes that of the society more effectively than when he really intends to promote it. I have never known much good done by those who effected trade for the public good.[19]

According to Smith, everyone pursuing his or her interests best serves the common interest. Individual self-interested actions will naturally bring about social harmony. As a result, he sees only three tasks for government: national defense, law and policing, and certain public works and public institutions. Smith borrows the justification for the third task from utilitarianism, one of the theories we will discuss in the next chapter. The government must limit itself to those public institutions and public works that one individual or a small group of individuals cannot undertake. "[T]he profit could never repay the expense to any individual or small number of individuals, though it may frequently do much more than repay it to a whole society."[20]

Interestingly, the idea of the "invisible hand" also opens up a movement beyond normative egoism. Smith justifies his encouragement of the pursuit of self-interest on the basis that society is indirectly served by it. The criterion for judging actions is not self-interest, but rather the interest of society. It follows that as long as everyone pursues profit, ethics in economic exchange is superfluous. The adage *laissez-faire, laissez-passer* from the eighteenth-century orthodox liberals is a more radical version of Adam Smith's basic ideas.

Criticism of the neoclassical vision of corporations

The distinction that can be drawn between facts and values does not imply that arguments based on values and standards are no longer valid. Values cannot simply be cast aside as irrelevant. Values fulfill an important social role and have a significant impact on the way corporations operate. The distinction between facts and values does not diminish this at all.

The demand for efficiency and functionality (which, if we recall, was introduced with the rise of modern scientific thinking) reduces the manager to an instrument of others, his objective being to achieve predetermined corporate targets without assessing these on the basis of personal moral convictions. However, this view does not preclude corporations from being faced with moral demands. As a result, moral questions are transposed to those who set targets and direct the manager.[21]

Adam Smith's notion of the "invisible hand" itself is value laden. To achieve maximum prosperity, moral demands in the market should be refrained from. Yet, some corrections are necessary, such as the limited functions assigned to the state. There are thus limitations to what can be entrusted to market forces. The role of the government is to create a framework within which the market can function. Finally, in his *Theory of Moral Sentiments*, Smith names those sentiments that are required for self-restraint. According to Smith then, market forces must be corrected in two ways: through government intervention and self-regulation.

From the above it is clear that the arguments that moral questions concerning corporate functioning are illogical, undesirable, and even unnecessary can each be shown to be untenable. Nevertheless, this analysis does show that there is something unique about the actions in the business context from a moral point of view. This explains the ambivalence toward corporate morality both in theory and in practice.

THE GROWING INTEREST IN THE ETHICS OF BUSINESS

Despite the historically rooted ambiguous conceptions regarding business and ethics, a growing interest in the ethics of business is developing. What are the reasons for this? What is changing and why? Is the growing interest just hype or is it a structural development? To start answering these questions, Table 1.3

Table 1.3. The state of business ethics

State of the Art in the Year 2000	
What stakeholders in fact do: several indicators	
Capital providers	Almost 350,000 unit-holders and policyholders in ethical funds with a total value of $3.5 billion;[22] and the use of investment guides such as *Ethical Investing*,[23]*The Better World Investment Guide*,[24]*The Ethical Investor*,[25]*The Corporate Report Card*,[26] and *Proxy Voting Guidelines & Social Screening Criteria*.[27]
Employees	Books like *The 100 Best Companies to Work for in America*[28] and *The* 100 Best Companies for Gay Men and Lesbians,[29] journals like *Working Mother* and *Black Enterprise*, and ILO conventions like the *Tripartite Declaration of Principles Concerning Multinational Enterprises and Social Policy* (1977) and the *Declaration on Fundamental Principles and Right at Work* (1998).
Consumers/customers	Books like *Shopping for a Better World*,[30]*The Green Consumer Guide*,[31]*The Ethical Consumer Guide to Everyday Shopping*,[32] the growing use of the SA 8000 social accountability standard of the Council on Economic Priorities for screening the ethics of suppliers, and the presence of alternative consumer groups in many countries.
Governments	Standards like *The Foreign Corrupt Practices Act* (1977), *The Federal Sentencing Guidelines for Corporations* (1991), *European Parliament Code of Conduct for MNCs Operating in Developing Countries* (1999), the OECD *Guidelines for Multinational Enterprises* (2000), and *Combating Bribery of Foreign Public Officials in International Business Transactions* (1997) of the OECD.

Table 1.3. (*Contd*)

	State of the Art in the Year 2000
Business associations	The International Chamber of Commerce (published the code on *Extortion and Bribery in International Business Transactions* (1977) and the *Business Charter for Sustainable Development* (1992)), European Business for Social Cohesion (1995), the Caux Roundtable (published a model code), Business for Social Responsibility (provides tools and guidance), the Business Roundtable (since 1972), the Business of Social Responsibility (since 1993), and the World Council for Sustainable Development (1995).
Non-Governmental Organizations (NGOs)	26,000 NGOs, including Amnesty International (published *Business and Human Rights Guidelines*), Greenpeace, Friends for the World, and Human Rights Watch.
Universities	Fifteen business ethics chairs in Europe,[33] more than a hundred business ethics chairs in the Unites States and business ethics often a core part of the curriculum at business schools.
Networks	Several networks and institutions include the Center for Business Ethics, the Ethics Resource Center (since 1977), the Conference Board (since 1916), the European Business Ethics Network (since 1987), the Institute of Business Ethics (since 1987), the Cambridge Centre for Business and Public Sector Ethics (since 1990), the Institute for Social and Ethical AccountAbility (since 1996), and the Global Reporting Initiative (1997).

What companies in fact do: several indicators

Codes of ethics	United States: 78% of Fortune 1,000;[34] Canada: 85% of top 1,000 companies;[35] India: 85%[36] Germany: 54% of top 1,000;[37] Australia: 50% of the larger firms;[38] the Netherlands: 38% of top 100 companies;[39] England: 33% of top 500 companies.[40]
Ethics training programs	70–75% of employees of Fortune 1000 companies receive ethics training or education;[41] 65% of Canadian companies have formally established training programs for communicating compliance standards and procedures.[42]
Ethics officers	US Association for Ethics Officers with more than 700 members,[43] 51% of large US corporations have special telephone numbers for reporting ethical concerns, 30% of large US corporations have offices for dealing with ethics.[44]
Ethics reports	Various companies publish external reports on the degree to which they uphold ethics. For example, SBN Bank (since 1993), Ben & Jerry's (since 1995), Body Shop (since 1995), British Petroleum (since 1996), British Telecom (since 1998), and Shell (since 1998).

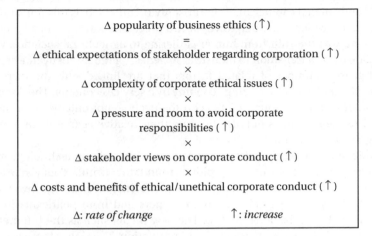

Δ popularity of business ethics (↑)

=

Δ ethical expectations of stakeholder regarding corporation (↑)

×

Δ complexity of corporate ethical issues (↑)

×

Δ pressure and room to avoid corporate
responsibilities (↑)

×

Δ stakeholder views on corporate conduct (↑)

×

Δ costs and benefits of ethical/unethical corporate conduct (↑)

Δ: *rate of change*　　　　　　　↑ : *increase*

Fig. 1.2. Determining factors for the popularity of business ethics.

illustrates the manifestations of business ethics at the beginning of the third millennium.

The interest in the ethics of business can be ascribed to a broad range of developments of the past decades. Although these developments are distinct, they are all interlinked. Five such clusters of factors can be identified as determinant of the interest in business ethics and are illustrated in Figure 1.2.

In this section, we will discuss how these factors have stimulated the growing popularity of business ethics. While corporations have been incurring greater ethical responsibilities, the issues corporations are confronted with have also become more complex. The opportunities and pressure for corporations to behave unethically have also increased. The growing power and influence of public interest groups who demand greater corporate accountability have also fueled the popularity of business ethics. Finally, the benefits of ethical conduct against the growing costs of unethical behavior have also stimulated the interest in business ethics. Growing stakeholder willingness to reward ethical behavior and punish unethical conduct also stimulates the corporate interest in ethics. One way for stakeholders to achieve their objectives is to pay more for products (as customers) or to show greater commitment to their jobs (as employees). They can also punish corporations by turning down certain products or by leaving the company. Below we discuss the social and economic context in which these developments are embedded.

The Information Age

During the second half of the twentieth century, industrialized countries gradually entered what is referred to as the "information society," the "Information

Age,"[45] and "digital capitalism."[46] Futurist Alvin Toffler labels this transition the "third wave," which is the outgrowth of two preceding waves of social progress. First, there was the shift from hunter gathering to agricultural societies, which was followed by a transition to industrial societies.[47] Francis Fukuyama ascribes this shift to a number of related factors that are linked with the increasing displacement of a manufacturing economy by a service economy. The dominant position of factories in our society is on the decline, not only because they lie beyond residential areas but also because their relative economic importance has significantly declined.

Production is being globalized as inexpensive information technology makes it easier to move information rapidly around the world. Today's world is characterized by a constant and high level of information exchange involving all kinds of players, from producers to consumers and from politicians to non-governmental organizations (NGOs). The new media such as the Internet give stakeholders rapid access to a wealth of information. These developments have transformed the social order from a centralized, rational, bureaucratic hierarchy to a decentralized network society. The sociologist Max Weber argues that rational bureaucracy was in fact the very essence of the industrial age.[48] Because of the information explosion, hierarchies of all sorts have come under pressure and are crumbling.

Large, rigid bureaucracies, which sought to control everything in their domain through rules, regulations, and coercion, have been undermined by the shift toward a knowledge-based economy, which serves to "empower" individuals by giving them access to information.[49]

In an information society, corporations and governments can no longer rely exclusively on formal, bureaucratic rules to organize their "subjects." Instead, power is decentralized and devolved to self-organizing individuals over whom they have nominal authority. A precondition for such self-organization is internalized rules and norms of behavior. These norms will play an increasingly important role in the twenty-first century.[50] The New Economy[51] requires a new or different type of business ethic. The trend of decentralization has brought greater social responsibility for business, which is, in turn, devolved to employees lower in the organization. The result is an increase in social responsibility among employees and a greater interest in business ethics as a key coordination instrument.

The rise of expectations

While the regulatory and guiding role of the state was relied upon in the 1970s, in the 1980s it soon became apparent that the complexity of social problems (such as environmental protection, technological development, social integration, etc.) required solutions that government alone could not provide.

Addressing these problems would require a colossal and therefore unaffordable and unworkable controlling government apparatus.

With the collapse of the socialist and communist economies that began at the end of the 1980s, and the wave of privatization that followed, the business community received fresh impetus to shoulder greater responsibilities. At the same time, the distinction between business and government has become less pronounced. The free movement of capital, information, labor, and goods weakens the regulatory power of nation states along with the will to initiate global change. Corporations are now called upon more than ever to account for their conduct, to become socially engaged, and to regulate themselves. This is succinctly illustrated by civil society organizations' shift in focus from national governments to corporations. At the global level, intergovernmental organizations are gaining in stature, although even on this level, initiatives focus primarily on stimulating corporate responsibility.

The "one-way governance" approach, which entails an essentially hierarchically structured relationship between regimes and corporations, is also declining. In this approach, the government ultimately directs the social parties. These parties are assumed to act largely on impulses from above. The social parties have always had a power of their own. They, too, have aims and by using this power they attempt to direct others so as to achieve their objectives.

Although the government is still viewed as the representative of society, it is increasingly operating as one among a number of social parties. To realize social goals, governments are compelled to enter negotiations with other social players. This results in "two-way governance," in the sense that the government manages consensus and takes in emphatic positions that are defended in the negotiation process. Because governance is a two-way process, corporations are increasingly asked to shoulder their responsibilities. In this setting, it is more difficult for corporations to hide behind the government's responsibilities. In the case of a one-way governance structure, the corporation cannot be held liable as long as it operates within the stipulated boundaries. That which is not regulated is not prohibited either. Complaints in this model are directed at the government, given its responsibility for formulating adequate regulations.

Another separate development is that NGOs (such as consumer interest organizations, the environmental movement, and human rights groups) have gained a stronger voice. Aided by growing support, these public interest groups (also called "public policy networks") are operating more effectively and are better equipped to voice their concerns—largely as a result of technological advancements such as the Internet. They also seem to be playing more of a governance role. Whereas 6,000 NGOs were operational in 1990, a decade later the world counts more than 26,000 such organizations.[52] In many countries, the largest five NGOs have more members than all political parties together. This form of democratization is stimulated not only by greater cooperation between governments and NGOs but also because of greater social awareness.

Partly as a result of growing prosperity and widely publicized corporate scandals, the public has developed a critical attitude towards business. Cynicism is rife and has manifested in a contemptuous mistrust of business.[53] Increasing numbers of companies thus feel compelled to examine how they could function more responsibly. While corporate power has increased, corporations have also become more vulnerable to public campaigns against them. Small groups are capable of bringing large corporations to their knees and forcing them to transform radically. Power, in short, has become diffused.

The complexity of issues

At the beginning of the third millennium, corporations are being confronted with issues of such a complex nature that it is sometimes difficult to determine what the appropriate response could be. The Information Age has produced different organizations with different structures of responsibility. Compared with traditional organizations, it is now more difficult to determine who is responsible for what and where in the network of actors the boundaries of business lie. How far does a corporation's responsibility extend if its products or services are embedded in a complex network of organizations? In such networks, who, if anyone, can be seen as representing the corporation? Management is not the only party that upholds the organization's image and it is not employees alone that create that image. Other stakeholders also mirror the corporation's image. In a network corporation, the corporation shrinks on the one hand while it expands on the other.

The Information Age also brings new modes of communication between corporations and the outside world. Knowledge and information have become core business. This leads to ethical issues such as what information is confidential and who really owns it. We are thus faced with questions of how to protect stakeholder privacy and where the lines can be drawn. Moreover, we must also contemplate how confidential information can be protected and under what circumstances it is justified to leak confidential information (i.e. whistleblowing). Thought must given to appropriate methods for collecting stakeholder information. As a potential Orwellian Big Brother, where does the corporation draw the line?

Two complex issues that should be noted are the questions of cultural relativity and stakeholder identification. Both these issues play an important role in the interest in business ethics. Partly owing to the information revolution and the free market economy, the world is gradually turning into a global village. As a result of their growing international character, corporations are facing not only new issues (such as the extent to which profits earned abroad may be funneled back to the home country) but also different customs and traditions. The world had 7,000 multinational corporations in 1970. In the year 2000, the number had climbed to 60,000.[54] Questions that multinationals are confronted with concern the extent to which local norms and customs of host countries should be adopted and to what extent multinationals should be governed by the standards of their home base. Or do universal standards exist that can be applied?

These questions are raised with respect to issues such as child labor, health and safety standards, investment in countries with corrupt regimes, investment in environmental protection, and wages in the developing world. Which standards should prevail? How does one make a choice in cases of conflict? How relative are norms and values? How far can a corporation apply a single general ethics code in an international context? And to what extent can stakeholders criticize a corporation for its behavior in another country where its actions reflect local standards, which just happen to lag behind those of its home country? The tendency toward concentration (partly as a result of mergers and acquisitions) has also made it clear that corporate cultures can differ vastly from one another, even within the same society. Cultural diversity requires modern corporations to adopt a position on how far they can and may go along with different customs and habits.[55]

One of the consequences of internationalization is that the world around corporations has grown more turbulent. Changes take place faster than before and the world has become extraordinarily complex. The perforation of geographic boundaries implies that people all over the world may now consider themselves stakeholders in decisions of corporations in far-away countries. Contact with stakeholders is often quick and anonymous. The world of e-commerce, for example, operates without any face-to-face contact whatsoever between buyer and seller. All in all, the corporation's relationship with the positive and negative effects of its policy and the products and services it markets has undergone a significant change. It has become more difficult to determine who one's stakeholders are. This requires corporations to become more adept at interpreting their external environment and its expectations. In this regard, modern information systems offer scores of ways to explore and learn about the world in a different—and perhaps better—fashion. Accordingly, ethics is an important instrument, both for contemplating where the next stakeholders might come from and for legitimizing stakeholder claims.

Greater stakeholder expectations with respect to corporations' responsibilities, the complexity of ethical issues confronting the business community, and the decline of the norm-setting role of government all lead to a greater need among corporations for instruments to regulate themselves. While the business community might prefer a moral vacuum (giving them more leeway), it does present a risk as corporations may find themselves at the mercy of fickle stakeholders.

The scope and pressure to shirk responsibilities

Many organizations nowadays are moving away from traditional bureaucratic structures toward more flexible, decentralized, and flatter structures such as matrix organizations, adhocracies, and networks. The new competitive environment requires more independence of employees and cooperation with stakeholders. Internal decentralization and de-layering ("leaner and meaner") that widens the span of control, requires greater employee autonomy and discretion. Employees have greater access to company resources such as regular and mobile telephones, fax machines, desktop and laptop computers, Intranet, and the Internet. The opportunity and temptation to use these for personal gain is likewise all the greater. Information networks are more vulnerable than industrial networks given that the links are more fragile and the degree of interdependence greater.[56] Information is also easier to manipulate and harder to safeguard. Where physical tools, for example, can be locked up after use, information can generally be found in scores of places. Moreover, it is much more difficult to register the use of information than the use of equipment.

This goes far beyond information that can be stored physically (on paper, in computers); it also includes the knowledge embodied by each employee. Every time someone leaves employment, the corporation not only loses labor potential, it might also lose valuable, sometimes irreplaceable, knowledge, for example of markets, products, or people. The loss of an employee can also mean the loss of his or her network. Precisely because of the increased complexity of personal actions and a decrease in their tangibility, direct management control diminishes. To put it briefly, corporations are becoming more dependent on the intentions and intuitions of their employees. And as supervision and monitoring become more difficult, trust gains in importance. If there is no trust, network organizations quickly revert to traditional hierarchical structures or fall apart altogether.[57] Good ethics builds trust in the company.[58]

Tougher competition, greater emphasis on the financial bottom line, and the mobility of capital places limitations on tending to a broad range of responsibilities.[59] The more global the market, the more competitors, and the more important one's competitive edge. These factors restrict the scope to attend to those activities that society sees as desirable but that fail to contribute to corporations' competitive edge. Recently privatized corporations in particular have become familiar with the discipline of the market and the necessity of limiting social responsibilities. Moreover, those business parties who feel competitors breathing down their necks will exert greater pressure on the corporation to turn a blind eye to such responsibilities. For example, a supplier whose future is on the line is more likely to appease its potential customers in all kinds of dubious ways than one who has a portfolio brimming with orders.

Stakeholder access to corporate information

Decentralization and increasing complexity make it more difficult for corporate management to know what their employees are up to. While the employee, as a provider of services, is frequently in contact with customers, management's ability to exert direct influence on employees has diminished. At the same time, the outside world has acquired an even better view inside. Society is now more capable of evaluating a corporation's behavior than ever before. The "media-zation" of society is typical of the Information Age. Organizations of the future will distinguish themselves by making information virtually completely acces-sible to practically everyone who has a direct stake in the corporation. This will be necessary since in many cases it will be impossible to establish in advance what information might or might not be relevant.

Corporations are increasingly operating in a global fishbowl,[60] making it more difficult to hide incidents from the public. Shady practices that come to light in distant countries make the international news in no time. In addition, the public's heightened awareness of the wheeling and dealing of corporations has made it easier for them to compare corporations on all accounts. Since the end of the 1990s, we have seen an interest developing in establishing a set of indicators for gauging corporate ethics.[61] Stakeholders are using this informa-tion to compare, benchmark, and rank the performance of competing com-panies. Areas of interest include who emits the most CO_2, which corporation has the most legal transgressions on its record, and which corporation has the lowest absenteeism rate due to sickness.

The increased access that stakeholders have to information about corporate activities, especially in far-away places, is linked to the growing demand for corporations to account for their conduct. A significant shift has occurred in the relationship between stakeholders and corporations. The culture of "trust me" has given way to a culture of "show me."[62] The collapse of many forms of traditional authority structures is accompanied by the demand of a wide range of stakeholders for information on what business is doing and planning to do. It is not only external stakeholders who have become more articulate; corpora-tions' own employees, too, have become more vocal. Employees have not only been given more room to maneuver—they have actually claimed it. High levels of education and flatter organizational structures stimulate critical thinking and independence. The information revolution has facilitated this development. A democratization of morals has ensued where moral standpoints are formed in debates between participants who all claim the right to voice their viewpoints. Ethics, or the development of moral standards, itself, is becoming an informa-tion and communication process.

The costs and benefits of irresponsible and responsible corporate conduct

The last factor that has contributed to greater corporate responsibility (which might seem to contradict the above) is the increased legal risk that unethical conduct involves. Ethical transgressions can lead to hefty fines. Mitsubishi, for example, agreed to pay $34 million to several hundred women whose claims of sexual harassment were ignored throughout many years of work at its assembly plant in Illinois. Especially in the United States, the view is held that the continuity of the free-market economy depends on the ability of corporations to place limits on themselves. This means that corporations and their representatives can be held legally liable for all the damage caused by the corporation. A number of huge scandals in which the court awarded substantial damages have forced people within the business community to start thinking about corporate responsibility.

Rather than limiting the damage after the fact—before a court and using complicated legal procedures—would it not be better to see how problems can be prevented instead? In the 1970s, the *Foreign Corrupt Practices Act* came into force following a number of sensational bribery scandals. In accordance with this law, corporations can be held liable if they make contributions to political parties, politicians, or government employees to gain their favor. The year 1991 followed suit with the *US Federal Sentencing Guideline for Organizations*, which prescribes a proper compliance program—in mitigation—to address damage caused by corporations. These laws have a global impact since they also apply to non-US parent companies with offices in the US or with a New York Stock Exchange listing.

Greater costs are involved not only concerning legal repercussions but also in terms of the scope of the organization. The wider the influence of the corporation or the greater the network of mutual relations, the greater the consequences (the trigger-effect). In addition, stakeholders have more and better means at their disposal to counter irresponsible corporate behavior. Greater mobility generally renders stakeholders more capable of exchanging one corporation for another. This includes switching brands as well as jobs. Employees today have better legislation working in their favor and access to more and better means of transportation, and they may be financially less vulnerable than before. Educational levels also render them intellectually less dependent (employability). Given this new self-reliance, it is not difficult to see why employees are nowadays less committed to their employers than before. Company loyalty is no longer automatic.[63]

Finally, the increased mobility of capital providers and consumers means that they have more options at hand for sanctioning a corporation for reprehensible practices. On the other hand, good corporate ethics can work like a magnet on stakeholders. Empirical studies show that stakeholders feel attracted to responsible companies.[64] This is reason enough for corporations to prevent irresponsible behavior and to stimulate responsible conduct.

The great social disorder?

The question that we, albeit at another social level, could pose together with Fukuyama is to what extent we are dealing with a great social disorder. The extent to which ethics is violated within the corporate domain is not insignificant. Moreover, various studies show that the scope of ethical misconduct grew during the last decades of the twentieth century.[65] Corporate ethics is thus on the verge of taking a turn for the worse. This is the downside of recent developments. Nevertheless, the interest in business ethics is growing with the aim of closing the gap between expectations and actual practice. As Fukuyama observes:

[S]ocial order, once disrupted, tends to get remade once again, and there are many indications that this is happening today. Human beings are by nature social creatures, whose most basic drives and instincts lead them to create moral rules that bind themselves together into communities.[66]

Societal, academic, and corporate attention to business ethics can be viewed not only as a reaction to the doubts surrounding the ethics of business but also as a response to the quandary of the business community as to how to organize its ethics. Whatever the future may hold, a concerted effort to improve corporate social performance will lead to a decline in the scale and scope of such violations. As the gap between norms and practice closes, the role of business ethics as an academic discipline will change with it. At present, however, it is important to determine what role business ethics as an academic discipline can play in actually bridging this gap between norms and practice.

BUSINESS ETHICS AND THE MORAL DEBATE

It is undeniable that ethics plays a role in a multitude of business issues. That corporations have a certain ethical responsibility is now more or less accepted in society as well as within corporations. A certain degree of ambivalence does, however, exist in attributing ethical responsibilities to corporations. This ambiguity can be understood against the backdrop of the neoclassical tradition that rejects the idea of corporate ethical responsibility. Nevertheless, contemporary society is confronted with a number of issues that make the demand for corporate ethics urgent. What remains unclear is the precise nature and extent of this responsibility.

Ethics belongs to a branch of philosophy that systematically focuses on human behavior in so far as it is driven by principles, doctrines, and norms. Business ethics is applied ethics that reflects on the moral issues that arise within the business environment. As an academic discipline, business ethics develops concepts and theories better to understand concrete moral problems and dilemmas, and to offer guidelines for behavior in the corporate context. "Business ethics to business needs ethics that emerges from, is related to, and can contribute to the actual reflection, decisions, and actions of business."[67]

Business ethics as a reflection on actual practice begins as soon as we progress beyond the stage of being led by dictated and internalized norms and start thinking in critical and general terms. Business ethics is both an activity (i.e. the reflection process) and a qualification for practice (i.e. the outcome of such reflection). The reflection process is conducted in academic circles, society, and the business community itself. Business ethics can also be regarded as a management discipline, referred to as "ethics management"[68] that involves the activities undertaken by managers and employees to structure the ethics of an organization. The task of academic business ethics is to provide organizations with the conceptual tools to reflect on their responsibilities and to translate their ethical responsibilities into daily organizational processes and practices.[69] The importance of business ethics for scholars and practitioners lies in the fact that it involves a reflection upon the legitimacy of the corporation as a social institution. This covers specific business sectors or corporations, their relationships with stakeholders, and how dilemmas are dealt with. Besides raising awareness and facilitating moral judgment, reflection also produces tools for ethics management.

Descriptive, normative, and meta-ethics

Business ethics is generally divided into descriptive, normative, and meta-ethics. Descriptive ethics describes facts: how people in the corporate domain actually justify their opinions, principles, and rules and how corporations manage their ethics. Normative business ethics focuses on prescriptions, not facts. The primary question pertains to the principles and rules that *should* be endorsed. Meta-ethics concerns the clarification of ethical concepts and theories.

The aim of this book is to identify norms for corporations (normative business ethics). In order to formulate moral norms that are appropriate for corporations, we need to develop adequate concepts and theories that would enable us, for example, to conceive of corporations as moral subjects (meta-ethics). At the same time, we will draw upon the intuitions, insights, and perspectives that have developed in practice (descriptive ethics).

Moral pronouncements

At what point does an issue become the subject of moral reflection and, with it, a moral issue? What is the nature of moral issues? Moral pronouncements exhibit a number of features.[70] Here, we will discuss six such features.

A moral pronouncement is first and foremost a normative judgment in that it expresses approval or disapproval. A second feature is that moral pronouncements call for general consent. It is in this regard that moral judgments differ

1. A normative judgment.
2. The judgment appeals to general consent.
3. The judgment is accompanied by feelings of shame or pride.
4. The judgment concerns actions and attitudes.
5. Interpersonal.
6. Fundamental individual interests.

Fig. 1.3. Features of moral pronouncements.

from expressions of taste. The latter fall beyond the domain of moral discussion as there is no disputing taste (*De gustibus non est disputandum*). The call for general consent implies that a moral pronouncement applies to everyone in similar circumstances. Even in the absence of consensus, the expectation of agreement by those who make the pronouncement still exists. Debate on moral issues is unavoidable as an opinion on moral issues implies a judgment, hence more than a subjective opinion. Issues become the topic of discussion when judgments are communicated to others through reasonable arguments. The appeal to general consent also implies a willingness to forgo one's judgment for the sake of a better one.

A third feature is that moral judgments evoke feelings of shame or pride, the one sometimes also replacing the other. The pronouncement of a moral judgment arouses these feelings. One feels shame when disapproved of and pride when approval is expressed. Sometimes it involves the one feeling substituting the other. For example, feelings of embarrassment among onlookers are evoked if the person to whom the negative judgment pertains does not feel accountable. One can relate to someone who is given praise.

A fourth characteristic is that moral judgments concern actions and attitudes. An action has to be conscious and free to qualify for moral judgment. Freedom and consciousness are the prerequisites for individual autonomy. Concepts like "conscious" and "willing" cannot be attributed to situations that simply arise or happen. The decision to abstain from action can also be morally relevant. If someone freely decides to refrain from doing something, the resultant inaction, too, can be judged in moral terms. Often, ethics is restricted to the domain of action. However, actions are also motivated by intentions or are the result of certain attitudes. It is thus possible to subject mere attitudes and intentions to moral evaluation even if no action is involved. This is possible on the condition that the requirements of freedom and consciousness are met. In the case of natural persons, the character of the person becomes the potential object of moral evaluation. This feature of moral pronouncements is of particular significance to corporations. In this way, corporate processes become the objects of moral evaluation (which we will discuss in detail in Chapter 3).

The fifth feature of morality is that it involves the interests of others.[71] The other is conceived as possessing inherent value. The treatment of animals and nature has generally fallen beyond the domain of ethics, but an increasing number of ethicists criticize the underlying assumptions of this tradition. These ethicists advance arguments to substantiate the inherent value of the natural environment and animals. In their view, the value of nature and animals cannot be reduced to the (instrumental) value they have for humans. A sixth characteristic of moral pronouncements is that it involves issues where fundamental interests are at stake. These interests are related to the basic conditions for individual self-realization. Trivial actions, such as offering someone a drink, fall beyond the domain of morals. In some contexts, where someone is dehydrated by the elements, for example, even these can acquire fundamental importance.

Objectivism and relativism in business ethics

The claim is often made that ethics is ultimately a subjective matter. People's backgrounds differ and they perceive the same issue from different perspectives. Ethics is thus portrayed as a question of taste. In the corporate context, this radically relativist perspective raises fundamental questions. How to deal with a multitude of moral viewpoints within one corporation? Are the norms a corporation observes simply a matter of adding different viewpoints or is it a question of power, where the top manager determines the norms of the corporation?

The appeal to "cultural differences" is often made to justify the differences in norms. This position is known as cultural relativism. Ethics is closely connected to the nature and problems of the society and industry it applies to. The ethic of a farming community differs vastly from that of a shipping or trading nation. What we regard as fitting in antique dealing is not necessarily appropriate for the insurance branch. Moreover, the norms and values we uphold change over time. Computerization has necessitated new interpretations of privacy protection. Moral norms simultaneously express and shape social developments. For this reason, it is mistaken to construe morality and society as separate spheres. One of the most important methods we use to draw a clear distinction between societies is to point out moral differences. In Chinese culture, gift giving is an expression of appreciation and it is regarded as highly inappropriate to refuse a gift. In Western societies, people are quick to associate such offerings with bribery. The tensions and conflicts that result from the diversity of moral norms and values are inherent to a pluralist society and increasing globalization.

A number of perspectives exists on the relation between morality and the person making a moral judgment or the context that norms function in. Ethical objectivism holds that "the right" or "the good" exists independently of time, place, or interests. Stealing is wrong irrespective of time or place. Shell's intention to dump the Brent Spar was right or wrong whether Greenpeace and the media paid attention to it or not. According to the ethical objectivist, ethics can uncover true morality (approximately) and justify it.

In opposition to ethical objectivism, ethical relativism denies the possibility of a single "true" morality. In this perspective, morality is always connected to the culture in which norms and values are upheld. If giving and receiving lavish gifts is regarded as appropriate in Chinese culture, it follows that it is also morally acceptable in this culture. Some relativists link morality to (class) interests. Some go as far as arguing that the basis of morality simply lies in the choice of the person in question.

The objectivism–relativism question creates serious problems in the corporate domain. What is to be made of the diversity of cultures that are represented within a single corporation? Employees with different cultural backgrounds observe different customs and traditions. Should they be respected without question or can everyone in a company be expected to conform to a specific set of norms and values? How can different customs in the respective sectors be dealt with? If corruption is common in the weapons industry, should companies in this market adjust their norms accordingly? How should internationally operating firms deal with the diversity of cultures they are confronted with? Should corporations respect discrimination against women when they do business in countries where it is justified on the basis of religious convictions? "When in Rome," it is said, "do as the Romans do." The Western belief in gender equality does not necessarily mean that other cultures may not subscribe to other values. What, then, to do about child labor in countries where it is regarded as acceptable?

For the purpose of this discussion, it is important to draw a distinction between descriptive ethical relativism and normative ethical relativism.[72] Normative ethical relativism, we will show, is inconsistent. Descriptive ethics refers to assertions that are made about the norms and values of other cultures with the aim of describing and understanding such a culture. To criticize the accuracy of a description does not amount to a moral judgment of the appropriateness of these norms and values. Statements about the norms and values of other cultures can, however, also be normative in nature (normative ethics).

Some people hold that doing business in another culture requires one to adapt to the norms of the culture in which one is a guest. Conversely, this viewpoint usually also maintains that immigrants should subscribe to the ethic of their newly adopted home. The view that corporations should respect the customs and traditions of their immigrant employees also tends toward a form of relativism. Having grown up in another culture, people were taught different norms and values. The weakness of normative ethical relativism lies in its formulation of the norm that we should respect the ethics of different cultures on the basis of the fact that different cultures subscribe to different norms and values. Apparently, then, there is one norm that is not context bound! The fundamental criticism of ethical objectivism against ethical relativism is that norms are derived from facts. The fact that norms are culturally diverse provides no basis for their acceptability, nor does it render a critical engagement with other cultures' norms and values meaningless.

A moral judgment is a pronouncement that prescribes the same conduct for everyone under comparable conditions. Such a judgment is not determined by the situation that the person making the pronouncement happens to find himself/herself in. The intention to rise above the level of intuition or personal opinion has to be present. The latter implies that the person making a moral pronouncement makes herself vulnerable to criticism. A willingness to engage in discussion is therefore crucial.

Hypernorms and moral free space

Does the departure from a universal and absolute ethic mean that everyone is master of their own truth and that no generally applicable pronouncements whatsoever can be made that are valid irrespective of context? Tom Donaldson and Tom Dunfee[73] offer a solution to this dilemma by grounding the norms that are applicable in local communities in two types of social contract: the hypothetical universally valid macrosocial contract; and the factually valid microsocial contract of local communities. The theory that links these two types of moral contracts is called Integrative Social Contracts Theory (ISCT).

The macrosocial contract can be deduced from a thought-experiment. In the same way that one cannot establish the rules of a game while playing it, when one sets out to establish the rules for governing global society, one has to construct a hypothetical situation where rational actors have limited knowledge of their social standing. In this way, they are able to come to an agreement on the norms for regulating economic exchange relationships. These rational economic actors occupy a position behind a "partial veil of ignorance." The ignorance of the actors in this thought-experiment is partial because they do know how the economy functions. They are also motivated by a need to establish fair norms. These actors are aware that they are restricted by "bounded moral rationality" in that they are unable to oversee all moral aspects. In addition, they grasp the necessity of a framework of morality as a foundation for economic exchange. According to Donaldson and Dunfee, these rational economic actors behind the "partial veil of ignorance" would formulate the following universally applicable moral norms:[74]

1. Local economic and political communities may specify ethical norms for their members through social contracts. They therefore have moral free space. These are the so-called microsocial contracts that are applicable in these communities.

2. Norm-generating microsocial contracts must be grounded in informed consent buttressed by rights of voice and exit.
3. In order to be obligatory, a microsocial contract norm must be compatible with hypernorms.
4. In the case of conflict between norms satisfying terms 1–3, priority must be established through the application of rules consistent with the spirit and letter of the macrosocial contract.

An important concept in Donaldson and Dunfee's theory is the notion of moral free space. Local economic and political communities have the right to choose distinctive conceptions of appropriate economic behavior within certain boundaries. These are the so-called microsocial contracts. An example of norms that are established by such a microsocial contract is "implicit agreements" on fees that can differ by branch or industry and also by country. Another example is agreements that have a binding effect. The settlements involved in buying a house are different from those in the cattle market. It also follows that the way in which the camel trade is established in Egypt differs from the way in which horses are traded in the US.

Hypernorms are generally applicable norms that restrict the moral free space of communities to agree on norms by means of microsocial contracts. In this respect, Donaldson and Dunfee refer to norms such as respect for human dignity and keeping promises. That corruption is unacceptable is also regarded as a hypernorm as no society condones corruption and giving and receiving kickbacks takes place in secret.

ISCT is a pragmatic business ethical theory that renounces the relativist view that ethics is based in subjective judgments that are context-specific. On the one hand, this approach allows for norms that apply in local communities, and on the other, it acknowledges those universal norms that everyone has to observe.

Value pluralism in business ethics[75]

Value pluralism is an approach of particular relevance to the objectivism–relativism debate. The objectivist view of morality departs from the assumption that one supernorm or one internally consistent and rational set of generally applicable norms can be identified. Donaldson and Dunfee's pragmatic ISCT also presupposes the consistency of hypernorms. Value pluralism departs from such a monistic view on norms and values without lapsing into moral relativism or moral subjectivism. According to value pluralism, fundamental values and norms can be identified but it is also acknowledged that these norms and values may conflict or be mutually exclusive. Since different norms and values can be valid at the same time, it is sometimes difficult to determine which is to receive priority. Often it is impossible to establish "the" correct answer. In the value pluralist perspective, no absolute criterion exists on the basis of which a decision can be made. This, however, is not to imply that all perspectives are equal and that the norms and values that apply in different cultures are always equally acceptable. An inability to prioritize may be due to the fact that our knowledge is insufficient to make an adequate choice between the values at stake. The impossibility of prioritizing may also be due to the incomparability of the values at stake or to the fact that they are mutually exclusive.

Following Martin Benjamin,[76] Theo van Willigenburg[77] regards the impossibility of determining which values to prioritize as an argument for striving for a compromise between the values that are at stake. Choosing for one specific value amounts to choosing against other conflicting values that are also valid. Passenger safety is one of the most important values for an airline. Most airlines demand that their crew refrain from consuming alcohol for a number of hours before flying and alcohol tests are performed to enforce this policy. Airlines are, however, expected to protect the privacy of their employees. In order to do justice to both values, some airlines have decided that only those in charge would undergo the test in exchange for the assurance that the tests are used only for the purpose intended. These airlines therefore accept a degree of risk by subjecting only those in charge to the test, whereas the pilots accept that their privacy is violated to a certain extent. Achieving a moral compromise can take on the form of negotiation: giving and taking by the parties involved.

Van Willigenburg distinguishes two requirements that the process of moral negotiation must meet. In support of the autonomy of all involved a proportional distribution of benefits and burdens should be strived for. The compromise of all parties should therefore be more or less the same. This is nicely illustrated by the example of the alcohol test, where all parties compromise to a certain degree. The second condition that moral compromising has to meet is in fact at odds with the requirement of striving for a proportional distribution. Some values are of such importance to certain parties to the debate that these are experienced as determining of their identity. In the search for a compromise, a more than proportional weight should be attributed to this identity-determining value. A corporate canteen can choose to serve vegetarian meals. Even though all tastes cannot be catered for, meat-free meals could be of such fundamental importance to vegetarian employees that a company might have to relinquish efficiency considerations to honor these values. Within a company, a discussion can start about the smoking habits of employees and the subsequent passive smoking of other employees. A healthy work environment for asthmatics is of such importance that a compromise would at least have to assure a smoke-free work environment for those employees who cannot tolerate tobacco smoke.

The notion of integrity that we develop in this book for the corporate context leans strongly on a value pluralist view of morality.

Ambitions with this book

We hope that this book contributes to the development of a model for analyzing the ethics of corporations so as to establish business ethics as an independent discipline. One can only speak of an independent discipline if it concerns a separate object of study that is characterized by a number of unique elements and a related set of interconnected issues. To achieve this, we must make clear that these issues cannot be sufficiently analyzed on the basis of general ethical or general management theories.[78] The concepts and theories developed in business ethics should be customized to suit the business context. Furthermore, they should provide better instruments than would be the case if general concepts and theories were used.

That it is desirable and possible to develop customized ethical concepts and theories for the business context that produce better results than general theories is not to suggest that they are so special that they cannot be compared with issues in other contexts. Some scholars prefer "regionalization,"[79] which implies that the issues that arise in the business context require a unique approach. We view regionalization as delineating (albeit temporarily)[80] an independent area for ethical reflection on the basis of which it is acceptable to develop unique concepts and theories. Defining an independent field for reflection does not deny the value of general ethics. In the same way that the infrastructure of a geographic region is linked to the surrounding provinces or countries, business ethics is not isolated from general ethics. Business ethics is still ethics. Moreover, ethics is by definition already "applied" in its conception.[81] Business ethics is concerned with what the business context complements to the individual moral arena. What are the moral demands that can or should be placed on managers within the business context? How should a corporation be organized? What moral demands should be placed on that context? How should employees be stimulated and how should one deal with all those justified but sometimes conflicting claims? Finally, business ethics also concerns the demands that can be placed on all stakeholders who contribute to the continuity of the corporation.

The objective of this study is to develop a model that will enable us better to understand and acknowledge the ethical responsibilities of corporations. By uncovering the nature of corporate functioning, we can examine how moral questions arise in this context and the kind of moral criteria that can be applied to corporate practices. It is especially from an auditing and reporting perspective that it is necessary to seek quantifiable criteria for morally evaluating corporate performance. The model we develop can also be used as a basis for adopting proper measures to improve the ethics of business. It is an aid for developing ethical practices (prospective/proactive) and its usefulness exceeds merely providing an answer to the question of accountability in hindsight (retrospective/passive).[82]

In our view, a model of corporate ethics should provide criteria that are applicable to business practice. The new perspective on the corporate function must be useful in concrete situations. This means that the model must be suitable for analyzing and engaging with the problems that managers encounter. In addition, it should be able to capture the experiences of business people in contemporary society. The gut feelings of most managers harbor a certain degree of truth. These people have had years of experience to develop a set of intuitions about what is responsible and what is not. This experience should not simply be cast aside. Our aim is to reveal the reasoning behind their intuitions and to link it to our criteria. This does not mean that we seek to use "intuition" to limit corporate responsibility. Even managers are prone to systematic "corporate blindness." In this sense, our model has the aim of pointing out the possible "blind spots" in the vision of those managers who seek to act responsibly. It should help them to identify those responsibilities that either have not been acknowledged or that have been inadequately recognized in the past.

KPN

In September 1999, KPN Telecom's Board of Management adopted its draft corporate code entitled *What Unites Us*. In four pages the code sets out the company's mission, its core responsibilities, and core values. The code was the result of the *Ethical and Socially Responsible Business* project that was initiated in early 1998. Its purpose was to establish KPN's position in the face of society's changing views and its changing role as a result of market liberalization and further privatization.

At the end of 1999, KPN, a company offering a wide range of telecommunication services, had 34,000 employees. With more than 8 million customers on its regular network and more than 2 million customers who use its mobile telephone services, KPN is the market leader in the Netherlands. KPN was privatized in 1989 although 44 per cent of its shares were still held by the government at the end of 1999. The company is listed on the stock exchanges of New York, London, Amsterdam, and Frankfurt.

Developments

The reason for KPN to put its code of conduct in writing and to review its own responsibilities was based on important organizational changes along with the company's changing position in society. At the end of the 1990s, KPN was confronted with three key developments:

1. *The privatization* of KPN in 1989 from a state-owned to a private company shifted its external focus from politics to the market. Stakeholders appealed to the company directly instead of using politicians to plead their case. New stakeholders (such as private stockholders) also entered the scene.
2. *The liberalization and dismantling* of KPN's monopoly position in 1997 (i.e. an increase in the number of providers in the telecommunications sector) and the related intensification of competition on the telecom market. This, on the one hand, put the profit margins under pressure, and, on the other, made it necessary for KPN to remodel its image.
3. *The splitting off* in 1998 of the subdivision that was responsible for postal services. By shedding half of the company, the question arose at KPN as to what the shared values of the company were and what it is that makes it unique.

These three changes took place against the background of the character of a public utility and the increasing impact of the telecom sector on society. Typical product- and sector-related developments increased both the interest in and importance of ethics. These developments are as follows:

1. The telecom sector and especially KPN, was marked by a higher degree of *product penetration*. There was an absolute and relative increase in the influence of telecom products and services on general and personal welfare. This meant that people could actually die if the national alarm network went down. This made KPN's impact on society quite profound.
2. The frequency of *product innovation* was on the rise in response to the growing supply and demand of telecom services. This increased the risk of dangerous or inferior products reaching the market. The growing use of mobile phones got people thinking about the related health risks for consumers and people living in the vicinity of mobile phone antennas. Automobile accidents caused by people engaged in phone conversations behind the wheel also became an issue.
3. The *blurring of social norms*. The scope of fraud and the misuse of telecom products by consumers were on the rise. Using a whole range of constructions, criminals succeeded in billing their telephone expenses to others. KPN customers received bills for calls they never made. Even though the root of the problem could be found largely outside KPN, people still perceived KPN as lax in its attitude. KPN was expected to take a proactive stance.
4. *A more critical public*. Consumers were making new demands of KPN products and services. Chiefly as a result of the importance of telecommunications in the New Economy, it was almost as if KPN had become a community service, which implied that telecom products and services had to be accessible to all echelons of society.

Other relevant changes in the environment within which the above processes unfolded, also played a role.

1. Owing to various *reorganizations*, KPN had become more horizontal, with greater responsibility located at lower levels of the organization.
2. Greater *employability* among the staff. Given the entrance of new companies onto the Dutch telecom market, employees had greater opportunities to switch employers.
3. The rapid *internationalization* of KPN meant that employees were confronted with a whole different set of mores. They also needed to "fight" harder to succeed in other countries.
4. *Mediazation*. The media was increasingly replaying the conflicts between the company and the world around it. In such situations, it became virtually impossible for KPN to defend itself. From the very first reports in the media, things looked bad for KPN.

Incidents

Numbers of incidents are linked to the above developments and emphasize the importance of a clear business ethics policy. For example, when KPN acquired a stake in the privatized SPT, a telecommunication company in the Czech Republic, rumors surfaced that agents working for KPN had resorted to bribing politicians to clinch the deal. Even though there were no facts to support these accusations, the media reported in detail on these supposedly corrupt practices at the outset of 1999. KPN was swamped with bad press. To put an end to this deluge of unfounded allegations and rumors, KPN engaged two outside auditors to remedy the situation. Neither of them could find any evidence to support the accusations. Two years later, the judge ruled that the broadcasting corporation that uttered these accusations had been wrong. Neither a parliamentary inquiry nor a police investigation of the Czech Republic could find evidence to substantiate the alleged bribes.

Three months later a new incident occurred. This time the television broadcast suggested that KPN had bribed Indonesian officials. Viewers in the Netherlands were told that KPN was guilty of bribery, that KPN had "rewarded" key government officials in Indonesia through various constructions, and that influential persons in President Soeharto's entourage had pocketed millions from KPN. In addition, KPN was accused of having used a "sly stock construction" to win over the key players in Indonesia that entailed taking an unacceptable risk with $94 million. Various political representatives ended up questioning ministers in the Dutch parliament for quite some time. To the horror and indignation of KPN, these questions were formulated in a tone that suggested the accusations to be true, which only exacerbated the scandal. According to KPN, the broadcasts caused major damage, not only financially, but also to its reputation.

The summer of that same year KPN became the talk of the town once again. The World Bank decided to exclude Nepostel, a consultancy division linked to the KPN Group, from tenders for a period of three years on the basis of alleged fraudulent practices. This news also caused quite a stir. KPN refuted the allegations in an investigation it conducted itself. KPN also lodged an informal complaint with the World Bank in Washington as well as with the Dutch Government for not being able to appeal against this decision and in particular with regard to the questionable definition of fraudulent behavior the World Bank employs.

All in all, KPN was criticized on all fronts and although unjustified—as we can now safely assume was the case in all matters—this did not become clear immediately.

More pressing was another allegation that concerned KPN's dominant position as official operator on the Dutch telecommunications market. The complaints covered its excessively high rates for telephone services, fraud with prepaid cards for mobile phones, spoiling the view of many people with all its mobile telephone antennas, the poor quality of the mobile network, and the misuse of its market position.

Despite the fact that KPN was already making a significant contribution to society, the company undertook to develop a proactive policy to address new issues instead of taking a reactionary stance. The process of drawing up a company code was much accelerated by these incidents but the positive attitude remained, as is evident from the tone of the code and the design of the implementation phase. All of the members of the group responsible for formulating the code as well as the Board of Management were acutely aware of the fact that international accusations of bribery and corruption were something a company like KPN was evidently vulnerable to. This was the result of a few factors in particular:

- business is always being done with government;
- long-standing licenses are always involved that need a long time to secure;
- licenses are worth billions of dollars;
- political decision-making processes are always involved whether the telecom sector is liberalized or not; and
- at the time, KPN was focusing on countries that no other big telecom companies had entered yet. Often market liberalization was new to these countries and lacked a democratic political and judicial system.

A fundamental strategic dilemma

What do these developments have in common? What sort of perspective and policy could be expected from KPN? What this all came down to was a fundamental strategic dilemma for KPN. On the one hand, the need to become socially engaged was pressing. On the other, KPN had less leeway to achieve this.

Stakeholder expectations of KPN were sky high in comparison with those of other companies. This was because of its roots in Dutch society, having been the provider of public utilities for over a hundred years. KPN's social function had grown more important as a result of the increasing impact of telecommunications on people and society. This was strengthened by KPN itself by implicitly claiming a social function with its prominent image. The use of the term "royal" in its name and the significant advertising it makes with the message "always nearby" are contributing factors. KPN also sponsors the most widely viewed sports program in the Netherlands and links its name to the annual national soccer match and other important eye-catching events. In many aspects of its business, KPN positions itself as an organization with a high profile in Dutch society.

At the same time, the chance of failing to meet the expectations was on the rise. This had to do with factors such as growing profitability requirements, regular product innovation, the blurring of norms inside and outside the business community, its internationalization and the uncertainty of the financial success of this international strategy, and the disappearance of the unconditional political support that KPN once enjoyed.

In short, whereas KPN had less room to maneuver in the area of social engagement, its stakeholders demanded KPN to become more socially engaged. This was the central dilemma. The challenge was to express clearly, vividly, and recognizably what KPN really stood for and also what it regarded to lie beyond its responsibility.

An example of this dilemma KPN was confronted with concerned the church phone. If the phone (which allows 80,000 people to listen to the church service of their choice from the comfort of their own homes) were offered below cost for social reasons, KPN's profits would either fall or its rivals would have good reason to accuse KPN of unfair competition. If the telecommunications supervisory body (OPTA) forced KPN to deliver this service at cost (which would amount to a 300 per cent increase in rates), great resistance among the churches would have been unleashed.

Employees at all levels experienced comparable dilemmas. Ambiguity was present in almost all the public debates in response to major or minor incidents concerning KPN (such as the reproach from OPTA that KPN's profits were too high and that it charged its consumers too much). KPN recognized its social task but was also under pressure to act as a company capable of taking on the fierce competition that arrived in the Netherlands earlier than in the rest of mainland Europe. As a result, KPN employees found themselves less than capable of convincingly refuting the criticism that friends and acquaintances had of KPN.

On the basis of its forecast of the future, the Board of Management recognized that this problem was more likely to take a turn for the worse rather than for the better. KPN is probably the company with the greatest public exposure in the Netherlands. As a result, KPN cannot allow itself to make as many mistakes as other companies. Or as one employee put it: "Whenever a major company makes a mistake everyone says, 'that was to be expected.' Yet, if KPN makes a mistake, they all of a sudden think, 'we didn't expect that at all.'"

The solution to this strategic dilemma can be located in achieving a balance between the various contradictory demands placed on KPN. The company had to obtain a clear view of the responsibilities it was willing to take on. On the other hand, stakeholders needed to accept that the responsibilities that the company could and would shoulder were limited and needed be balanced in order to match KPN's responsibilities as a business. This led the company to the conclusion that it would be desirable to develop a clearer understanding of its social responsibilities (and their limits), to ensure that this view was shared by as many employees as possible, and to present it to the outside world in a corresponding manner. The corporate code is an important instrument in this process. In little more than a year a company code was drafted and adopted by the Board in September 1999. It was published in October 2000 after the implementation process was agreed upon, a compliance structure was under way, and (top) management was informed what was expected of them.

Crucial questions that were posed during this process are:

- What should be included in the code and what should be left out? How "free" should a code be?
- How does a code come about? Is it the responsibility of senior management to draw it up, should the employees be involved, and are outside stakeholders also important sparring partners? And who finally adopts the code?
- How should a code be implemented once it is adopted?
- What are the under-performance risks of such a process? Would that not just increase the expectations of stakeholders? And is there any way back?

At this point, the question for us within the context of this book reads: which theoretical views are available for getting an ethical grip on these ethical issues and dilemmas? As a step in this direction, the chapter that follows gives an overview of the commonly accepted, general theories of ethics.

2

General Theories of Ethics

The three competing approaches to ethical analysis are consequentialism, deontology, and virtue ethics.[1] In consequentialist ethics, the moral content of an action is determined by the real and expected consequences of an action.[2] Deontological ethical theories regard the action itself as the object of moral evaluation, whereas virtue theory is concerned with the intention behind the action.[3] The difference in the object of analysis and evaluation of the respective approaches is illustrated in Figure 2.1.

This chapter consists of a discussion of the three approaches, on the one hand as a framework for "solving" ethical dilemmas and on the other, as a stepping-stone for the ethical analysis of corporate practices. We conclude this discussion with an exposition of the Integrity Approach that integrates consequentialist, deontological, and virtue ethics.

CONSEQUENTIALIST ETHICS[4]

According to consequentialist ethics, the moral content of an action is determined by the real and expected consequences of that action. An action is morally good if its consequences are desirable and bad if they are not.

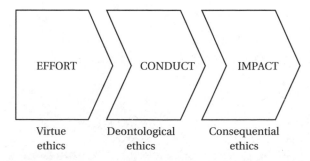

Fig. 2.1. The general theories of ethics.

Consequentialist ethics employs a certain standard (the purpose or end) against which the consequences of an action are judged. This is why it is also referred to as teleological ethics (from the Greek *telos*, "end"). Actions are taken to achieve a certain end, often with a view to a more distant goal. When ends are a means to a more distant goal, they are referred to as instrumental ends. Ends that are achieved for their own sake are intrinsic.

Teleologists are particularly interested in the latter kind of ends. One or more of such ends are chosen as a standard for judging the moral content of actions. The ends that function in teleological theories are not moral in themselves. They become morally charged in their use as a standard for the moral content of actions.

Depending on the number of intrinsic ends that a teleological theory employs, we call it either monistic or pluralistic. Monistic theories hold that there is only one intrinsic end to which all other ends lead, and on the basis of which all actions can be morally evaluated. Pluralistic teleological theories hold that there is more than one such intrinsic end. Teleological theories are also subdivided according to the nature of the end employed. Hedonism, for instance, holds that this end is pleasure or delight. This criterion for action dates back to the beginning of classical antiquity.

One problem that the hedonists have been up against is how to rank different dimensions of pleasure. How is it possible to compare a brief, yet, intense, pleasure with one that lasts longer but that is not quite so intense? The Greek philosopher Epicurus (342/341–270/271 BC) draws the conclusion that the end is not physical pleasure but the satisfaction of the needs of the spirit. As powerful as physical pleasure may be, it remains short lived. Moreover, the pursuit of physical pleasure as an end would lead to all kinds of evil. Feeding one's spiritual pleasure is, to his mind, significantly more valuable and leads to a lasting sense of well-being.

Teleological theories center on this targeted end, which can differ from person to person. As individual ends often conflict with each other, the question arises as to which end should be employed as the criterion for moral action. This question subdivides teleological theories once again. At this third level, ethical egoism (a theory we reject as a normative ethical theory given that it falls short on generalizability) holds that individual pleasure and pain should serve as the ultimate criteria, whereas utilitarianism holds that the common good forms the true end.

Classical utilitarianism

Adam Smith advocated the pursuit of individual self-interest in the belief that this would indirectly serve the common good. According to utilitarianism, the criterion for evaluating actions is the welfare of society. Utilitarianism is the general term for all ethical theories that hold that actions should be judged on the basis of their total costs and benefits for society. The action that produces the greatest benefits at the lowest costs for society is the action we are morally obliged to follow.

Jeremy Bentham

Jeremy Bentham (1748–1832) is widely considered the father of utilitarianism. Just as in the case of most other theorists Bentham, too, relied on a number of pioneers such as Francis Hutcheson (1694–1746), David Hume (1711–76), and Adam Smith. Bentham was a true revolutionary of his times. His theory of utilitarianism constitutes a break with ideas on social status common at the time. His criterion is the "greatest pleasure for the greatest number" on the basis of which all actions must be judged. In this regard, he considers the pleasure of a vagabond just as important as that of a well-to-do citizen. Everyone counts as one and no one counts for more than one. The core of his universalistic hedonism is articulated in several passages in *An Introduction to the Principles of Morals and Legislation*, published in 1789.

Nature has placed mankind under the governance of two sovereign masters, *pain* and *pleasure*. It is for them alone to point out what we ought to do, as well as to determine what we shall do. On the one hand the standard of right and wrong, on the other the chain of causes and effects, are fastened to their throne. They govern us in all we do, in all we say, in all we think: every effort we can make to throw off our subjection, will serve but to demonstrate and confirm it...The principle of utility seeks to rear the fabric of felicity by the hands of reason and of law...By utility is meant that property in any object, whereby it tends to produce benefit, advantage, pleasure, good, or happiness, (all this in the present case comes to the same thing) or (what comes again to the same thing) to prevent the happening of mischief, pain, evil, or unhappiness to the party whose interest is considered: if that party be the community in general, then the happiness of the community: if a particular individual, then the happiness of that individual...The community is a fictitious *body*, composed of the individual persons who are considered as constituting as it were its *members*. The interest of the community then, what is it? The sum of the interests of the several members who compose it...Of an action that is conformable to the principle of utility one may always say either that it is one that ought to be done, or at least that it is not one that ought not to be done.[5]

For Bentham it is possible to formulate the utilitarian criterion in quantitative terms. Ethics in his opinion is simply a matter of counting. The meaning of the "greatest pleasure" can be explained in quantitative terms. Happiness lies in the greatest possible amount of pleasure and the absence of pain. To achieve the greatest pleasure for the greatest number, he devises a hedonistic calculus to weigh pleasure and pain. To Bentham's mind, pain and pleasure are quantifiable units. He sets this out as follows:

To take an exact account of the general tendency of any act, by which the interests of a community are affected, proceed as follows. Begin with any one person of those whose interests seem most immediately affected by it:

- Take account of the value of each distinguishable *pleasure* that appears to be produced by it in the *first* instance.
- Take account of the value of each *pain* that appears to be produced by it in the *first* instance. (...)
- Sum up all the values of all the *pleasures* on the one side, and those of all the pains on the other. The balance, if it is on the side of pleasure, will give the *good* tendency of the act upon the whole, with respect to the interests of that *individual* person; if on the side of pain, the *bad* tendency of it upon the whole.
- Take an account of the *number* of persons whose interests appear to be concerned; and repeat the above process with respect to each. *Sum up* the numbers expressive of the degrees of *good* tendency, which the act has, with respect to each individual, in regard to whom the tendency of it is *good* upon the whole: do this again with respect to each individual, in regard to whom the tendency of it is *good* upon the whole: do this again with respect to each individual, in regard to whom the tendency of it is *bad* upon the whole. Take the *balance*, which if on the side of *pleasure*, will give the general *good tendency* of the act, with respect to the total number or community of individuals concerned; if on the side of pain, the general *evil tendency*, with respect to the same community.[6]

The significance of this empirical theory of ethics is that it was formulated primarily to serve state policy and legislation, especially criminal law. The way in which Bentham argues about the function and the severity of punishment is characteristic of the classical utilitarians.[7] The aim of legislation is to promote the well-being of citizens. Care must be taken that laws are not used to other ends, such as to enforce divine or natural rights. Punishment is, in and of itself, suffering. Accordingly, the punishment should fit the crime: it may not cause more suffering than that caused by the crime. Nor is punishment justified if no one has suffered any damage caused by the crime. In this, Bentham turns against punishment for sexual "offences" committed by consenting minors, a position rather progressive for those times.

Another significant feature of his theory is that punishment is not justified if it is not effective in preventing the same offence from being committed again. This also applies if other (cheaper) means are available for achieving the same effect, such as corrective instruction. Most importantly, there must always be a relation between the gravity of the crime and the severity of punishment. The gravity of the crime is determined by the harm caused by the crime. With respect to the severity of punishment, Bentham applies the fundamental rule that punishment must be severe enough to counteract any benefits that the perpetrator may have gained from committing the crime. At the same time, it must not be harsher than necessary to keep the offender from committing the crime again.

John Stuart Mill's criticism

It is probably because of John Stuart Mill's (1806–73) criticism of Bentham that his work was forgotten and Mill came to be seen as the key exponent of utilitarianism. In *Utilitarianism* (first published in 1861), Mill argues that it is not only intensity and duration that have to be taken into account in measuring pleasure. The nature of the pleasure itself is also relevant. Pleasure, according to Mill, to his mind is largely *qualitative*. The pleasure of Socrates cannot be compared with that of a pig. Pleasure can be divided into higher and lower pleasures.

The intrinsic good

Utilitarianism is a term that covers many theories. The different strands of utilitarianism share a number of features. All utilitarian theories depart from the assumption that an intrinsic good exists that can serve as a criterion for evaluating actions. Monistic utilitarianism holds that there is only one value that should be used as a criterion: pleasure or enjoyment. Pluralistic utilitarians reject the idea that all values can be reduced to one value, holding instead that there are several values that are intrinsically good. According to preference utilitarianism, a value is that which people find valuable.

Bentham and Mill are known as hedonistic utilitarians. They hold that there is only one intrinsic good: pleasure or enjoyment. Pleasure is a good unto itself. Pleasure and enjoyment are synonymous to them. Pluralistic utilitarians disagree with the assumption that all values are a means to pleasure. Aesthetic values and knowledge (for example, a researcher who examines something out of scientific curiosity) can be pursued for their own sake as well. An exponent of pluralistic utilitarianism is George Edward Moore (1873–1958). His *Principia Ethica* (1903) gives an account of the intrinsic good and the actions that should be promoted to further these intrinsic goods.

Besides the hedonistic and pluralistic variants of utilitarianism, preference utilitarianism is another dominant strand in utilitarian thinking. Preference utilitarianism has its origins in neoclassical economics and game theory. Instead of using certain desired states or situations (such as pleasure) as the criterion for moral action, this variant of utilitarianism is based on the satisfaction of individual needs. People's actions are a reflection of their needs and the value or utility of a good can be inferred from the price that someone is willing to pay for it. If the buyer pays a given price for something instead of using the money for something else, the product apparently represents so much utility that he or she is willing to pay the price. Preference utilitarianism holds that people strive to achieve the greatest satisfaction of their individual needs with as little means possible (the principle of efficiency).

There are several problems with this perspective. Preference utilitarianism fits in well with the market system. However, not all needs can or may be expressed in this system. The need for love, friendship, recognition, health, and a clean environment can only be factored into this system to a limited extent— or perhaps not at all. Consequently, they run a high risk of falling by the wayside.

The second problem with preference utilitarianism is the question of whether all needs are fit to be satisfied. What about the needs of a perverse sadist? In one way or another, a distinction needs to be drawn between preferences that are acceptable and those that are not. This calls for a moral criterion that can be used for selecting the "right" preferences.

Aggregating and comparing utility on an interpersonal level

A second feature that utilitarian theories share is the assumption that the intrinsic good or the common good can be aggregated. According to utilitarian thinking, it is possible to sum the different goods that people attribute to an action. Moreover, it is possible to compare the consequences of an action for some with the effects it has on others. The common good is thus comparable on an interpersonal level, which means that it is possible to aggregate the well-being of different individuals.

Utility as criterion for action

The third feature of utilitarian theories is that utility or the common good is used as the moral criterion for action. This means that people should act with a view to maximizing the common good of society as a whole. The consequences for all people, directly and indirectly involved, need to be factored into their actions. This drive towards maximization and the emphasis on efficiency is an essential feature of dominant Western economic theories. Our limited means of production (labor, capital, nature, and technology) need to be utilized in such a manner that they satisfy human needs to as great an extent as possible. The production requirements currently placed upon companies are a concrete translation of the utilitarian criterion for moral action.

We can distinguish two variants of utilitarianism: act-utilitarianism and rule-utilitarianism. The act-utilitarian judges every action separately on the basis of the criterion of the common good. Rule-utilitarianism tests each action against a rule that is evaluated against the criterion of utility. According to rule-utilitarianism, the right action is that action which conforms to the set of rules that, if accepted and acted upon by most people, would maximize utility.

Contrary to act-utilitarianism, not every action is judged separately. Instead, it is the rule, provided it is accepted by most people, that lies at the root of the act that is judged in terms of its utility for society. The final criterion is utilitarian in nature: maximization of the common good.

Rule-utilitarianism is much more practical than act-utilitarianism. For a rule-utilitarian, it is unnecessary to keep track of all the consequences of a particular action in order to evaluate an action. Well-founded and accepted rules can be relied upon instead. Besides its practicality, it also entails another dimension that can be best illustrated with an example. From an act-utilitarian perspective, it is strictly speaking better to leave an unsolved crime as it is. It is better to let the offender go free, particularly if a repeat of the crime by the same person is virtually impossible. After all, the crime has already been committed and damage or suffering has already taken place. Punishing the offender would only diminish the total welfare of the community. According to rule-utilitarian, it makes sense to have generally accepted rules in place that prohibit crime and make it punishable. Even though it might be better to deviate from the rule in certain situations for the sake of the common good, it is not desirable because such a rule would then tend to lose its authority. This could lead people to act contrary to the same rule in exactly those instances where following it would be better for everyone.

Comparing actions

Finally, the fourth feature of utilitarian theories is that the extent to which one action promotes the intrinsic (common) good is comparable with that of others. In this regard, preference-utilitarianism uses the price of the goods. The amount of money someone is willing to pay for a product is a quantitative measure that can also be compared from person to person. If two people are prepared to pay $2.50 for a particular item, preference-utilitarianism holds that the utility that both people believe they can gain from that product is the same. If the price were to rise to $3.00 and only one is prepared to pay, we can deduce that the utility of that item is greater for the one than for the other.

A practical and powerful theory

Consequentialism is a powerful theory that resonates well with our moral intuitions.[8] In everyday life, we very often think in terms of consequences for the persons involved. A common example illustrates this: anyone who buys a car and uses the highway system knows that he or she runs the risk of getting involved in an accident. Cars can be made safer for passengers by improving their brakes or adding air bags for the back seat. Yet, safer cars are more expensive. Everyone in the market for a car has to decide what is more important: safety or price. We weigh the extra cost of a safer car against the extra benefits of greater safety. The government often reasons in exactly the same fashion. For example, the benefits of giving the public the opportunity to view a painting by Picasso (by buying this artwork for a museum) needs to be weighed against the benefits of constructing a new hospital. Political decision-making often takes place along consequentialist lines of reasoning.

Objections to consequentialism

As remarked above, consequentialism is a powerful theory that resonates well with our moral intuitions, particularly within the corporate context and with regard to state policy. Nevertheless, it still has two practical and two very fundamental problems (see Figure 2.2).[9]

In the first instance, consequentialism faces a problem of measurement: is it desirable to quantify the costs and benefits and by implication, the common good? A real danger exists that non-quantifiable consequences fall to the wayside. Mill criticizes Bentham on this point in particular. If we were to follow Bentham's train of thought, a happy pig would be preferable to an unsatisfied Socrates. In Mill's opinion, it is primarily the qualitative pleasures that play a role in happiness. A quantitative method would not do anyone much good. To conceive of pleasure in qualitative terms, however, is also problematic. How can it be determined which situation contributes most to the common good? How for example, do we calculate damage to people's health in qualitative terms?

The problem of comparison follows from the above point of criticism. How is it possible to compare fundamentally incomparable goods in order to determine the extent to which they promote happiness or the common good? For example, how is it possible to compare health with employment? In order to determine which situation represents the greatest common good, we have to be able to make a comparison between different goods.

The response to these objections (an answer that Mill actually already provides) is that the idea is to weigh up the pros and cons of various alternatives as conscientiously and accurately as possible, given our limited time and

---

Practical problems
1. The problem of measurement.
2. The problem of comparison.

Fundamental problems
1. The problem of justice.
2. The problem of rights.

Fig. 2.2. Objections to consequentialism.

knowledge. For this purpose, we may rely highly on our common sense and experience. After all, in everyday life we are able to choose between the most incomparable of options. If it turns out that the wrong decision was made, it does not necessarily follow that an action was not responsible. To judge an action gone wrong we must look to the intention behind the action.

Of a more fundamental nature is the problem of justice. How can the benefits for one person be weighed against the costs for another? The utilitarian criterion of the greatest pleasure for the greatest number says nothing about how the costs and benefits of that pleasure must be distributed. Bentham himself recognizes this problem. In a thought-experiment, he reflects on how a society consisting of 4,001 people should be judged if the total amount of happiness of 2,000 people is taken away and awarded to the majority. This can be achieved if 2,001 people take the remaining 2,000 people into slavery. Would the total amount of happiness remain the same? According to Bentham, it would decrease. However, this does not lead him to advance a non-utilitarian criterion such as the principle of distributive justice. Bentham's response is that utilitarianism also places demands on how pleasure is distributed in society. The aim remains the greatest pleasure for the greatest number but he fails to indicate at what point this maximum spread is reached. As we shall see in Chapter 4, this fails to resolve issues such as how many Jews or homosexuals we can allow to be discriminated against in the name of securing the jobs of 10,000 others.

The problem of rights corresponds to the problem with justice. On what grounds can people's rights be abused in the name of serving the common good? Is it acceptable simply to push aside rights that are based in a contractual agreement or in the *Universal Declaration of Human Rights* (adopted by the General Assembly of the United Nations in 1948) if it promotes the common good? A rule-utilitarian would try to elude this criticism by asserting that the common good is served by accepting such rules. Nevertheless, it still fails to address the fundamental problem. As soon as a principle of distributive justice or rights proves to be generally detrimental to the common good, the same rule-utilitarian would change his mind and revise his rule.

Conclusion

Of the various theories we have covered that focus on realizing a particular end, we can eliminate the theory of egoism (see Chapter 1) on the grounds of internal inconsistency. Rule-utilitarianism and preference utilitarianism (which is well suited to neoclassical theories) in particular are two powerful variants for determining what morally responsible action actually means in concrete situations. This is certainly true with regard to state policy and corporate functioning. In many cases, these theories place clear limits on actions. However, consequentialist theories (and this applies to the above two variants, too) fall short where justice needs to be done to certain principles such as people's claim to rights and fairness.

DEONTOLOGICAL ETHICS[10]

Duty-based or deontological ethics solves a number of problems associated with consequentialist ethical theories such as utilitarianism. According to deontology, all persons have certain obligations. These obligations are non-negotiable: they cannot be bought off or disposed of. Different kinds of inalienable rights form the basis of these obligations.

Rights, obligations, and justice are concepts that consequentialism has no answer to. In a duty-based ethic, however, this is the focal point. According to this theory, an action is morally good if it honors a given obligation (which does not depend on the consequence of the action). Such a theory entitles certain people or groups to rights or a claim to justice. Deontological theories stipulate duties that must be observed irrespective of their consequences: legitimate rights must be respected and unjust action is prohibited. The word "deontological" comes from the Greek *deon*, "one must." The essential difference between deontological and teleological theories lies in the role that is attributed to the consequences of the action under review.

Principles of deontology

The fact that an action's consequences do not determine its moral character does not imply that deontologists (or at least most of them) do not take consequences into consideration. An action that violates a moral obligation is immoral without doubt. However, acting in accordance with moral obligations does not necessarily mean that such actions are always morally right. In a secondary sense, the consequences of a given action could very well be factored into the obligation itself. However, a deontologist would not go as far as committing himself or herself to a specific, superior consequence. The action's correspondence with certain principles is primarily what determines whether it is morally right or wrong. Keeping a promise is important because it is a moral duty, and not because of the consequences.

What principles do deontologists use to judge people's actions? In the course of history, a divergent variety of theories and imperatives has been formulated. Examples include "Do unto others what you would have them do unto yourself" and "Don't do to others what you would not like done to yourself." This principle is known as the golden rule. A promise made is a promise kept. Equal treatment for equal cases. This forms the basis for various theories of justice.

The foundation of the principles

An important difference between the various deontological theories concerns the foundation of these principles and how they can be identified. Three types of deontological theories can be distinguished in this regard. The first holds that duties are God-given; the second that they are based on common sense; while the third holds that they are founded by a social contract. The basis for a deontological theory can be sought in God's commandments. Frequently, the rightness or wrongness of an action can be sought in the nature of the action itself. Some deontological theories appeal to a kind of social contract as the foundation for the principles that are endorsed. Most religions of revelation rely on a kind of deontology. The rules are God-given and communicated in the Bible or the Koran, for example. It is our obligation to follow these revelations because it is the will of God.

When the moral rightness or wrongness of an action is based on the nature of the action itself, the question shifts to how it can be determined whether an action is moral or immoral. Some deontologists hold that this insight can be obtained from rational arguments (this is the view of Immanuel Kant), intuition (the golden rule), or by following the "voice of one's conscience." By grounding principles in a social contract, one presumes the implicit consent of all parties involved. The basis of the obligatory principles thus lies in the mutual consent to the conditions of the contract.

Act-deontology and rule-deontology

Just as with utilitarianism, we can draw a distinction between act-deontological and rule-deontological theories. The act-deontologist holds that every situation is unique so that it is undesirable or even impossible to formulate general rules of action. One must determine in each individual situation which action is morally obligated and how it should be judged. The agents in such situations normally proceed on the basis of their intuition or "listen to their conscience." Act-deontology is generally seen as a weak basis for normative judgments. For example, how is it possible for a Board of Management to reach consent on the basis of intuition in deciding whether or not to sink an oil platform in the ocean? That is why deontologists generally advocate a form of rule-deontology.

The rule-deontological variant holds that we should not evaluate actions individually but rather that we should judge types of actions on the basis of general principles or rules. The advantage of the rule-deontological approach is that it is much more practical for the purposes of decision-making. It is virtually impossible to contemplate every single aspect of each and every decision. Reliance on a number of rules of conduct makes it possible to implement the deontological approach in practice. Moreover, the use of rules in society helps us to understand better what we mean to one another. The moral judgments on the basis of act-deontology are too fickle.

Monism and pluralism

Another distinction that can be drawn between various deontological theories concerns the principles that are applied as criteria of morality. In monistic theories, all moral judgments can ultimately be related back to one universal principle. Kant's theory is an example of a monistic theory. In opposition to this, pluralistic theories employ various principles—not necessarily corresponding with one another—together.

The advantage of a monistic theory is that it excludes a conflict between principles. There is ultimately only one principle for judging all actions. Pluralistic theories must therefore provide an answer to the question of what we should do if there is a conflict between principles. Which principle should be given precedence? David Ross (1877–1971) developed a pluralistic theory that addresses precisely this problem.[11] According to Ross, a distinction can be drawn between "prima facie" and "actual" duties. Our intuition allows us to acknowledge various general obligations to which we are morally bound. Only, we do not know which obligation is right for which situation. This is where our ability to reason comes into play. In each concrete situation, we have to look for the most powerful obligation. This is the obligation that, if discharged, will lead to the greatest preponderance of good over evil. If more than one principle is relevant in a given situation, we have to examine which would yield the best result.

According to Ross, moral principles fall under a prima facie duty that must always be honored unless they conflict with other, more weighty obligations in a given situation. The *actual* duty is the highest and most binding obligation in a given situation. According to Ross, always being on time for one's appointments is a prima-facie duty. This is generally binding. It is only in extraordinary cases that we are relieved of this duty. Take the example of someone on her way to an appointment coming across a person in dire need of medical attention. It remains her duty to keep the appointment. However, at this time she is bound by a more pressing obligation: to help the wounded person.

Kant's categorical imperative

Kant developed a powerful theory in which moral rules are based in pure reasoning instead of intuition, our conscience, or the consequences of action.

His theory can be characterized as a monistic, rule-deontological theory. That is to say, Kant does not subject incidental actions but rather types of actions (such as lying, keeping promises) to moral judgment. All moral rules can be traced back to a general rule: the categorical imperative.

Kant (1724–1804) is without doubt one of the greatest philosophers in the history of Western philosophical thinking. He was a true representative of Enlightenment thinking and active in various fields. His writings covered physics, gnoseology, ethics, and peace issues. He was able to resolve—or at least shine a new light on—many of the problems Enlightenment philosophers contended with.

In the field of epistemology, for example, he was able to bridge the gap between empiricism and rationalism. Radical empiricists such as Hume hold that all knowledge comes from sense experience. On the other hand, exponents of rationalism such as Descartes, Spinoza, and Leibniz argue that truth, as opposed to appearance, is arrived at through reason. Thus, true knowledge depends on reason. Since Kant, speaking of the way knowledge is acquired purely in terms of either rationalism or empiricism is no longer possible. He argues that our observation of the world is more than the passive function of the mind; there is always an aspect of reason involved. This is first of all because experience is located in space and time. These are not properties of the things themselves but of the intellect. He calls these "forms of observation." Second, the intellect presides over a number of categories—such as "unity," "denial," and "causality"—which make knowledge of experience possible. The nature of reality itself, the *Ding an sich* ("the thing-in-itself") cannot be known. All knowledge of experience relies on our forms of observation and the categories.

Kant's ethic is similar to his epistemology on several points. Moral law is not something that can be deduced from reality, or that is imposed from the outside. Instead, morality is part of human nature. People are human precisely because they know and acknowledge moral law. For Kant, humans are distinct from the material world because apart from being biological beings, we are also spiritual beings. As natural beings, people are heteronomous. That is, they are subject to the physical laws of nature. As moral beings, they are autonomous: they are rational and free and can thus be held responsible for their actions. As Kant presupposes the existence of true knowledge in his epistemology (which would include Newton's laws, for example), he also presupposes the existence of a moral conscience. What he seeks to achieve in his normative ethics is simply to identify those suppositions that reinforce existing moral rules.

Kant maintains that there is one principle at the root of all moral rules. As such, Kant's normative ethic can be classified as a monistic deontological theory. Instead of judging the actions themselves, this general principle is used to evaluate the underlying concrete rules of action (maxims). This is therefore a clear case of rule-deontology.

According to Kant, every action, no matter how trivial it may be, falls under a certain rule of action or maxim. No action is without a maxim. For example,

"If I have to work tomorrow, I'd better not stay up too late tonight" and "I don't usually eat breakfast because I'm never hungry that early." A maxim is morally neutral. It is a rule that categorizes an action into a group of actions. The fact that every action is driven by a maxim is the crucial difference between behavior and action. Beings that are not able to act are not able to develop guidelines for their actions and cannot be judged in moral terms. This applies to animals and the mentally disabled. A maxim describes actions and they are formulated on a descriptive level. The aim is to find the right criterion on the basis of which it can be asserted which maxims should or should not be followed. The term "should" suggests the normative nature of this endeavor.

Kant formulates a moral principle as a kind of "moral litmus test" for determining whether or not a maxim is to have moral status. The general principle at the root of all moral rules, according to Kant, is "the categorical imperative." This is an imperative—a command that is unconditional or categorical. Kant sets "categorical" off against "hypothetical." An imperative would be hypothetical if its validity were tied up with specific conditions. For instance, "If you want to achieve this or that goal (for example, succeed in your job), then you need to do such and such (for example, work hard)." These rules of behavior are not unconditional in nature; they apply only if the relevant conditions are established, in this example, the desire to succeed in one's job.

The categorical imperative applies to everyone in all situations. A categorical imperative often takes the form of "Thou shalt..." for example, "Thou shalt not tell a lie." Commandments like these are unconditional. What exactly is the categorical imperative? Kant formulates this general moral law in several different ways. The most formal variant reads: "Act only in accordance with that maxim through which you can at the same time will that it become a universal law."[12] Another formulation of the categorical imperative is: "Act as if the maxim of your action were to become by your will a universal law of nature."[13] To act morally, the agent must determine whether it is reasonable to expect others in a similar situation to follow the maxim that he is about to follow. What if an immoral maxim is considered as a law of nature? In this regard, Kant points out that to elevate an immoral maxim to a universal law would be contradictory. Promoting immoral maxims to universal laws should be refrained from, as it is logically inconsistent.

Kant's examples

Kant employs several examples to illustrate the moral nature of actions. His examples are quite extreme. However, this is a conscious strategy to capture the essence of morality. In his first example, he poses the question as to whether a person weary of life may kill himself. His maxim would be: "From self-love I make it my principle to cut my life short when its extension threatens to bring more misery than happiness."[14] The essential question is whether this maxim may be elevated to a universal law. Kant's thoughts on this are as follows:

[A] nature whose law it would be to destroy life itself by means of the same feeling whose destination is to impel toward the furtherance of life would contradict itself and would therefore not subsist as nature; thus that maxim could not possibly be a law of nature and, accordingly, altogether opposes the supreme principle of all duty.[15]

Kant thus assumes that self-love ultimately serves to preserve humanity. If this first example concerns the agent's duty to himself, the one that follows entails a duty toward others. Say someone finds herself forced by circumstances to borrow money. She is well aware that she will not be able to repay the debt. However, she realizes just as well that no one would lend her money if she does not solemnly swear to pay it back. She is on the verge of making this promise, yet her conscience is bothering her. She also ponders whether freeing herself from distress in this manner does not run counter to her duty. Let us assume that she decides to take the money after all. The maxim behind this action would then be: "If I believe I desperately need money, I will borrow money and promise to pay it back, even if I know that that will never happen." Can I will that this maxim should be made a universal law?

For, the universality of a law that everyone, when he believes himself to be in need, could promise whatever he pleases with the intention of not keeping it would make the promise and the end one might have in it itself impossible, since no one would believe what was promised him but would laugh at all such expressions as vain pretenses.[16]

In the third example, Kant poses the question as to what a person stands to do who is extremely talented and who could be of great service to society but who would rather spend his time on the pleasures of life? It is impossible to elevate "neglecting to develop one's natural talents" to a law of nature. According to Kant, a rational being will necessarily aspire to developing his or her potential. It can serve a person in all sorts of ways, which is why he or she was endowed with it the first place.

Finally, in his fourth example, Kant examines what someone who has run into good fortune should do for those who are less fortunate. Can we assert that it is morally justified not to help others who are less fortunate than ourselves? According to Kant, we cannot will such a maxim to be made a law of nature.

For, a will that decided this would conflict with itself, since many cases could occur in which one would need the love and sympathy of others and in which, by such a law of nature arisen from his own will, he would rob himself of all hope of the assistance he wishes for himself.[17]

The version of the categorical imperative quoted above is relatively formal in nature. A more practical variant Kant formulated reads as follows: "So act that you use humanity, whether in your own person or in the person of any other, always at the same time as an end, never merely as a means."[18] Kant holds that this version has the same meaning as the first one above. A key term in the first two versions of the categorical imperative is the word "will." The categorical nature of the imperative suggests the autonomy of this will, which means that there must be no outside force upon which this will depends. Humans (both the agent and the receiving party) must thus be viewed as an end in itself, as inherently valuable. Kant contends that the latter formulation is merely another way of stating the categorical imperative.

This new formulation of the categorical imperative can be employed to reflect on the examples above. Suicide as way to escape difficult circumstances does not withstand the test of treating a person as an end in itself. A human being is not simply a means to a life filled with pleasure from beginning to end. In the second example of making a promise in bad faith, the person lending the money is reduced to an instrument if she is unaware of the actual plans of the person borrowing the money. And while neglecting to develop one's talents in order to dedicate oneself to the pleasures of life may not necessarily threaten the future of the human race as a goal in itself, it would not promote it either. That would be improper from a moral point of view. Helping others to reach their potential can be seen a similar light. It furthers the human race as an intrinsically valuable goal, thus rendering it a moral duty.

The above version of the categorical imperative does not suggest that people may never be used as a means to an end. If I sell a product to a customer, I use the consumer partly as a means to boosting my sales and to help secure the future of my business. However, people may never be used solely as a means to others' ends; they must also be treated as an end. This implies that I also need to see my customer as a person with a legitimate claim to all the information he needs. I must also refrain from trying to pass off a hazardous product to him, at least not without informing him of the danger. This more practical version of the categorical imperative resembles the golden rule to a certain extent: "Don't do to others what you would not like done to yourself." However, it is not exactly the same. One could regard the golden rule a special instance of the categorical imperative. After all, the golden rule says nothing about one's duty to one's self.

John Rawls

With *A Theory of Justice*, John Rawls established himself as a contemporary normative political philosopher.[19] In his theory of justice as fairness, Rawls departs from the assumption that people are motivated by self-interest. With the view to formulating the fundamental principles for regulating society, he constructs a hypothetical contracting situation called the "original position" in which contracting parties set down the basic principles behind "a veil of ignorance." Parties behind the veil of ignorance are bereft of knowledge about their position in society and the position they will occupy after the contract has been concluded. Due to the veil of ignorance, the contracting parties are free of unbridled self-interest. It is still assumed that they will do their best to secure their own interests but with the qualification that they will take into consideration all the possible positions they might occupy once the veil is lifted.

Absence of knowledge about social circumstances, gender, or natural endowments therefore ensures the fairness of the terms of the contract. As all rational, free, and equal people can consent to the principles of justice, the legitimacy of the institutions that embody these principles is secured. The principles of justice read as follows:

1. Each person has an equal right to the most extensive basic liberties compatible with similar liberties for all (the principle of "equal liberty").
2. Social and economic inequalities are arranged so that they are both
   (a) attached to offices and positions open to all under conditions of fair equality of opportunity (the principle of "fair equality of opportunity") and
   (b) to the greatest benefit of the least advantaged persons (the "difference principle").

The first principle comprises the fundamental political and civil liberties and includes the right to hold property and freedom of expression. The second principle concerns the distribution of wealth. According to Rawls, these principles of justice apply to a society that has reached a sufficiently high standard of living. This is the case where basic needs of the poorest level of society have been adequately satisfied. In such a society, these principles are lexically ordered: the first principle takes precedence over the second, while the principle of fair equality of opportunity takes precedence over the difference principle. The difference principle takes priority over efficiency and wealth maximization. Rawls holds that in sufficiently wealthy societies, citizens are capable of making effective use of their political and civil rights. In this context, a rational agent has no interest in exchanging his or her political and civil rights for an increase in wealth. For Rawls, less-affluent societies are governed by a more general principle of distributive justice. All social goods (freedom, equal opportunities, income and wealth, and the bases of self-respect) need to be shared equally, unless an unequal share of these goods would be to the benefit of everyone.

The two principles of justice mentioned above can be seen as special variants of this general principle of justice, the former of which only takes force in sufficiently affluent societies.

Deontological ethics and consequentialism

A fundamental shortcoming of consequentialism concerns the problem of measurement. Others include the assumptions that all consequences of an action can be measured against one criterion (the problem of comparison) and that the effects of a given action are easy to predict. Consequentialism also fails to take the historical context into account and neglects issues of rights and justice. Deontological ethics overcomes most of these problems. The measuring problem and the uncertainty of an action's consequences have nothing to do with deontological ethics. An action either does or does not honor a given principle. In addition, deontological ethics allows for a whole range of obligations in special relationships. For example, the relationship between employer/employee, buyer/seller, lessor/lessee, and parent/child all imply special obligations. Consequentialism recognizes only the relationship between the agent and the recipient of the benefit or disadvantage. Deontological ethics also takes the past into consideration. Actions in the past can engender obligations in the present. Finally, a deontological ethical approach also makes possible an evaluation of the intentions behind an action. For the consequentialist, only the anticipated results count. Rule-utilitarianism is incidentally a response to the criticism advanced by deontologists. In concrete situations, rule-utilitarianism and deontological ethics often lead to the same conclusion. Nevertheless, the ultimate criterion remains of a fundamentally different nature.

Objections to deontological ethics[20]

A point of critique that Mill in particular raises against Kant's deontology, is that in the final analyses, Kant still reverts to ends or goals. Mill illustrates this by pointing out that lying is immoral because it undermines the trust we place in one another, which is vital to society. The final criterion that is thus employed is goal-orientated: the well-being of society. This observation can be countered by pointing out that although it is evident that deontological ethics also includes ends of an action in moral evaluations, the moral content of an action is not *conclusively* determined by its consequences.

The second objection to deontological ethics, especially as Kant formulates it, is that all moral judgments seem to be either/or judgments. A moral principle is either violated or not. As such, a deontological ethic like Kant's leaves no room for exceptions. Exceptions to each and every rule are, however, very well imaginable. For example, if a murderer were to ask where his potential victim was hiding, the universal duty to tell the truth would no longer apply. In the case of pluralistic deontological theories in particular, it is impossible to determine which duty should be honored in a conflict. The introduction of prima-facie duties seems to remedy this situation, although it remains unclear how a trade-off between different obligations can or should be made.

The final objection to deontological ethics is that, like consequentialism, this approach is at a loss when it comes to altruism and exemplary behavior. Deontological ethics requires one to act simply in accordance with certain principles, doing more than one's duty is never necessary. Everything beyond moral obligations cannot be captured in moral terms.

In conclusion, we can assert that deontology is a powerful approach to ethics and that it resonates well with accepted (even religious) moral intuitions. The main disadvantage of this approach is that it easily leads to a rigid application of rules. The introduction of the concept "prima-facie" duty addresses this shortcoming. However, it remains inadequate, especially in situations where major economic interests and specific principles are at stake. In situations like these, deontological ethics offers no adequate, watertight solution.

VIRTUE ETHICS[21]

In addition to the theories of moral obligation that focus on action as the object of moral evaluation, there is another where the agent, not the action, takes center-stage. In this approach, it is not the action or the consequences that are evaluated but the person in question. Instead of judging what people do, it looks to who people are. The object of analysis is the qualities of a person.

A person can be ascribed a wide variety of characteristics. These are not only physical attributes like age, height, and size but also intangible ones such as abilities, intentions, and motives. It is particularly the latter class of traits that is relevant from a moral perspective. These qualities determine how an individual will act in morally problematic situations and can be evaluated in moral terms. For example, it is possible to say someone is honest, just, or reliable. These are morally desirable traits that are traditionally designated as moral virtues.

The concept "virtue" has its origins in classical antiquity. The etymological origin of the term "virtue" can be traced back to both the Greek *arete* and the Latin *virtus*. *Arete* means "virtue" and "excellence." This refers to someone's or something's ability to achieve a specific goal. The Latin *virtus* means "manliness" or "bravery." This also refers to an ability or capability. *Virtus* thus refers to a person's capacity to perform what is expected of him or her. An ethical theory that formulates norms that are related to the moral characteristics or qualities of a person is called "virtue ethics" or "aretical ethics." This approach in ethics dates back to classical Greek philosophy. In addition to virtue ethics, one can also refer to it as "quality ethics." Virtue or quality ethics refers to every ethical theory that formulates norms on the basis of human characteristics or qualities.

Virtue ethics in Greek philosophy

The Greek concept of *arete* is, as mentioned above, rather broad in meaning. It refers to a quality (virtue, excellence, and perfection) which can in principle be ascribed to almost anything, including people and states of affairs. It designates a state of affairs or a person as good or virtuous. A knife is good (or bad) but that can also be said of a school. Goodness or virtue is that which makes a knife or a school stand out or excel. In the same way, one can say that a person is good or bad. In this context, "good" is not used in an absolute sense. A person is good or bad in comparison with other people. Nevertheless, goodness is a decisive characteristic. Whether a knife or a person is good or bad is determining for that knife or that person's character.

Still, people and objects do differ. A person can stand out in various ways, while a knife can only excel in one particular manner. A person could, for example, be good at cooking or writing. Someone is a good cook if he is able to combine various ingredients in a way that produces a fine meal. Someone excels as a writer if she is able to captivate people with the written word. In both these areas, it is possible to specify how a person can be good. These qualities do make a person a good cook or a good writer, but not necessarily a good person. A good writer can be a bad person at the same time. What makes a person good? This is one of the most fundamental questions the philosophers of Greek antiquity wrestled with.

It was Aristotle who synthesized the ideas about virtues that were current among the Greeks at the time in a comprehensive theory. Aristotle is the founder of practical philosophy that was practiced until long after the Middle Ages. Practical philosophy embraces both ethics and politics as both are concerned with gaining insight into and achieving the good life as well as attaining the means to do so. Aristotle's virtue ethic is part of his philosophy of the good. With this, he takes a stand against the Platonic teachings and its focus on ideas. For Plato, the "good" as such exists—but as an idea. The idea of good exists not only as an intellectual concept but also as an independent, actual object.

According to Aristotle, however, the good does not exist independently of concrete reality. It is only with the help of reason that it can be abstracted as a concept, a thought constructed on the basis of concrete reality. By using the term "good," we apply a norm to that which we regard as "good." To deem something "good" implies for Aristotle that it is desirable or that it is strived for. All human conduct focuses on the achievement of certain goals:

Every art and every scientific investigation, and every action and every conscious decision strives, according to men, towards some good. That is why people have correctly called good that what everyone strives for.[22]

The various objectives that people pursue are hierarchically ranked. Most goals are pursued because their achievement is a means to reaching an even higher objective. Everything in nature harbors a specific goal. In pursuing that goal, nature strives to realize its potential to the best of its ability. For this reason, Aristotle's philosophy is teleological, which should not be confused with contemporary consequentialism. What is being pursued is not an external objective. It is already present, a potential. Aristotle calls the highest human good *eudaemonia*. This is often translated as "happiness." For Aristotle, *eudaemonia* has both an objective and a subjective dimension toward an inner state of contentment while it is also externally recognizable. In English, the concept "flourishing" best approximates the broader meaning of *eudaemonia*. The greatest good that a person can achieve is to give expression to her own, typically human, nature. The ultimate goal of a human life is to realize this "highest good," which is attainable through virtuous activities. Virtues are the necessary condition for achieving the highest good, *eudaemonia*. It is unclear whether Aristotle also considered acting virtuously as a sufficient condition for achieving the highest good. We suspect not. That also goes against common sense: virtuous conduct is not a guarantee for success. What then, is a virtue precisely?

In every action and situation, it appears to be something else: something different in medicine, something different in strategy, and so forth. What is, then, the good of each one? Is it not that for which everything else is done? In medicine, this is health, in war, victory, in construction, the house, etc., in all actions and designs the goal, for this is the reason why everyone does everything else. If there is, therefore, a goal for all our actions, this will be the good we are able to achieve, and if there are more than one, then these will determine the good.... Because there are apparently multiple objectives and we want one objective above the other, such as, for example, wealth, a flute, a tool in general, it is clear that they are not all ultimate objectives. But the highest good is apparently something ultimate. If there is, however, only one ultimate objective, it will be the ultimate of it. Now, we call that which we pursue on its own merits more ultimate than that which is pursued in the pursuit of something else and never is chosen for something else, more ultimate than something that is chosen on its own merits and can be chosen because of something else, and so, we call something that consistently is chosen on its own merits and never in the pursuit of something else completely ultimate. According to common wisdom, happiness is the highest of these. We seek this at all times on its own merits and never because of something else. We also choose honor, pleasure, insight and all the virtues, because of themselves (because even if nothing should result from them, we would still choose them for themselves), but we also choose them in pursuit of happiness, because we believe we can become happy through them. In contrast, happiness is desired by no one because of the other things mentioned or for anything else.[23]

A virtue is a state of character, a necessary condition for being happy. A virtuous person derives pleasure from acting virtuously. A person is virtuous when acting correctly has become habitual. In human activities or, better yet, typically human behavior (as distinct from how plants and animals live), two levels can be distinguished: a lower level of activity that obeys reason; and a higher level of activity that possesses reason and also exercises it. Parallel to these two levels of human activity, virtues can also be divided into two groups: intellectual virtues (such as wisdom) and moral virtues (such as moderation and generosity). Characteristic of intellectual virtues is that they grow through training, while moral virtues arise and develop through habit or custom. Virtues are acquired by using them, as is the case with all skills:

Because what we must learn to do, we learn in the doing: we become a master builder by building and a zither-player by playing the zither. So, too, do we become just by carrying out just deeds, moderate through acts of moderation, brave through acts of bravery.[24]

Virtue is a certain condition that renders good that of which it is a virtue. Furthermore, this condition ensures that the subject or object also carries out its function well:

[A]nd so the virtue of the eye makes both the eye itself and its functioning good, for through the virtue of the eye, we see well. Equally, the virtue of the horse makes the horse itself good, and that it runs well, that it carries the rider well, and stands well against the enemy. If this is so for every case, then the human virtue will also be a condition by which the person becomes good and by which he carries out his own tasks well.[25]

A virtue is a mean between two undesirable extremes. The two extremes are vices, which are diametrically opposed to each other and which, together, stand in opposition to virtue. Courage is the mean between fear and recklessness and generosity is the mean between wastefulness and greed. What a moral virtue precisely consists of in a concrete situation cannot be described in general terms. That depends on the nature of the person involved. Depending on the inclination toward a given extreme, one must strive in the direction of the opposite extreme.

Virtue ethics in the history of Western philosophy

Although great differences exist between classical philosophers such as Plato and Aristotle, they shared the same cultural frame of reference. Virtues played a central role in this context and were common in ancient Greek thought. In the various ethical theories of the time, the concept has more or less the same meaning. The double meaning of "virtue," both in its more technical sense as "capability for a particular goal" and, in the moral sense, one's "capability as a person," is characteristic of these classical Greek theories. The discussion was never really about what this concept meant or should mean. Everyone knew what virtues were. Plato and Aristotle's dialogues were more concerned with the characteristics of virtues and whether virtues can be learnt or not.

During the Middle Ages, the theological framework borrowed from scholastic thought—also shared by virtue ethics—was more or less commonplace. Although the technical meaning of virtue was pushed to the background, the moral meaning of the term remained intact. Just as in classical thought, virtues were viewed as those qualities that make a person fit for his destination. However, for Christian theologians and philosophers in the Middle Ages, humankind's destination was divine in nature. Because the human destination is not realized here on earth, but in the hereafter, the nature of the virtues changed radically. Humility, meekness, and the recognition of human weakness and sin were the qualities that encouraged people to focus on the divine, the perfect, and the transcendent. In his time, the apostle Paul identified the divine virtues by which people could submit to the power of God: faith, hope, and love. Together with the classical virtues (wisdom being replaced by practical insight or prudence) these three divine virtues make up the seven cardinal virtues of medieval Christian theology and philosophy: prudence, courage, moderation, justice, faith, hope, and charity.

Thomas Aquinas may be considered the greatest neo-Aristotelian thinker. He wrote not only the very influential *Summa Theologiae*, but also a number of philosophical texts such as *De Virtutibus*. Because virtues were an integral part of the prevailing cultural climate and thus fulfilled an important guiding role, it made sense for most of the ethical theories from that time to devote attention to virtues. Contemporary virtue-ethical theories have to make do without such a commonly accepted framework. In everyday usage, virtuousness is predominantly associated with the *bourgeoisie*. When the term is used, it encapsulates rudimentary references to the scholastic tradition from before 1800. In a theory where virtues play a role, no special justification is required.

Various Renaissance philosophers (including Machiavelli, Campanella, and Telesius) explicitly rejected the scholastic school of thought. In doing so, they fell back on the concept of virtue as derived from Roman philosophy. Campanella even goes as far as saying that virtues are limited to those qualities that serve the self. Although the concept of virtue continued to play a role in modern philosophy (after 1600), it gradually came to be seen as less of a guiding principle, and virtue ethics also began to lose ground.[26] Aristotelianism and the scholastic framework were forced to give up ground bit by bit. Especially the distinction between facts and values, and the increasing importance attached to facts (this happens to an extreme degree in neo-positivism), led to the situation where the primary interest became discovering natural laws. Normative questions were no longer regarded a suitable subject in the realm of scientific thought.

These developments have led to a situation where modern virtue ethical theories have to make do without a generally accepted framework. As a result, supporters of a virtue ethical approach face a number of questions. What characteristics or qualities can be called virtues? What are these moral virtues based on? How do moral virtues relate to other (amoral) characteristics? Can the moral subject influence virtues? How do virtue ethics relate to or how do they differ from the common ethical theories of moral obligation?

Despite the fact that the concept of virtue is no longer a dominant guiding principle in Western thinking, ethical theorists have taken up the study of virtue ethics anew. Contemporary virtue ethical theorists include Elizabeth Anscombe, Peter Geach, and Alasdair MacIntyre. MacIntyre has rekindled public interest in virtue ethics with his highly acclaimed book *After Virtue*.

Characteristics of virtues

A broad range of virtues features in the various virtue ethical theories. Depending on the basis of the theory, different tableaux of virtues are advanced.

Plato recognized four cardinal virtues, those virtues to which all other moral qualities can be traced. These are wisdom, courage or bravery, moderation, and justice. Plato devoted several dialogues to virtues: courage in *Laches*, friendship in *Lysis*, and wisdom in *Charmides*. In the dialogue *Meno*, Plato attempts to describe what virtues actually are. Virtue appears to be neither an innate characteristic nor something that can be acquired through instruction. He relies upon a sort of divine inspiration:

SOCRATES. We shall only have certainty when we, before asking the question of how virtue comes to a person, first attempt to ascertain what the virtue—taken purely of itself—might be.[27]

In *Republic*, Plato also devotes some attention to human virtues, which could be realized both in the individual and in the ideal state. Plato uses the state as a model for natural persons. The virtues can also be found in natural persons. In this way, he distinguishes four principal virtues. Aristotle draws a distinction between intellectual and moral virtues. He classifies the moral virtues according to his division of desires and passions. The moral virtues include, for example, courage, sobriety, generosity, and justice. Friendship lies on the dividing line between the intellectual and the moral virtues.

What qualities or characteristics (virtues) should a person possess? According to Plato, virtue or excellence is expressed in the proper execution of a specific function or task. For Aristotle, a virtue is a characteristic, a "state of character,"[28] which renders a person good and able to carry out his function well.[29] Hume considers every quality of the spirit which results in "love and pride" a virtue. Among the vices, Hume includes those qualities of the spirit that foster hatred and cause humiliation.[30] Kant offers an interesting definition. A virtue is *"die festgegründete Gesinnung seine Pflicht genau zu erfüllen"* (an internalized inclination properly to fulfill one's duties). Here, the concept of virtue is synonymous with morality. MacIntyre describes virtues as a type of "obtainable human qualities."[31] That the concept of virtue is used in various ways is apparent from its wide variety of definitions.

Five characteristics of moral virtues can be distilled from the various theories of virtue. Moral virtues are characteristics or qualities. These qualities

(1) are desirable, they are perceived as worthy of pursuing and therefore imply a moral norm;
(2) are expressed in actions;
(3) have a more or less stable, durable character;
(4) are constantly, albeit often latently, present; and
(5) can be influenced by the subject.

Moral virtues express a moral norm. Virtues presume a goal or ideal that is worthy of being pursued. Virtues are those qualities that contribute to the realization of the ideal, or, more concretely, the goal. For Aristotle, virtues rely on a reasonable order (the Logos), which is present in nature. Everything—people and objects—plays a special role in that order. For people, it is the destination of being a person. Fulfilling that role well makes a virtue of the thing or of the particular person. For Aristotle, order resides in concrete everyday reality. Plato, on the other hand, locates virtues in a transcendent order. The good exists as a transcendent reality. A thing is good to the extent that it expresses the idea of "Good." The virtue of a thing is the excellent fulfillment of its specific function. In his writings, Thomas Aquinas links Plato's transcendent order to Aristotle's order of reason. Like the contemporary ethical theorist Geach, this medieval theologian and philosopher places virtues in a divine order. Virtues rely on a divine hierarchy. Only if we allow ourselves to be led by these virtues are we able to live in a state of love of God or in accordance with God's will. Campanella and Hobbes value virtues as functional for the self-preservation of mankind. MacIntyre paints virtues against the background of a social order, which exists thanks to the exaltation of these virtues.

The ideal that is being pursued is not necessarily an external goal that applies in all circumstances and for everyone. The standards of excellence for people differ from culture to culture, and perhaps even from individual to individual. Moreover, to name a person good or bad, just or unjust, is something other than describing an actual state of affairs. A number of arguments can be used to make this clear.[32] For instance, someone who formulates his goal in life also says something about himself. In making a statement about the goal of a person, it is impossible to abstract from the fact that we ourselves are people. Secondly, knowledge about the meaning or goal of human life is not theoretical in nature. It is practical wisdom that also implies action. Insight into the aim of human life has direct consequences for what people do and how they live their lives. The practical nature of this knowledge also implies that it cannot be universal in nature. The ideal for a person is always concrete and related to the context.

Moral virtues are expressed in action. A second characteristic of virtues is that they pertain to a person's actions. This refers to the capabilities a person has and, therefore, indirectly to the actions he or she is capable of. How will the agent act in morally critical situations? Characteristics that cannot be or are not expressed in the actions of the subject are, in fact, morally irrelevant. Characteristics are judged as good or bad to the extent that they are related to actions that we conceive of as good or bad:

There is no such thing as a good tree producing bad fruit, or a bad tree producing good fruit. Each tree is known by its own fruit: you do not gather figs from brambles or pick grapes from thistles. Good people produce good from the store of good within them; and evil people produce evil from the evil within them. For the words that the mouth utters come from the overflowing of the heart.[33]

Virtues have a more or less stable and long-lasting character. A third important characteristic of moral traits is that they make it possible to focus one's attention on the more lasting, structural, bases of behavioral expressions:

Human good consists of the activities of the soul in accordance with virtue, and, as there are multiple virtues, in accordance with the best and most perfect. That must go on for an entire life. A single swallow doesn't make a spring, or a single day; equally, a single day or a short period doesn't make a man content and happy.[34]

The key to virtue ethics lies not in isolated actions but in the structure that is recognizable in the actions and that is related to the qualities (the virtues) that an agent has developed. People trust each other when they experience the trust-inducing action of the other as a disposition rather than whimsical or opportunistic.

Virtues exist in a latent form. A fourth trait of moral characteristics is that they relate to capabilities and dispositions. The subject has certain qualities, which may never have to be expressed. However, if they are needed (in morally precarious situations, for example) they can and will be used. Someone can be described as reliable only if they have resisted opportunistic behavior under circumstances where unfair benefit or breaking one's word were tempting. We say someone is reliable on the basis of past behavior even though the person cannot prove it at the moment it is said of him or her. By calling someone reliable we express the expectation that the person will be worth the trust we place in him in situations where his reliability has to be trusted. We call someone courageous only if someone has proven to be courageous in circumstances that required courage.

Virtues are subject to influence. A fifth trait of moral characteristics or virtues is that they can be cultivated to a certain extent. In this regard, virtues differ from passions. Passions are based in overwhelming emotions. The concept "passion" suggests, furthermore, a sort of determinism. We can say, for example, that someone "acts in a fit of rage." Virtues, by way of contrast, can be cultivated to become habits. If one has cultivated certain character traits, they can start to function as embedded habits. Virtues, are, however, closely related to passions. They give emotions and passions shape.

According to Aristotle, it is a parent's task to raise children to acquire certain virtues so that these become habits. It should not be necessary to decide whether you are going to tell the truth or not. Honesty must come automatically, something you do not have to think about. This can coincide with a feeling of happiness. The reverse is also true: for the virtuous person for whom acting virtuously has become a habit, acting improperly results in discontentedness.

Not all habits are virtues, they can also be bad character traits or morally neutral. Taking sugar and milk in your coffee is a morally neutral habit. Virtues are moral qualities that are developed, that people are aware of, and that can be influenced. With regard to unconscious characteristics, people need to be able to become aware of them and to influence them.

Consciousness and freedom are preconditions for morality. The qualities we classify as moral are therefore distinct from innate characteristics. Qualities that are "imposed" by caregivers, that have become habits, also fall beyond the category of moral qualities. If one speaks of qualities or habits that are passed on through child-rearing practices, one must also speak of qualities that can be influenced by the person in question. The way a child is reared does shape its character. Nevertheless, he or she can very well decide to change by developing other character traits. That there exists the possibility of learning and that a subject can undertake this out of his or her free will implies—partially at least—consciousness and a focused choice.

THE INTEGRITY APPROACH

In this section, we examine the extent to which the three ethical approaches above are complementary and how the integrity approach can effect coherence between these three approaches. First, we address the question of the extent to which a deontological approach contrasts with a consequentialist ethic, and the extent to which virtue ethics precludes an action-orientated approach.

Deontological ethics versus consequentialist theories

Consequentialism, especially the utilitarian strand, and deontology are powerful ethical theories that generally capture our moral intuitions well. In utilitarianism and other consequentialist theories the danger exists that the end can be used to justify the means. The objection to deontological ethics lies in the risk of rigidly holding on to moral principles and losing sight of the consequences of actions. Acknowledging the pitfalls of both approaches, John Dewey asserts that we should learn to think more technically about ends and more ethically about means, and avoid investing all ethics in ends and all technology in means.[35]

Often, both deontological and consequentialist arguments play a role in discussions about a controversial moral issue. No general rule can be formulated to indicate when one approach should be favored above another, or when another line of argumentation should be employed. Sometimes the consequences of an action should be considered and sometimes an appeal to principles is most suited for analyzing and evaluating the issue at hand. The choice for a given approach is not arbitrary. A deontological approach is most appropriate in the event that the fundamental rights or the distribution of benefits and burdens among different (groups of) people are at stake. If people's well-being is threatened, a consequentialist approach should also be included in the argumentation. The two approaches frequently complement each other well. Often a number of minimum requirements will be formulated on the basis of deontological arguments that set the boundaries within which, on utilitarian grounds, a course of action can be carved out that contributes optimally to the general welfare of all parties involved.

Action-orientated theories versus a virtue approach

Virtues become visible in actions. Why do we need virtue ethics? Is a theory of action not sufficient?

Given the relationship between obligations and virtues, it is understandable why theories of moral obligation focus on virtues. Virtues are regarded as a predisposition to act in keeping with moral obligations. The value of virtues lies in their contribution to making moral obligations concrete. The utilitarian John Stuart Mill sees virtues as internal sanctions that lead to desirable actions. In general, however, virtue ethics goes much further. Proponents of a virtue ethics approach presume that virtues have intrinsic value, that is, that their moral value does not depend on anything else.

If one considers actions only, one runs the risk of losing sight of the intentions that lie at the base of an action. Consequently, whether a given objective is realized intentionally or by coincidence or whether a principle is respected is irrelevant. A somewhat related argument—which holds that in addition to criteria for action, characteristics also merit attention—is that acting purely according to the letter of the law is morally defunct. Morality also concerns the spirit in which one acts. A moral system of rules of conduct must be based in a predisposition to act according to moral rules. Geoffrey James Warnock (1923–95) therefore considers virtues fundamentally as moral standards that provide arguments to justify given obligations.[36] In general, a theory of moral qualities supplements a theory of moral obligations.

For William Klaas Frankena (1908–94),[37] virtues and moral obligations are two sides of the same moral coin. Every obligation has a corresponding virtue. For every principle, there is a characteristic, which often has the same name and which motivates people to act morally. The reverse is also true, as for every virtue there is a moral obligation. Principles without character attributes are powerless and character attributes without principles are blind.

Frankena attributes to moral qualities a corresponding moral obligation and to obligations a corresponding moral quality. The question is whether this is necessary. Some virtues have no corresponding moral obligation. This applies, for example, to the virtues of self-control, diligence, and courage. No obligations that meet the criteria of morality (universally applicable, reversible) correspond to these virtues. These examples concern qualities that give direction to life in that they describe a particular ideal. In that sense, they describe a norm. However, one may never impose an ideal that may be achievable only for a select few as a general norm for everyone.

Frankena posits that moral virtues can be reduced to two fundamental virtues: benevolence and justice. These two cardinal virtues correspond to moral obligations. According to him, any quality that defies this classification is not a moral virtue: "Having accepted that, it still seems to be that, if someone's ideal is really a moral ideal, there will be nothing in it that cannot be covered by the benevolence principle and the justice principle."[38] This seems rather simplistic. Virtues such as diligence, courage, and self-control cannot be universalized; therefore, they do not qualify as moral virtues. Frankena in effect places the burden of proof on the critics. It should be noted here that Frankena assigns a broad meaning to the concept of the word "must" and by analogy, to duty ethics. A second shortcoming of Frankena's theory is that his quality ethic rather thinly reproduces what theories of moral obligation already do. Virtues only describe those characteristics that move one to act in accordance with moral obligations. Thus, a theory of moral qualities is worth while only as a supplement to theories of moral obligation. With the help of a virtue ethical approach, something can be done that cannot be done well or at all by the commonly accepted theories. The way Frankena engages with virtue ethics actually renders this approach superfluous.

Virtue ethics should do more than simply provide a reason for an agent to act morally. A set of moral characteristics cannot be reduced to obligations to act. Although virtues often correspond to a given obligation, they cannot be reduced to obligations.

Some authors go much further than Frankena and hold that virtue ethics is a moral theory that can and should replace the commonly accepted concepts. Exponents of this vision include Anscombe, Prichard, MacIntyre, Foot, and Gauthier.[39] In a controversial article written in 1958, Elizabeth Anscombe writes: "[I]t is not profitable for us at present to do moral philosophy; that should be laid aside at any rate until we have an adequate philosophy of psychology, in which we are conspicuously lacking."[40] In this article, theories of moral obligation in particular are rejected in no uncertain terms. If possible, the term "obligation" should be thrown overboard completely. In fact, these concepts are the remains of outdated ethical theories that no longer apply in contemporary society.

In reviewing these contributions, one can assert that Anscombe goes too far in saying that virtue ethics can and should replace the commonly accepted set of instruments. Acting cannot simply be reduced to qualities of the agent. Theories are instruments that can be used in an ethicist's analytical and norm-ative work. Where the instrument set of the duty-based ethic fails, virtue ethics can jump in. Similarly, duty ethics can supplement where virtue ethics fails. Because all moral norms (both with respect to qualities and with respect to obligations) ultimately rely on moral values, a theory of moral qualities does not necessarily exclude a duty ethic. Ethical theories are, just as other scientific theories, instruments that ethical theorists use in their analytical and evaluative research. It is therefore understandable that they want to avoid relinquishing tools unless they are forced to do so.

Monism, pluralism, and dilemmas

In the preceding sections, we presented the three ethical theories as competing approaches, each with its own dominant point of view. In practice, these the-ories are not necessarily mutually exclusive. Deontological and consequentia-list theories complement each other in many instances. Criteria for action and virtue ethical norms are often two sides of the same coin and support each other. Virtue ethics describes the disposition or character that is required to satisfy the action-orientated norms. At the same time, the one cannot be reduced to the other. Moreover, the choice for one criterion is no arbitrary choice. Arguments can be given to substantiate when a particular criterion is appropriate or not.

The more use is made of ethical theories to back up a moral choice, the stronger its basis. The question, however, is what to do when prescriptives of these theories conflict. In real-life situations, this means that one must first acknowledge and appreciate the value of each concept. Then one must apply these respective concepts to the situation at hand and pay close attention to their discrepancies and how they complement each other. If the situation is clear cut (i.e. if the different theories all point in the same direction), a well-founded and clear standpoint can be formulated. In conflicting situations (i.e. if the different theories advance different alternatives), well-considered and sometimes refreshing insights are the outcome.

A person is often called to account precisely when others feel that he or she should have adopted a more appropriate approach—or the one they advocate themselves. Lack of understanding of such requests can easily lead to resistance and even condemnation from others. To enter into a constructive discussion is to set aside personal and preconceived opinions and to be receptive to others' viewpoints. To understand truly the "counterparty" is to appreciate their stand-point and arguments against the background of the theories set out above. Being equipped to give an account of the three different approaches, both individually and comparatively, is an indispensable skill in the field of morals. So is the ability to explain in a conflict situation why the one approach is preferred over the others or why a compromise is called for. Individuals therefore need to be aware of the correlation between the three perspectives and why the one sometimes excludes the other.

It thus appears that we are dealing with a diverse range of norms and values, each of which can be appropriate depending on the circumstances. This points in the direction of value pluralism. Is it not possible to weigh the different criteria up against each other in a suitable fashion? If action is urgent and the different theories all point in different directions, is it not possible to justify the chosen action? In other words, does an eventual choice not show that an all-encompassing or ultimate norm for testing everything against can be found? If such an ultimate norm or value does exist, which is it? And is it utilitarian, deontological, or of a virtue ethical kind? Along with the utilitarians, both Kant and Aristotle's approach is monistic. For Aristotle, the virtues ultimately form a coherent whole. For Kant, the categorical imperative ensures that all moral duties are consistent. For utilitarians, the unifying criterion is the common good. Do situations arise where moral demands are truly mutually exclusive? Do dilemmas truly exist? Or are these situations that just require proper reflection to come up with an all-embracing criterion?

Dilemmas, in our view, are not simply difficult issues. A dilemma concerns situations where we are morally obliged to act and to refrain from acting at the same time. It may be that we are required to act to achieve a certain end but that other counter-effects render the action unacceptable. One of the important duties of a doctor is to relieve terminal patients of pain. If it results in ending a life, the doctor has consciously taken someone's life. Dilemmas of this kind form the central theme in many literary works. In Dostojevski's *Crime and Punishment*, the student Raskolnikow takes his landlady's life, an impossible woman who made life unpleasant for everybody. Dilemmas can also involve situations where honoring an obligation can prevent one from honoring another for the simple reason that it is practically impossible to perform both actions at one and the same time. You may have promised your partner that you would leave work early to fetch the children from school without realizing that you had an appointment with a client to discuss a report you compiled. Your partner is counting on you and you have a duty toward your client, especially since the appointment was difficult to arrange with everyone's schedules being so full. Not only is your spouse relying on you but your company and your client are also counting on you. In situations like these conflicting demands are made of the person involved. It is in cases like these that "real" dilemmas present themselves.

It is sometimes possible to resolve a dilemma by prioritizing (see the discussion of Ross and the prima-facie character of duties), but often it is impossible. Practical hurdles can make it impossible to prioritize. Perhaps there is an order of priority and good reasons to make trade-off, but we lack sufficient knowledge, insight, information, and the analytical skills successfully to make such a trade-off. In that case, we could try to resolve these dilemmas with still further research to fill the gaps in our knowledge and insight. This impossibility to come to a rational decision can also be due to the incomparability of the values, norms, and ideals that are at stake. In that case, we are dealing with what we referred to as a "real" dilemma.

"Real" dilemmas are present in situations where:

- resources (time, money) are scarce, and/or
- we lack the knowledge and insight to make a responsible choice, and/or
- incomparable values, norms, and ideals that are mutually exclusive are at stake, and
- it is imperative to choose.

Thomas Nagel identifies five different types of moral criteria that can cause conflict between different demands: obligations, rights, utility, personal commitments, and perfectionist ideals.[41] In his view, these moral requirements are incomparable. He is also of the opinion that we cannot expect our moral system to always be consistent.

There is quite a bit of discussion about the question of whether dilemmas truly exist. Are we faced with conflicting moral obligations that cannot be realized simultaneously and where the realization of the one offers no excuse for neglecting the other, or is it a case of difficult issues that we simply have to think through better in order to judge which deserves priority?

One argument against the existence of true dilemmas is that to do so would amount to a logical inconsistency. On the one hand, obligations have to be honored. On the other hand, "ought implies can." We are not bound by impossibilities.[42] Another argument that is often advanced against the existence of true dilemmas concerns the unacceptable consequences of accepting their existence. To do so would undermine all ethics. According the critics, we should hold on to the ideal of coherence, as without it ethical reflection is meaningless or even impossible.

For Bernard Williams,[43] true moral dilemmas do exist. In his view, norms and values that clash should be compared with desires and not with beliefs. In choosing between two beliefs, no regret is felt at relinquishing one of the two. With desires, it is different. Sometimes one has to choose which need to satisfy. In doing so, the need that cannot be satisfied remains. Usually, one would experience regret at not having been able to satisfy the unfulfilled need. In the event that one has to choose between conflicting demands one would feel uncomfortable and perhaps even guilty. This feeling of guilt shows that meeting one of the obligations is not to imply that it is justified not to meet the other. Williams offers an interesting argument but it is not conclusive. Regret is a psychologically complex feeling. It is possible to make the right moral decision and still feel regret. Besides, the feeling of regret does not necessarily mean that there is not one ultimate moral criterion for evaluating action.[44]

The question as to whether real moral dilemmas exist where a choice has to be made between values and norms is not yet resolved. On the one hand, we argue that different norms and values apply that cannot be reduced to one measure. On the other hand, ethical reflection requires that decisions be made rationally. If the choice for a given criterion is ultimately arbitrary, both the meaning and possibility of ethics are undermined. From a theoretical perspective, it is difficult to place dilemmas. In everyday practice, however, a pressing need for placing dilemmas is felt. As McConnell observes, "Common sense and ordinary moral discourse are on the side of the friends of dilemmas."[45]

The question of dilemmas arises in applied ethics in particular. In this context, concepts and theories are employed that render classification in terms of one of the previously discussed approaches difficult. The concept "responsibility" is a good example.[46] "Responsibility" can be a characteristic of a person, for example: "she is a responsible person." The concept "responsibility" can also be used with reference to an action, for example: "he acts responsibly." One can also talk about "responsibility" with reference to the effects of actions, for example: "we think it is a responsible use of resources." In applied ethics in particular, concepts are employed in a manner that integrates the respective approaches.

In our view, "integrity" is a concept that is well suited to be used in the analysis and evaluation of organizational functioning and functionaries within an organization. This concept, too, is multi-layered and makes possible the integration of the different approaches. We view the notion of integrity as offering a way to move beyond the monism–pluralism debate. It is a concept that is rich in meaning and one that promotes the pursuit for coherence.

The integrity approach advocates the simultaneous and balanced use of the three ethical approaches. Sound decisions based upon integrity preclude the denial of moral complexity or settling for a simple, narrow-minded resolution based upon less than the three key ethics approaches. An understanding of ethics can be achieved only by grappling with the diversity of perspectives it offers. Moreover, the integrity approach comes down to guaranteeing wholeness in instances where one or more of the theories of ethics have been violated. A compromise may still preserve one's integrity. Or as ethicist Linda Sharp Paine succinctly states: "When dilemmas arise, integrity requires that individuals deal with such conflicts and overcome the tensions inherent in them."[47]

Integrity

The concept "integrity" is derived from the Latin word *integritas* and also means "wholeness," "completeness," and "purity."[48] The everyday usage of the term "integrity" (in a moral sense) generally centers on lapses or deficiencies in integrity. Integrity is thereby defined as "unimpeachable," "intact," or "incorruptible."[49] From this perspective, integrity comes down to safeguarding against infringements: making sure that one does not become tarnished or corrupted or that one does not overstep the mark. "Wholeness" can also be given a positive meaning. From this perspective, integrity refers to the implementation of good practices to ensure that one remains whole, in one piece, or unblemished.

"Wholeness" concerns the values and principles a person upholds. Later in this chapter, we will argue that the values and norms that guide the conduct of a person of integrity are complete and consistent. That is, that the values and principles, actual conduct, and the consequences that are strived for form a coherent whole. The words and deeds of a person of integrity conform with each other. Integrity concerns the degree to which people are integrated, both on a personal level (toward oneself) and in relation to society (toward others).

In our view, integrity is not limited to one aspect of human character, such as the inclination not to get involved in corruption or—in positive terms—being honest. Nor do we see integrity as something solely related to character in the sense of integrity being the catch-all for all virtues.[50] Integrity refers to the integrative judgment and control of character, conduct, and consequences.

Prototypes that fall short of integrity

In outlining the contours of the concept of integrity, we follow Martin Benjamin's approach by first studying the ways individuals are customarily said to fall short of integrity.

[L]ike the darker parts of a black and white photograph, the network of negative characterizations may, by contrast, throw into relief a more positive and literal understanding of what we mean by it.[51]

It is possible to distinguish several prototypes that fall short of integrity.[52] In practice, those who embody these characteristics do so in very subtle, varied, and complex ways. Moreover, these characteristics appear in varying combinations and degrees. The aim here is to distinguish the hallmarks of integrity.

(I) A person can lack integrity or fall short of integrity when the values, norms, and ideals the person upholds are incomplete or inconsistent. The moral chameleon is a person without strong personal convictions. He is someone who is anxious to accommodate others and inclined to evade moral controversy and disagreement. The moral chameleon is quick to modify or abandon currently held principles in order to placate others. He will "change colors" for the sake of fitting in. The moral chameleon lacks a coherent and stable set of values and principles.

Similarly, the opportunist will alter his beliefs and behavior whenever he thinks that doing so will lead to personal gain or advancement. What he does and aspires to depend entirely on the circumstances. Both the moral chameleon and the opportunist lack a stable and substantive set of values and principles. The opportunist lacks a set of values and principles that takes precedence over self-interest.

A narrow-minded person adopts a narrow point of view simply by opting for one line of reasoning. He does not take the trouble—generally owing to prejudice or a lack of competence—to engage with other moral points of view. Instead, he looks for quick fixes to complex moral problems, which often finds its expression in rigidity. The narrow-minded person lacks a well-considered set of values and principles.

The pragmatist has put aside all values and ideals. He no longer believes in values and ideals, and his conduct is led purely by pragmatic considerations.

(II) A person's integrity also falls short or lacks because the values, norms, and ideals are not consistent with actual conduct and actual effects that are strived for in conduct.

In contrast to the moral chameleon and the opportunist, the hypocrite has a more determinate center, in the sense of being calculating and manipulative. A deliberate inconsistency between words and deeds can be identified in the hypocrite. "The hypocrite pretends to live by certain standards when in fact he does not."[53] Hypocrites may be "rotten to the core," but they are not wholly without center. Hypocrites have two different sets of principles, one for public consumption and one that actually guides their behavior. From the outside, the hypocrite is not "all in one piece."

Weak-willed persons have a reasonably coherent set of principles but lack the courage of their convictions or fail to make a conscientious effort to act in accordance with these principles. Their words or deeds will deviate from these principles in the face of external, but not irresistible, pressure or constraints. The weak-willed person lacks any real commitment, resolution, or tenacity regarding the chosen values and principles.

The self-deceiver lacks self-understanding. A discrepancy exists between the values and principles he likes to think he is acting upon, and the different, incompatible interests and desires that actually motivate his actions. To resolve this tension and to preserve his idealized self-image, he deceives himself about what he is in fact doing. For this reason, he is able to retain his internal integrity. From an external point of view, the integrity of the self-deceiver is everything but intact.

The capricious (unreliable, whimsical) person is led by his mood and coincidence. His actions are characterized by *ad hoc* decisions.

The pawn shifts the responsibility for his deeds onto others. He perceives himself as driven entirely by forces beyond his control and sees himself as a slave to his desires.[54] He seeks exoneration with excuses such as "he made me do it," "I was just following orders," and "I had no choice."

An alienated victim of external coercion is a person who is coerced into acting and speaking in ways that are at odds with his deeply held and cherished convictions. The alienated victim experiences an inconsistency between

I.	Absence of a coherent or complete set of values:
	1. The moral chameleon
	2. The opportunist
	3. The narrow-minded person
	4. The pragmatist
II.	Incoherence between values and deeds:
	5. The hypocrite
	6. The weak-willed person
	7. The self-deceiver
	8. The capricious person
	9. The pawn
	10. The alienated victim of external coercion
	11. The traditionalist
III.	Disconnection from the environment:
	12. The rigid dogmatist
	13. The rigid bureaucrat
	14. The hypochondriac

Fig. 2.3. Prototypes of persons lacking in integrity.

internal convictions and words and deeds. This person is in some ways the opposite of the hypocrite, who may be consistent from his point of view but not from others'. The alienated victim of external coercion differs from the pawn in that the latter is not conscious of any deeply held and cherished convictions.

Customs and traditions lead the conduct of the traditionalist: "This is the way we have always done it" and "Everyone does it this way."

(III) A person's integrity can fall short or even be lacking because he takes no account of the environment and the role he plays in it.

The rigid dogmatist follows his or her own values and principles, and races after his or her own ideals. The dogmatist is not receptive to the questions and expectations from the environment.

The rigid bureaucrat is simply led by the rules and is insensitive to signals from his or her environment.

The hypochondriac wears blinkers and is not receptive to signals from his or her environment. The hypochondriac does not consider the effects of his or her actions on the environment.

Characteristics of integrity

How can we, following the advice of Benjamin, "by contrast, throw into relief a more positive and literal understanding" of what we mean by "integrity"? Three positive aspects of meaning can be deduced from the negative meaning of the concept "integrity":

1. A person of integrity is an autonomous thinker; he or she has a stable set of values and norms, and what he or she promotes is authentic: he or she stands and strives for something and is true to his or her ideals;
2. A state of internal integration: the words and deeds of a person of integrity conform;
3. A state of external integration: a person of integrity pays attention to social issues and is willing to account for himself or herself.

1. *A person of integrity is first and foremost autonomous and authentic: he or she stands for something, strives for something, and is true to his or her ideals.* First of all, we can say that a judgment of integrity is a judgment of character.[55] Persons of integrity have a set of steadfast beliefs that define who they are and what they stand for. They have a high degree of self-control, self-awareness, and autonomy.[56] In contrast with the moral chameleon, external forces do not sway them. Integrity stands for the wholeness of motives. As the psychoanalyst and developmental psychologist Erik Erikson states in his book *Childhood and Society*,[57] integrity can be regarded as an encompassing wholeness and as the final and highest stage of personal development. Accordingly, persons of integrity accept responsibility for themselves, for what they do, and what they have done. They rarely appeal to external forces to explain or justify their behavior. The norms and values of a person of integrity flow forth from the individual and are determining of his or her character. The norms and values of the person of integrity are autonomous and authentic.

2. *A person of integrity is capable of integrating his or her values, deeds, and their effects in his or her life in a natural way.* Integrity is not a matter of intentions alone.[58] Intentions are a necessary but insufficient condition for speaking of integrity. Integrity is also a matter of conduct. Good intentions alone are a job half done.[59] Not only is the quality of one's intentions evident from one's actions, but the quality of one's actions is evident from one's intentions. A good deed that lacks substance is as empty as no good deed in the presence of substance. Persons of integrity match their intentions with deeds. They conscientiously translate their intentions into actions, which can be traced back to good intentions. To say that a person has integrity is to judge not only specific actions but also the extent to which the actions flow from commitments that are integral to a person's self-understanding. Bernard Williams observes that "one who displays integrity acts from those dispositions and motives which are most deeply his and has the virtues that enable him to do that."[60] Someone who acts merely out of habit or on impulse is not a person of integrity. A person of integrity acts from a sense of what is right. "Persons of integrity generally strive for harmony between principle and practice, and for coherence among who

they are, who they perceive themselves to be and how they present themselves to the world."[61] A person with integrity does the right thing for the right kinds of reasons. Even though it is not always possible systematically to translate intentions into actions, they at least offer stability. Conduct must be consistent with commitment and vice versa.[62]

Also significant when we speak of integrity is that whereas a single action can betray a lack of integrity, no single action can definitively establish a person's integrity. A single slip can be fatal whereas a lifetime of good deeds can still leave one's character open to question.[63]

Thus, integrity is about constant alignment. It is not an *ad hoc* affair. It has diachronic as well as synchronic dimensions in the sense that it involves a pattern, stability, and self-integration. Persons of integrity alter their behavior only for very serious and well-considered reasons. That means "certain underlying principles of judgment, principles on which, at the deeper level, their ongoing stability of character is founded" are present.[64] At the same time, stability requires courage (the will to do what one knows is right) in the face of external, but not overwhelming, pressures, temptations, or constraints. According to Benjamin, integrity is precisely the ability to remain oneself in trying situations. It is exactly in situations like these that integrity materializes. For him a "person of integrity does not have the split in the timber which would cause him or her to break under pressure."[65] The way in which events unfold may serve either to reinforce one's integrity or to jeopardize it. That is why it is so much easier to point out a person who lacks integrity than one who has integrity.

The strength of a person's character that is revealed in moments of pressure enables us to predict future action. Not surprisingly, integrity is about an integrated life. The unity of the self "resides in the unity of a narrative which links birth to life to death as narrative beginning to middle to end." MacIntyre continues, "Given the constraints of biology, society, and fortune, what will my life as a whole look like when it is nearly over?"[66] Solomon is perfectly right in saying that integrity goes beyond resisting temptation. Integrity more often requires action and proactive behavior. It is not just a matter of "not giving in."[67] Integrity must therefore be continually affirmed in action. It follows that the motivational self-sufficiency of a person of integrity surpasses by far that of a reasonably decent person.

3. *A person of integrity is integrated into his or her environment and sensitive to social issues, and willing to account for himself or herself.* Integrity also means wholeness in the sense of being an integral part of something larger than the individual.[68] Not only are persons of integrity internally consistent—both at certain points in time and throughout time—they are also in harmony and connected with others. Others who depend on such persons therefore have reason to trust them.

Being integrated into one's environment also means making a contribution to the smooth functioning of the whole. In the society and organizations in which we function, everyone fulfills specific roles. Persons of integrity fulfill their social roles and tasks. The question of whether a functionary acts with integrity depends on the function the person fulfills. If conflicts arise between the various tasks that someone fulfills, a clear and unprejudiced choice must be made. The fact that a mixture of motives plays a role in actions is not necessarily unacceptable and does not raise questions with respect to a person's integrity as such. However, the situation changes when a function is used—or misused—to realize other (covert) ambitions. Because integrity is related to tasks or functions carried out, the demands that are placed on people are achievable. Integrity requires of each person to do what is necessary to fulfill the function as well as possible.

The business ethicist Henk van Luijk[69] argues for an operational notion of integrity. What he has in mind is integrity principally as the responsibility for fulfilling a given role. A person of integrity accepts the responsibility that comes with his or her function. For van Luijk, this involves among other things that the person is willing to account for the manner in which he or she gives content to his or her responsibilities. Accountability for actions is central along "with the willingness to take other views on proper conduct seriously, to the point of acknowledging that one's interpretation of integrity is less defensible than the alternatives offered."[70]

Integrity not only involves an individual's commitment to principles that are in accordance with personal or public opinion. Integrity also implies loyalty to those principles that can be consented to on legitimate grounds. Contrary to the arguments of some scholars,[71] integrity requires more than adherence to some arbitrary set of values and more than adherence to a set of values acceptable to some other individual or group. Integrity refers to an express commitment to a morally justifiable set of principles and values. For example, we cannot label a guard at a Nazi concentration camp as a person of integrity if he ebulliently escorted Jews and gypsies to the gas chambers. Integrity means acting in accordance with the *legitimate* expectations of those around us. Integrity means wholeness in conduct also from an outside perspective. As Bob Solomon puts it, "Integrity does not mean being the moral rock around which the rest of the earth revolves."[72] Solomon's view of integrity encompasses an understanding that one's principles are not necessarily universal. Different people of integrity might very well subscribe to different principles. Nevertheless, cooperative relationships with other people and conforming to legitimate principles remain of primary importance. At the same time integrity also implies independence and may sometimes even require disobedience and disloyalty. As a result, people of integrity may not always be particularly likeable. Integrity requires flexibility, an ability to adjust to some situations while holding onto one's norms and values.

Characteristic of a person of integrity is the will to make a contribution to the greater whole. According to van Willigenburg, it is in this aspect of meaning that the moral character of the concept of integrity lies.[73] It is not only about a formal alignment of values, norms, and effects. A person of integrity has the expectation that the norms and values that she upholds are also subscribed to by others. That implies a willingness to analyze and discuss the norms and values that are advanced and to relinquish them for better norms and values should it be necessary.

Integrity and the "resolution" of dilemmas

Previously in this chapter, we gave an overview of two types of dilemmas. In the first, deontological duties and consequentialist criteria conflict with each other. In the second, requirements for actions clash with desirable characteristics. The question is whether it is possible to resolve these kinds of dilemmas by formulating one fundamental criterion against which all values and norms can be weighed. If this is not possible, it seems that we will have to accept that norms and values are ultimately relative or subjective in nature. Dilemmas put people's wholeness (and as we will see below, also that of organizations) in question. People who are confronted with dilemmas oscillate between conflicting demands.

The notion of integrity offers a way out of this choice. Integrity means "working on wholeness" in three respects. First, by aligning values, norms, and ideals. Second, by striving for coherence between words and deeds. And, finally, by making a contribution to the greater whole. What does this mean in concrete terms? Do the dilemmas that arise between values, norms, and principles get solved of their own accord as long as we are dealing with persons of integrity?

It seems that even by choosing for the integrity approach, we are making things very difficult for ourselves. Integrity, after all, seems to be incompatible with making concessions and compromises. According to van Willigenburg, it is

[N]ot only a matter of our personal integrity being at stake, it concerns "the matter" itself. It is about upholding moral norms and values. It is not only about staying true to commitments that are determining of identity, it is about being true to that which counts for all of us or should count for us all. How could one compromise on that?[74]

A "real" dilemma can be "resolved" in several ways:

- A simple choice can be made for one of the two values.
- Another possibility is to do nothing. None of the conflicting values are realized.
- Sometimes a compromise can be sought where both values are partially realized. It implies falling short with respect to both values at the same time.

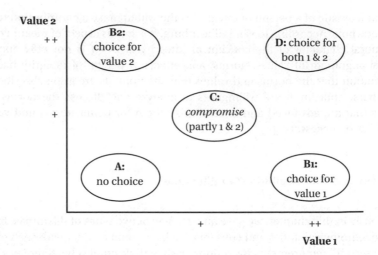

Fig. 2.4. Alternative solutions to dilemmas.[75]

- A compromise can be optimized where solutions are sought that realize both values to as great an extent as possible and an optimal situation is achieved.

Figure 2.4 depicts the logical possibilities for solving dilemmas.

An important reason for the acuteness of moral dilemmas can be found in the fact that we tacitly assume that honoring one of the conflicting values is to reject the other value.

However, we believe that in the face of dilemmas, value pluralism can ensure "wholeness" in the three senses discussed. Value pluralism recognizes the validity of a plurality of values, norms, and ideals. This is not to suggest that all values, norms, and ideals are equally good or that mistaken responses to moral issues are no longer possible. Value pluralism should be distinguished from moral relativism and moral subjectivism. Value pluralism holds that people find valuable a diverse range of irreducible values, norms, and ideals that regularly clash. This, in short, is what lies at the basis of moral dilemmas. That a choice has to be made, for example, due to a scarcity of resources (time, money), does not imply that the obligation that is not fulfilled or the value that is not honored is no longer valid. Choosing for one value does not necessarily imply a choice against the other conflicting value.

Value pluralism holds that norms (of both the utilitarian and deontological kind) and ideals ultimately rest on values. Characteristic of values is that they are not mutually exclusive.

Charles Hampden-Turner and Fons Trompenaars, both experts in the field of strategic intercultural management, have conducted extensive research on managing intercultural differences. In their view, values exist by virtue of differences. Something is a value because it possesses a distinguishing feature we deem valuable. Tension can arise between the things we value. This can readily be seen in products:

Consider the differences incorporated into an automobile. We wish it to be *high-performing* yet *safe*, to *economize on fuel* yet *accelerate sharply*, to be *sporty* yet *reliable*, to give *freedom* to the driver *yet reassert control* in emergencies, to be *compact* yet *roomy* inside, to *absorb* the impact of a collision so that occupants *escape* that impact. We want it to be *low-cost* yet *distinctive*. Clearly this list of values is full of contrasts. A car that performs more sluggishly is safer; acceleration uses up fuel; a compact car, all things being equal, is less roomy; and so on. These values are in tension with each other. The conventional wisdom is that we must choose between these values, so that a Volvo, for example, is safe and reliable but not high-performing and sporty. But if we look deeper, we see that despite some trade-offs, automobiles are considerably safer *and* better performing, more fuel-saving *and* more responsive to the throttle than they were just a few years ago. The industry consistently improves *both* values-in-tension.[76]

According to Hampden-Turner and Trompenaars, the tension between values is the source of value creation. Conflicts between values should thus be seen as a challenge. This applies not only to products but also to processes aimed at producing these products.

Value conflicts and clashes emerge within research, development, manufacturing, marketing, distribution, and after sales service departments, and many conflicts erupt *between* them.[77]

In launching a new pharmaceutical product on the market, the approach of a marketer is different from that of a medical researcher. Every professional has his or her own values and with it, his or her own professional culture. Value conflicts can arise not only between national cultures but also between corporate cultures. In most instances, it is possible to search for optimal situations where the different values at stake can be honored as best as possible. For the process aimed at uniting clashing values Hampden-Turner and Trompenaars use the term "reconciliation", which entails thinking together these conflicting values to as great an extent as possible.

Hampden-Turner and Trompenaars' description of conflicting cultural values also applies to conflicting moral values. Conflicts between particular rights and the common good, for example, can often be "resolved" in practice. The solution has to be sought in reconciling clashing demands. In so doing, it is important not to treat each situation as an isolated case. The reconciliation of clashing demands can consist in frankly admitting to the impossibility of meeting all demands, expressing regret, showing compassion for the victim, striving for minimum damage, and seeking a way to compensate damages. It can also involve seeking creative compromises. This approach often means making oneself vulnerable, being willing to learn from mistakes, and being open to better ideas.

Dealing with moral dilemmas places demands on behavior but in particular on the disposition of the person involved. This person is to stand up and make known the values he believes in. The person of integrity does not hide behind others and makes sure forces beyond him do not control him. Over and above this, he has the disposition to search for unity in the different demands. A person of integrity strives toward understanding and realizing the respective conflicting values, norms, and ideals as an interconnected whole.

Against the background of the alternative responses to dilemmas, we can now describe the choice a person of integrity would make.

For a person of integrity, alternative (A) is a never acceptable. The person in question actually leaves the choice to others and in doing so, he actually relinquishes his autonomy. He becomes a plaything of the forces around him and lets it happen.

Alternative (B) is unappealing to a person of integrity. It implies that only one value is realized and the other is negated, which raises doubts about how strongly one feels about the value that is not realized. A choice for (B) requires a clear explanation for the absolute importance of the one value or interest over and above the value that is ignored.

The compromise (C) is similarly unattractive for a person of integrity if it leads simply to appease others superficially. In seeking a compromise so as to realize an optimal solution (alternative (D)), it must be clear that the person in question is confronted with a tragic dilemma that forces him to choose but that he is trying to fulfill all moral obligations to the best of his abilities. Only if these requirements are met is it clear that he takes both values to heart. The search for the correct balance is expressed in the willingness to enter into dialogue and to subject choices to discussion.

Integrity concerns a disposition that is aimed at holding on to values, norms, and ideals. The search for an appropriate course of action involves a willingness to analyze and discuss one's choices and to seek richer solutions. "Richness" refers to finding solutions that do justice to the different values at stake. By combining where possible the positive dimensions of the one-sided (B) alternatives, we gain sight of an optimal solution (D). Integrity is visible in a disposition, conduct, and ambitions that are aimed at continuous improvement and in striving for a (more) optimal solution. Integrity implies holding on to values, norms, and ideals; openness to other values, norms, and ideals in words and deeds; and striving for improvement. Integrity is therefore expressly non-relativist. The notion "improvement" is an explicitly normative concept. Integrity leaves room for other norms and values.

In this chapter integrity was analyzed from two perspectives. On the one hand we examined the different types of moral criteria that could involve mutually conflicting prescriptions in practice. From this point of view, an appeal is made for value pluralism. From this perspective, integrity is described as striving for coherence between values without suggesting that differences should be erased. On the other hand integrity was analyzed as coherence between input, conduct, and outcome. The two perspectives in fact form two layers of the notion of integrity. The coherence between qualities, principles, and objectives is repeated as coherence between input, conduct, and outcome.

Conclusion

Individual integrity requires that one's words and deeds conform to a substantive, coherent, and relatively stable set of qualities, behavioral principles, and goals/ideals to which one is genuinely and freely committed.[78] The call for "integratedness" does not exclude conflict between the different ideals and commitments of one and same person. Sometimes, one has to let go of one goal to be able to retain another. A compromise need not threaten one's integrity. In fact, it may even be called for to a certain extent to safeguard "integratedness."[79] At the same time, there are some ideals and goals that are so intertwined with one's identity that renouncing them would result in "losing face" or the trust of others. Integrity therefore requires a certain degree of integration and standing strong in the convictions and values that make one unique. At the same time, limitations and responsibilities do exist that have to be respected by everyone irrespective of individual identity or principles—even if it requires sacrifice. Sometimes it may even be important *not to do* something. To say someone has integrity is not to suggest that outsiders necessarily approve of a person's convictions and conduct. Aspiring toward something (having goals), standing for something (being steadfast), and feeling concern for something (having affinity with the outside world) are key elements of a person of integrity.

A life is "whole" when it is integrated from both the point of view of the agent and from the perspective of others. Integrity regulates the connection between intentions, deeds, and consequences. Integrity requires consistency in thoughts and action. Moreover, it requires sincere dedication to convictions.[80] The three chief characteristics of the concept of integrity are as follows:[81]

1. internal coherence in the motives for what one would like to be, what one will (not) do, and what one would like to realize
2. coherence between motives (what one is), actions (what one does (does not do)), and the effects of these actions (what one achieves)
3. coherence in motives, actions, and effects with respect to the outside world.

The concept of integrity is not entirely distinct from consequentialist, deontological, and virtue ethics. In consequentialist ethics, moral judgment is based on the effects of an action whereas in deontological ethics, the nature of the action itself is evaluated. In making a moral judgment, virtue ethics looks to the character of the actor, the motives and intentions behind the action. The integrity approach emphasizes the coherence between these approaches. The integrity approach takes seriously the whole: the individual, the context, and the past. The concept is flexible in the sense that it does not take an initial stand by prioritizing virtues or principles or consequences. The integrity approach offers connections for an exchange of ideas among the advocates of the different perspectives. Another advantage of the concept is that it does not make unrealistic demands but achievable ones that are related to the function people perform. In this approach, an action is chosen which is justifiable but not totally determined by others' expectations. In theory, a person who fulfills a role according to the book could be viewed as a person of integrity. However, because situations arise that cannot simply be resolved by following the rules, practical wisdom is required in performing a function properly. To be able to assess a situation and determine a sound course of action in the light of the nature of the role and its moral dimensions, the appropriate values and principles must be internalized. When a person has the knowledge and skills to interpret rules, he or she is also able to use his or her critical faculties to determine his or her own position in relation to the conventional interpretation of the rules.[82]

The main question is whether or to what extent this theoretical framework can be applied to the corporate context. What do terms like "unity," "completeness," and "integration" mean to corporations? Do corporations have "motives" and, if so, where are these located? Is it possible to characterize corporations as having a high degree of self-control and self-awareness? If so, exactly what does that mean? What moral expectations of corporations are reasonable and legitimate, and how would they relate to corporate roles and tasks? Can a corporation defy the moral expectations of its stakeholders and still retain its integrity? What kinds of moral criteria can be formulated with the help of the three general ethical theories and how are they related? Is it possible to apply the concept of integrity to business organizations? These in short, are the fundamental issues that we shall examine in the next chapter.

IHC Caland

In 1998, IHC Caland was in the process of constructing a floating storage and offloading system 120 miles off the coast of Myanmar (the former Burma) for more than $100 million, with plans to lease it to Premier Oil. IHC took a beating from the public since, at that time, Burma was in the hands of a particularly repressive military regime with an atrocious record of human rights violations.

IHC Caland

IHC Caland is primarily a supplier of offshore services and dredges with worldwide operations. The products of IHC are mainly "custom-built" to meet the special requirements of its customers. This means that the number of projects it can carry out is limited to a certain capacity. IHC is the leader in this small international market. This dominant position constitutes a strategic risk for the corporation. IHC could not afford to let a single tender go by, because there are only a few big projects each year, and, as a spokesperson stated at the time "if we don't do them, somebody else will."[83] Given its fixed annual expenses and obligations, missing out on a single project could have had serious repercussions for the corporation. The necessity to do its utmost for each and every project was exacerbated by the major subsidies granted to shipbuilders in certain countries. Other factors included the protectionism prevalent among certain governments regarding shipbuilding in their own countries and the entry of new market players.

Burma[84]

Burma became independent in 1948 following a period of British colonization. A new state was formed with a parliamentary democracy. In 1962, the Burma Socialist Program Party seized power in a military coup. Under this dictatorial regime, free elections and freedom of speech came to an end and torture became common practice.

On 8 August 1988, the citizens of Burma took to the streets to demonstrate and demand that the Burma Socialist Program Party make way for a democratically elected parliament. The demonstration resulted in many civilian casualties. On 18 September 1988, the army conceded and established the State Law and Order Restoration Council (which was later renamed as the State Peace and Development Council). Free elections were held in Burma in 1990, with the National League for Democracy (NLD) winning 82 per cent of the seats in parliament. Despite the fact that these elections were free and unbiased, the military junta refused to accept the new government and continued its undermining activities. During the 1990s the NLD was increasingly threatened. Some of its members were forced to leave the "political" arena and most of the NLD's offices were closed down. The junta's political opponents were killed, tortured, or locked away in dreadful prisons. Many thousands of people perished. By the time people started focusing attention on IHC, Amnesty International estimated that there were about 2,000 political prisoners detained in abominable conditions. In order to force the military into a dialogue with the opposition, the leader of the Democratic Party, Aung San Suu Kyi, appealed to foreign companies to stay out of Burma. The United States outlawed new investments in Burma in May 1997. Canada also put trade sanctions in place on Burma. Many European corporations (such as Ericsson, BHS, Heineken, Carlsberg, and Philips) also took heed and left Burma. One of the corporations that stayed was IHC Caland. What was IHC's reason for staying?

The situation of IHC in Burma[85]

The Yetagun natural gas field lies in the Golf of Martaban, 260 miles south of Yangoon, the capital of Burma. The field is operated by British Premier Oil, Nippon Oil, the Petroleum Authority of Thailand, and Myanmar Oil and Gas Enterprise (MOGE, a Burmese state-owned enterprise). Since the beginning of 2000, this consortium has been pumping 200 million cubic meters of natural gas a day to neighboring Thailand. The pipeline runs across land adjacent to the Yadana gas field pipeline—a second natural gas field operated by Total, Unocal, PAT, and MOGE. The extraction of natural gas from the two fields represents the largest foreign investment in Burma. The total investment represents one-third of all foreign investments secured. The Yadana alone generates more than $200 million a year for the Burmese junta. The two natural gas fields therefore form the financial backbone of Burma's military regime.

The standpoints

IHC could not afford to let projects such as that for Premier Oil go by. "We are no political party. We are interested in business—nothing more. Let's not convolute matters." Those were the words of Bax, chairman of the board at IHC until the middle of 1999.[86] In Bax's opinion, it was not IHC's duty to change public opinion within Myanmar or any other country. IHC had signed a contract and it was too late to pull out. "If you sign a contract, there's no way back. And if you do decide to pull out, you'll look ridiculous. You might as well close down shop."[87] Langeman, president-director of IHC, added: "If the situation were to repeat itself, we'd accept the order all over again. We are active in a lot of countries where human rights are violated. If the government does not ban investing in such countries, we see no reason to be more reticent. If we did, we'd go under."[88] Langeman stated in clear terms that it was up to the government to decide whether to ban investments in a certain country. "If the government decides not to boycott, then the decision is up to us as to whether or not to invest. If we fail to invest, someone else will instead. In that case, the ruling regime is not any better or worse off. We intend on going forward with our business policy wherever we are able to tender without government sanctions."[89]

Partly at the insistence of the pension fund ABP, one of its stockholders, IHC started to draw up a corporate code.[90] ABP requires the companies it invests in to have a clear framework against which investments in politically sensitive areas can be checked. According to a representative of the pension fund, "investments in countries where human rights are violated present a gray area where the company's own management needs to take the responsibility. In such cases, it is not right to draw the line at what the government prohibits or allows."[91] However, IHC's senior management was of the opinion that the corporate code will not change a single thing regarding the investment—after all, it had already been made. They decided that the corporate code would state that such investments would be called off only in the case that government sanctions are put into place.[92]

One of the NGOs, the Burma Committee, blamed IHC for ignoring the negative consequences of such investment and asserted that "This storage platform plays an important role in the extraction of natural gas. Even though IHC is a subcontractor for this project, the platform is leased to Premier Oil, which forms a direct link with Burma. All of the proceeds from these natural gas fields are siphoned off to Burma's department of defense. It uses these funds to buy weapons to use against its own people and for keeping its ethnic minorities under control."[93] At the time, the Burmese regime spent 50 per cent of the state budget on weapons, 24 per cent on social services, and 14 per cent on education. In an interview, director Bax acknowledged this: "Of course the money is going to the colonels."[94]

Arguments

The demand for investment/divestment in countries with repressive regimes is a fundamental dilemma for many multinationals. Corporations like IHC Caland that operate in countries where human rights are, or might be, violated are often and justifiably asked to defend their position. With this, the integrity of the company comes under scrutiny. The discussion normally does not center so much on whether the current regime can be justified (it is usually condemned) but instead on the issue of how to deal with the situation as a corporation. Consequentialist, deontological, and virtue ethical arguments are usually advanced during the public debates on such issues.

Some NGOs point to the negative impact of a corporation's presence on human rights in a given country. The corporation, in turn, points out that pulling out would only exacerbate the local situation. Moreover, the presence of a Western business could play a positive role through its business activities in such a country. Just like IHC, the company Unocal decided not to pull out of Burma, since it was convinced that its presence there had more of a positive than a negative impact on the Burmese people. Opinions on the effectiveness of the various alternatives are widely divergent. Some opt for a unilateral boycott and sanctions, while others hold that sanctions would be counter-productive and that silent diplomacy would be the most tactful approach (as opposed to screaming headlines). Some people believe that outside pressure is the only way to bring about change, whereas others advocate the "change from within" model. Moreover, a modicum of financial welfare would be necessary for opposition parties to exist. If the country as a whole were denied all income from the outside, it would be very difficult for other—democratic—parties to achieve a secure footing.

It is also possible to hold on principled grounds that corporations are entitled to do business with whomever they like, as long as this is not against the law. Furthermore, it is argued that corporations should keep out of host government policies as long as these do not directly influence their own operations. Likewise, on the basis of another principle, it can be maintained that it is the duty of corporations to refrain from violating human rights—whether directly or indirectly.

From a virtue ethical perspective, it is the purity of the motives behind the action that is the determining factor. Some people consider divestment merely a public relations tool. They see companies driven purely by their fear of negative press and boycotts. Divestment therefore becomes an exclusively opportunistic affair. Others see the refusal to pull out of such countries as a sign of courage— the bravery and spirit of CEOs to stand up for their principles under pressure. Giving in to public opinion could also be interpreted as signifying weakness. At the same time, others may perceive a corporation's willingness to change in accordance with the wishes of the public as an indication of its human side, making it worthy of praise. In response to attacks from NGOs, some companies have been questioning the soundness of NGOs' motives. According to them,

NGO arguments are unsophisticated and their appeals to the press are solely aimed at boosting their own image and satisfying their supporters' craving for sensation.

In cases where all sorts of ethical arguments can be posited both for and against investment and divestment, the question of what we can reasonably expect from a corporation looms even greater. And what role does the corporate context play? To what extent is "preserving the continuity of the corporation" a legitimate reason for letting other responsibilities fall to the wayside? To what degree is it acceptable for a corporation (in this case IHC) to allege that a "contract is a contract" and that terminating it (in this case with Premier Oil) would tarnish its reputation, thereby disqualifying it as a business partner? Where does the integrity of IHC lie and when are we justified in condemning the corporation? These are some of the questions that we shall answer in the next chapters by means of an analysis of the fundamental dilemmas facing corporations today. First of all, we shall examine the extent to which the concept of integrity can be applied to corporations as distinct moral entities.

ETHICS OF BUSINESS

INTRODUCTION

In Chapter 1, a range of moral questions that arises in the corporate context was discussed. These issues render a moral analysis of the functioning of corporations urgent.

Chapter 2 gave an exposition of the three generally accepted ethical approaches, namely consequentialism, deontological ethics, and virtue ethics. A number of theories can be distinguished within each respective approach and an overview was given of a few of them. Each theory can be used to analyze and evaluate particular aspects of human functioning. Every theory has its strengths and weaknesses, and the different approaches are often combined in practice. Sometimes, however, the theories appear to articulate moral demands that are mutually exclusive. The integrity approach, that is in keeping with the tradition of value pluralism, was introduced to make it possible to understand the connection between the conflicting demands that are formulated on the basis of the respective approaches.

In Part II, the question of whether ethical criteria can be applied to corporations is examined so as to formulate in Part III the criteria that can be employed to analyze and evaluate the functioning of corporations.

As a field of applied ethics, business ethics generally departs from the assumption that general ethical theories (as described in the previous chapter) can simply be applied to corporations and the people who act within the corporate context. Where general ethics formulates criteria for the conduct of persons, business ethics is the discipline that formulates requirements for corporations and managers who act on behalf of the corporation. The company is generally regarded as a small and simple entity in which the director (usually the owner) can be directly addressed regarding every decision made, the actions carried out by employees, and their effects. Shell's plan to sink the Brent Spar oil platform into the ocean and IHC's decision to continue doing business in Burma can be evaluated as good or bad, responsible or irresponsible, in the same way that we evaluate the actions of natural persons. The corporation is identified with the owner/director. If we recall the case of IHC, it was the opinions of people (such as Bax, De Ruiter, and Langeman) that were central to the moral evaluation of the company. Conflating the decisions, actions, and effects of corporations with those of individuals negates the unique character of the corporation and hinders an adequate moral evaluation of the corporation. In our view, the task of business ethics is to take the collective and complex character of corporations into account when subjecting this domain to moral evaluation.

An important problem with applying general ethical concepts and theories to corporations is the individualistic (atomistic) nature of the dominant ethical theories. Since the seventeenth and eighteenth centuries, moral judgments have focused on (actions of) natural persons. Moral demands can be placed on natural persons because they have a conscience and act voluntarily. They are able to distinguish between right and wrong and between responsible and irresponsible conduct. In addition, they are able to discern the consequences of their actions in advance and they are able to choose to act differently. Concepts such as "conscience," "free will," "intentions," and "deliberate actions" cannot be applied directly to corporations. In this atomistic orientation in ethics, a distinction must be drawn between methodological atomism and ontological atomism. Ontological atomism (nominalism) holds that only the individual exists. Methodological atomism does not deny the existence of social phenomena, but social reality is conceived as composed solely of individuals. Social phenomena are thus viewed as the result of the actions of individual agents.

A corporation consists of a multitude of individuals. Corporate functioning is based on the support of a great number of interested parties and takes shape internally through the concerted efforts of its employees. By attributing moral responsibility to natural persons (as the methodological atomists and to a certain degree ontological atomists do), responsibility for collective action cannot be adequately conceptualized. To acknowledge collective responsibility does not, in our view, necessarily detract from individual responsibilities. Instead, a new type of responsibility is created. The "total amount" of responsibility involved in collective action modifies and broadens its character. For the purpose of further analysis, methodological atomism fails to clarify the connection between different actions and their consequences.

This is not to suggest that we should adopt abstract or metaphysical concepts that are removed from reality. An alternative can be found for the choice between a logical-positivist or empiricist methodology and an aprioristic methodology. As a basis for an ethical theory that aims to take social action into account, these two scientific traditions are inadequate. The logical-positivists consider a concept or theory a logical construction of elementary assertions, each pointing toward reality. In this perspective, moral concepts such as "responsibility" fall beyond the theoretical domain. We also reject the other extreme— that the content of the concept "moral responsibility" is already established a priori—as a basis for our study. Here, we shall define a concept as a thought construction that contributes to clarifying problems as they are experienced. The basis and the test for concepts are the intuitions and experiences of those involved. The value of any concept depends on the extent to which it clarifies and sharpens our intuitions.

Business ethics as an academic discipline focuses on developing a moral perspective on the functioning of corporations. An atomistic/individualistic interpretation of the concept of responsibility (as is common in the dominant streams of contemporary ethics) prevents us from examining and judging the functioning of corporations in its full complexity. The concept of corporate integrity attempts to address this shortcoming. The criteria developed in business ethical theories have to contribute toward clarifying concrete issues and providing the means to evaluate corporate functioning consistently.

The question that is examined in Part II is where exactly the integrity of the corporation can be located. In this regard, we propose two theoretical anchor points.

In order to analyze and evaluate corporations in moral terms, it is necessary to establish why the corporation can be seen as a moral entity. In Chapter 3, three common models for locating corporate responsibility are discussed. These are the amoral, functional, and autonomy models of corporate responsibility. Our aim is to substantiate the autonomy model that posits that the corporation can be conceived as an independent moral unit. This is the first theoretical anchor point. An analysis of the corporation in terms of moral practices reveals the coordinating mechanisms of employee conduct. These mechanisms make it possible for us to regard the corporation as an autonomous moral entity, rendering the corporation itself an object of moral evaluation. In addition, we localize the integrity of the corporation in its moral character and in the moral cohesion of the relations between the corporation and its stakeholders.

Three types of relationship are identified that characterize corporate functioning: the relationship between the corporation and a diverse range of stakeholders; the relations of cooperation within the corporation; and the relations of individual employees with the corporation and third parties. Each of these relationships can generate tension. Chapters 4 and 5 consist of an in-depth discussion of the dirty hands, the many hands, and the entangled hands dilemmas. The three types of dilemmas are determinant of the corporate condition, that is, the preconditions for the functioning of corporations. We argue that the tension that arises in the relationships above can be made manageable by conceiving these relationships as contracts.

The second theoretical anchor point is that relations within the corporate context can be seen as contracts and that the corporation itself can be interpreted as a nexus of contractual relationships. From a social contract perspective, corporate responsibility is the effect of these contracts. In Chapter 5, we argue that the corporation can be conceptualized as a focal point within a network of contractual relationships. The suitability of the contract model lies in the fact that the aim of a contract is to satisfy optimally the rights (deontological perspective) and interests (consequentialist perspective) of all parties

involved. By viewing the corporation as a relatively long-term multiparty contract, it is morally desirable to pursue the corporate interest and honor stakeholder rights simultaneously. By conceiving the corporation as a contract and
its relations with stakeholders as contracts, we can deduce the criteria for their
moral legitimacy. On the one hand, these criteria will concern the contracting
process (deontological perspective). On the other, they will apply to the contracting parties (virtue perspective).

In Part III, we will develop criteria for corporate integrity to address and
resolve the three fundamental dilemmas on the basis of the theoretical study of
the moral dimensions of corporate functioning.

3

The Corporation as Moral Entity

Large corporations usually consist of a conglomerate of corporations each with its own management. All sorts of units or departments headed by a management team can be found in corporations. It is ultimately the individuals within each unit or department that forms the corporation. We speak of the cooperation of a team or the supervision of the Board of Directors or management team, but within each of these collectives it is ultimately individuals that take decisions, make compromises, and implement decisions on the basis of their responsibilities.

Is it justified to conceive of corporations as moral subjects? If this question can be answered in the affirmative, what is the relationship between the moral responsibilities of natural persons and that of their employer? To what extent can the representatives of a company who are involved in an incident hide behind the organization's responsibilities? And to what extent can the organization hide behind the responsibilities of individual employees?

The use of the concept of integrity in connection with the functioning of corporations appears contradictory. How is it possible to speak of a stable set of norms and values in relations of cooperation when individuals all have their own norms and values? What guarantees the coherence between the words and deeds of corporations? What guarantees the external integration of a corporation? How can "wholeness" and "unity" be guaranteed if a corporation is represented by a multitude of individuals and if individuals can join and resign at will? On what grounds can we view the corporation as a unit on the basis of which we speak of its integrity?

These questions ultimately turn on the localization of the moral responsibility of corporations. To distinguish the integrity of a corporation from the integrity of individual employees, it must first be shown that it is justified to conceive of the corporation as a moral subject. In answer to the question of the localization of the moral responsibility for corporate activities, three positions can be distinguished:

1. The *amoral model* does not acknowledge corporate moral responsibility as a meaningful concept. Moral responsibility in the corporate context is

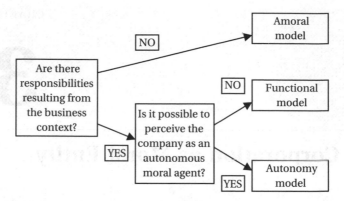

Fig. 3.1. Three models for localizing responsibility.

conflated with the personal responsibility of natural persons within the company.

2. The *functional model* of corporate responsibility acknowledges that the organized character of actions within the organizational context results in responsibility, but reduces it to the individual responsibility of company representatives.

3. The *autonomy model* portrays the corporation as a social entity. Corporate responsibility is viewed as separate from the individuals who represent the company.

The amoral perspective, the traditional view of corporations, generates a number of problems. The functional model succeeds in addressing these inadequacies but leaves a number of other problems unresolved. The autonomy model solves the problems that the amoral model and functional model fail to overcome. The autonomy model enables us to ascribe the responsibility for a company's total operations to an independent moral entity. This model also allows for drawing a distinction between actions undertaken by the staff on behalf of the company and actions undertaken by the staff on the basis of intentions that are at odds with their role as employee. In this chapter, we will show that the autonomy model can be further developed as a basis for applying the concept of integrity to corporations.

THE AMORAL CORPORATION

According to the amoral model, moral responsibility cannot be ascribed to the corporation or to people who fulfill certain functions. The ideas of Friedrich Hayek and Milton Friedman, and the reasoning of John Kenneth Galbraith are in keeping with a neoclassical conception of the corporation. They argue that one cannot ascribe responsibility to the corporation or to certain stakeholders (on the basis of their function within this context) who constitute the corporation. The difference between Hayek and Friedman, on the one hand, and Galbraith, on the other, is not to be found in the way they conceptualize the corporation, but in how they *value* it. Hayek and Friedman see something of value in the amoral character of the corporation. It is the guarantor of a free society. For Galbraith, the amoral ideal is only a cover for the actual immorality of corporate functioning, which leads him to argue for mechanisms to control and correct corporations. Despite the great differences between these scholars, all three are exponents of the amoral model.

Hayek

Friedrich Hayek[1] perpetuates classical economic thinking and is primarily concerned with safeguarding the free society. For Hayek, freedom and morality are two sides of the same coin. Freedom is the precondition for morality since people can only be held morally accountable for their actions if they are free. A free society depends on society's general acceptance of certain moral values such as the value of the individual.

For Hayek, "freedom" refers to freedom of choice. A society is free if people have freedom of choice. Two conditions have to be satisfied for a society to be free: *individual responsibility* and *an amoral market*.

First, people must believe in individual responsibility. An individual's personality (which develops over a lifetime), as opposed to outside circumstances, ultimately determines action. Praise and criticism, both of which are received from society on the basis of actions, influence the individual personality. In this way, a kind of "indirect guidance" of individual action occurs. It is a form of "indirect" determinism that Hayek accepts and which gives rise to individual responsibility.

Second, people must receive compensation for their work in accordance with the value it has for others. It is not a person's moral value (good motives and intentions) but rather his or her contribution to the prosperity of the community that is the correct criterion for the distribution of wealth. If people are free to decide how to apply their abilities, it follows that they should be rewarded according to the value of their services. The market price expresses the value of services. People are thus stimulated to make optimal use of their knowledge and abilities.

Hayek does not consider corporations to be autonomous moral entities. They are the instruments for the efficient organization of the market. The market itself must be considered an amoral arena. The free society would be undermined if corporations were to pursue autonomous moral objectives. People would be able to hide behind an anonymous collective and individual responsibility would disappear.

Hayek acknowledges that the corporation may be identified with the interests of its employees. This would mean that the group of employees could be viewed as a collective with its own personality. Employees pursue a common goal and they share collective experiences, thereby creating a collective with similar traits. For Hayek, however, it is not acceptable to identify the corporation with this collective. This would amount to interfering with freedom and, in turn, the efficient use of the means of production. Here he is referring, for example, to the freedom of employees to leave and find a new job, and the freedom of employers to fire employees if they become superfluous or when their skills are no longer needed. He writes:

[I]n a free system (i.e., in a system of free labor) it is necessary in the interest of the efficient use of resources that the corporation be regarded primarily as an aggregate of material assets. It is they and not the men whom the management can at will allocate to different purposes, they which alone are the means which it is the task of the corporation to put to the best use, while the individual must in the last resort himself remain free to decide whether the best use of his energies is within the particular corporation or elsewhere.[2]

Hayek does recognize the importance of the role that employees can play. He even admits that there may be cogent arguments to identify the corporation at least partially with the employees, but he maintains that this would be undesirable. To guarantee as free an economy as possible, he certainly does not want to link moral consequences to this conceptualization since it would put the free society at risk.[3]

Friedman

Milton Friedman, too, echoes the classical economic thinking of Adam Smith. For Friedman, a corporation cannot have moral responsibilities because a corporation is at most an artificial person. Only people—the directors—acting for the corporation could possibly be held morally accountable. Moreover, a corporate director must refrain from basing his decisions on moral considerations. He is an employee who owes a responsibility to the owners, the stockholders. In general, they are after as much return on their capital investment as possible. On the basis of his freely accepted contractual relationship with his employer, a director is obliged to pursue this goal of the owners. Naturally, a director may, as a private person, invest money or energy in public causes. In that case, he is spending his money or time and not that of the corporation. A director who does not pursue the objectives of the owners is in fact robbing them. Friedman formulates his argument as follows:

What does it mean to say that the corporate executive has a "social responsibility" in his capacity as a businessman? If this statement is not pure rhetoric, it must mean that he is to act in some way that is not in the interest of his employers. For example, that he is to refrain from increasing the price of the product in order to contribute to the social objective of preventing inflation, even though a price increase would be in the best interest of the corporation. Or that he is to make expenditures on reducing pollution beyond the amount that is in the best interests of the corporation or that is required by law in order to contribute to the social objective of improving the environment. Or that, at the expense of corporate profits, he is to hire "hardcore" unemployed instead of better qualified available workmen to contribute to the social objective of reducing poverty. In each of these cases, the corporate executive would be spending someone else's money for the general social interest. Insofar as his actions are in accord with his "social responsibility" to reduce returns to stockholders, he is spending their money. Insofar as his actions lower the wages of some employees, he is spending their money.[4]

To the extent that a director runs a company on behalf of the stockholders, he must consider himself to be their personal instrument. He therefore has only one responsibility and that is to the owners. This responsibility is set down in a (partly implicit) contract. Thus, a director does indeed have responsibilities: to fulfill the terms of an explicit and implicit contract. To a certain extent, this is also a moral obligation. The moral duty of a corporate director is, according to Friedman, to act amorally. If the director sees himself destined to serve the public interest, he "taxes" certain groups, as it were, for the sake of achieving public aims. He thereby takes on those tasks that actually belong to democratically elected bodies. It is the responsibility of these institutions to decide which social objectives to target and which taxes to impose. The director should stay clear of tasks that are proper to the political arena. After all, he was neither hired nor paid to dabble in politics.

Friedman in fact shifts the problem of corporate responsibility onto the stockholders—the ones who give the orders. Are they not morally accountable for the corporation they own? Can and should they not feel morally obligated? Say the stockholders happen to be satisfied with lower profits in order to be "socially responsible," who is to oppose them? Friedman acknowledges this point of criticism and replies that stockholders will not and should not act in this way. He believes that whenever terms such as "social responsibility" are used, stockholders are trying to cover up their unbridled self-interest. Such refined tactics almost qualify as fraud. Stockholders should, therefore, not act morally because such actions undermine the foundations of the free society. The market system and the political system become intertwined at this point. The political system would dominate the market system, leading to a collectivist doctrine. The doctrine of the social responsibility of companies is therefore extremely subversive. In a free society, business has only one social responsibility and that is

...to use its resources and engage in the activities designed to increase its profits so long as it stays within the rules of the game, which is to say, engages in open and free competition without deception and fraud.[5]

In his conception of the corporation as merely an artificial personality, Friedman still fails to show why corporations *cannot* be held responsible and he fails to convince that organizations *should not* be held responsible. This position can only be maintained if ethics is purely and exclusively related to natural persons. This is precisely the point in question but Friedman's assumption precludes a discussion of corporate responsibility altogether.[6]

Corporate morality as a reflection of the norms and values of society

A variation on the amoral model holds that a corporation is no better or worse than the society within which it functions. A corporation consists of and sells to people. It passively reflects the values and norms people uphold.

Corporations function amorally. It is society that forces them into moral or immoral "action."[7] The corporation is thus viewed as a plaything of market forces; it is completely heteronomous. If this were a normative proposition, the corporation would be obligated to submit to market forces entirely. In that case, the corporation would have both limited freedom and the ambiguous obligation to surrender its freedom, rendering it a voluntary plaything. Is it possible to speak of corporate responsibility under these circumstances? Does the corporation not remain accountable for its actions? If this is not a normative standpoint, but purely a descriptive proposition, it becomes significantly more difficult to parry. The validity of this reasoning depends on the question of whether viewing corporate action as a reaction to market stimuli is an accurate description of the corporate function. Moreover, to accept this proposition does not mean that the corporate function can be completely explained in terms of market stimuli. Market stimuli are important, but they do not completely explain the corporate function. There is, therefore, room to speak of freedom and moral responsibility.

Galbraith

In their criticism of the corporate manner of production, the critics of the neoliberal market system indirectly reinforce the amoral view of the corporation. According to the institutional economist John Kenneth Galbraith, the free corporate production method praised by the classical and neoclassical economists has engendered today's large multinational corporations. These are managed by technocrats, the officials just below the directors in the corporate hierarchy. On the basis of their know-how, they are the ones who actually make decisions and do not have to account to anyone—nor can they be controlled. Galbraith calls this group of people the "technostructure." As a result, neither the government nor the stockholders have any grip on the corporation. For

Galbraith, the "idealistic image" of the classical economists represents merely a cover. It is a myth behind which the real powerbrokers are able to hide.

From our view of UGE and Phillips [the two corporations that Galbraith used as examples in his study] we can see how great the conflict is between myth and reality in the modern corporation and how this generates unease and suspicion. Where the myth departs so sharply from the reality, it is only natural to suppose that its purpose is to conceal. No one can believe that UGE is the powerless and passive instrument of market forces. No one with the slightest knowledge of UGE's Washington operations can believe that it is without power in the state. No one can believe that its management is the responsive servant of directors and stockholders. Yet all these things the myth affirms. Where so much must be done to conceal power, only one conclusion is possible. The exercise of power must surely be malign.[8]

The arms race (especially in the 1980s) in particular is the damaging result of the uncontrolled power of the technostructure. It is maintained by the entanglement of the government apparatus and the technostructure (the military-industrial complex) with the exclusion of Third World countries that do not have the power to offer sufficient opposition.

According to Galbraith, there is only one remedy for the immoral functioning of corporations: more, and more effective, control. Society should limit the freedom of movement of corporations through government instruments and state controls so that the interests of the anonymous technostructure can no longer dominate the general interest. According to Galbraith: "[T]he only answer is a strong framework that aligns the exercise of corporate power with the public purpose."[9] Another possible way to achieve this goal is to replace the Board of Directors, which actually has no function since the technostructure makes all the real decisions, with:

... a board of public auditors, which would keep out of management decisions, but ensure the enforcement of public laws and regulations, report on matters of public interest, otherwise keep management honest and ratify or, in the event of inadequacy or failure, order changes in the top management command.[10]

Galbraith therefore indirectly reinforces the idealistic notion of the amoral corporation. His version can, however, only be realized through a controlling government or in some other way. The implication is therefore that corporations should bear certain moral norms in mind. Since corporations function in a market, that seems unrealistic to him. As a result, he places no moral demands on corporations.

Room for personal responsibility

From an amoral perspective, the question of corporate responsibility is rejected as nonsensical. In the different variations on the theme, localizing the moral responsibility at the level of or in the corporation is either rejected as undesirable or exposed as a justification for corporate immorality. People are able to do good or bad things. These concepts do not apply to corporations and actions taken on behalf of corporations. A corporation does not act morally or immorally, but amorally. From an amoral perspective, corporate responsibility is an empty concept; it cannot be localized.

Various motives and considerations play a role in the arguments of the proponents of the amoral model of the corporation. Some acknowledge that corporations should indeed keep certain obligations in mind. The responsibility toward stockholders, for example, takes precedence over all others. This responsibility is moral in nature as management has a contract or agreement with the owners of the corporation. They have to keep this agreement by generating as much profit as possible. In general, however, those who deny corporate moral responsibility do not view the fulfillment of this agreement as a moral obligation. They equate morality with the pursuit of social ideals. Moral responsibility in this view is lumped together with idealism and political activism.

The various versions of the amoral model all agree on one point: there is no place for moral considerations in the corporate context. In most of the versions, however, a certain degree of morality does creep back in through the side door. A distinction that is not explicitly advocated or explored by the proponents of this approach, but that plays an implicit role in most of the theories, concerns the degree to which personal responsibility is acknowledged. On the basis of this criterion, two types of amoral models can be distinguished: the completely amoral model and the model of personal responsibility.

The most extreme position in this regard is the completely amoral stance that holds that the corporate context leaves absolutely no room for moral responsibility. From this perspective, all corporations relentlessly pursue maximum profits. The only way in which corporations will take norms into consideration is if they are forced to do so by legislation and government control or by economic need. A director cannot and may not allow himself moral standards. The position he holds offers no room for personal responsibility.

The personal vision of moral responsibility denies that the corporate context entails special responsibilities but accepts that the personal responsibility of every natural person also plays a role in the corporate context. Both Hayek and Friedman's line of reasoning actually contain elements of this variation. They reject morality, as they perceive it as the pursuit of social ideals. All other obligations are subsequently viewed as personal moral obligations.

Criticism on the amoral position

Several considerations from various perspectives have been advanced for viewing corporations as amoral. None of the arguments in favor of this position is, however, sufficiently persuasive. The need to separate values from facts does not imply that one cannot argue in the realm of values or that values are irrelevant for the corporate context. If the manager is regarded purely as an instrument of the owners of the corporation (as in the neoclassic economic vision of Hayek and Friedman), it does not necessarily follow that absolutely no responsibility rests with the corporation or its owners.

Adam Smith's theory of the "invisible hand" alludes indirectly to a moral responsibility of corporations. Hayek's argument that the free society is threatened by acknowledging corporate moral responsibility can just as well serve as an argument against the amoral model. The fact that a corporation is not the appropriate institution for pursuing social ideals (as Hayek and Friedman propose) does not mean that no norms at all should apply to the business context. There is a difference between the social responsibility and the moral responsibility of a corporation. The former points toward the reach of corporate moral responsibility, whereas the latter concerns the question of whether a corporation can be regarded as an independent moral entity.

The main problem with the amoral model is that it fails to take the role of the corporate context into account; that is, when someone's moral obligations are the direct or indirect result of the job the person holds. Proponents of the amoral model are inclined to view moral obligations as general human obliga- tions. From this perspective, child labor is unacceptable because it violates a right that must be honored. It does not matter whether one is a director of a corporation in a developing or in an industrialized country. By shifting the moral problems in the business setting to the private arena, the "real" business ethical problems are neither acknowledged nor addressed. As we have observed, most problems are about a dilemma in the form of a choice between two values: for example, to protect jobs (a responsibility toward employees) or the environment (a responsibility toward society and future generations). People find themselves in such dilemmas due to their position within the corporation. These positions are extremely relevant for judging whether a decision is acceptable or not. Labor representatives and directors do not have to meet the same expectations. The idea that a general human perspective must serve as a guide for moral evaluation presumes that it is possible to make decisions without taking one's function or profession into account.

Advocates of the amoral model do acknowledge this sort of obligation. The problem is that they do not acknowledge its moral character. For them, morality is synonymous with the pursuit of lofty social ideals with the result that morality is banished from the corporate context. Equating ethics with the pursuit of social ideals does not do justice to the nature of an ethical evaluation of corporations. Business ethics is concerned with the daily functioning of corporations and not with saints. By drawing a distinction between moral ideals and the moral obligations associated with the corporate context, it is possible to show what the moral obligations of a corporation are without undermining the corporate pursuit of profits.

THE FUNCTIONAL MODEL

With the rejection of the amoral model of the corporation, the question arises as to how one can localize the moral responsibilities that corporations obviously can have. What exactly does corporate responsibility mean? The function-related model of responsibility offers an answer to these fundamental questions. In the functional model[11] of corporate responsibility, the corporation is seen as an association of persons: "[A] corporation is in fact an association of individuals who are entitled to the same rights and legal protections which apply to all other individuals and organizations."[12]

This is still not to suggest that the corporation is a moral agent. The model refers to cooperation among a number of individuals who, out of practical, economic, or legal motives voluntarily join an association. The term "corporate responsibility" is used as a practical but also risky way of referring to the responsibility of some or all of these persons. In contrast to the amoral model, the functional model acknowledges that moral responsibilities arise in the context of the corporation. In other words: the corporate context is relevant for the evaluation of actions in and on behalf of the corporation. The corporation can, however, only be responsible to the degree that there are *persons* who can be held morally responsible.

Manuel Velasquez defends this position in his provocative article "Why Corporations are not Morally Responsible for Anything They Do."[13] According to Velasquez, a corporation cannot be held morally responsible because it cannot act. It is always people who act *on behalf of* the corporation. He formulates his position as follows:

Although we say that organizations "exist" and "act" like individuals, they obviously are not human individuals. Yet our moral categories are designed to deal with individual humans who feel, reason, and deliberate, and who act on the basis of their own feelings, reasoning and deliberations. So how can we apply these moral categories to corporate organizations and their "acts"? We can see our way through these difficulties only if we first see that corporate organizations and their acts depend on human individuals: organizations are composed of human individuals and they act only when these individuals act. We can express this precisely in two somewhat technical claims:

  I. A corporate organization "exists" only if
    (1) there exist certain human individuals placed in certain circumstances and
    (2) our linguistic rules lay down that when those kinds of individuals exist in those kinds of circumstances, they shall count as a corporate organization.
  II. A corporate organization "acts" only if
    (1) certain human individuals in the organization performed certain actions in certain circumstances and
    (2) our linguistic rules lay down that when those kinds of individuals perform those kinds of actions in those kinds of circumstances, this shall count as an act of their corporate organization.[14]

In the functional model of corporate responsibility, two broad variations can be distinguished: the management and the participants perspective. The difference between these two variations turns on the question whether corporate responsibility can be reduced to the responsibility of the decision-makers (the management approach) or to the responsibility of all the employees involved (the participants approach).

The management perspective

The management approach is grounded in the classical model of the corporation. In this model, the corporation is identified with one or several persons. The businessperson is the corporation. In sole proprietorships and partnerships, the owner or owners are directly liable for the corporate function. According to the management perspective, the relatively simple corporate structure as object of analysis is only slightly altered by the distinction between ownership and management (in the private limited and public limited company) and the growth and increase of complexity within corporations. In principle, the owners remain liable. The directors are employees to whom the moral responsibilities of the owners (the stockholders) have been delegated. In his dissertation *Responsibility in the Corporation*, Cobbenhagen[15] observed as early as 1927 that the public limited company, which made possible the distinction between management and ownership, can lead to the erosion of responsibilities. For him, moral responsibility within the corporation has to be retained and he emphasizes that persons within the corporation are and should remain responsible.[16]

The management approach is defended by people like Peter Kuin, the former Unilever CEO.[17] For him, corporate responsibility refers to the responsibility of management. For Kuin, however, moral responsibility is not derived from the owners' obligations. The corporate managers need a mandate from society. Kuin seems to be referring to the form of "social contract" that is used by John Locke. The legitimacy of management is based on the silent consent of all. The clear-cut role and function of corporate leaders can be based on this "social contract".

...in the comprehending acceptance of it by the community. In return, the corporate leaders would have to meet the expectations that the community in our time has of them. Their mandate can never be anything but conditional, but they do need a mandate in order to fulfill their function...[18]

The leadership within the corporation has an important social function. Much in society depends on the responsible performance of this function. Leadership derives its legitimacy from society's acceptance. In return for this mandate, the corporation must be prepared to carry out a socially responsible policy and justify it to society.

The management variation of the functional model contains an odd inconsistency, at least if one thinks of management as a team. This, too, is a collective—but one that seems less problematic because it is easier to watch over. In fact, the same problems as with the amoral model apply here: why is it acceptable to speak of the collective responsibility of the team and unacceptable to speak of an autonomous corporate responsibility? Can this team responsibility be reduced to individual responsibilities or does the team have an autonomous responsibility? If one opts for the latter (if the influence exerted by regular management team meetings is acknowledged and individual moral responsibility remains intact), one opts for a form of autonomous corporate responsibility.

The participants approach

The participants approach applies Kuin's reasoning to all employees. Managers are also employees of the firm. Everybody contributes to the overall result. All participants have a degree of responsibility for the functioning of the corporation. This is the reasoning of people such as the former CEO of Shell, Gerrit Wagner:

The persons in the company are personally responsible for ensuring that their actions meet ethical standards. They must ensure that the organization as a whole acts in a manner acceptable to society. There is, of course, a gradation of responsibilities, and higher-ranked functionaries bear more responsibility for the corporation than others do in ethical and social areas as well.[19]

A powerful argument in favor of the participants approach is advanced by the sociologist Henk van Zuthem. He argues that employees bear a moral responsibility for the products they help to create. The causal relationship between labor and the final product makes the employees co-responsible. Van Zuthem criticizes contemporary labor relations on these grounds. Because no conclusions are drawn from the causal relationship between labor and products, employees are neither taken seriously nor respected. He argues his point as follows:

There is...a noteworthy and radical contradiction in our system of labor relations. On the one hand, employees create by their labor products and services and, as a result, positive and negative consequences for others. On the other, their formal influence in the existing power structure is extremely limited. The cause of this contradiction lies in the way power and morality relate to each other in our system. Industrial morals are such that no consequences are drawn from the causal relationship between labor and products. As a result, the interests of others are not given their proper attention and personal responsibility does not extend to those others.[20]

The practice of whistle blowing also departs from the assumption that contributing to production or services implies a moral responsibility.

Problems with the functional model

The functional model of responsibility recognizes that moral responsibility cannot be separated from the corporate context. Ultimately, however, this model traces all responsibility back to natural persons. According to this model, the "actions" of a corporation must be traced back to its functionaries. The functional model fails to recognize the relevance of the structure and culture of a corporation. Moral problems are treated as problems for individuals within the corporation. The context itself remains unexamined.

Three problems can be identified in the functional model:

1. The *transfer problem*: is responsibility transferable throughout time?
2. The *dispersion problem*: how is responsibility divided at a given moment?
3. The *complexity problem*: how should one cope with the complexity and difficulty of overseeing the contemporary corporation?

Let us first examine the transfer problem. What are the implications for the responsibilities of a corporation if the managers and employees are suddenly replaced? As extreme as this example might seem, the problem is real. What remains of the responsibility of the various German companies who used forced labor during the Second World War? Those companies have become what they are today partly because of their success at that time. The extent to which companies are responsible for pollution raises similar questions. During the 1950s and 1960s, various companies polluted the environment relatively unhindered. In many cases, the consequences of what they did surfaced only decades later. This is not a purely theoretical question, as someone actually has to bear the burden of cleaning up polluted areas. If people took risks in the 1950s and 1960s, the companies in question retain a certain moral responsibility even today. This holds true even if it was management who ignored the signals or even if people underestimated the possible cumulative effects of their work (with remarks such as "the amounts are negligible" and "it will be okay during my lifetime"). It is reasonable to say that these companies are at least obliged to repair the damage as best they can and to take sufficient organizational measures to prevent similar problems in future. In the functional model, this responsibility disappears.

A second problem with the functional model concerns the question of the distribution of responsibility at a given moment. Let us say that a corporation's management comes to the conclusion that large-scale cutbacks have to be made and a number of people have to be laid off. This thankless task falls on the shoulders of the personnel manager. Who can be held responsible for the decision? Perhaps the manager involved doubted the appropriateness of the decision. Perhaps he abstained from voting or even voted against the decision. Regardless of what he thinks of the decision, he will have to carry it out. Only in clear-cut situations and where fundamental issues are at stake might one expect a manager to refuse to go along with a decision to which he is fundamentally opposed. What the manager can be held responsible for is not clearly defined in a case of collective decision-making. It is a responsibility that cannot be traced back to individual responsibilities. As we saw in Chapter 1, higher levels of education and computerization have contributed significantly to the dispersion of responsibility.

And, finally, the functional model of responsibility cannot escape the exponential increase in the size and complexity of corporations. Acquisitions, mergers, and joint ventures have led to colossal amalgamations of companies. Complex organizational structures have also developed in order to react efficiently and adequately to signals from a turbulent market. An increase in size and complexity has radical consequences for how a corporation can and should deal with its responsibilities. Managers must to a great extent place their trust in the employees who represent the corporation. The simple organizational structure, where management bears the ultimate responsibility for what the corporation does and where employees are only responsible as woodcutters and water-bearers, no longer applies to modern corporations. Many corporations have achieved such a size and complexity that it is no longer possible to hold management morally responsible for everything the corporation does.

The problems of transfer, dispersion, and complexity point toward the relatively autonomous processes that also take place in corporations. A multitude of actions (based on the limited knowledge of individual players, the multiplicity of reactions to what is undertaken without the effects of the actions being sufficiently clear) has turned corporations into cumbersome social entities, which, once started, are difficult or nearly impossible to control.

The functional model of responsibility tries to resolve these problems by linking responsibilities to jobs and to distinguish them from personal responsibilities: obligations created by one's predecessors often stay part of the job forever. Two sources of responsibility are thus acknowledged. Every person has a personal responsibility that does not disappear when participating in a corporation. A person also has an additional responsibility related to the function fulfilled. The content of the functional responsibility grows over time, partly through the various functionaries that carried out the job in the past. Furthermore, the content of one job is defined in relation to other jobs. The functional model thus includes an organizational component. To resolve the transfer problem, the dispersion problem, and the complexity problem an autonomous organizational component has to be acknowledged.

To hold individual functionaries accountable for the functioning of the corporation is an attempt to salvage individual responsibility. People are reluctant to hold collectives responsible because individuals could use this to pass their responsibilities on to the collective. Relating responsibility purely to the functions individuals perform does not capture the nature of corporate responsibility. It therefore offers no adequate solution to the problem. To the extent that a job is defined within the context of an organization, the corporation as such is also at stake.

Ontological individualism

Both the amoral and the functional model of corporate responsibility rely on a form of ontological individualism. *The* corporation does not exist and can, therefore, not act. All that really exists are the individual employees, managers, stockholders, etc. *The* corporation is nothing more than the sum of a number of individuals. Likewise, the actions of the corporation are nothing more than the actions of individual employees or managers, which renders the concept of corporate morality null and void. Ontological individualism is more radical than methodological individualism. Ontological individualism acknowledges only the individual. Methodological individualism recognizes the existence of social reality although it is understood as an expression of individual actions. Consequently, neither the independent existence nor the absence of social phenomena is addressed.

The functional model of corporate responsibility is clearly somewhat ambiguous. Responsibility can be identified in the corporate context but there is no overall corporate responsibility. To ascribe moral responsibility to functionaries is, nevertheless, to advance an organizational approach to the corporation. The proposition that individuals have certain responsibilities on the basis of their jobs signifies a departure from an individualistic theory of the corporation.

Moral responsibilities are *partly* linked to the job performed, and by linking responsibilities to jobs, the corporation's responsibilities are brought into view. The content of the job is partly determined by the corporation. The corporation does not only define the distribution of functional responsibilities. It also creates expectations as to how to realize them. These expectations are expressed in a particular manner. To recapitulate, the functioning of persons within a corporation cannot be viewed in isolation from the context in which they operate. Once this step is taken, a purely individualistic view of corporations is no longer possible. We then proceed to an organizational ontology: the whole is more than the sum of the parts. If we accept that a corporation is not simply the sum of its individual members, it also becomes possible to speak of a kind of corporate morality that cannot merely be traced back to individual responsibilities.

THE AUTONOMY MODEL

The autonomy model proposes that a degree of irreducible responsibility can be localized at the organizational level as well. The corporation is an independent social entity that can be held responsible for the effects of its actions. Consequently, the corporation cannot be understood simply as a plaything of market forces or completely determined by the actions of one or more individuals.

As observed earlier, even advocates of the amoral model do not wholly dispute this argument. Hayek makes a strong case for partly viewing the corporation as an autonomous collective. On the basis of common experiences, the corporation develops a common body of knowledge and a number of customs that remain in place even after operations have ceased. In this regard, Hayek writes:

The corporation tends to develop from an aggregation of material resources directed and operated by a body of men hired for that purpose into what is primarily a group of men held together by common experience and traditions, and even developing something like a distinct personality. It is an important and probably inevitable fact. Nor can it be denied that some of the features which make a particular corporation especially efficient do not rest entirely with the management but would be destroyed if a new workforce replaced its whole operating personnel at a given moment. The performance and very existence of a corporation is thus bound up with the preservation of at least an inner core of men right down the line who are familiar with its peculiar traditions and concrete tasks. The "going concern" differs from the material structure which will still exist after operations have ceased mainly by the mutually adjusted knowledge and habits of those who operate it.[21]

He is, however, quick to reject the idea of the corporation as an independent entity. Ascribing autonomy to the corporation would undermine the conception of the free society he upholds. Nevertheless, Hayek fails to advance substantive arguments against acknowledging an autonomous corporate responsibility. His argument rests on the idealistic individualistic society he envisions. His rejection is, therefore, based in ideological prejudice.

Both the amoral model—the variant in which personal responsibility is acknowledged—and the functional model, are grounded in ontological individualism. In contrast, the autonomous model as discussed below opens the way for adopting a holistic methodological approach.

We shall outline three variations of the autonomy model here. Each conceptualizes the autonomous responsibility of the corporation in its own way.

1. Goodpaster and Matthews's *projection approach*. In this approach, a corporation shares a number of characteristics with individuals. On the basis of this analogy, we are justified in projecting moral autonomy onto the corporation.
2. Werhane and Spit's *secondary moral actor theory*. A corporation can act secondarily by virtue of a powerful and effective management. Corporate actions can be judged in moral terms because the management of the corporation is in the hands of moral players (Spit). The "moral awareness" of the natural persons involved makes it possible to apply this to a corporation (Werhane).

3. French's *corporate internal decision structures theory*. The individual actions of functionaries can be viewed as the actions of the corporation due to the existence of a decision-making structure. Because the actions of the corporation are based on autonomous corporate intentions, they can be judged in moral terms.

We propose an *integrated corporate moral practices theory*. Corporations are moral entities because they consist of independent practices that can be subjected to moral evaluation.

The projection approach

According to Kenneth Goodpaster and John Matthews Jr,[22] corporations possess a number of core characteristics that are also found in natural persons. On the basis of this analogy, corporations can be viewed as moral agents just like individuals. The analogy justifies the projection of "moral responsibility" onto corporations.

We call an individual a moral person because he or she is capable of acting rationally and of showing respect for others. To act rationally refers to the individual's ability to consider alternatives, to weigh up the consequences of different courses of action, to set goals, and endeavor to realize them. Showing respect for others implies that others are not regarded purely as instruments for achieving one's goals. Human beings have inherent value on the basis of which their interests must be taken into account. Like individuals, corporations too are capable of acting rationally and respectfully:

Hence, corporations that monitor their employment practices and effects of their production processes and products on the environment and the human health show the same kind of rationality and respect that morally responsible individuals do. Thus, attributing actions, strategies, decisions, and moral responsibilities to corporations as entities distinguishable from those who hold offices in them poses no problem.[23]

For Goodpaster and Matthews, concepts that are employed to discuss the moral responsibility of individuals can, by analogy, be applied to corporations. An individual person has the capacity for self-control, to be honorable, and mindful. These qualities can also be found embedded in corporate reward systems, internal control systems, and R&D programs. Just as an individual, the corporation can have a certain character. In the same manner people gradually develop moral responsibility as they grow into adulthood, so too does the moral character of corporations grow in stages.

The arguments of Goodpaster and Matthews are instructive, but analogous reasoning in itself proves nothing. It shows only how the actor perceives something. Such reasoning is useful in formulating ideas, clarifying theories, and persuading others. To derive premisses from it is not wise.

A serious objection that can be raised against the reasoning of Goodpaster and Matthews is that they infer that a corporation actually possesses certain personal characteristics. Some of the characteristics they refer to are, for example, the development stages and learning processes that a corporation can go through and the self-control it can possess. Here, Goodpaster and Matthews commit an elementary error in reasoning. They in fact "discover" something that was "hidden" from others before them. In the past decades, organizational theories frequently projected personal traits onto corporations in order to make certain issues clear through comparison. For instance, we all have a grasp on what learning means for natural persons. We can also identify certain processes in organizations that resemble human learning. By using the term "learning" in this context, the question remains whether the instruments of the pedagogue can be applied to organizations. By using insights into learning processes, one hopes, as it were, to understand the related processes of corporations. However, the corporation does not "learn." At best, what it does can be described as similar to learning. If we propose that the instruments of the pedagogue can/ should be applied to the corporate context and that corporations are indeed capable of learning, we presuppose that which still needs to be substantiated. One cannot deduce from this form of analogous reasoning that the corporation actually possesses personal characteristics.

As a result, the assertion that a corporation possesses sufficient personal characteristics to qualify as a moral person remains dangling in the air. Goodpaster and Matthews write:

Goals, economic values, strategies, and other such personal attributes are often usefully projected to the corporate level by managers and researchers. Why should we not project the functions of conscience in the same way? As for holding corporations responsible, recent criminal prosecutions such as the case of Ford Motor company and its Pinto gas tanks suggest that society finds the idea both intelligible and useful.[24]

In this quote, another type of argument enters the discussion: society finds the concept of corporate morality intelligible and useful. This also offers insufficient grounds for holding a corporation morally responsible. Even if it may have a certain appeal, it is a pragmatic consideration that lacks sufficient grounds for justification.

The arguments of Goodpaster and Matthews are valid only if it can be shown that the grounds for ascribing moral responsibility to natural persons are also applicable to corporations. Goodpaster and Matthews set out to do so, but only up to a certain point. Individuals act responsibly, they say, when their actions are rational and respectful. They neglect to show how or why corporations meet these criteria. Can one speak of corporate actions, and, if so, can they be viewed as intentional (i.e. conscious, intended, and free)? The theories that follow attempt to answer these questions.

The secondary moral actor theory

The way Ireneus Spit localizes moral responsibility in the corporation more or less serves as a standard for the system of reasoning advanced by a number of others (especially Patricia Werhane). He follows two distinct and logical steps. First, he poses the question whether a social reality is composed purely of individuals or whether collectives (such as a corporation) have their own separate ontological status. The second question Spit poses is whether collectives can act. This he answers in the affirmative by pronouncing the corporation a social entity. What, then, is the basis for judging corporate actions on moral grounds?

Both Spit and Werhane employ the concept "secondary action" to show that corporations can act. Spit applies the concept to all sorts of collectives. Werhane focuses solely on corporations. Both come to more or less the same conclusion: a corporation can act secondarily and this action can be judged in moral terms. A corporation is, therefore, a secondary moral actor.

In his dissertation *Multisubject Activity and Moral Responsibility*, Spit investigates how moral responsibility can be ascribed in situations where people act collectively. Spit calls this "multisubject" action. He distinguishes four types: joint action, the actions of the collective, the activities of the group, and mass activities.

Joint action. First, he defines the joint actions of a number of individuals, for example, two individuals who play chess or commit a robbery together. This joint action (also referred to as collective action and not to be confused with the actions of a collective) is a form of cooperation where individual actions are directed toward a common goal. In joint action, the contribution of everyone involved is required to achieve the goal. Moreover, this form of cooperation relies on communication and is incidental in nature. In addition, there is no intention or expectation that the relation of cooperation will continue. This joint action of individuals has traits that are unique to acting: conscious intervention in the course of events where each individual has control over what he or she does. There is also an element of freedom. Those involved could have decided not to take part in what they are doing.[25]

Actions of the collective. A strike called by a union or the dumping of environmentally harmful refuse by a corporation are examples of actions of the collective. A collective can also be an acting subject. The collective has the ability to act if several members of the collective make decisions for the whole and are able to carry them out (in cases of powerful leadership and effective coordination). Here, too, the characteristics of action are applicable: conscious and causal intervention; control and freedom.

Activities of the group. In the third instance, Spit identifies the activity of the group. An example is a group of individuals who spontaneously plunder a store or vandalize a bus without prior consultation or any other joint decision-making process. Vandalism of this kind cannot be seen as a group "action." Because there is no coordination or leadership, activities developed in the context of a group cannot be classified as action. The group does not consciously intervene in society and no control is exercised. Nevertheless, they are free, as they are not being coerced into doing what they do. Still, it cannot be described as action. At most, the group is simply demonstrating its own type of behavior.

Mass activities. Finally, we have mass activity such as a public demonstration or vandalism committed by soccer fans. For the same reasons as for the group, one cannot speak of mass action.

Only the first two forms of multisubject activity can, according to Spit, be judged in moral terms. The joint action of individuals can qualify as morally good or bad. It is reasonable to hold the individuals morally responsible for their particular contribution to the joint action. The actions of some collectives can also be judged in moral terms. These collectives can, therefore, be held morally responsible for their actions. The behavior of a group or a mass of people, however, cannot be judged in moral terms, as this behavior does not qualify as conscious action. Thus defined, neither a mob nor a group is a moral actor.

The second type of multisubject action, the actions of the collective, is particularly important. These actions can be distinguished from the actions of the members of the collective. This is the category corporations belong to. According to Spit, corporations can be viewed as autonomous actors. Corporate action displays characteristics on the basis of which it can be morally evaluated. Spit argues that although collectives are composed of individuals, they are unique types of entities that must be distinguished from the individual members of the collective. A collective is a moral actor if it meets two conditions:

(1) it must be an actor (rational, free/intentional);
(2) a number of members of a collective must be moral actors.

The first condition requires actions to be performed by the collective. Only if it is an actor can it be a moral actor. It must be shown that collectives actually act despite the very significant differences between a natural person and a collective. A collective can act only through its members. Moreover, in contrast with a natural person, a collective does not have a single, undivided body or a single, undivided consciousness.

To meet the first requirement, Spit borrows the concept "secondary action" from David Copp. This is an action that is carried out by an actor on behalf of another. Copp describes this concept as follows:

An agent's action is a secondary action if, and only if, it is correctly attributable to this agent on the basis of either an action of some other agent, or actions of some other agents.[26]

Secondary action can apply to a natural person who is represented by another person, but it can also apply to a collective that is represented by others. In the case of the latter, it is the collective that is acting secondarily. If, for example, the director of a corporation enters into a contract (in his capacity as director) on behalf of the corporation, the corporation is bound to it. Although the director is the one who actually signs the contract, the ensuing rights and obligations are incumbent upon the corporation. The natural person thus carries out the physical act of signing but the collective acts in a secondary, indirect sense. Natural persons can act in both a primary and a secondary sense; a corporation only in the latter.

The requirement of a free will and consciousness places a demand on a corporation's leadership. If a collective has a powerful leadership and effective coordination, it can justifiably be viewed as an actor, as an entity that acts. Due to a powerful and effective leadership, its behavior can be qualified as the "conscious intervention of the collective in the course of events."[27] Given such a powerful and effective leadership, the collective possesses the characteristics that are unique to action. The collective expresses an autonomous will in the activities that are developed and the leadership that makes decisions on behalf of the collective embodies this will. We can also consider this a form of collective consciousness. After all, it encompasses control, supervision, and the possibility of correction. And, finally, the collective has freedom of choice: it can decide not to act or to act differently. The ability to act is a precondition for qualifying as an actor. A powerful and effective leadership makes meeting this precondition possible.

If the second condition (a number of the members of the collective must be moral actors) is met, the decisions of a collective can be morally assessed. Only when individual leaders are also moral actors does the collective actor also become a moral actor. A collective actor is a moral actor only in a secondary sense. Due to the moral competence of the decision-makers, moral considerations can play a role in the decision-making process. If a collective is a moral actor, the actions of this collective can be judged in moral terms and the collective can be held morally responsible. It is therefore reasonable to expect it to be collectively accountable. The collective can thus be praised, blamed, and held liable (for example, by claiming compensation or reparation) for its actions.

Usually, a corporation meets these two requirements: it has a powerful and effective leadership and managers are moral actors. For these reasons, a corporation can be seen as a collective that acts instead of consisting purely of the joint actions of individuals. A corporation has moral competence and is, therefore, morally responsible for its actions.

Patricia Werhane[28] holds that a corporation can be viewed as a moral actor and, like Spit, she employs Copp's concept of secondary action in her argument. Because corporations can act in a secondary sense, they are regarded as secondary actors. A corporation can be regarded as a moral actor because its actions are based on corporate intentions. These are secondary intentions. The objectives of stockholders, management, managers, employees, and external advisors constitute the primary intentions. Not all intentions of constituents are part of the corporate intentions. A corporation possesses a selective system of intentions. An intention is only "corporate" if it helps the corporation achieve its corporate objectives. Just as with Spit, however, the moral responsibility of a corporation ultimately rests in the role of natural persons. Werhane writes:

Corporations as secondary collectives made up of persons who can "act" as moral agents, and therefore are morally responsible. Moral awareness, however, is dependent upon the moral input of corporate constituents. If corporate constituents are rational free adults, and one must assume they are, their crucial input into corporate decision-making is such that moral blindness does not excuse a corporation from moral responsibility just as it does not excuse rational free adults.[29]

For Spit, the moral competence of a corporation is based in the moral competence of management, while for Werhane corporate "moral awareness" is based in the moral input of its constituents. In both cases, corporate morality is located in the moral abilities of individual constituents.

Because both Spit and Werhane ultimately fall back on the moral competence of natural persons in establishing the moral character of the corporation, the question arises whether this does not amount to a variation on the functional model. Werhane acknowledges this problem and argues that this is not the case. According to Werhane, it is possible to combine ontological individualism and methodological collectivism. Moreover, Werhane maintains that to view the corporation as a secondary moral actor is not to ontologize the corporation. Corporations are not a reality besides or above their constituents. Natural persons create corporations and they function through natural persons only.

In Werhane's view, ontological individualism does not completely eliminate the possibility of corporate action. Not only is it difficult to reduce the actions of a corporation to the actions of natural persons who represent the corporation, sometimes it is even impossible. To illustrate her point, she recalls the accusations of discrimination against women and minorities that were brought against AT&T. Although relatively large numbers of women and members of ethnic minority groups were hired, only a small percentage was promoted to management positions. Even if no one inside the company consciously discriminated against them, the company was still guilty of structural discrimination. Werhane argues the point as follows:

A re-analysis of what happened at AT&T in terms of constituent and agent actions will not yield the proper explanation of the behavior in question in every case. Or, to put what I want to argue differently, the analysis of discrimination at AT&T in terms of individual actions will uncover the causes and necessary conditions of that "action" but not the reasons for it.[30]

The first step in localizing corporate moral responsibility is to acknowledge the corporation as secondary moral actor. Besides ontological individualism,

Werhane also employs methodological collectivism. For Werhane, it is not necessary to attribute moral autonomy to a corporation to say something meaningful about the corporation's actions. On this point, Werhane departs from Spit. The first step in Spit's reasoning specifically concerns the ontological status of a corporation. In his view, the corporation can justifiably be viewed as a social entity.

Spit, too, balances on the edge of the functional model and the autonomy model. His reasoning centers on the moral competence of a number of individual members or, rather, the collective's leadership. The moral competence of the members of the collective is the only necessary condition for conceiving a collective actor as a moral actor. In principle, it is not necessary for the executive members of the collective (i.e. the rest of the employees) also to be moral actors. It is sufficient that they stick to the decisions that have been taken by the leaders of the collective. A powerful and effective leadership guarantees this. According to Spit, the moral competence of a collective can be seen as a derivative of the moral competence of the leaders of the collective:

Collectives are not freestanding social entities. Collectives owe their possession of certain social characteristics and abilities—such as reasoning and formulating goals, being able to act, being able to act morally and so on—precisely to the fact that its members themselves (the individuals) possess these. Anyone who disputes this would need to show another way—and via another path than that of the characteristics and abilities of the members— that one could arrive at a situation in which collectives are able to act morally.[31]

Here, it seems that Spit departs from the management approach of the functional model. Corporate morality, according to him, cannot be reduced to individual morality as responsibilities are coupled to jobs. The responsibilities that are linked to particular jobs are partly determined by the way these jobs have developed over the course of time, and the structural and cultural framework in which they are carried out. It is, however, the person on the job who in the final analysis gives shape to that position. The moral competence of the corporation is, therefore, based in the individual conscience of its employees. On this basis, the corporation cannot be held morally responsible as well.

The secondary moral actor theory advocated by Spit and Werhane offers a sounder analysis than Goodpaster and Matthews's projection model. It also differs from the functional model in that it ascribes independent knowledge and intentions to the corporation. Because people embody the knowledge and intentions of the corporation, corporate morality ultimately rests on the individual awareness of the natural persons within the corporation. Despite their fundamental points of difference, the criticism against the functional model is to some extent also applicable to the theories of Werhane and Spit.

Although the historical, structural, and cultural context within which the corporate leadership functions can be named, no further moral implications are linked to them. As in the functional model (especially in Spit's vision and, to a lesser extent, Werhane's), a relatively simple and easily managed collective is assumed. Many modern corporations no longer fit this image. The three features of the modern corporation that were named earlier—the problems of complexity, the inability to oversee everything, and the distribution of responsibility—raise questions about Werhane and Spit's theories. What should be done if the leadership of a corporation is not powerful and effective enough to coordinate and manage the various activities that are undertaken on behalf of the corporation? Does incompetent leadership make the corporation an amoral entity? Does incompetence relieve one of one's responsibilities? In that case, all immorality could be ascribed to incompetence. This objection is also applicable to Werhane's argument. If the "moral awareness" of the constituents does not extend beyond what is physically possible, what are we to make of the possible gaps in the moral map of the corporation and its leaders?

A key concept in Spit's reasoning is "powerful and effective leadership." A collective, that is the management team, generally forms the powerful and effective leadership in a corporation. In one way (however cryptically formulated it may be) the leadership of the collective rests on another, smaller collective. Is the leadership an independent moral actor? Spit would say yes, at least if a moral person powerfully and effectively leads this collective. In this way, the moral responsibility of a corporation ultimately rests on a single person, the CEO.

We have seen that for Spit, the status of decision-makers as moral actors is a necessary condition to ascribe moral responsibility to a corporation. Werhane speaks of "moral awareness" because a corporation has moral competence through its members. The characteristics of action, such as knowing, wanting, and managing, are applicable to the corporation only through the individual members. Only through the members (the management) does moral reflection on action take place. By not adequately addressing the role of the structure, culture, and history of a corporation, Spit in effect isolates the role of the individual decision-maker from these distinguishing features of the corporation. In an organizational context, people think and behave differently from the way they do as individuals. That a corporate tradition, structure, and culture can be identified is of crucial importance in considering the corporation a social entity. In Spit's model, the influence of history, structure, and culture disappears from view. These attributes play a role only to the extent that natural persons are aware of them. The features themselves are never subjected to moral examination.

It would be a misconception to see power and effectiveness as human characteristics only. Modern organizational theories are more inclined to view these as organizational characteristics. The power and effectiveness of the leadership are in the first place located in the organizational structure and culture. Whoever obtains a leadership position in an organization is strongly dependent on the selection and promotion procedures of the corporation. Cultural acceptance of the leadership forms to a significant extent the basis of power and effectiveness. A corporation is a secondary moral actor because it can act only through its members. Knowledge is also secondary. In our view, however, it is useful to see the rationality and intentions of the corporation as independent of its individual constituents. Werhane's example is instructive in this regard. That natural persons express intentions does not mean that these intentions exist through them alone. Spit shows that corporations possess knowledge that exists independently of their constituents. This relates, for example, to knowledge stored in files or computers.

A crucial point of criticism pertains to the link between acting and morality. According to Werhane and Spit, responsibility can be ascribed to the corporation because the corporation acts secondarily. In the corporate context, a distinction can be drawn between primary actions (for example, signing a document) and secondary actions (by signing, the corporation is bound to a contract). Spit and Werhane thus show that a corporation can act. How primary and secondary actions can also be distinguished in practice, remains unclear. What does the corporation do and what can be ascribed to the individual person? Acting, for Spit and Werhane, is a condition for morality. This is why they would gladly localize something like a corporate ability to act independently. Because this point of criticism is also applicable to French's model, which will be addressed below, we shall return to it in more detail later.

The corporate internal decision structures theory

A large part of the work of the philosopher Peter French is devoted to the moral responsibility of collectives.[32] As early as the beginning of the 1970s, he became involved in the discussion on collective responsibility. This was initiated in response to the massacre perpetrated by US soldiers in My Lai. At the beginning of the 1980s, he started looking into corporate responsibility.

According to French, persons acting collectively can be divided into two types: aggregates and conglomerates.[33] These two types of collectives respectively refer to an unstructured and structured collection of individuals. Aggregates can be divided into coincidental aggregates and statistical aggregates. A coincidental aggregate refers to a more or less coincidental group of people, for example, the residents of a street or spectators at a sports event. In the latter, interest in the same game brings people together. In a statistical aggregate, people are categorized on the basis of a given characteristic, for example, people of a certain age group or the unemployed in a region. It is characteristic of all sorts of aggregates that there is no question of cohesion or structure. Nor is there any solidarity. In these respects, an aggregate differs from a conglomerate.

A conglomerate is an organization of individuals. The identity of a conglomerate cannot be comprehensively described by adding the identities of the individuals together. What can be attributed to the conglomerate cannot necessarily be ascribed to the members. Members joining or leaving the conglomerate do not necessarily affect its identity. Because an aggregate can be comprehensively described by putting the characters of the individual members together, the moral responsibility of an aggregate is nothing more than the sum of the individual responsibilities. The moral responsibility of an aggregate can be described only in a distributive sense: each member is responsible according to his share. Here, methodological individualism applies. By way of contrast, the moral responsibility of a conglomerate cannot be distributed among its members. This is because the characteristics of a conglomerate cannot be reduced to the sum of individual characteristics. In a situation where all the members of a conglomerate quit and are replaced by new members, the responsibility of the conglomerate remains unaltered.

Usually, two objections are raised against attributing moral responsibility to conglomerates such as corporations. The first is that a corporation consists of persons. The employees, stockholders, suppliers, banks, etc. collectively create the corporation and keep it going. The corporation can, therefore, be seen as the product of human efforts. Moreover, people also safeguard its future. In response, French argues that recognizing a separate moral actor is not to suggest that the individual members change their identity. A common criticism against positing a supra-individual entity is that individual identity would be radically altered as a result. French argues that attributing moral responsibility to a conglomerate does not automatically imply that the individual identity, and therefore individual responsibility, changes.[34] The second reservation that is often voiced is that it would be unfair to blame well-meaning constituents for things the conglomerate does. For French, this reservation is unfounded. His theory does not suggest that the responsibilities of the conglomerate and those of the constituents are one and the same thing. The distinction between individual and collective responsibility prevents this confusion.

According to Peter French, the corporation is a moral person that is capable of acting. The actions of the corporations can, therefore, be analyzed and judged in moral terms. Briefly summarized, French reasons as follows:

1. A metaphysical person is always a moral person.
2. A corporation is a metaphysical person and, therefore, a moral person.
3. It is justified to speak of the actions of a corporation.
4. Conclusion: the corporation is a moral person who is able to act. In other words: the actions of a corporation can be judged in moral terms.

A moral person is an independent, irreducible subject to whom moral responsibility can be ascribed.[35] When we ascribe moral responsibility to a person, notions of "being accountable" and "owing an explanation" are invoked. Moral responsibility is, in the first instance, localized in the intentions of the subject. A person can only be held morally accountable (moral personality) in the presence of self-awareness or self-consciousness. The subject must be capable of giving answers and seeing his or her own actions objectively. A metaphysical personality implies that an occurrence can be justifiably described as an intentional act by the subject. The intentionality of a subject is a necessary and adequate condition for the moral personality of that subject. Consequently, only a metaphysical subject can be a moral subject. In French's words:

To be the subject of an ascription of moral responsibility, to be a party in responsibility relationships, hence to be a moral person, the subject must be at minimum an intentional actor.[36]

An event can often be accurately described in various ways. "Monica's hand touched Bill's face" can be reformulated as "Monica touched Bill." Certain events that can be seen simply as movements of natural persons can also be described as the actions of subjects that arise from the intentions of those subjects. In this way, an action can be described as that of a functionary and, at the same time, as that of a corporation. The corporation can have intentions that do not coincide with the intentions of the functionary.

According to French, it is due to the Corporate Internal Decision (CID) structure that the actions of an individual functionary can be reformulated as those of the corporation. On the basis of the CID structure, a distinction can be drawn between the intentions of the corporation and the intentions of the individual members constituting the corporation. The CID structure consists of a formal decision-making structure and of recognition and acknowledgement rules:

1. The *formal decision-making structure* is usually represented using an organizational flow chart that delineates stations and levels within the corporation. The organizational chart of a corporation distinguishes players and clarifies their rank and maps out the interconnected lines of responsibility within the corporation. For French, this is not simply an idealistic concept conceived at the office desk, but the structure of responsibility as it actually exists.
2. The *recognition and acknowledgement rules* are the rules by which decisions can be recognized and acknowledged as corporate decisions. These rules determine the intentional character of the actions of the corporation. They consist of procedural and policy recognition and acknowledgement rules. Procedural acknowledgement rules indicate which competence belongs to whom, who must take which decision, and whose approval is needed. It is not sufficient for the proper person to take a decision according to the proper procedure. This decision must also fit into the corporate climate and the company objectives. Members must feel that the decision is one that serves the corporate interest. The policy recognition and acknowledgement rules implicitly refer to the company interests and, therefore, the corporate intentions.

Thanks to the CID structure, a corporation has its own interests. On this basis, its intentions are distinguishable from those of the individual functionaries. As such, decisions of the individual functionaries are literally incorporated into those of the corporation. The CID structure makes it possible to view individual decisions as corporate decisions under certain conditions. Also, owing to the CID structure, the corporation has its own intentions that cannot be traced back to the intentions of individual persons.

Donaldson criticizes French's "redescription" theory on a fundamental point. He agrees with French's proposition that a corporation can act, but questions the moral character of these actions. According to French, the action of a corporation can be judged in moral terms because it is intentional: it is conscious and focused. In response, Donaldson asserts that showing that a corporation has intentions is not to prove that a corporation is also a moral actor:

Sometimes entities appear to behave intentionally which do not qualify as moral agents. A cat may behave intentionally when it crouches for a mouse. We know that it intends to catch the mouse, but we do not credit it with moral agency...A computer behaves intentionally when it sorts through a list of names and rearranges them in alphabetical order, but we do not consider the computer to be a moral agent. Perhaps corporations resemble complicated computers; perhaps they, according to a complicated inner logic, function in an intentional manner but fail altogether to qualify as moral agents...One seemingly needs more than the presence of intentions to deduce moral agency.[37]

French attempts to set Donaldson's criticism aside by formulating sharper criteria for intentional action. The behavior of a cat or a computer cannot be regarded as a primitive form of intentional action because the focused character of this behavior is entirely a function of the cat's instinct or the computer's program. The intentions of corporations, however, cannot be traced back to individuals. Intentionality is characterized by self-awareness. An intentional subject is capable of selecting a specific objective among others, of choosing between different actions to achieve the intended result, and evaluating the value of the intended result against the effort required. Just as Donaldson's computers, cats, and other lower animals cannot be seen as intentional actors, corporations, on the other hand, can.

The possibility of abuse

One of the considerations for opting for the functional model (or the amoral model) is the fear that something like a separate corporate responsibility could be misused to evade individual responsibility. This reasoning makes sense only if the total "quantity" of responsibility is fixed and a greater corporate responsibility automatically leads to smaller, individual responsibilities. If accepting a new level of responsibility cannot be used as a basis for excusing individual actions, this problem is avoided. This is the case when it is clear that corporate responsibility and individual responsibility are of a different type.

The opposite risk cannot be ignored either. If it is not materially justified to hold natural persons at least partly responsible, and one is not prepared to speak of responsibility at any level other than that of the individual, the risk exists that the functioning of corporations can be analyzed only superficially. As a result, a moral vacuum is created.

CONSEQUENCES OF THE CORPORATE AUTONOMY MODEL

Should theory and object not agree with each other, we can either redefine the object or modify the theory. In the case of the former, the description of the aspect of reality selected for examination is modified in such a way that it is possible to apply a general ethical theory to it. In the latter case, the theory is adjusted to the object, which is taken as a given. General theories are not so much rejected as incorrect or untrue, but as inadequate for the analysis and evaluation of the social phenomenon under examination. The new theory involves supplementing the existing theories to facilitate the analysis and evaluation of those aspects of reality that cannot be adequately understood and analyzed by utilizing the common concepts and theories.

The advocates of the autonomy model opt for the first alternative as the object of analysis and evaluation is made accessible to existing theories. While the existing theories are left intact, the approach fails to do justice to the object under examination. As a result, the social reality under examination is unacceptably reshaped to fit the common action-oriented theories. Our criticism relates especially to the artificial manner in which the concept of action is incorporated into the arguments of the proponents of the autonomy model. Goodpaster and Matthews, Spit, and French all try to discern an autonomous corporate responsibility. They assume that to achieve this, it must be shown that a corporation can act. For them, the action of the corporation is a necessary condition for holding this entity morally responsible. In order to apply common action-oriented theories in the corporate setting, something resembling action on the part of the corporation must be "constructed."

In our opinion, it is unnecessary to link morality with the concept of action. To conceive a corporation as a moral subject, one must not only look to the actions of the persons who represent the corporation (secondary action). The framework within which action occurs is also of fundamental importance. It is especially this framework, which ensures unity and directs the individual representatives, that deserves assessment.

Modifying the object of evaluation to the theory

The concept of action plays a central role in a much-cited article by Goodpaster and Matthews.[38] The question they address is whether it is meaningful to apply moral concepts to actors who are not persons but who are composed of persons.

If a group can act like a person in some ways, then we can also expect it to behave like a person in other ways. For one thing, we know that people organized into a group can act as a unit...If we can say that persons act responsibly only if they gather information about the impact of their actions on others and use it in making decisions, we can reasonably do the same for organizations.

Ethics is apparently only possible when actions are involved. In order to be able to hold a corporation morally responsible in a way analogous to natural persons, the corporation must be able to act. Elsewhere,[39] Goodpaster puts the crucial role of actions into its rightful context. In later publications, the analogy no longer relies on the ability of corporations to act, but on certain characteristics or qualities that can be ascribed to corporations and which, by way of analogy, are also found in persons. On the basis of this analogy, corporations can be held morally responsible in the same way as natural persons. Spit, too, links moral responsibility to actions. In his dissertation, the question of the moral responsibility of a collective is immediately translated into the question of whether "hold[ing] a collective morally responsible for what it has done" serves any purpose.[40]

French, too, immediately establishes the link between the concept of a "moral person" and the concept of action:

Our primary interest is in moral...personhood and the question of whether corporations can pass standard tests of moral responsibility...It involves metaphysical problems of identity, agency, and the like. Attention must be directed to those questions, if the moral-person status of corporations is to be settled.[41]

If we take into account that general ethical theories were developed to evaluate actions, the attempts made by Goodpaster, Matthews, Spit, and French are understandable. In order to apply ethics to corporations, actions that can be evaluated must be localized. If this is achieved, the ethical concepts do not require modification. Only the way in which the functioning of corporations is described and analyzed must be modified. This research objective is posited explicitly by French:

I am convinced that the primary problem of business ethics is not to identify ways of applying the traditional moral theories and principles in order to evaluate the actions of corporate managers. That, unfortunately, has been the characteristic approach in the field. Instead, the concept of the business corporation needs to be examined metaphysically and, I am convinced, the outcome of such work will not be an attack on the old moral principles. It will be the innovative application of those principles to the corporation treated as itself a full-fledged moral person. My work has focused on both that anchor and course.[42]

Problems with the concept of corporate action

The exponents of the autonomy approach are of the opinion that the concept of action can and may be usefully employed with respect to corporations. Because corporations do not possess hands and cannot, therefore, act like natural persons, an artificial handle is required. Certain actions of natural persons who represent the corporation must be designated as corporate actions. Spit uses the concept of primary and secondary action (i.e. the "secondary actor" approach). French, Goodpaster, and Matthews propose that one and the same action of a person can, in principle, be described in multiple ways without having to trace the different descriptions back to one another (the "reformulation" approach). In so far as the actions of representatives of the corporation can be understood as actions on behalf of the corporation (i.e. they agree with the corporate objects; in French's terms they are justified by the CID structure), one may speak of corporate action. In that case, a moral evaluation of that action also implies a moral evaluation of the corporation!

A consistent thinking through of the autonomy model shows us that it is not enough to submit the actions of a corporation's representatives to moral evaluation. What about blame of the corporation as a whole where no single action can be called blameworthy? The problem with French and Spit's approach is that in situations where "corporate action" is difficult to identify, we can no longer apply moral norms. This applies to situations in which corporate action is new and not purely a reformulation of a complex of primary actions. This applies to several situations, such as when the actions of an individual functionary are finely interwoven with those of the corporation. Or consider, for example, the case where no clearly objectionable action flows from the corporate intentions. And what about corporate "non-actions" owing to a lack of power (unintentional passivity) or negligence (unconscious passivity)? In situations where it is difficult, if not impossible, to identify the actions of the corporation, we must look for a new object of evaluation and for concepts that make moral evaluation possible.

Secondary action is new action

The autonomy theories presume that it is possible to define corporate action clearly. They posit that an action by a natural person that is based on the intentions of the corporation can be regarded as a corporate action. In practice, however, things are not so clear. A corporate activity is the result of the cooperation of people. People are able to achieve efficiency through cooperation. It is, therefore, generally not possible to consider a corporate action as the sum of a number of discrete primary actions by corporate representatives. This can be illustrated with two examples:

1. Two men, A and B, are carrying a metal bar. The joint activity cannot be fully described as a series of actions by A and B that can then be reformulated as individual acts of the collective. In describing the primary action, one must also refer to how A and B coordinate their actions and the objective they are trying to achieve by cooperating with each other. This is required for understanding it as a collective action. Only then is it possible to describe the joint activity adequately: their lugging the bar.
2. A management team makes a decision: hundreds of people must be laid off. The decision is a compromise. The corporate action cannot, then, be described as a series of primary actions that can be reformulated as corporate action.

A corporate activity is a series of primary actions that can be developed at various places and at various times and that usually resists simply being reformulated as a corporate action. Such primary actions become a new action because they are developed in relation to one another and with a joint objective in mind.

The entanglement of primary and secondary action in practice

Both Spit and French neglect the connections between various events that result from the mutual interweaving of the various types of actions. Functional (secondary) action may be distinguishable from individual (primary) action in abstraction but, in practice, such a distinction is virtually impossible. A corporation's ability to act does not mean that we can distinguish the actions of the corporation from the actions of the individual members. If analyzed from an autonomy perspective, individual and corporate actions are often so entangled that it becomes impossible to determine exactly what actions can be attributed to the corporation and what to the individuals. If corporate actions cannot be clearly localized, it is also impossible to apply action-based theories.

For example, say a personnel manager abuses his position during a performance review of a female employee by making unsolicited sexual advances. Can we view this as a corporate action? No, French and Spit would say, at least, not unless unwanted sexual advances are common during performance reviews. That the functionary is abusing his position cannot be blamed on the person being interviewed or on the corporation. It is clear that the action flows from the intentions of the personnel manager, which can in no way be designated as reasonable or as in the interest of the corporation. Still, it would not be justified to exonerate the corporation completely in this case. It is reasonable to expect a corporation to be organized in such a way that this sort of abuse does not occur. This might mean preventing situations where only one person is in charge of performance reviews. It would also be reasonable to expect the corporation to have set procedures for submitting and handling complaints in such cases. An institution that takes these matters seriously would certainly radiate a pre-ventative aura. In appointing the personnel functionary, one would also expect a corporation to appoint people who have learnt how to deal adequately with authority.

Secondary action that does not flow from corporate intentions

French's theory leaves more room for corporate action only in so far as it can be seen as a result of corporate intentions. When someone acts without the necessary authority or in conflict with the corporate objectives, we cannot speak of corporate action. This means that almost no immoral actions of cor-porate functionaries can be held against the corporation. If an employee released poisonous waste into the environment, the company can only be held responsible if this action conforms to corporate policy. Seen in this light, the concept of corporate responsibility is rather hollow. In French's approach, virtually every immoral action is ascribed to the individual.

The criterion of corporate intentions makes it possible to ascribe almost all immoral actions of the corporation to natural persons. Only when the cor-poration pursues immoral objectives and when corporate actions are based on clearly formulated corporate intentions, can immoral actions be blamed on the corporation itself. The corporation's responsibility for secondary actions where immoral objectives are consciously (thus, intentionally) pursued is clear.

The difficult cases concern situations where the corporation pursues com-mercial objectives where insufficient account is taken of the fundamental interests of others. This involves not the conscious pursuit of immoral object-ives, but the unintended neglect of the moral aspects of a given issue. The corporation can argue its responsibility away by treating the action of the functionary as an action taken on personal authority. In doing so, the corporate responsibility disappears.

The conduct of employees acting on their own authority belongs to this category. As will be mentioned in the discussion of the problem of entangled hands in Chapter 4, employees sometimes abuse their positions in pursuit of other than corporate interests. Such people may represent the corporation, but their activities cannot be designated as corporate action. At the same time, while employees might not abuse their positions, they might not act in the interest of the corporation either. For example, employees sometimes mis-interpret the corporate interest. In such cases, the position of the employee is not abused. The employee is acting on the corporation's behalf, although no actions flow from the intentions of the corporation. To evaluate the corporate function, it is necessary to find out if the corporation consciously does not want to know what the employee is up to.

Unintentional inaction: corporate impotence

Inaction is generally treated as action.[43] Here, a distinction is drawn between "intentional passivity" and "unintentional passivity." We are dealing with abstention or intentional passivity when people opt for inaction or expressly resist a certain action. "Unintentional passivity" crops up when lack of awareness of reasonable expectations results in inaction. Intentional passivity or abstention can be treated in the same way as action:

In abstention, an element of control plays, just as it does in action, an important role. Where in one instance one intervenes in the world in a controlled fashion, in the other instance, one does not do this in an equally controlled way. How close the link is between the two concepts is apparent from the fact that some actions can be carried out by abstention; you can insult someone by not shaking his hand, or by not taking your hat off for him.[44]

There is a degree of intentional passivity in action if the person involved has knowledge of the consequences and the will to achieve them. The difference between abstention and unintentional passivity lies in the presence or absence of certain mental or psychological characteristics of the agent. Unintentional passivity and abstention cannot be distinguished by appearance. It is through the psychological aspect of abstention that it can be dealt with as a sub-set of action: is the agent aware of what is expected and has he or she the will to act in accordance with expectations?

French pays almost no attention to the inaction of collectives. Spit gives some attention to inaction. He even acknowledges that the relationship between action and the failure to act of a collective, on the one hand, and of the members of the collective, on the other, is not a simple one. He draws no further con-clusions, however. For him, it only leads to a refinement of his model.[45]

Corporations are "guilty" of abstention whenever the corporate intention—the psychological aspect of corporate action—is evident. Inaction in the sense of intentional abstention can be treated as a form of corporate action. It is important to highlight the secondary nature of abstention. Such would be the case if a corporation instructs its employees not to act. Here, abstention can be traced back to the corporate aims, the grounds upon which the internal actors reconcile themselves with the consequences of this inaction. Corporations that consciously and intentionally fail to report income in order to lessen their tax burden (thereby maximizing profits) can be blamed for abstention. The inaction of the accountant must, therefore, in the first place be blamed on the corporation. This is not different from intentional action. Usually, it will also result in the blame being placed on the person who acts in a primary sense, in this case the accountant. The corporation is blamed for the abstention arising from the corporate objectives (intentions). One can speak of abstention in a secondary sense that is consciously developed by the corporation.[46]

The situation becomes more problematic if the corporation intends to do something but fails. In that case, one is dealing with corporate impotence. The corporation is dependent on its employees for the execution of the corporate objectives. Insufficient employees could, for example, be available, or the company's employees may simply be incapable of carrying out their work. Or some employees could refuse to conform to the corporate intentions. Environmental factors can also make the organization unmanageable. A dramatic example of this came to the fore during the inquiry into the bankruptcy of RSV, one of the largest shipyards in Europe, when president Stikker gave an account of the unmanageability of this company. He saw the corporation as a car in which the Board of Directors turned the steering wheel without any response from the wheels. In an emotional testimony during the inquiry, Stikker said:

...I can still feel the shivers running down my spine...We discovered that we no longer had any grip on the organization. You are completely right in holding the management primarily responsible. I want, however, to express once more that the conditions under which these projects had to be completed were among the most difficult a person could imagine in an industrial environment...You would be surprised to learn how impossible these projects were in terms of delivery times, costs and, sometimes, technology. They could run terribly out of control....The company was damaged and battered and in some ways humiliated. It was dominated by a complete lack of motivation. The management was worn out...In that situation RSV was no longer able to steer and manage the process.[47]

In a number of cases, corporate impotence can be traced back to the responsibility of its managers. However, when it concerns a failure that the corporation was aware of, but did not intend, the corporation is not guilty of intentional inaction.

Unaware inaction: corporate negligence

"Unintentional passivity" suggests that the remaining category (all inaction that is not abstention) might be relatively insignificant or unproblematic. The philosopher Hart has paid particular attention to this form of inaction. According to

Hart, inaction whose consequences were unknown and unintentional can lead to blame.[48] This category includes negligence, inaction by mistake or misfortune, and inaction as a result of thoughtlessness or recklessness. Suppose that a signalman, whose job is to service a number of railroad signals to prevent train collisions, "forgets" to switch on the "unsafe" sign. We would not accept the excuse that he was playing cards and that in the heat of the game he simply did not think of switching on the "unsafe" signal. The signalman may not realize, at least at the moment of inaction itself, the consequences of his action. There is also no intention to do harm, yet the signalman is still to blame. For corporations, the grounds for blame for this type of *in*action differ from the grounds for blame for harmful consequences of action. Not having taken the right measures to prevent damage is blameworthy:

After all, a hundred times a day persons are blamed outside the law courts for not being more careful, for being inattentive and for not stopping to think; in particular cases, their history or mental or physical examination may show that they could not have done what they omitted to do. In such cases, they are not responsible; but if anyone is ever responsible for anything, there is no general reason why a man should not be responsible for such omissions to think or to consider the situation and its dangers before acting.[49]

The demand that people must be attentive implicitly refers to a norm or standard: what can reasonably be expected from the agent in this situation? When someone is blamed for negligence, it means the person failed to take the preventative measures one would expect from a reasonable person with normal capacities under the given circumstances. This norm describes not only which preventative measures a reasonable person should consider but also the capacities of the person involved (including the circumstances).

Corporate inaction, even if it occurs unconsciously or unintentionally, can imply blame. As was indicated above, negligence cannot be viewed as a sub-set of action because the psychological aspect that characterizes action (knowledge of the consequences and proceeding from a will) is missing. Nor is it possible to use the reformulation theory advocated by French, because there are no corporate intentions to be found at the root of negligence. The justification for the blameworthiness of negligence in the case of the corporation is that no adequate preventative measures were taken. The demands that can be made of natural persons (primary negligence) differ, however, from the conditions under which corporate negligence (secondary actors) becomes blameworthy. Hart has formulated two conditions for blameworthy negligence by natural persons:

(1) one may expect a reasonable person to take relevant preventative measures; and
(2) the person involved must possess the mental and physical capabilities required to take such measures.

Insufficient capacity can be considered a reason for exonerating a natural person. However, it is not as simple for corporations. If a pharmaceutical corporation markets a medicine without having carried out sufficient research, it can be blamed regardless of whether or not it was on the verge of bankruptcy at the time. Within the corporation, persons would undoubtedly have felt "compelled" to bring the medicine onto the market without the necessary tests. Possessing insufficient knowledge of the possible risks is blameworthy regardless of the financial position of the corporation. In the case of corporations, only the first of Hart's conditions is valid: what can we reasonably expect from a corporation?

The corporation as moral subject

If there is—in a secondary sense—either action or clear and intentional inaction/abstention (with the latter ensuing from the intentions of the corporation where the decision-makers have insight into the situation and have a goal in mind), we are justified in calling the corporation to account. Under these circumstances, a corporation's secondary actions can be distinguished from the primary actions of its representatives. The corporation itself deserves the blame or praise.

In this situation marked by concrete corporate action or a lack thereof, it becomes necessary to look at the intentions behind the action should we hope to make a moral judgment. Corporate action takes place in a cooperative context. Corporations are created to generate a "surplus" through cooperation. Even where it is possible to relate corporate action to a number of subsidiary actions of the personnel, the way in which their actions is coordinated is what qualifies this series of primary actions as a corporate action. These actions (just as an obvious lack of them) can be attributed to the corporation because they direct or guide employees. It is also on this basis that corporate action is called "secondary" in such situations. This directive role opens the corporation to potential criticism. What is the intent of the direction given? Are employees given responsible directions?

Even though no clear corporate action can be discerned, the issue of the corporation's culpability still remains. Nor does the lack of concrete action rule out the possibility of moral judgment. Only the corporation, where the intentions (the will) can be localized, can be held accountable for partial (in)action or the lack of an adequate reaction.

THE CORPORATION AS AN AUTONOMOUS MORAL ENTITY

If it is clear that the corporation as such can be held morally responsible, it must be established what this really means. Responsibility is at least a three-way relationship: corporation (A) is responsible to stakeholder (B) for action/situation (C). What is corporation (A)? What are the grounds for morally evaluating (A) as an autonomous entity? Where is the moral responsibility located within corporation (A)? Only when these questions have been answered can we determine which aspects of action/situation (C) stakeholder (B) can hold corporation (A) accountable for. In turn, it is possible to show how the organization of corporation (A) can be tailored to bear these responsibilities (as we shall do in Part III).

Corporate practices

A corporation is a social entity that presents itself both internally and externally through various "expressions." A corporation expresses itself through the behavior of its managers and employees, in its verbal and visual messages, and its symbols. The patterns in these expressions make it possible for internal and external parties to recognize and distinguish a corporation from others. The identity of a corporation is manifested in a multitude of expressions that can be understood as a coherent whole.

Here we are especially interested in the cohesion of a corporation's expressions. We will refer to this with the term "corporate practice(s)."[50] A practice is a more or less stable and coherent pattern of expressions in a cooperative context. With respect to corporations, it relates to the complex of corporate actions that form patterns that fulfill a guiding role. It refers to those aspects of the organization that actually guide or direct employees. With practices, we are neither concerned with the rules, procedures, and power relations as they are set down in an organizational chart nor with an explicit code of conduct formulated by the organization's management. Rather, practices include the tasks, responsibilities and procedures, relationships, norms and values, etc. that are *actually* expressed in the actions of organizational members.

Internal (the way the internal stakeholders experience the corporation) and external (the way external stakeholders experience the corporation) structural mechanisms exist that give directions to employees. These practices form the grounds upon which a corporation can be regarded as a moral entity. This concerns the conditions, rules, habits, the ingrained customs, incentives, and stimuli that structure individual actions and that become visible in individual actions. The object of evaluation is not incidental actions, but rather the context that compels, stimulates, or tempts people to act. It is precisely this organizational context that is susceptible to change. Moral qualities or characteristics are those relevant and desirable contextual standards that can be institutionalized.

Corporate practices do not exist in the way tables and chairs do.[51] The multiplicity of corporate expressions displays a regularity that an observer can recognize. The observer can draw one aspect from one corporate expression and connect it with another.

In a certain sense, an "organization" is formed whenever two people meet for the first time. If this meeting is coincidental in that no roles have been pre-established, no actions need yet be coordinated. There is no joint objective yet, let alone a social institution. Such initial contact involves more than just physical actions. During such a meeting, people form an image of each other and they try to convey a certain image of themselves. Both people eventually walk away with a certain idea of the other. As quick and unconscious as it may be, every person forms an image of the other: "What is she like, what can I expect from her, and what role might I want to play?" On the basis of initial contact, people have expectations that direct their actions toward the other person. Every time these people meet, the image and the expectations of the other are modified. The image takes on more nuances. As more facets of the other person become visible, the corresponding expectations are increasingly based on experience. In each meeting, the shared history is present and grows and develops into a new history. As soon as mutual expectations are formed and people have developed a certain way of behaving, it is difficult to act in a way that runs counter to these expectations. When actions are directed even a little—in one way or another by the expectations of those involved—a practice is born: a pattern of expressions that can be recognized by others.

The interaction described above is always partly influenced by the reactions and actions of other people. In interaction with third parties, similar ways of behaving gradually develop. People usually fulfill a role that is recognizable to others, which often forms their reason for seeking contact. A policeman is recognizable by his uniform. The person standing behind the counter is the salesperson. This type of (job-related) role generates predetermined expectations. The circumstances under which people come into contact also play a large role in their expectations. In major train stations, for example, people generally do not ask strangers to keep an eye on their belongings. In hotels, however, receptionists are asked to do this all the time. The expectations with respect to the receptionist are based partly on the fact that he or she represents an institution.

The dimensions of corporate practices

When we speak of a corporation as a social entity, we presume that we can identify a pattern in its expressions. This regularity does not arise of its own accord. One presumes that something lies at the basis of the regularity that directs the various expressions. Corporate practices, the pattern that is recognizable in the expressions of the corporation, are "caused" by two usually connected types of organizational structuring mechanisms. First, the tasks and responsibilities, rules and procedures (i.e. corporate structure) structure the actions of individual members of the organization. Secondly, this regularity arises through ideas, expectations, and customs (i.e. corporate culture) that are shared among those involved. The corporate culture and structure are the result of developments that the organization has undergone in the past (i.e. corporate tradition) and are, in addition, aimed at achieving the actual corporate goals (i.e. corporate strategy).

Corporate structure

The patterns that can be recognized in the actions of persons within an organization have both formal and informal aspects. The formal dimension (the organizational structure) concerns the jobs that persons or groups of persons fulfill in the organization. The function—not the person who fulfills it—is key. The organizational structure directs the tasks and responsibilities that belong to various functions and determines the relationships among these. The distribution of tasks and responsibilities is usually at least partly set down in a sort of organizational chart and in corresponding, explicit decision-making procedures. These concern formal responsibilities, tasks and rules that set down who makes what decisions, what responsibilities belong to which functions, and which procedures should be followed. (For example, a decision is made by majority vote or by management after consultation with the staff council, etc.) It is the corporate structure that establishes the content of the jobs and that regulates the formal coordination among the various functions.[52] The corporate structure provides the formal acknowledgement of a decision made or an action carried out by the right person in the right way. In addition, it provides clarity and predictability for the person in the job and the stakeholders who deal with the functionary.

Often, this explicitly formulated organizational structure fails to correspond with the corporation's actual structure. Because the actual corporate function is key to making a moral judgment, the actual structure is very important. Accordingly, the following section on the culture of corporations pertains to this "actual" structure.

Corporate culture

The corporate culture concerns the way of thinking, feeling, and doing unique to the corporation. It concerns the manners particular to a corporation. The corporate culture consists of things such as recognition and acceptance rules that reflect what can be designated as corporate interests and corporate actions for those involved. These rules for recognition and acceptance imply that decisions are also recognized and accepted by the corporation as corporate decisions if they are made by the appropriate decision-maker using the correct procedures. In this way, the organizational culture contributes to distinguishing jobs or functions and coordinating them among the individual members.

The culture of an organization provides the informal recognition and acceptance of an action or decision as a corporate action. To take an example, a director is authorized to buy and sell stocks, and uses this authority to sell these stocks at a nice price to himself as a private person. Although he is formally acting on behalf of the corporation, most people would not see this as acting in the interest of the corporation. To them, this would not qualify as legitimate corporate action.

The culture of an organization is not something that simply happens. It is not an uncontrollable natural phenomenon. Sometimes, organizations even use their culture to motivate and stimulate their employees with the aim of achieving corporate goals.[53] The organizational culture develops where members of the organization are confronted with dilemmas and where the choices that are made introduce new patterns of expectation and new "ways of doing." When choices are made with respect to dilemmas, a framework is created that can be used to understand and evaluate other similar situations.

Corporate tradition and strategy

The corporate culture and structure are linked.[54] Together, they form corporate practices. The tradition and strategy of a company stand out in its culture and structure that develop throughout time. Therefore, regularity in corporate expressions should generally be understood against an organization's historical background. In general, new employees and managers undergo a process of socialization. They internalize the way things are done as they have developed in the corporation. In addition to the historical aspect, there is also a strategic dimension: a leaning toward the future. The regularity in corporate expressions arises partly because the actions take place in order to achieve future corporate goals. Long-term cooperation indicates that stakeholders have expectations that must be achieved in future.

The justification for evaluating corporations in moral terms

Corporate practices make it possible to conceive the multitude of internal stakeholder expressions as cohesive and, therefore, as constitutive of the corporation. Due to the culture and structure that make up the core of corporate

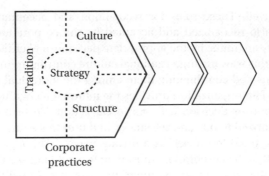

Fig. 3.2. Elements of corporate practices.

practices, the corporation is an autonomous social entity with its own intentions and history. On these grounds, the corporation can be viewed as a moral subject. The corporate culture and structure provide the basis for judging a corporation in moral terms. They can, therefore, also be the objects of evaluation. The structured nature of corporate cooperation allows us to distinguish a corporation from an unstructured group of individuals or a mass of people. In the absence of such structure, one is dealing with a collection of individual moral subjects.

A corporation originates and exists as a result of the cooperation of a number of people. Thanks to the corporate culture and structure, a corporation is an autonomous entity. If the corporation is criticized, it cannot simply hide behind other parties. It is thus possible to distinguish corporations from their individual stakeholders: as independent entities. Autonomy implies that what the corporation does, or is, cannot be derived from other entities, at least not completely. For a full explanation of the characteristics a corporation exhibits and what the corporation does, one must look to the corporation itself. It is by virtue of its autonomy that a corporation can be regarded as a moral entity. This is a crucial moral feature: corporate moral responsibility cannot exist if the source of what the corporation is and does must be sought outside the corporation.

A corporation as an intentional subject

Corporate functioning can be read from a corporation's intentions. The latter form the basis for complimenting or criticizing the corporation. Issues such as IHC Caland's investment decisions that involved human rights issues and Shell's management of its environmental impacts are relevant in this regard. Criticism or praise are not given because there have been no incidents. The issue is the intentions of the corporation: what it is working toward; and what it does to protect its stakeholders from harm. In order to make corporate intentions visible the context within which the actions of the corporate representatives do or do not occur has to be studied. Does the context promote an acknowledgement of the responsibilities toward stakeholders? What is really done to ensure that employees' human rights are honored? What is done to protect the environment? The real intentions of the corporation must be read from the activities developed by the employees.

The intentionality of a corporation entails that the corporation has its own will and that it is able to reason. A corporation can only be held morally responsible if it knows what it is and what it is doing. Without any kind of self-awareness, corporate integrity is an empty concept. Corporations have a will, an orientation toward certain objectives. Corporations make conscious choices that allow us to address them as corporations and as moral subjects. Thanks to corporate intentions that are embedded in the culture and structure of a corporation, it is possible to establish whether certain actions can be regarded as flowing from the corporation or not. In view of corporate intentionality, it can be asserted that a corporation stands for something, strives for something, and that it possesses ideals.

In order to function effectively and efficiently, the corporate structure sets down who should make what decisions, as well as how and when these need to be made. Decisions are usually made after a number of meetings with various groups within the corporation. In such situations, the collective decision-makers generally see these decisions as compromises. The decision-making process contributes to the optimal realization of corporate intentions and decisions. Likewise, it confirms the existence of corporate intentions and the corporation's capacity for reasoning and decision-making.

Empirical research also points in the direction of the existence of autonomous corporate thinking and reasoning processes. Argyris and Schön have shown that individual learning may be a necessary condition for corporate learning, but that is not a sufficient condition. This knowledge must be embedded in the organizational structure and culture:

We can think of organizational learning as a process mediated by the collaborative inquiry of individual members. In their capacity of organizational learning, individuals restructure the continually changing artifact called organizational theory-in-use. Their work as learning agents is unfinished until the results of their inquiry—their discoveries, intentions and evaluations—are recorded in the media of organizational memory, the images and maps which encode organizational theory-in-use.[55]

Only if the subject were the same then as it is now are we justified in addressing a corporation in moral terms (calling it good or bad, giving praise or blame). The structured character imparts a certain durability to the corporation that enables us to distinguish it from a number of people who incidentally work together. Cooperation within a corporation implies a certain tradition—an established way of doing things. These corporate practices guarantee a kind of internal alignment. The durability of the cooperative context is a necessary condition for being considered a trustworthy partner by stakeholders. In the absence of such a durable character, no stakeholder would be prepared to take risks such as investing capital. Customers would hesitate from buying a car if it did not come with a warranty and a guarantee on service. Nor would society have much trust in this framework if it were not possible to hold a corporation accountable for consequences that become evident only after a period of time. The corporate practices distinguish the corporation from individual internal and external stakeholders. At the same time, corporate practices constitute the basis for stakeholder trust and support of a corporation. In this manner, corporate practices contribute to a corporation's integration into its environment, and to the possibility of judging and questioning a corporation on its integrity.

THE CORPORATE INTEGRITY APPROACH

Since the middle of the 1990s, the term "integrity" became increasingly used within the business context.[56] This is quite understandable as the concept of integrity as applied to natural persons is linked to carrying out a particular job or task. It is an appeal not to pursue lofty ideals but rather achievable aims. The integrity approach takes account of the conditions under which corporations operate, rendering it well suited for application to organizations.

Applying the integrity approach to corporations

The first step in applying the concept of integrity to corporations is to apply the features of the integrity approach to this context. In the discussion in Chapter 2, we showed that natural persons (agents) of integrity have a set of anchoring beliefs. They accept responsibility for themselves and their actions (they have a high degree of self-control and self-consciousness), they are aware of the connection between intentions and deeds (through repeated alignment), and they are perceptive to those who make legitimate demands on them (integrated with others). Integrity comes down to the internal integration of intentions, conduct, and consequences in and of themselves; the integration between these three factors; and their integration into the world around them. Yet, what exactly does corporate integrity mean?

Corporate integrity relates to the corporate efforts that are localized in the corporate culture and structure

Just as improper conduct can raise doubts about the integrity of a natural person, abuses by an employee can also raise doubts about the integrity of the corporation.

The saying "one rotten apple spoils the whole barrel" captures this succinctly. Is the proverbial bad apple really representative of the rest of the barrel? Does it indicate systematic abuse or just an incident? Is the organization systematically focused on meeting its responsibilities? What are the anchoring beliefs of the corporation? Does the organization encourage its employees to meet responsibilities or does it pose obstacles? To pick up on the rotten apple analogy, does the harvester actually pick the apples with care or are they simply shoveled off the ground and then carelessly stored and shipped? The organization itself can play a significant role in stimulating or discouraging responsible employee behavior. This guiding role is localized in the culture and structure of the corporation.

Its own efforts make the corporation a moral entity

The basis for taking decisions with respect to fundamental moral dilemmas is embedded in the culture and structure of a corporation. The structure and culture organize the multitude of corporate expressions into a coherent whole and harbors the moral autonomy of the corporation. Given its autonomy, the corporation bears responsibilities and can also be called to account. Even if there is no concrete proof of objectionable behavior, corporations can still be held accountable. The organization can even be reproached for unintentional inaction if it fails to embed adequate measures to prevent possible unethical action of managers and employees. An organization can thus be called to account for reprehensible behavior of employees and managers if greater efforts at prevention could reasonably have been accepted. In the face of dilemmas, the corporation retains the responsibility for deciding which stakeholder rights and interests should take precedence over others and which must suffer. The corporation of integrity does not pass its responsibility to resolve dilemmas on to its employees or other stakeholders. Rather, through its culture and structure, it creates conditions that stimulate the careful consideration and resolution of moral problems.

Corporate integrity refers to the coherence between corporate efforts, conduct, and consequences

The corporate culture and structure greatly influence the way in which relationships with stakeholders are maintained. Employee conduct and actions build and give content to these relationships. The integrity of their behavior lies in the extent to which conflicting interests are treated with care. The integrity of the outcome of corporate conduct is determined by the extent to which stakeholder interests are respected or neglected. This requires an examination and evaluation of the period during which actions occurred instead of treating conduct as isolated events. On the one hand, integrity is about realizing legitimate moral expectations in a coherent manner. A corporation with an excellent environmental program that subjects its employees to poor working conditions cannot be regarded as a corporation of integrity. A good environmental program does not justify poor working conditions. On the other hand, integrity is about the possibility that a company's integrity can remain intact even in the event that stakeholder expectations are not fully satisfied. This can be achieved by paying sufficient attention to preventing dilemmas from arising and to engaging with them adequately when they do arise. A corporation's integrity is therefore also located in the way its efforts, conduct, and consequences are integrated. In this approach, corporate conduct should be based on good intentions. These, in turn, should be reflected in the consequences of conduct. Corporate integrity differs from the three general ethical theories in that it applies all three approaches simultaneously instead of judging organizations from one particular standpoint or another.

Corporate integrity is about repeated alignment and can be developed

In the integrity approach, the idea is not only to judge a corporation in one particular situation but rather to base an evaluation on a longer period of time. Integrity is about repeated alignment. The corporation's intentions, related conduct, and their consequences are prominently expressed in the way it deals with major dilemmas. The greater the dilemma, the more the chosen course of action says about a corporation's integrity.[57] Corporate integrity can be developed, guided, and improved precisely because it lies in those elements that corporations themselves can influence.

Corporate integrity is grounded in its social function

The requirements for corporate integrity should be based on the social role corporations fulfill. This social function brings with it difficult dilemmas that need to be resolved in order for the corporation to carry out its tasks properly. It is precisely in these kinds of situations that integrity requirements prove their worth. That a dilemma can be seen from different perspectives does not mean that we cannot distinguish more and less responsible responses. In situations where stakeholder expectations conflict, or are mutually exclusive, reasons can be advanced why a given course of action is better or less painful than other alternatives. Even if a corporation is unable to satisfy each and every stakeholder, it can act responsibly. The integrity of the corporation lies not only in the choices that are made but also in how they are arrived at. What values were involved in the balancing process? Were the rights and interests of the stakeholders taken into consideration? How does the choice relate to the identity of the corporation?

To apply the integrity approach to the business context, we have to examine what the social function of an organization is, the nature of the corporate condition, and the dilemmas it generates. These questions will be discussed in the next chapter. On the basis of this, we will be able to develop the behavioral principles and qualities that are applicable to organizations.

The Herald of Free Enterprise

On 6 March 1987, right on schedule, the *Herald of Free Enterprise* set sail for Dover across the English Channel from the port of Zeebrugge. The weather was calm and everything appeared to be running according to the normal routine. Shortly after leaving the harbor, the ferry capsized and vanished under the waves in less than a minute. Everything happened so quickly that a large number of passengers did not even have time to make it safely on deck. A rescue mission was basically out of the question as the ferry had already found its tragic resting-place at the bottom of the ocean. All the authorities could do was to rescue the scant number of survivors who had managed to jump ship. The weeks following the disaster bore witness to a number of bodies washed ashore. Most of the 193 bodies could be buried only after the ferry was recovered from the seabed several days later.

Right before the disaster, P&O (Peninsular and Oriental Steam Navigation Company) acquired Townsend Thoresen, the original owner of the *Herald*. After the disaster, P&O immediately changed the old company name from Townsend Thoresen to P&O European Ferries Ltd. With 23 vessels and a market share of more than 50 per cent, it is the largest enterprise (still) operating on the English Channel.

The cause of the disaster became clear relatively soon: the crew had forgotten to close the bow doors of the car deck before setting sail. The *Herald of Free Enterprise* was built for what is known as roll-on/roll-off transport. Passengers drive their cars and trucks into the ferry, where they park their vehicles, and leave again by car or truck. Because the bow doors were not closed when the ferry set sail, the sea flooded that part of the ferry causing it to roll and capsize. According to the report from the official investigating committee that was commissioned by the British government to conduct a judicial inquiry into the tragedy, three crewmen had not performed their duties as required. The assistant boatswain who was responsible for closing the bow doors was asleep at the time the ferry set sail. It was initially the responsibility of the 23-year-old assistant boatswain to close the hydraulic doors, but he had had a busy day before and was given permission by the chief officer to get some rest. However, the chief officer neglected to arrange for someone else to close the doors. According to the regulations, he was supposed to check to make sure that the doors were closed before setting sail. According to those same regulations, however, he was also supposed to be on the bridge at the same time. Before giving permission to set sail, the captain should have asked the chief officer if everything was ready for departure. But he neglected to do so. At first glance, it appeared that a number of human errors was responsible for the disastrous results.

According to the special investigating committee's report, much more was involved. We already saw that the chief officer should have checked whether the bow doors were closed but that—according to one of the other official procedures—he was also required to be on the bridge at the same time. It was not possible to check the doors from the bridge. If he were to conform to all of the procedures required of his function, the chief officer would have had to be in two different places at once at the time of departure. The procedures stipulated by headquarters were clearly inconsistent. It came to light that the crew had asked management to install warning lights on the bridge to remedy the situation. Their suggestion was dismissed as ludicrous.

The investigation also showed that this was not the first time that the ferry had set sail with its bow doors open. It appeared that this had happened—purposefully—before as a means of quickly ventilating the parking deck of the gasoline fumes from the parked vehicles. This practice was undertaken five or six times within a period of three years. The captain testified in front of the investigating committee that he knew nothing about this "ventilation method." Although the issue of open bow doors was reported to management a number of times, the board of directors never took the trouble to investigate the cause of these incidents. Not to mention that, by looking into these problems, they could have found a way to prevent such incidents from occurring again.

Finally, it became crystal clear that management did not care much for safety. No safety system had been developed to guarantee adequate safety standards on the boats. The investigating committee was of the opinion that one would expect a company that was responsible for so many people's lives to have a system in place that minimizes the risk of danger.

These points led to the investigating committee's conclusion that: "The underlying or cardinal faults lie higher up in the company. The board of directors did not appreciate their responsibility for the safe management of their ships. They did not apply their minds to the question as to what orders should have been given to ensure safety on their ships. The directors have no understanding of their duties. It appears that no consideration was given to the way in which the *Herald* ought to have been organized for the Dover/Zeebrugge run. Everyone involved, from the members of the board down to the junior superintendents, are guilty; they all are responsible for the management failure. From top to bottom, the body corporate is infected with the disease of sloppiness... The failure on the part of the shore management to give proper and clear directions contributed to the disaster."[58]

According to the investigating committee, it was clear that up until the disaster, P&O placed its commercial interests above the safety of the passengers.

This information was enough for the public prosecutor to institute criminal proceedings against P&O. The company was charged with involuntary manslaughter. In addition, three employees (the assistant boatswain, the chief officer, and the captain) and four managers were summoned to appear in court. That the company was considered guilty of criminally *negligent* homicide was particularly interesting. The company was at fault and was therefore considered guilty by the public prosecutor.

It is important to separate the question of liability (under civil law) from that of negligence. Even if a company is not at fault, it can still be held liable. In that case, we are dealing with strict liability. This usually involves establishing who should pay the damages. A good example of this is a multiple car collision. Somebody has to pay for it; the only question is who. In such a complicated situation, it is almost impossible to determine who is guilty of negligence (at fault). An accident can also be caused by conditions beyond one's control. A strong gust of wind, for example, can cause a collision between two or more vehicles. In accidents involving a motorized vehicle and a pedestrian or bicycle, the driver of the vehicle is liable for any damages under the premise of strict liability. This rule is justified as a means to stimulate automobile drivers to exercise the utmost care. It also ensures a speedy settlement. For such situations, rules have been made to ensure that damages can be paid irrespective of who is at fault. When the issue of negligence is at stake, we are presented with a legal question, just as in cases involving strict liability. However, the case of negligence also involves a moral question. The concept of negligence always has a moral side. Why are certain actions or behavior considered reprehensible? And, is culpability an issue? In penal law, moral condemnation is translated into grounds for punishment. The moral aspect of negligence in particular is what is at stake here. The question of whether P&O, on the one hand, or the managers or the captain, on the other, can or should be held accountable to one extent or another on the grounds of their official responsibilities, is first and foremost a moral issue.

On the basis of research carried out by a special commission, the state prosecutor held P&O partly responsible for the disaster of the *Herald of Free Enterprise*. The corporation was charged with *culpable* homicide. Even though certain people, especially the boatswain and the first officer, received a share of the blame, the responsibility for the disaster was, according to the prosecutor, located higher up in the organization. Among those singled out were the captain and a number of on-shore managers. According to the prosecutor, that the disaster happened also touched on the organization as such. P&O maintained procedures and a culture that reflected an attitude primarily oriented toward achieving commercial success. The safety of passengers and the crew came second. This was expressed in inconsistent procedures and a slack organizational culture (including ignoring signs and suggestions). The corporation was therefore also responsible for the disaster. On these grounds, the prosecutor decided to prosecute P&O as well. With this, he reasoned in accordance with the autonomy model that considers the corporation a moral subject.

However, the criminal proceedings that began on 10 September 1990 ended quickly. The judge agreed with the prosecutor about the obvious risk of a ferry sinking if it departed with its bow doors open. That was, however, not clear to the corporation, the management, or the captain until it actually happened. According to the judge, no guilt could be ascribed and, therefore, there was no real case. In contrast to US criminal law specifically, in England it was and still is quite difficult to prosecute a legal entity such as a corporation, a hospital, or an educational institution. The court requires that the Crown shows the crime was committed by the "hands and mind" of the perpetrator. In other words, a corporation can only be condemned when it can be shown that people were *consciously and completely* involved in the crime. According to the judge, P&O did not meet this criterion. P&O did not consciously do or fail to do anything that led to the disaster. Because the corporation, the management, and the captain had no knowledge of the risk, both guilt and punishment were out of the question. The judge ruled that since the corporation, the management, and the captain could be not charged with culpable homicide, no one could be punished. So, P&O was acquitted. The prosecutor then decided to withdraw the charges against the boatswain and the first officer. He found it unacceptable that punishment should be meted out only at the level of the operational staff.

If one follows the judge's reasoning, one can only morally accuse a corporation that is established with the goal of committing crimes. The consequence of this perspective is that the moral responsibility of corporations disappears almost entirely from sight. The fear of individuals hiding behind collective responsibilities produces a situation where corporations hide behind individual responsibilities. Corporations are constantly boosting their efficiency by integrating staff activities. This makes it increasingly difficult to reduce corporate responsibility to that of the individual. As a result, it has become more important to look into how that responsibility can be localized in corporations. The autonomy model (and especially the reasoning of French) offers a suitable starting point.

In adopting the autonomy model, we can morally evaluate not only the actions of the corporation, but also the corporation itself. After all, the corporation provides the framework that directs the persons who represent it and that stimulates or hinders them from fulfilling their responsibilities. Consequently, the corporation is a social entity that exists autonomously with its own intentions (it is a structured and goal-oriented cooperation of persons) and its own history (the cooperation has a long-term character). The corporation can thus be seen as a moral subject that can be judged in moral terms.

4

The Corporate Condition

The difficulty with assessing corporations in moral terms is that the dominant ethical theories have been developed to evaluate human action. Since it is awkward clearly to identify corporate actions in practice, applying these theories runs into difficulties. This is an important reason why many ethicists argue that the corporation as such cannot be subjected to moral judgment. In Chapter 3, we showed that the corporation can be conceived as a moral subject. We now have to determine which ethical concepts can be applied to the functioning of corporations. For this purpose, the moral questions typical to the corporate context need to be carefully examined.

Three morally significant features of the corporate domain require us to tailor general ethical concepts to this context. In this chapter, we describe the "corporate condition," or the nature of the corporation, and discuss the implications of these defining characteristics for subjecting corporate functioning to moral judgment. The content we give to the "corporate condition" is derived from "the theory of the firm." This theory was developed by the economist Ronald Coase and formed the basis for a completely new approach to economic theory. Coase, who formulated his ideas in the 1930s, was not set on developing a moral theory. His objective was to understand what transpires when people cooperate within the corporate context. Before we discuss Coase's theory and deduce from it three fundamental dilemmas for corporations, we would like to present the mountain climber's dilemma.

THE MOUNTAIN CLIMBER'S DILEMMA

To start off, let us take an example from a completely different context: mountain climbing. As extreme as the situation and the context of this case might be, it illustrates a dilemma that serves as an excellent analogy for the functioning of corporations.[1]

Climbing Mount Everest

In 1992, a team of experienced mountain climbers led by Ronald Naar attempted to climb the highest mountain in the world, Mount Everest. Reaching the summit of this mountain is the ultimate goal of many ardent mountain climbers. Climbing at that height is risky business. Each step requires an immense amount of effort because of the thin air. Altitude sickness is not uncommon. In addition, the weather can be atrocious. Temperatures of around 20 or 30 degrees Celsius below zero are common. Moreover, the weather can change in a flash. Snowstorms and mist where people are barely able to see their hands in front of their own face sometimes take people by surprise. Major parts of the trip are made on glaciers that can shift tens of centimeters a day. Avalanches can also catch people off guard. These are the reasons why so many accidents happen at those heights.

About 10 per cent of all mountain climbers perish during the climb, especially during the descent. That is because after having reached the summit, they tend to be overconfident in addition to being twice as exhausted as during the ascent. Any mountain climber who decides to attempt the climb knows and accepts these risks. Ronald Naar's team also considered the risks during their preparations. One way to limit them was to train physically and mentally, take the proper equipment, and prepare well for the expedition in advance. The home front of Ronald Naar's team was also aware of the risks and was involved in the team's preparations.

As is usual in such expeditions, base camp was pitched right below the summit and a few team members were chosen to attempt the climb to the top. In this decision, Ronald Naar took the physical and mental condition of his team members into account. The idea was to select a group of people that was fit and able to support each other so as to secure the best chance of success. The team also included two local Sherpas.

The team set off. Under normal conditions, the journey from base camp to the summit takes about six days. However, the weather took a turn for the worse, snowstorms and mist making things quite difficult for them. Halfway there, they ran into a completely demoralized Indian team. They related that they had had to give up their attempt at reaching the top. In addition, they explained that they had been forced to leave two of their people behind who were unable to carry on. Ronald Naar's team was shocked but they decided to push on. They felt in good enough shape and with the final goal in view, they were not willing to give up.

At the end of the day, they pitched camp. When one of the team members went outside for a second during the night, he saw a figure in the mist about 20 meters away from the tent. He assumed it to be a member of the Indian team. To his horror, he suddenly saw the man move his arm in an attempt to wave for help. Even though he was "only" 20 meters away, at 8,000 meters it takes a lot of energy to walk that far. And it is extremely risky; mountain-climbers sometimes get lost and stranded even when covering such short distances. He returned to the tent to discuss the matter with his team.

They went through all the questions as to what to do, whether to drag the Indian to the tent to see if he could be saved and what they would do if he came to. Trying to save the Indian would have meant abandoning the attempt at reaching the summit altogether. Every delay meant a greater chance of the temperature rising and less of a chance of continuing the expedition. Bringing the man back down was also out of the question. If he were to survive, he would be in such bad shape that he would never be able to descend the mountain on his own. Nor was dragging him down a sensible option either. Every climber needed all the energy he had just to take care of himself. Fortunately, they were able to contact base camp to discuss the problem. They gave him a zero chance of survival. They estimated that his body temperature had probably already dropped to around 28 degrees Celsius. At that temperature, the Indian's organs would have been permanently damaged already. Bringing him into the tent and warming up his body would thus only have postponed his inevitable death. As difficult as it must have been, Ronald Naar decided to leave him outside. The next day they took a look at the Indian's lifeless body. To Ronald Naar it was simply awful, but, all things considered, there was nothing they could have done to help him.

Ronald Naar decided to go through with the expedition and two other team members followed him. One of the team members decided to return to base camp with the two Sherpas, who regarded the incident as a bad omen. A team that is split up and without any guidance has little chance of reaching the top of the mountain. Sufficient support at that time is crucial. The severe weather, small size of the team, and their demoralization eventually forced the remaining team members to give up.

Later, after the team had returned home, the expedition received wide media coverage and emotional images of the dead Indian were broadcast on television. Ronald Naar and his team became the topic and target of a lot of debate and criticism. Joe Simpson, himself a mountain climber who was once left behind by his team after he had fallen and broken his leg, was particularly vehement in his criticism. He viewed the incident involving Ronald Naar's team as an example of the degeneration of mountain climbing as a sport. He saw it as a distressing sign that all that counted in the sport was reaching the summit—nothing else seemed to matter any more.

Criticism

According to Joe Simpson, Ronald Naar was solely interested in reaching the summit.

Simpson: Helping a dying man would have reduced your chances of success.... You were there with your oxygen and tents and not even one of you was willing to walk twenty meters to lend a hand. All you cared about was reaching the peak.

Naar: Oh, come on. We scrapped our shot at reaching the top then because of the bad weather. We didn't reach the summit until eleven days later. The dead Indian wasn't holding us back at all.

Simpson: Well then how can you justify...

Naar: We couldn't afford any risks.

Simpson: What risk? To go out twenty meters?

Naar: Yes.

Simpson: Nonsense!

Naar: If we had run into the same situation in camp three, at 7,200 meters, of course we would have left the tent. There is a big difference between 7,200 and 8,000 meters. The difference is so great, so incredibly great.

Simpson: But I'm talking about ethics.

Naar: For me, ethics means preventing accidents. If you take risks, you have to accept the consequences...I was the leader of the group of climbers. That was my responsibility. If I had returned with an injured member of the expedition, now then they really would have given me hell. Nowadays a lot of untrained people go up. Is it my duty, as someone who is well trained and properly prepared, to save those people? Do you want me to endanger the people in my party? I spoke to one of the team members about this yesterday. We realized that taking pictures of the dead Indian—and our openness—worked against us.

The dilemmas

The expedition of Ronald Naar's team illustrates several difficult dilemmas. Ronald Naar and his team had to weigh the "cry for help" from the dying Indian against their drive to reach the peak and all the extra risks rescuing him involved. What made this difficult was that Ronald Naar and his team had to weigh up different possibilities: the chance of helping the dying Indian and him actually surviving, and the chance of something happening to the team members.

The team was put together with the goal of reaching the peak. That would only have been possible with teamwork, with everyone giving 100 per cent. At the same time, the team members all had their own ideas about how to achieve that goal and how to balance the risks and options they faced. The Sherpas had other aims. For them, the Naar expedition was just one of many they guided. Their cultural background was different, which meant that they interpreted critical situations somewhat differently.

There was also the question of teamwork between different teams. It is a good custom for teams that run into each other in the mountains to give each other the necessary help. Yet, how far did the responsibility of Naar and his team extend to someone who got left behind by his own team? Can others be responsible for someone who sets off on such an expedition without the necessary preparation and clothing?

Ronald Naar was in a special position. As the leader of the team, his task was to take them to the summit while keeping their safety in mind and avoiding any unnecessary risks. He was also responsible for keeping the team together, since that is the only way to reach the peak and keep risks to a minimum. There is a big difference between the way a leader and a team member see the same situation. Individuals tend to take greater risks in these circumstances. For those who are responsible for making decisions and weighing risks on behalf of others under their supervision, circumstances like these can really take their toll.

Climbing as a business

The expedition of Ronald Naar and his team can in fact be seen as a business based on a temporary venture (project organization) to realize a joint aim. Of course, there are differences. The project goal was not related to economics, but a number of contracts or agreements were involved in this endeavor. People who join an undertaking have a common goal in mind that can be more effi-ciently and effectively realized through teamwork. The dilemmas that Ronald Naar and his team members faced also surface by analogy within the corporate context. There are always people or groups with expectations that stand in the way of the corporation achieving its goals. Teamwork is key to reaching such goals. Corporations generally receive a plethora of opinions on which choice to make in the event that people's interests conflict with the corporate objective. Teamwork also carries the risk of people passing their responsibilities on to others. Working for a corporation means dealing with role conflicts. A single person can represent a corporation, be the mother of a family, and be a member of a certain association. Working for a corporation adds an extra role to one's load of general responsibilities. This can place conflicting demands on the other roles one has to fulfill.

Hereafter we refer to these dilemmas as the problems of dirty, many, and entangled hands. These three dilemmas are characteristic of the corporate context. Anyone who works within the corporate context eventually comes to face these three quandaries. In the section that follows, we analyze the nature of the firm to explore and describe the "corporate condition."

THREE FUNDAMENTAL DILEMMAS OF THE CORPORATION

By uncovering the nature of the corporation, we can deduce the defining features of corporate functioning. These insights are subsequently used to examine how ethical questions arise in the corporate context. This is a study of companies that operate within an economic order that can be characterized, at least in part, as a market economy. This assumption makes it possible to consider the decisions that entrepreneurs are confronted with in creating products or services. The question is whether they should produce them inside their own company or procure them on the market. That is, the question of "to do or have done."

It is precisely because Coase's "theory of the firm" was not developed for submitting corporations to an ethical analysis that this theory offers a powerful point of departure for exploring the corporation from a moral perspective. Coase's theory of the firm borders on a neoclassical economic approach. Neoclassicists view the corporation solely as a market player. Coase moves beyond this restricted view. Nevertheless, he draws no distinction between the corporation and the entrepreneur. Coase's theory has had an enormous impact due to its great many applications (including the "behavioral theory of the firm" and "transaction costs" theory).

This does not, however, imply that we can uncritically embrace Coase's theory of the firm. A careful examination of Coase's account of the nature of the firm shows that he employs a very narrow conception of contracts. For Coase, contracts are simply transactions. In Chapter 5, we shall show that a broader conception of the contract is more suitable for understanding the responsibilities of the corporation. We use Coase's theory to deduce three fundamental problems for corporations and refer to them as the dirty hands, the many hands, and the entangled hands dilemmas. Together, they define the corporate condition that refers to the preconditions for corporate functioning. Any adequate business ethics model should take these three fundamental issues into account.

Efficiency

In an influential article "The Nature of the Firm", Coase gives an exposition of the basic tenets of his "transaction costs" theory. The question Coase examines in this article is why corporations exist in a free-market economy.[2] According to the basic premisses of neoclassical economics, an optimal allocation of the means of production can be created through the price mechanism. Yet, corporations make the price mechanism inoperative to a certain extent. Resources within corporations are not allocated by the price mechanism but rather by entrepreneurs who direct them in accordance with their aims.

According to Coase, at the basis of corporations lies efficiency. Corporations owe their right of existence to the efficient production of goods and delivery of services. Focused and coordinated teamwork is the key to achieving efficiency. Entrepreneurs are prepared to set up activities in corporations because of the advantages that stand to be gained. The social legitimacy of corporations is grounded in the fact that an optimal level of prosperity can be achieved in this way. Prosperity is seen as a higher level of production of products and services in both a quantitative and qualitative sense. Efficiency is the reason why entrepreneurs are interested in taking the initiative to incorporate their activities, and why society accepts the phenomenon of corporations.

This function points toward both the scope and limits of corporate moral responsibilities. Corporations exist in order to produce goods and services in the most efficient way possible. This curtailment of the responsibility of corporations ultimately rests on rule-utilitarian thinking: the general interest is usually best served when corporations limit themselves to the efficient production of goods and services.

Specialization

According to Coase, there are certain costs involved in using the price mechanism as a means of allocation. The creation of corporations can therefore be explained in terms of a simple cost/benefit analysis. Where it is more efficient to create goods and services in a corporation than through transactions on the market, there is room for corporation-based production and service.

[T]he operation of a market costs something and by forming an organization and allowing some authority (an "entrepreneur") to direct the resources, certain marketing costs are saved. The entrepreneur has to carry out his function at less cost, taking into account the fact that he may get factors of production at a lower price than the market transactions which supersede it, because it is always possible to revert to the open market if he fails to do this.[3]

To incorporate a given activity within the corporation, the related organizational costs must be lower than the costs involved in allowing the transaction to go ahead using the price mechanism. And it must also be lower than the costs that other corporations would incur in rendering the product or service. An entrepreneur will create a corporation and incorporate as many activities as possible up to the point that the marginal costs of a new activity are equal to the organizational costs of another company or to the transaction costs involved in creating the product in a non-corporate fashion.

Such efficiency, which can be seen as the *raison d'être* of the corporation, is achieved by the division of labor, specialization, and cooperation. Specialization and the related phenomenon, the division of labor, occur internally and externally. The external division of labor and specialization occur when an individual or a cooperative group applies itself to the production of certain goods and services. These individuals or cooperatives opt to supply a product or service because they believe that they possess certain capacities (expertise, resources) that will allow them to realize this economic goal better than others on the market will. The internal division of labor occurs when the various types of activities within a cooperative group are divided among a number of specialists with the aim of achieving a collective result.

Efficiency can be achieved by using external specialists. By applying himself to the production of certain goods or services or even to a part of a production chain, the entrepreneur capitalizes on the advantages of his own position. The corporation's production costs are therefore lower than the cost of procuring the same products and services on the market or having another corporation produce them. For a corporation striving to achieve efficiency, the availability of external specialists is important. A consequence of external specialization is that a large number of parties operate outside the corporation and develop activities that the corporation can no longer carry out efficiently, although they are necessary for its success. This is how corporations become dependent on capital providers (venture and non-venture capital), employees, suppliers, nearby residents, the government, and other stakeholders. A situation then arises where the corporation has to ensure that these parties remain available while achieving this under the most favorable conditions possible.

Efficiency is further achieved through economies of scale, which is made possible by internal specialization and the division of labor. Economies of scale arise when advantages can be gained through cooperation. By purchasing collectively, for example, one can secure better terms. Or by collectively purchasing machinery that would be unprofitable for one user alone, everyone can reduce production costs. In this way, it is possible—purely through economies of scale—to reduce the unit cost of a product.

Corporations consist of people who are prepared to work together in an organized fashion to achieve collective objectives and to work as efficiently as possible by coordinating their individual and collective activities. At the same time, relationships of dependence arise where people's interests do not necessarily converge. External specialization, on the one hand, and internal specialization and the distribution of tasks, on the other, lead to three dilemmas that are determinant of the "corporate condition" of contemporary Western corporations.

The Dirty Hands Dilemma

An entrepreneur cannot do everything himself. His gain lies in organizing the work of others. Whatever he is incapable of achieving efficiently inside his own corporation can be acquired from the outside. An entrepreneur depends on employees and on other specialized corporations. In creating a specialized product or service, he must acquire the support of employees and market parties to create and maintain the corporation.

The only way for an entrepreneur to succeed in incorporating activities is by attracting stakeholders. To make things interesting for the stakeholders, he must share advantages with them. He must succeed in satisfying those stakeholders who are necessary for the future of the corporation. Corporations that generate insufficient means in this regard run the risk of losing stakeholder trust, which could ultimately lead to bankruptcy. Doing business must also be sufficiently attractive for the entrepreneur. Profits must be adequate to compensate for all his efforts and risks.

Those stakeholders that are necessary for the functioning of the corporation and who only receive compensation for this at a later time must be convinced of the corporation's importance as a long-term partner. Only then will these parties be prepared to contribute to its continued existence. For example, employees will not be prepared to invest their energy in their corporation (by following training programs necessary for carrying out their jobs, working overtime, etc.) unless they are convinced that they will eventually profit from this. Consumers will only purchase a product from a corporation if they know they can expect reasonable after-sales service.

In order to ensure the future of their corporation, entrepreneurs must also try to meet justified stakeholder demands as minimally as possible where these involve costs for the corporation. After all, if the entrepreneur is unable to produce products or services at less cost than on the market (the transaction costs), the corporation's reason for existence disappears. In order to realize the primary function of the corporation—in the sense of producing goods and services efficiently—the corporation must secure both the fundamental rights and interests of the stakeholders as far as possible while honoring those of the individual stakeholders as minimally as possible. In other words, in order to function responsibly (ensuring the continuity of the corporation so as to secure the rights and interests of the collective stakeholders), one must act immorally (with regard to the individual stakeholders) at the same time.

Is it acceptable, given the drive to produce goods and services efficiently so as to honor the rights of the collective stakeholders, to refrain from (sufficiently) honoring the rights and interests of certain individual stakeholders? That is, to dirty the corporation's hands? Is it acceptable to ignore the stakeholder who waves for help in a failed attempt to reach the summit? An entrepreneur must continuously find a balance between the conflicting demands of stakeholders. As a result, unrelenting pressure bears down on the entrepreneur to opt for the greater or more powerful interest and turning his back on certain lesser stakeholders' rights or demands.

The position corporations, entrepreneurs, and all those who represent the corporation find themselves in, is therefore ambiguous. In order to ensure the continuity of the corporation, they must secure the support and goodwill of the internal and external stakeholders. This requires exerting maximum effort on behalf of stakeholders' rights and interests. At the same time, the legitimate claims of individual stakeholders must be honored as minimally as possible.

Only then can the continuity of the whole, and by extension, the rights and interests of the collective stakeholders be best assured. These are the broad contours of what we call the Dirty Hands Dilemma.

I. The corporate dilemma of dirty hands: in order to safeguard the continuity of the corporation and, thereby, the rights and interests of the collective stakeholders, these rights and interest must be honored as minimally as possible. Running a business thus requires dirtying one's hands. Here the corporation encroaches upon legitimate stakeholder interests and expectations in order to realize other legitimate interests and expectations that are seen as more important in keeping the corporation afloat.

Examples of the Dirty Hands Dilemma are when corporations consider firing employees to increase returns or when a decision has to be made about whether environmental investments that exceed the law are justified if it is at the expense of profits. When companies make use of child labor in order to produce competitively priced products, they are dirtying their hands to do good. The same applies to corporations that use dubious means to obtain information about rivals so as to secure their competitive edge. Another example concerns the extent to which corporations should take measures to rule out the improper use or deliberate misuse of products that could present a public health threat if it would entail higher prices and diminished product convenience or use.

An adequate corporate ethics model must take account of the context that corporations and their representatives function in. It will have to indicate which stakeholder demands the corporation should honor and it must show how a responsible choice can be made in cases of conflict between different demands. Moreover, such a model must show how a balance can be achieved between the legitimate claims of individual stakeholders and the corporate interest to the extent that the latter is derived from the legitimate claims of collective stakeholders.

The Many Hands Dilemma

Internal specialization and the division of labor, and the related requirements of coordination and cooperation to realize the efficient production of goods and services, point toward the dilemma of many hands. Given the number of individuals involved and the effects of collective corporate action, it becomes difficult to locate the responsibility for the activities undertaken.

As was observed in Chapter 3, corporate responsibility can in many instances not be traced back to the sum of individual responsibilities. Just as a product as the result of teamwork and cooperation defies an easy breakdown into its constituent parts, responsibility, too, is difficult to trace back to individual components. Effective integration of the actions of internal stakeholders introduces a shifting mechanism and an opaque responsibility structure with respect to the result achieved. This will be true especially of failures where damage is caused or rights violated. In this regard, the expression "success has many fathers, failure is an orphan" certainly holds true.[4]

The successful integration of the actions of the individual members of a corporation (employees, managers, staff council, Board of Directors, etc.) into a cohesive whole implies that it is no longer possible to show who is accountable for particular effects of corporate functioning. One cannot unproblematically equate the responsibility of the entrepreneur for the functioning of the corporation with his personal responsibility.[5] The complexity of the organization and the increase in individual discretion and autonomy at lower levels have led to a situation in which the model of the bureaucracy (with its clear hierarchical structure) is largely no longer applicable to corporations. An atomistic approach to moral issues in the corporate context leads to a situation where the responsibility for corporate functioning seeps away, at least partly, between individual responsibilities. This gives rise to what we call the Many Hands Dilemma.

> II. The corporate dilemma of many hands: adequately carrying out a social task (the efficient production of goods and services) with effective and efficient teamwork dilutes the team's responsibility for the result. If a corporation acts responsibly, the collective moral responsibility can become diffused in that it disappears between the individual responsibilities of employees.

The Many Hands Dilemma can arise in organizations in different ways. First of all, multiple employees may have separate, uncoordinated perspectives on the corporate aims and responsibilities. Each of them feels responsible for the proper functioning of the organization and views his or her interpretation of the organization's future as accurate (even though this is done unconsciously and with all the best intentions). The Many Hands Dilemma can also crop up where responsibilities are shirked and stakeholders are left with no one to turn to. In such instances no one is willing to take on the task because they see themselves as unauthorized or lacking the necessary competence. When employees feel responsible only for their own tasks, the bigger picture simply fades away.

The many hands problem often turns the search for responsibility into a quest for the Holy Grail.[6] An inadequate distribution of responsibilities can result in certain corporate responsibilities slipping through employees' many "fingers" and getting lost. In assigning concrete tasks, corporations run the risk of their employees or departments doing their jobs wearing blinders. In that case, these people no longer concern themselves with the duties of others and lose the sense of the corporation as a corporate body. As a result, no one sees or takes responsibility for the bigger picture. Other many hands dilemmas include the extent to which employees should be collectively or individually rewarded and the degree to which internal teamwork or competition should be stimulated. Similar problems also arise in determining how to make decisions quickly and carefully, who should be responsible for what, and to what extent decision-making can be delegated without corporate responsibilities getting lost.

The many hands problem is not necessarily a matter for the organization alone. Collective responsibilities can get lost in joint efforts with external stakeholders as well. In a sense, close working relations such as joint ventures with their own aims, people, resources, and structures constitute separate enterprises. The more intense such efforts become, the more difficult it becomes to determine who is or was responsible for what. This makes the many hands problem even more poignant (although there is a range of alternatives for aligning responsibilities).

An adequate business ethics model should take account of the fact that the Many Hands Dilemma is inherent to the functioning of corporations. It also needs to present a possible solution for this dilemma. Organizing business processes not only contributes to the efficient production of goods and rendering of services but also has consequences for how moral responsibilities are given shape within the corporation. Just as the organization must ensure that the actions of the individual employees are coordinated to ensure effectiveness and efficiency, so too the various responsibilities toward stakeholders should be coordinated. Dividing the work among several people implies that the total corporate responsibility should be divided to as great an extent as possible among the various people involved.

The Entangled Hands Dilemma

By their very nature, corporations can act only indirectly, that is, through managers or employees. The actions of managers or employees are representative because they are undertaken on behalf of the corporation. An entrepreneur who assumes obligations toward stakeholders that he or she cannot realize on his or her own can still produce the desired output by hiring others to help him or her. As he/she subsequently delegates tasks and authorities to these employees, the entrepreneur is no longer the only one acting on behalf of the corporation. In order to do their work, employees have to have access to company assets such as information, funds, goods, equipment, and time. This places them in a special position. It makes them both principals (stakeholders) and agents (actors who realize stakeholder expectations). Employees always play at least two roles and, as a result, represent at least two kinds of interests. They have their own personal interests and expectations that do not necessarily coincide with the interests and responsibilities of the corporation.

Employee commitment and loyalty to the corporate interest is a necessary condition for the corporation's efficiency and effectiveness. At the same time, the optimal efficiency of employees can be at odds with their personal interests. As a special corporate asset, human capital falls into a class that is distinct from financial capital, goods, and resources. Employees have intrinsic value and their own preferences. Nor can they be programmed like machines. Whereas it is important for the corporation to deploy its employees efficiently, these employees, in turn, are served by using some corporate assets for private purposes. While it would generally suit the organization to draw the line for using corporate assets at zero and monitor employees to make sure they do not overstep the line, employees are likely to move this border up in order to secure as much freedom as possible. Moreover, a system of intensive control would compromise the efficiency of the business processes and the trust employees expect the corporation to place in them.

The dilemma at hand concerns the balance that needs to be found between entrusting responsibilities to employees and seeing to it that they are properly realized. The greater the employee's responsibility, the greater the opportunity, *ceteris paribus*, to misuse the means to realize them. Whereas the personal interest of the entrepreneur practically mirrors that of the corporation, this is not the case for employees. At what point does personal use becomes abuse and what constitutes a sound balance between personal interests and corporate interests? This problem we refer to as the Entangled Hands Dilemma.

> III. The corporate dilemma of entangled hands: for a corporation to function responsibly (i.e. properly responding to the changing expectations of stakeholders) it must delegate responsibilities. As these responsibilities are delegated and people are given access to corporate assets, the likelihood of them behaving irresponsibly increases. This is because employees have their own private responsibilities and interests that could be at odds with the interest of the corporation.

We use the Entangled Hands Dilemma as a metaphor for the conflict between the personal interests of employees and those of the organization where corporate assets are at stake. The private and corporate responsibilities of employees form a tangle that is either difficult or impossible to unravel. Some of the dilemmas that can occur concern the extent to which employees are allowed to make private use of the corporation's assets or to hold other jobs that are in conflict with the interests of the organization. Others have to do with the personal acceptance of promotional gifts, engaging in business with family members, and making private purchases from the corporation's suppliers.

The problem of entangled hands also arises in relations with external stakeholders where the latter misuse the corporate assets at their disposal or abuse the trust placed in them. For example, a contractor who is planning on placing a large order with a certain company can probably expect the price of the company's stock to rise. In that case, he might be inclined to purchase shares in that company on the basis of this knowledge. As long as external stakeholders cannot be seen as representatives of a corporation, their actions will continue to defy classification under the actions of the corporation itself. In this case, the situation cannot be seen as an ethical issue for the corporation. This changes, however, if the actions of the stakeholder reflect upon or are partly imputed to the corporation, and if the latter can be called to account. The issue can be subjected to moral judgment if a certain degree of complacence can be detected on behalf of the corporation. A corporation can be blamed for a supplier's systematic violation of human rights to the extent that it neglected to prevent this conduct or to record it in advance.

In the literature, this issue is indicated as the "agency problem," which asserts that the principal's use of an agent who acts on his behalf always involves agency costs. The difference between the Entangled Hands and the Dirty Hands Dilemmas is that in the case of the latter, stakeholders are the principals and the corporation the agent. The corporation acts on behalf of stakeholders. In the Entangled Hands Dilemma, the corporation is the principal and the employees are the agents. Employees act on behalf of the corporation. The Dirty Hands Dilemma requires that sufficient grounds exist for stakeholders to trust that the corporation is careful in managing their interests. The Entangled Hands Dilemma demands that sufficient grounds exist for the corporation to trust employees to be careful in their treatment of the organization's interests. In both cases, the key is to find the right balance between conflicting interests and, by implication, the responsibilities of the corporation.

An adequate corporate ethics model must address the Entangled Hands Dilemma. It has to formulate requirements both for the corporation and its individual employees. What can a corporation (and its external stakeholders, by extension) reasonably expect from its employees? And what can employees (and by extension, external stakeholders) expect from a corporation in order to engage responsibly with the Entangled Hands Dilemma—and be respected for their efforts?

The practical relevance of dilemmas

The above issues arise not only at a conceptual level, they also materialize in various forms at different levels within organizations. Nevertheless, the extent to which the three fundamental dilemmas come into play differs sharply from one organization to the next. The Entangled Hands Dilemma mainly occurs in organizations where employees or other stakeholders have access to valuable corporate assets (for example, information, goods, or money) or where they have extensive decision-making powers. These issues can play a role in companies where, for example, buyers in procurement departments have considerable decision-making powers, where wrong decisions may have major consequences, and where potential suppliers do everything to get in the buyer's good books. The Many Hands Dilemma generally occurs in large organizations that are characterized by both complexity and high levels of internal job-specialization and coordination. The complexity of the decision-making procedures, the distance between the top and bottom level, and the partially conflicting interests of various units have the effect that responsibilities in large organizations in particular are prone to get lost. Such organizations are therefore inclined to malfunction. Many network organizations face this dilemma where several people work together without an overall supervisor. In addition to afflicting those organizations with major losses or tight and shrinking budgets, the Dirty Hands Dilemma generally encroaches upon those that operate in culturally diverse or politically turbulent countries or those whose activities have a high impact on the natural environment. In order to comprehend their topical relevance, these three dilemmas can be related to the developments set out in Chapter 1.

Table 4.1. Topical relevance of the fundamental dilemmas

Developments	The Dirty Hands Dilemma	The Many Hands Dilemma	The Entangled Hands Dilemma
More corporate responsibilities	Expectations regarding the harmony between corporations and the world around them are rising while limited resources make choosing more difficult.	More unity expected of the corporation while greater responsibilities make coordination more difficult.	Employees are expected to show greater loyalty, commitment, and efforts in order to realize the corporate responsibilities while this is less of a 'given' than before.
Greater complexity of issues	Because of increasing (more complex and contradictory) stakeholder demands, balancing them becomes more difficult.	Because of the increasing complexity of the corporation and the need to resolve complex issues simultaneously, responsibilities are more difficult to locate and assign.	Because of the increasing responsibilities of employees, it is more difficult to keep the interests of the organization and those of the individual separate.
More room and pressure to shirk corporate responsibilities	More pressure to forgo meeting legitimate, non-profit-related stakeholder expectations.	More opportunities and reasons to shirk responsibilities or to refrain from accepting collective responsibilities.	Employees have greater access to corporate assets for private use.
Greater stakeholder access to information	More difficult to cover up the failure to meet legitimate stakeholder expectations, increasing the need to weigh these carefully.	More difficult to cover up those collective tasks that no one has taken care of, increasing the need for good organization.	More difficult to cover up employee misuse of assets, increasing the need to handle assets carefully.
Higher costs and benefits of irresponsible and responsible corporate behavior	Stakeholders are prepared to take an active stance with respect to damage caused or added value created by the corporation.	Because of increasing internal interdependence, the quality of the one part has greater consequences for the functioning of others.	Greater damage to the corporate image if employees misuse assets.

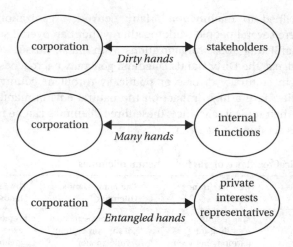

Fig. 4.1. Three fundamental dilemmas and the relations of and within corporations.

Fundamental dilemmas and the relations within the organizational context

The Dirty, Many, and Entangled Hands Dilemmas portray the fundamental tensions that arise in three types of relationships within the organizational context. The moment people decide to create products and services in a corporate context, three new relationships come into being: the relations of the corporation with stakeholders; the relation of cooperation within the corporations; and the private relations of the corporation's representatives. Often, a single moral issue will contain several dilemma structures.

The three fundamental moral dilemmas that arise in these relationships undermine the responsible functioning of corporations. An adequate model of corporate ethics should therefore take these obstacles into account and indicate how the problems outlined can be resolved. This requires a detailed analysis of the respective dilemmas.

A MORE DETAILED ANALYSIS OF THE DIRTY HANDS DILEMMA

The expressions "dirtying his hands" and "washing one's hands in innocence" come from the Bible. In times of yore, a local murder would require the city elders to kill a calf by slitting its throat and then washing their hands in its innocent blood. "And all the elders of that city nearest to the slain man shall wash their hands over the heifer.... and they shall testify 'Our hands did not shed this blood.' "[7] Likewise, Pilate absolved himself of responsibility for Jesus's death by publicly washing his hands. Although he was convinced of Christ's innocence, he agreed to his death sentence in order to prevent a riot. When Pilate saw "that he was gaining nothing, but rather that a riot was beginning, he took water and washed his hands before the crowd, saying 'I am innocent of this man's blood.' "[8]

In political theory, the term "dirty hands" is used with reference to the conduct of political leaders.[9] Set on furthering the general interest, politicians sometimes ignore moral demands. This is often difficult to understand especially for outsiders. It can also saddle an honorable politician with a conflict of conscience. The Dirty Hands Dilemma also plays an important role in the business context.[10] Corporate managers have a company to run, which means that painful decisions sometimes have to be made. They have to decide, for instance, whether to move operations to low-wage countries when it is bound to result in unemployment at home. Or they may have to decide what to do if paying a bribe can clinch a big business deal and secure the jobs of employees for years to come. Other examples of dirty hands dilemmas include the question of whether a cigarette manufacturer is responsible for the health problems of consumers. Or whether, due to the consequences of bad strategic management, it is acceptable to fire employees who have remained loyal for many years. Those charged with making these decisions usually find them painful. Ensuring the continuity of the corporation sometimes leaves no alternative to disappointing individual stakeholders.

These examples might seem dramatic but the fact of the matter is that corporate managers are continually faced with dilemmas. If managers do not consistently act in the corporate interest, they run the risk of being criticized for bad management at a later stage. This may require them to get their hands even dirtier. For example, failing to lay off a few employees in time to safeguard the corporation's profits can result in bankruptcy and everyone losing their jobs. For the corporate leader, corporate continuity brings a duty that often conflicts with other moral obligations. In the business context, the Dirty Hands Dilemma has not been acknowledged as such. In general, it is interpreted as a manifestation of egoism that is supposed to be the fundamental driver behind economic behavior.

The corporate interest and egoism

Trade (especially money lending) has traditionally been portrayed negatively. Both in classical antiquity and in the Middle Ages, traders were considered to be second-class citizens. Money lending was best left to the Jews. In Christian philosophy, commerce and charging interest on money lent in particular did not qualify as honest work and was deemed reprehensible. This was informed by the Biblical message that "Man should earn his living by the sweat of his brow."[11] In the fourth century, Church Father Chrysostomos proclaimed *"nulleus Christianus debet esse mercator"* (no Christian should be a merchant). To be sure, he who aspires to amass money scorns Apostle Paul's warning that "avarice is the root of all evil."[12] Christians were supposed to focus on the divine rather than on accumulating material goods because it stands in the way of serving God. Making money as such was thus considered reprehensible.

According to the thirteenth-century philosopher/theologian Thomas Aquinas, trade is not evil in itself. In daily practice, however, it is bound to lead to deception. In his time, the morally corruptive business of trade was the domain of non-Christians as they were more or less damned already. In his *Fable of the Bees*, Mandeville confronts his contemporaries with their double standards: they call themselves followers of Christ while they choose wealth as the highest fulfillment of life. According to Mandeville, the precondition for prosperity in any society is for people to be dissatisfied with what they have. To generate wealth, they must desire more and not bother with (Christian) morality that is based in sobriety and virtuousness. For Mandeville, a society that upholds high moral standards cannot be prosperous as, in order to achieve prosperity, one must compromise one's moral standards.

The solution to this dilemma between prosperity and virtue was discussed in Chapter 1. For Adam Smith, the founder of classical economics, the free market offers the solution to this dilemma since a "natural harmony" transpires through the collective pursuit of self-interest. The "invisible hand" coordinates all actions motivated by egoism, resulting in the optimal realization of the common interest. At an individual level, however, the tension between morality and prosperity remains, while at the macro level egoism seems to be effective.

In *Morality in Business* (1919), Rudolf Mees, businessman and Chairman of the International Chamber of Commerce, shows that egoism—so reviled in the Christian tradition—is the most important motive for the businessman. According to Mees, egoism is the source of all business virtues. "Nor is this egotistical element a stranger even to good faith."[13] But, he ponders, does that mean that trade is inherently bad?

A businessman who cares nothing for material possessions, who is immediately ready to leave his business over to a competitor, cannot remain a good businessman; business on that basis is impossible. That the Christian-feeling businessman must accept this is the moral tragedy of the character of his work.[14]

Furthermore, he asserts:

The businessman cannot exist, cannot carry on business, as long as he is unable to pursue his own interest. Concurrently, there is no virtue in business if it does not serve society.[15]

According to Mees, responsible business conduct implies that one must seek harmony, but in a manner significantly different from Smith's understanding of the concept. For Smith, harmony arises spontaneously when people are allowed to pursue their own interests without hindrance. In Mees's definition, harmony must be consciously and constantly pursued.

Both the individual and the community have their value, and that is why the development of the individual and serving the community are both our duty...Repeatedly, the businessman will face conflicts in which he cannot find unity; repeatedly, his personal interest will come into conflict with that of the community without being able to see a resolution of that conflict. But the moral strength of the businessman must lie precisely at this point. He doesn't have fixed values to which he can turn, and he will repeatedly have to decide afresh.[16]

The dilemma Mees is wrestling with concerns the choice between whether the businessman should pursue the corporate or the community interest. In this dilemma, it is clear that the motive of egoism is consistent with the Dirty Hands Dilemma. As representative of an organization, the businessperson's self-interest usually merges with the interest of the organization.

In an episode of the Dutch television program *The Flip Side of the Truth*, which covers ethical issues, the Dirty Hands Dilemma was staged convincingly. Presenter Marcel van Dam hosted a discussion between CEOs and labor representatives on whether it was acceptable to "sacrifice" a few employees to secure the continuity of a corporation, and, by implication, the jobs of the rest of the employees. To begin with, they debated whether it was permissible to fire homosexual employees or to exclude them from projects at the request of foreign clients. Subsequently, the "non-Jewish" declaration demanded by Muslim countries at that time was discussed. Is it acceptable or even possible for a businessperson to sign such a declaration to secure an order in the name of guaranteeing the jobs of one's employees? The following is an excerpt from this debate:

Van Dam: What do you think, Mr. Rijkse?
Rijkse (Member of the Board of a federal employers' association): I have a big problem with it, as you can well understand.
Van Dam: Yes, so does everyone...But do you think people should sign such a declaration or not?
Rijkse: In principle, no....
Van Dam: But just now [with respect to refusing to send gay employees on assignment] you said that you opt for safeguarding jobs.
Rijkse: Yes, but I think with this the limit is overstepped.
Van Dam: Mr. Ester?
Ester (Member of the Board of a Christian employers' association): Yes, I also have...
Van Dam: ...a problem with it?

Ester: Not only do I have a problem with it. I strongly object to issuing such declarations.

Van Dam: And if it means that ten thousand people will lose their jobs?

Ester: I believe there are limits to all conduct, whether that of an individual or of a corporation.

Van Dam: Yes, but in this case?...Ten thousand jobs. Yes or no?

Ester: In that case I must agree that a boundary is crossed.

Swarttouw (Chairman of the Management Board of an airline manufacturer): If you're facing a choice between the continuity of the company or sacrificing one or two employees, everyone knows which way the ball bounces. Being here on television is different from when you're in your office when you actually have to make such choices. The primary role of the businessman is to keep the company going. If he's interested in being everyone's best friend, he shouldn't go into business. If he wants to be respected, he has to keep his business running—but not at all costs!

Ester: I think this is exactly how we can describe a businessman.

Swarttouw: No businessman with some ten thousand jobs on his mind would think twice about signing some stupid declaration. No one willing to sacrifice ten thousand jobs in the name of such principles should be in charge of a corporation.

According to Swarttouw, the moral principle against discrimination on the basis of race or sexual orientation must yield to another: "keeping the corporation going for the sake of the livelihood of a great number of people." The continuity of the organization sometimes compels managers to ignore the legitimate rights and interests of individual stakeholders and even to switch off their conscience for a moment. In the business context, the Dirty Hands Dilemma expresses the paradoxical demand that is placed on the corporation and its representatives. In order to give shape to a function in a responsible manner—to serve the corporate interest, social interests (indirectly) and stakeholder interests—management has to act irresponsibly. To be competitive and to function efficiently, corporations must minimize their costs. This is also a stimulus for corporations just barely to meet the responsibilities that involve higher costs.

That corporations should function and survive in a competitive environment is grounded in a rule-utilitarian argument. Society is best served when corporations limit themselves to providing goods and services in the most efficient and effective way possible. When a corporation no longer meets the needs of society or no longer meets them in the most efficient way possible, it loses its right to existence. The efficiency requirement can, however, be in conflict with other moral demands. Ethical dilemmas that occur in a corporate context are quite often the result of the ambiguity of the moral demands placed on the corporation. In the business context the Dirty Hands Dilemma arises because the corporate interest, as derivative of the general interest, is granted a status independent and sometimes in opposition to the rights of individual stake-holders. At the same time, the corporate interest also represents the collective interests of stakeholders. Where the rights of the individual stakeholders are at odds with the corporate interest, managers frequently give precedence to the corporate interest.

By locating the Dirty Hands Dilemma also in the corporate context, the proposition (which is often unconsciously supported) that doing business is inherently immoral or that it carries at least a certain degree of immorality, is brought into focus. This raises the question whether immorality is unavoidable in the corporate context. To acknowledge the existence of the Dirty Hands Dilemma in the corporate domain makes clear that managers often come to stand before different, mutually conflicting, moral demands. Which moral criterion must prevail in the inevitable choice that has to be made?

Machiavelli's challenge

It was the Florentine political philosopher Nicollo Machiavelli (1469–1527) who helped to clarify the Dirty Hands Dilemma for political leaders in a particularly confrontational way.[17] It is, in fact, a central theme in his political writings. In his book Il Principe, he argues that in exercising his authority, a sovereign must not let his actions be dictated by moral principles. A prince

...must not flinch from being blamed for vices which are necessary for safeguarding the state. This is because, taking everything into account, he will find that some of the things that appear to be virtues will, if he practices them, ruin him, and some of the things that appear to be vices will bring him security and prosperity.[18]

The French philosopher Jean-Paul Sartre uses the term "dirty hands" to describe the dilemma of the political leader. In his play Les Mains Sales (Dirty Hands), an old communist leader accused of collaborating with the bourgeoisie to fight the Nazis defends himself by pointing out the necessity of getting one's hands dirty as a political leader:

How tightly you hold on to purity, boy! How afraid you are to dirty your hands! Fine, you remain pure to the bone! What use is that to us? Why did you come to us? Purity is something for yogis or monks... Do nothing, don't move, don't lift a finger, keep your ice cream gloves on. I, however, have dirty hands. The dirt goes up to my elbows. I have dipped them in filth, plunged them into blood. But what are you hoping for? Do you really think you can govern in innocence?[19]

More recently, Michael Walzer[20] and other political philosophers[21] have revisited the question posed by Machiavelli. Walzer discusses the Dirty Hands Dilemma with reference to a specific problem political leaders face. Is it, for the sake of society, justified to start a war that will result in the loss of life and much suffering of civilians and others who had no say in it? The politician sees it as his duty to realize the general interest in so far as it is possible. The Vietnam War was regarded as justified on the basis that it was the only way to keep communism from gaining further ground in Asia. The war against Iraq was justified by pointing out the world's interest in the uninterrupted supply of oil and the protection of the sovereignty of a UN member state. Can politics be reconciled with ethics? A discussion of this issue is tied up with the question of whether governance necessarily requires the use of immoral means. Is there a responsible way out of this dilemma?

The assumption that immoral or amoral conduct is inherent to the political domain suggests that whoever enters politics must be prepared to set their morals aside. From this point of view, the role of ethical analysis is to legitimize the amorality or immorality in this context and to determine where the boundaries lie. If we do not dismiss the possibility of moral responsibility in the political arena, we have to examine the dilemma and establish how it can be addressed. The Dirty Hands Dilemma can be viewed as a conflict between two types of moral demands: a consequentialist demand on the one hand, and a principled demand on the other. To resolve it, a way must be found to weigh the different types of demands in a responsible manner.

Some commentators[22] on Machiavelli interpret his discussion of the Dirty Hands Dilemma as the impossibility of imposing moral standards on political conduct. Machiavelli separates politics from the moral sphere and especially from the Christian ethic. In this popular interpretation of Machiavelli, morality and politics are mutually exclusive. Whereas some ultimate values are pursued for their own sake in the moral sphere, only technical skills are relevant in the political domain. As discussed in Chapter 2, Kant identifies these obligations with the term "hypothetical imperatives": if you want to achieve X, you must do Y. The question of whether X is worth pursuing is not raised. As such, the Dirty Hands Dilemma does not contain a true conflict. Ethics makes demands that are not applicable in the political arena. Dirty hands only become a true dilemma when technocratic conduct in politics is elevated to the status of a moral duty. The question then becomes whether one is morally obliged to behave amorally or even immorally.

When and why is it justified to make an exception of the political arena? Machiavelli is interpreted as holding the view that extreme situations require extreme measures. If the future of society is at stake, "immoral" conduct is justified. Commentators who believe they see Machiavelli in this argument consider him an early advocate of the *raison d'état*. This in effect presumes the superiority of the moral sphere since the justification for behaving immorally is to end the situation that made the immoral behavior necessary in the first place.

According to the British political philosopher and historian Isaiah Berlin,[23] this interpretation does not wholly capture the significance of Machiavelli's theory. In the essay "The Originality of Machiavelli", he examines why countless commentators on Machiavelli's ideas consider them to be so threatening.

According to Berlin, the anxiety apparent in these reactions is more or less justified. Machiavelli's political theory undermines the very foundations of Western Platonic/Jewish/Christian morality. At closer examination, his theory is significantly more subversive than the interpretation above.

According to Berlin, Machiavelli does not seek to oppose Christian morality. Nor does he want to change Christian morality or replace it with another. He simply declares it unsuitable for the political arena, but he does not draw the conclusion that the political arena must be devoid of moral considerations. For Machiavelli, other moral standards apply in the political arena. According to Berlin, Machiavelli argues that an idealized view of mankind is misguided. Based on his own views and experience, and on those of great thinkers and political leaders, he offers an account of mankind as it really is and functions. According to Machiavelli: "Christian...men who in their practice actually follow Christian precepts are good men, but if they govern states in the light of such principles, they lead them to destruction."[24] If everyone followed these precepts (Christian and otherwise), political leaders could do so as well. However, not everyone is good and it would be naïve to think that it is possible for everyone to be good ("the conditions in the world won't allow it").[25] As a result, the politician must adhere to other principles. According to Berlin, Machiavelli argues that a particular ethic applies in the political arena.

It may be that Christians are right about the well being of the individual soul, taken outside the social or political context. But the well being of the state is not the same as the well being of the individual—they are governed in a different way.[26]

Berlin observes that politics is an inherent part of human life. In this regard, he also refers to Aristotle and Cicero who see humans as political creatures. Politics for them is an inescapable part of our nature. The demands formulated by a political ethic are therefore requirements inherent to our successful functioning as human beings.[27]

According to Berlin's reading of Machiavelli, there are at least two moral systems: a public and personal one. This by no means represents two complementary ways of thinking—one moral and the other technical—or two autonomous spheres capable of coexistence. Instead, they are two mutually exclusive and conflicting value systems. A compromise would damage both. One must opt either for the one or the other. Herein lies the subversive character of Machiavelli's thinking, which also explains his commentators' conscious or unconscious resistance to his writings. Machiavelli undermines the monistic pillars of the Platonic/Jewish/Christian tradition: the tacit assumption that all significant values are ultimately compatible.

In Berlin's interpretation, Machiavelli's stance presents a clear dilemma. There is, however, no question of "dirty hands." The behavior of a politician must not be measured according to standards that apply to persons. It is therefore the duty of the politician—at least one who wants to function responsibly—to behave in accordance with standards specific to the political domain. In such ethics, standards of individual excellence do not matter. In public life, another morality applies where the excellence of the state as the ultimate criterion is upheld. According to Machiavelli, this is the highest form of excellence. Berlin observes that, "The moral ideal for which he thinks no sacrifice too great—the welfare of the patria—is for him the highest form of social existence attainable by man."[28]

A Critique of Berlin's interpretation of Machiavelli

Much of Berlin's analysis of the Dirty Hands Dilemma is open to criticism. Berlin proceeds from the assumption that values are ultimately irreconcilable and that a choice has to be made. This assumption is understandable for standards governing conduct. No one can pursue two activities simultaneously, as it is impossible to do something and not do it at the same time. That makes opting for one of the conflicting standards (or formulating a compromise resulting in a new, more satisfactory, standard) unavoidable. In the domain of values, as opposed to conduct, this assumption is unnecessary. In the discussion of value pluralism in Chapter 2, we argued that people can be motivated by multiple values at the same time and that they may even conflict. The conduct that follows is the consequence of the various judgments at work behind the conduct. If a form of conduct is induced by a given value, a conflicting value can be adjusted to a certain extent. Both values determine the end result expressed in the conduct and both values remain fully operational. The fact that Machiavelli acknowledged at least two value systems does not necessarily imply that they cannot be operational at the same time.

A second problem concerns the definition of the social characteristics to which the leader aspires. Machiavelli's theory rests, to a certain extent, on political philosophy as developed in classical, particularly Greek, antiquity, where the community is the polis. Social organization has subsequently become significantly more complex. Everyone belongs to a multitude of communities such as a family, company, church, sports club, etc. An individual is also a citizen of a particular community, state, country, etc. and therefore has a multitude of potentially conflicting loyalties. It is the individual who is the link between the various communities. It is also the individual who, to a greater or lesser extent, chooses allegiance, for example in voting for a president and/or deciding which company to work for. Where there is freedom of choice, the question of responsibility crops up. Even in the face of multiple ethical systems, a choice based on reasonable arguments is not excluded. Neither is it unreasonable to request justification for choices made.

A third point of criticism against Berlin's reading of Machiavelli concerns the content of the proposed social ethic. Proceeding from the principle that other moral demands apply to leaders as community representatives, nothing has yet been said about their content. The chief moral demand on a leader is presumably to preserve the community and perhaps even to make it flourish. However, the well-being of a society does not equal the sum of individual levels of well-being. Whether a society is flourishing or not can be only partly derived from the level of satisfaction of the individual community members. The moral demands of a leader are not straightforward and require careful reflection. Berlin neglects to pay attention to this aspect.

The relevance of Berlin's criticism for business ethics

The criticism against Machiavelli's political theory does not detract from the fact that the question he examines poses an enormous challenge for ethicists. The fundamental question is whether a unique system of values applies to conduct on behalf of and within social communities such as the state and the corporation.

Business ethics can be considered a form of applied ethics that posits a consistent relationship between general ethics and business ethics. Is it, indeed, correct to assume the existence of one ultimately cohesive moral system? Or is it possible, and perhaps desirable, to reserve a separate moral system for the business context? And may that system be at odds with the morals that apply to natural persons? If unique ethical standards apply to the business context, what are the moral demands that must be imposed on managers within that framework? How should a conflict of such different value systems be seen? How can people responsibly deal with conflicting demands?

The question finally presents itself as to how personal, corporate, and general moral values interrelate. In the chapters that follow, we will set down those ethical standards that are unique to the corporate context and that cannot simply be traced back to general ethical concepts. This does not lessen our conviction that a strong relationship does indeed exist between general ethics and business ethics.

The means–ends issue as an element of the Dirty Hands Dilemma

Berlin offers a radical and quite challenging interpretation of Machiavelli and, therefore, of the Dirty Hands Dilemma for the political leader. As argued above, this extreme interpretation is untenable. Walzer's interpretation of the Dirty Hands Dilemma is significantly less radical. He describes it as "the ends justifying the means" or as a conflict between two types of moral demands ("two spheres of justice"). Acting in conflict with a moral standard from this perspective is legitimate because it serves a higher goal. According to Walzer,[29] however, political conduct must follow a consistent set of principles. This is not to suggest that everything that can be shown to be consistent is also morally justified. Waltzer's is a partly principled argument that rejects the view that leaders must dirty their hands.

It is usually possible to evaluate people's behavior with reference to ethical theories based on prosperity (consequentialism) and on rights or justice (deontology). These concepts can also be applied to the corporate domain as corporations play an important role in creating wealth for society. Corporations should also respect rights and must test their own behavior against the principle of justice. At the same time, it has to be acknowledged that these criteria cannot unproblematically and universally be applied to corporations.

In a number of ways, we demand less of corporations than we do of natural persons. Suppose that a corporation is based in a region with high levels of unemployment. We would not expect such a corporation to employ local people if this is irresponsible from a business point of view. The consequentialist duty to contribute to the prosperity of society is therefore only applicable to corporations to a limited extent. Suppose that, in the fight against inflation, the prosperity of society is served by lower prices. In general, this would not imply a moral duty for corporations to set their prices below the market level. And to give another example, it is a generally accepted practice to fire employees who fail to do their jobs properly. Few people would go as far as severing ties with friends and family on the same grounds.

Sometimes we expect more of a corporation than of a natural person. When someone apologizes sincerely with the argument that she did not realize what the consequences of her actions would be, the excuse would be accepted in most cases. We are significantly stricter with corporations. If a corporation hastily markets a product that later proves harmful to public health, we regard this conduct as morally questionable. The excuse that the company did not know the product would be harmful is generally rejected. No one who markets a new product may cut corners with research into its potentially harmful effects. With today's technology, consumers generally trust corporations to conduct adequate research in advance. In the case of the sinking of the *Herald of Free Enterprise*, the reproaches directed at P&O Lines (the owners) were rooted in passenger expectations. The public assumed that the corporation would be structured in a way that reflected adequate attention to passenger safety. The crucial question is whether the safety policy of the shipping line meets these reasonable expectations. Whoever enters the market should at least guarantee that reasonable standards are met.

In a number of respects, we expect less of corporations than of natural persons. In other regards, our expectations are higher. Obviously, the context in which an issue arises is relevant to setting moral demands. What can be expected from a corporation, taking into account the special nature of this context? Similarly, it is possible to see the Dirty Hands Dilemma in the business context as an ends–means issue. When and to what extent is the use of immoral means justified in order to realize corporate interests? Or, is more perhaps at stake? Perceiving the Dirty Hands Dilemma purely in terms of a contest between two conflicting demands removes the dilemma's "sting." This means that we accept that just two demands are at stake and that we must find a way to choose between them. A balance must therefore be reached by weighing the moral standard against the general interest. This strategy presumes that one blanket criterion or another is at stake, with the result that an important dimension of the dilemma fades away.

The Dirty Hands Dilemma is not just about things like "lying with good intentions." An example can clarify this. If a prime minister or president tells untruths about intended actions in times of war or intended changes in the tax system, he does it to prevent a surprise attack or evasive behavior. The system he is part of (and especially the position he holds within it) demands that he speak untruths. If he were to answer the questions truthfully too soon (with the answer "no comment" also being quite informative), the whole political arena would be in uproar.

The role of context

The Dirty Hands Dilemma that leaders face is not purely about making difficult choices between consequentialist and deontological demands. The problem is partly due to the position of the person in question. The leader fulfills a social role, which makes it difficult, if not impossible, to give content to all the responsibilities he has to fulfill. Two features mark both the political and corporate context within which consequentialist and deontological principles are weighed. The first is the coercive nature of the social context within which the leader operates. The second is the representative nature of the leader's actions.

The compulsive conduct of the leader

The issue of determinism is essentially a question of to what extent a leader can be said to be free. Can a leader act autonomously or does he, as the Dirty Hands Dilemma suggests, play a predetermined role in society? That is, if you are a leader you *have* to dirty your hands.

This issue, in the form of the "determinism–autonomy" debate, has been analyzed by many philosophers and sociologists.[30] Freedom is a precondition for evaluating natural persons in moral terms. If a person, and therefore also a political leader, is seen as completely heteronomous (i.e. completely conditioned by external factors like natural, economic, social, and historical forces and heredity), there is no question of a free will. As we discussed in Chapter 1, a moral judgment is possible only if it involves an autonomous individual who can be held responsible for his or her actions.

When applied to the functioning of the leader, the "determinism–freedom" question takes on particular significance. In actual fact, it is a contradiction in terms. Is it possible to speak of leadership or freedom when a leader operates in a framework that forces him or her to place the common good above individual moral rights? A certain degree of freedom has to be assumed for the concept and function to have any meaning. If freedom were entirely absent, it would be foolish to place any moral demands on the leader. Can we say that a leader is free to make a choice between the common good and individual claims? In our view, we can indeed, since this expectation is inherent to the function the leader fulfills. Someone is elected because we expect him or her to be able to lead. The recognition of someone's leadership abilities implies that this person is not purely a plaything of the forces around them but that they are capable of giving direction (within certain limits). The debate about the deterministic nature of systems centers on two assumptions. Either someone is a leader and free and responsible, or this person relies on a coercive framework (that renders him or her unfit for the position in the first place).

How can we characterize the leader's freedom? Some philosophers view freedom as the absence of any form of constraints. Constraints can take the form of purely biological/physical compulsions (as Locke holds), or a socio-cultural compulsion (as Nietzsche holds, for example). Others define freedom as being able to agree with and act in accordance with a certain rationale, or a divine individual or group plan or purpose (as Spinoza, Rousseau, and Kant argue). Berlin defines the concept by drawing a distinction between negative and positive freedom. Negative freedom means a person is free "if and only if no other human being stands in his way, preventing him by force or coercion, by legal prohibition or private threat, from acting in a way he might otherwise act."[31] Lack of freedom in a negative sense occurs when someone prevents another from acting. Someone is free in a positive sense, "only when he is in charge of his life, master of his circumstances and able to do what he sets himself to do."[32] Freedom in this sense does not only mean the absence of external constraints, but especially the ability to pursue one's own goals.

Both the negative and the positive conceptions of freedom are interpersonal in nature and both recognize the equal right of others to be free. People can be free only if they can impose limitations on themselves and understand that their own freedom is not disconnected from that of others. Responsibility becomes pertinent especially where the freedom of others can be encroached upon by the individual's pursuit of freedom. This requires that individuals pursue their freedom within bounds and that individual conduct is coordinated with that of others.

The leader's freedom also does not require the complete absence of restraints. The role of the leader is to place the interests of individual members (citizens) in the broader organizational (social) framework. This framework offers a number of opportunities for development, but also a number of restrictions. A leader's task is to direct individuals' potential development while taking into consideration the possibilities and impossibilities of the organizational (social) framework.

In the face of the multitude of claims and expectations the leader is confronted with, a certain degree of independence is necessary if his/her conduct is to be subjected to moral scrutiny. In this way the leader is not stripped of their humanity or reduced to a robot. The question of the determinist nature of systems opens up the discussion of the relationship between the leader and the surrounding social framework.

The representative nature of the leader's conduct

Dennis Thompson[33] elaborates on the representative aspect of the Dirty Hands Dilemma. For Thompson, the Dirty Hands Dilemma is inextricably connected to the democratic character of society. If the leader carries out decisions taken in accordance with democratic procedures, he or she cannot be blamed for disregarding certain moral demands. He or she is, as it were, doing so on behalf of the community. It becomes difficult to blame a leader if they follow democratic procedures in decision-making. A politician can be blamed for the extent to which they allow themselves to be used to carry out immoral decisions. The nature of the decision itself, however, cannot be laid at their feet, as they are merely an instrument of the community.[34]

According to Thompson, a problem arises only where success depends on secrecy and democratic procedures are undermined. Thompson looks for the solution to this problem by formulating procedural requirements. The Dirty Hands Dilemma can be resolved by making the leader responsible after the fact, by delegating decisions to a commission with the authority to make decisions on behalf of his constituency or by establishing policy principles against which decisions can be evaluated. Thompson's solution focuses on the relationship between the leader and his people. It is the decision-making procedure that can contribute to the resolution of the Dirty Hands Dilemma. Under what conditions and within which limits may the leader speak on behalf of his constituency and act in the common interest without discussing matters with others in advance? What is the nature of the (implicit) "contract" between representative and the represented?

Just as the political leader, the corporate leader also represents a collective. The manager represents the corporation and is expected to serve the corporate interest. Managers (and the other employees) who (freely) represent the corporation externally and internally also commit themselves to the expectations of the external and internal stakeholders. The problem of representative action raises the question of the relationship between the corporation and its management and employees.

The fact that a leader acts on behalf of his constituency and in the common interest is relevant in evaluating his conduct. This is an issue that affects all those who have representative authority. Every manager, in the same way as every political leader, is faced with "the problem of representative action." When acting on behalf of the corporation, to what extent can actions of the manager be ascribed to the corporation and to what extent can the manager be held responsible for corporate actions? Representative action boils down to acting in a secondary sense, on behalf of the organization. This must be distinguished from acting in a primary sense, the physical action as such.

The structure of the three corporate dilemmas

The Dirty Hands Dilemma has a clear structure. It is characterized by two mutually exclusive values where a choice between the two is imperative. Moreover, clear social expectations exist regarding the manner in which the manager should engage with the dilemma and it involves representative action where the manager or employee represents the collective.

The structure of the Dirty Hands Dilemma can also be identified in the two other corporate dilemmas. The general structure of the three corporate dilemmas can be described in what follows. The essence of the three corporate dilemmas lies in the tension that can be identified between two or more fundamental values. This tension is often located in the inconsistency between the corporate objective and specific rights and interests. In the Dirty Hands Dilemma, the rights and interests of individual stakeholders conflict with the corporate interest. In the Many Hands Dilemma, the functionaries' restricted interpretations of the corporate objective conflict, resulting in less than optimal corporate achievements, and responsibility getting lost. In the case of the Entangled Hands Dilemma, private interests are in conflict with the corporate interest.

The corporate leader, but also the manager and other employees representing the corporation have limited freedom to act. Both internally as well as externally, expectations exist with respect to the role corporate representatives fulfill. The organizational framework limits the choices that can be made. Corporate leaders and managers in particular have the task to acknowledge these limitations (negative freedom) and to direct the actions of employees within these boundaries (positive freedom).

A manager or an employee's action with respect to a corporate dilemma is also a corporate action (in the secondary sense). The manager or employee represents the corporation. It is the corporation that acts in the secondary sense. To be sure, it is the manager or employee that directs the corporation in taking a decision with respect to the dilemma. Such a decision has to be recognizable to third parties as consistent with the corporate interest.

Real dilemmas or difficult problems?

In the general discussion of dilemmas (Chapters 1 and 2), the question was posed as to whether the demands that are made of those concerned are truly conflicting. This question needs to be posed once again in connection with the three corporate dilemmas. Are we dealing with demands that are made of corporate leaders and managers that are mutually exclusive, or are these simply difficult issues we have to think through thoroughly to find the right answer? In our view, real dilemmas do exist. Even if the decisions managers and employees take are not always as dramatic as the mountain climbing dilemma, they do share some crucial features that give them a similar character.

In corporate dilemmas the issue is about the conflict between the general interest (the corporate interest as the interests of all (directly) involved) and individual rights and interests. It concerns the different moral systems and the different moral levels within which the functioning of corporate leaders and managers is tested. The Dirty Hands Dilemma centers on the rights of individual stakeholders and the continuity of the corporation—the interest of the collective stakeholders. It is, for example, important for a company that an account manager builds and maintains good relations with his or her clients. Once such an account manager has successfully established a network of clients, one does not readily transfer him or her to another function. For the personal development of the employee, however, it is important to work on their career and grow into other functions. The interests of the respective parties clash. The Many Hands Dilemma is characterized by tension between the collective responsibility for the smooth functioning of the organization, on the one hand, and the individual responsibilities of functionaries and departments, on the other. Say, for example, an employee at a company is harassed to such an extent that he commits suicide. Many people could claim afterwards that they saw it happening but that they took no action. They were not in the position to do so. They did not know the details and did not dare to take action. People thought the human resources manager knew about it as everybody could see what was going on. Moreover, it is difficult to correct colleagues. If you do undertake something, you are interfering in business that you are not supposed to get involved in. The Entangled Hands Dilemma is characterized by tension between the private sphere and the corporate interest. This dilemma can be illustrated by the following example: a person in a leadership position falls in love with his secretary. Can he invite her for a date after hours? If a romance develops between them, can this private relationship be pursued? Transferring the secretary to another function would be degrading for her and a loss for the organization. Ending the private relationship would infringe upon the private sphere and would have a considerable impact on the personal happiness of two people.

The two other corporate dilemmas also possess the characteristics that make the Dirty Hands Dilemma so troublesome. The context plays an important role.

The determinist nature of systems and representative action both are present. As in the case of the Dirty Hands Dilemma, the manager or employee who is confronted with a Many Hands Dilemma or Entangled Hands Dilemma has to deal with demanding expectations regarding his or her role in connection with the dilemma. In the previously quoted television program *The Flip Side of the Truth*, CEO Frans Swarttouw succinctly expresses the pressures of the business environment:

If you're facing a choice between the continuity of the company or sacrificing one or two employees, everyone knows which way the ball bounces. The primary role of the businessperson is to keep the company going.

The freedom to choose against what is regarded as the corporate interest is perceived as (almost) non-existent. With regard to the three corporate dilemmas, the corporate leader or manager is under enormous pressure to make a decision that is in the direct interest of the organization and to sacrifice individual interests if necessary.

Representative action also features in the three corporate dilemmas. The corporate leader or manager acts as a natural person in the primary sense whereas the corporation acts in a secondary sense. Third parties perceive the act as an act of the organization. The choice that is made with respect to the corporate dilemma at hand depends on the formal and informal rules on the basis of which these can be regarded as corporate actions.

The three corporate dilemmas defy the integrity of a corporation. Dilemmas that are not properly resolved can erode the entity's wholeness and the integrity of the agent and/or the relationship with others. When the Many Hands Dilemma is inadequately addressed, the organization becomes fragmented due to a lack of integration of the actions of its various departments and officials. The corporation ceases to function as a unit. If the Entangled Hands Dilemma is not properly resolved, the organization becomes fragmented because the actions of employees and those of the corporation are not integrated. The employees are no longer intact (no longer people of integrity). If the Dirty Hands Dilemma is inadequately addressed, the moral integration of the corporation with its stakeholders is eroded. The corporation is no longer at one with the world around it. Given the fact that these three fundamental issues are inherent to corporate functioning—which means that damage to certain interests cannot be avoided—it is imperative to consider what an organization can do to retain or regain its integrity.

Corruption and Bribery

A manager accepted money from a supplier in exchange for using his influence to secure a large order for the supplier. A buyer was entertained by a supplier and allowed this to influence him in the selection of suppliers. A police officer ignored a traffic violation for a small fee. Reports like these appear in newspapers and magazines on a regular basis. It even seems that incidents of corruption are on the increase. Of course, it could also be that people nowadays are more willing to bring misconduct like this out into the open.

Corruption, bribery, and extortion have received a lot of attention in the past years. Most countries have laws that prohibit bribery of officials locally. Attention to corruption in foreign countries is relatively new. The US is the forerunner in this regard. The Foreign Corrupt Practices Act was adopted in 1977. This law made payments to foreign officials and politicians a penal offence. In 1997, the OECD adopted a convention aimed at combating bribery of foreign public officials. In the wake of this convention, a great number of OECD member states and also a few non-member states have now made laws to make bribery of foreign officials punishable. What does this mean for corporations and their employees?

Many corporate codes contain statements prohibiting the acceptance and payments of bribes. Confronted with business partners that attempted to bribe and corrupt its employees, Shell formulated a policy statement on bribery and corruption in its Business Principles. It reads: "The direct or indirect offer, payment, soliciting and acceptance of bribes in any form are unacceptable practices. Employees must avoid a conflict of interests between their financial activities and their part in the conduct of company business." Caterpillar states in its code that "we won't seek to influence sales of our products...by payments of bribes, kickbacks, or questionable inducements. Company employees are required to make good faith efforts to avoid payments of gratuities or "tips" to certain public officials, even where these payments are customary to expedite or secure performance of routine governmental actions such as processing visas or obtaining permits or public services. Where...unavoidable, they must be limited to customary amounts." ICI states in its code that "No employee should seek or accept a personal gift or entertainment which might reasonably be believed to influence business transactions."

In reading the legal documents and codes of corporations, it would seem that it is clear what is to be understood as bribery and corruption and what should subsequently be renounced as blameworthy. Whoever examines these texts more closely would quickly notice the complexity of the formulations.

Why are the OECD convention and many national laws regarding corruption restricted to bribery of officials and politicians? Is bribing someone in (another) organization not blameworthy?

- Many laws draw a distinction between facilitation payments, minor corruption (payments for routine activities of lower ranked officials), and grand corruption (payments to high-placed officials and politicians to exert influence over a decision). In practice, distinctions are not that easily drawn.
- What about payments to political parties?
- Should extortion be treated differently from bribery?
- When does a gift become a form of bribery?
- How should cultural differences be dealt with? In many Asian countries, gift giving and business go hand in hand.
- How should favors to family and acquaintances be dealt with?

What is corruption?

It is a matter of corruption:

- when an employee, an official, or a politician accepts money, gifts or illegitimate benefits or promises of these (passive corruption), or
- when an employee, an official, or politician gives or promises money, gifts, or illegitimate benefits (active corruption),
- where this payment, gift, or that benefit is given or accepted with a view to the employee, official, or politician abusing his or her authority,
- so as to serve the interests of a third party.

Characteristic of corruption is that it involves some sort of exchange. The employee, official, or politician does something for someone or refrains from doing it so as to benefit himself unfairly. It entails that something is or is not done that is expected of the person in question on the basis of his or her job in order to obtain a gift, benefit, or promise. This private benefit can take on many forms. A senior official that grants an assignment to a company in exchange for this company sponsoring the football club, of which he happens to be the chairman, benefits also in private sense. He may not become wealthier for it, but his status and honor as chairman of the football club is certainly promoted by it.

Abuse of authority refers to an employee using the freedom that he or she enjoys within an organization to do or refrain from doing something that is in conflict with a responsible fulfillment of his or her function. The abuse of authority is directed at unjustly benefiting third parties (often outside the organization). In exchange, the official, politician, or employee in question obtains illegitimate benefits, gifts, or promises.

Dilemmas

Although bribery is deemed unacceptable, many situations are less clear cut than the OECD convention, the legislation of many countries, but also the codes of corporations seem to suggest. The definition given is simple. When concrete situations are examined, it appears more difficult to indicate when relationship management is still acceptable and whether it has turned into corruption. Corruption, bribery, extortion, accepting and giving gifts, tips, payments to political parties, donations, and doing favors for friends and acquaintances are all themes in the field of relationship management that are difficult to distinguish sharply from forms of corruption. In practice, these themes also imply troublesome dilemmas for companies and their employees. Dilemmas can arise in situations such as those where the interests of employees are at odds with those of the company and where serving these interests is logical, condoned, or even required (the Entangled Hands Dilemma). While personal benefit stands to be gained from accepting payments, employees who do so run the risk of making poor decisions, for example, when it comes to selecting suppliers. Dilemmas can arise in situations where employees must weigh up the interests of the company and those of other parties. Moreover, it is not unimaginable that the company itself may benefit from paying the right bribes (the Dirty Hands Dilemma). Corruption-related issues arise also in relations of cooperation within the company. A boss can benefit employees in exchange for personal favors. Often corruption as an entangled hands issue is accompanied with issues of cooperation and the question of who is responsible for what (the Many Hands Dilemma).

In practice, it is difficult to draw a clear line to indicate when relationship management turns into corruption. At the same time, corruption has negative consequences for the employee in question (he or she becomes vulnerable to blackmail) and for the company he or she represents (the best and most profitable decisions for the company are not taken). It also has a negative impact on society (diminishing transparency of the market involves social costs that can ruin whole economies and corruption leads to injustice in a society where, for example, financial development assistance does not reach the areas where it is most needed).

Corruption as an Entangled Hands Dilemma

Corruption is in question the moment that roles conflict where people have the authority to represent an organization. Corruption is often an instance of the entangled hands issue. The representative role an employee of an organization fulfills is entangled with other roles. Each role makes demands on the person who fulfills it. Sometimes, these roles are in conflict with each other. Choices then have to be made. As such, that is no problem. The boundary is crossed when the organizational role is covertly, and in conflict with the task one fulfills within the organization, used to the advantage of the private roles one fulfills.

Some Entangled Hands Dilemmas include the following examples:

1. The head of the department of internal training frequently organizes courses at luxury conference centers. The manager of one of these centers that he incidentally uses for work invites the head and his family to spend a weekend at a hotel that belongs to the complex.
2. A buyer is a private customer at the garage where the company he works for has a lot of maintenance done. It does not seem to do him any harm. The price he recently paid for replacing his car tires is far below the market price.
3. One of the regular suppliers of medical equipment to a large hospital invites the director to sit on their board. With this, the director receives $10,000 for three evenings of meetings a year.

Corruption as a Dirty Hands Dilemma

It is noteworthy that the transparency that some companies observe concerns especially those forms of corruption where the company is the victim of the benefit that an employee or a supplier, for example, could gain. In some annual social or sustainability reports, mention is made of the number of corruption cases that have been detected. We hear much less about incidents where bribes have been paid to benefit the company. These kinds of cases come to light in the company that has been duped or that the authorities question. These concern payments to officials or politicians to obtain a concession, to influence a judge's ruling, or to speed up the clearance of goods at customs. Here the boundaries of acceptable forms of relationship management are also difficult to draw. Companies stimulate employees to maintain good relations with the parties they are dependent on. Business dinners and special treats form part of this.

Examples of corruption as a Dirty Hands Dilemma:

4. An employee who works for an operating company in an African country has purchased special equipment in Europe for the company site's security system and is waiting for customs to release it. Such procedures take a lot of time in this country. The official in charge tells him that paying a commission could accelerate the process considerably. He asks for $100 in addition to the official clearance fees. Compared to the actual cost of the equipment, this is relatively little money and such payments are not uncommon in this country. In fact, these officials are "expected" to supplement their salaries to an acceptable level by requesting such payments.

5. A company is trying to get one of the minister's officials to grant a concession. The country's government is also in discussion with a rival who, according to reliable sources, does not shy away from buying off politicians. In this country, bribery is the rule rather than the exception. The company learns that one condition for obtaining a concession is to donate a substantial sum to the president's campaign fund.

6. An oil company is considering a joint venture with a local company that has a substantial amount of tax credits from the government and wants to use these for domestic offshore exploration. The local company, a family-run business like many in this area, is a large conglomerate with many different business interests. It has a reputation for wheeling and dealing and maintaining close connections with many influential government figures. Partnering with this company could mean a lot to the oil company as far as its competitive edge is concerned. If the exploration were successful, the oil company could gain access to valuable oil and gas resources. Competition for access to such acreage is fierce and few foreign companies are successful in this country.

Corruption as a Many Hands Dilemma

The Many Hands Dilemma actually forms part of all the above examples. They all concern the question of who is responsible for resolving these dilemmas, who can be blamed in case of a poor resolution of the dilemma, and who is responsible for developing a policy for preventing corruption and bribery. A number of questions are significant in relation to the examples described above.

7. To what extent is the head of a department accountable for what his staff does? For example, in most instances the person in charge of employees in cases 1, 2 (the private benefit accruing to the person who has the authority to decide) and 4 (the payments to customs) is responsible for the conduct of the employee. Can one expect the person in charge to anticipate possible appealing but troublesome situations the employee might become involved in? Where does a superior's responsibility for the actions of his staff begin and end?

8. To what extent are employees jointly responsible for preventing and correcting unethical conduct, and for stimulating ethical conduct of their colleagues? Many instances of bribery show that people's immediate colleagues are generally aware of their shady practices, sometimes even at quite an early stage. If employees do have effective means at their disposal for exposing such practices, should they not also be held jointly responsible for bribery and corruption of their colleagues?

9. To what extent is the parent company in case 4 responsible for the unethical conduct of companies in host countries and to what extent are local companies accountable for centralized actions (case 5)? Does it mean that as local companies receive more decentralized responsibilities the parent company has proportionally fewer responsibilities to shoulder? If so, which responsibilities are retained at a central level if subsidiaries are largely autonomous? Or does the central level always maintain a certain degree of responsibility?

10. To what extent is the oil company in case 6 responsible for the unethical conduct of its partners in joint ventures? Imagine that the partner with whom the company is in a joint venture bribed some politicians in order to be granted a concession for the joint venture. Is the oil company responsible for these actions as long as it is part of the joint venture and profiting from the corrupt practices of its partner? At what point can the oil company wash its hands in innocence?

The Many Hands, Dirty Hands, and Entangled Hands Dilemmas can certainly be told apart in these cases. But that does not mean that they can be kept apart. These three issues are interrelated. One situation can also have a multiple dilemma structure. For example, those employees who dirtied their hands on behalf of the company by paying bribes could also be serving their own interests by increasing their chances of promotion. Ultimately, these dilemmas do not come down to individuals as such. Instead, they arise because of the corporate context within which the individuals function. Egoism is not the sole force that drives employees to bribery. Some people may merely seek to further the aims of the corporation. It is important for a company to make the bounds of its corporate interests clear to its employees. The fact that a company sees these situations as dilemmas implies that it acknowledges the existence of norms in this area; both for and against corruption and bribery. The question then is what theoretical concept lies at the basis of these norms? What can reasonably be expected of a company? To what extent can a company dirty its hands without losing its integrity?

The Corporation as Social Contract

When people cooperate in an organizational framework, three new relationships come into being: the relationship between the corporation and its stakeholders; the relations of cooperation within the corporation; and the relations between the different roles that representatives of an organization fulfill. Ethical dilemmas in the corporate domain arise as a result of conflicting value systems (virtues, principles, or interests) within these relationships. Sometimes, requirements for safeguarding the future of a corporation can clash with the fundamental rights and interests of particular stakeholders (the Dirty Hands Dilemma). The cooperation between units, departments, and employees can be hampered by the different interpretations each has of the corporate objective or responsibility for the overall results can be continually passed on to others (the Many Hands Dilemma). The different roles that an employee fulfills as soon as he or she acts within a corporate framework (for instance, the private–work relation) can be source of tension for employees (the Entangled Hands Dilemma). When these situations arise, corporations must find a way to honor conflicting obligations. A closer analysis of corporate relationships can illuminate the moral obligations of corporations. In this chapter, we argue that the different relationships of corporations can be understood as contractual relationships, which, in turn, denote their concrete moral responsibilities. In this way, a "solution" can be found for the Corporate Dilemmas. The aim of the contract is to do justice to the claims of all parties, including that of the corporation. This renders the notion of a contract eminently suitable as a conceptual model for formulating the moral standards appropriate to the corporate context.

Integrity is the disposition and behavior directed at realizing the wholeness of the organization. In this chapter we show that the concept of the contract as a heuristic device enables us to bring conflicting demands into relation with each other, thus serving as an aid for realizing the desired wholeness. For a relationship to qualify as a contractual relationship a corporation should not only fulfill the terms of its contract it should also meet a number of preconditions.

The concept of the contract facilitates the endeavor of giving concrete content to the notion of integrity.

CORPORATE INTERESTS

The notion "corporate interest" plays an important role in the three corporate dilemmas. The Dirty Hands Dilemma concerns the tension between the corporate interest and the interests of individual stakeholders. In the Many Hands Dilemma the corporate interest also takes central stage. Everyone that contributes to the realization of the corporate objective has a different interpretation of it. The Entangled Hands Dilemma concerns the tension that can arise between the different roles a manager or employee in a corporation fulfills. It refers to the tension between the demands of the role of manager or employee and the demands of other roles in the private sphere. In the Many Hands Dilemma the demands on a manager or employee reflect the concrete meaning of the corporate interest that he or she upholds. It is tempting to view the corporate interest as the interests of all the stakeholders. In our view, this does not provide adequate insight into the nature of the corporate interest. Interests do clash and when such conflicts occur, an independent decision has to be made. A corporation must also take the long-term effects of its actions into account. That which is undertaken today can affect stakeholders in future and has consequences for internal relations of cooperation. This also requires an independent choice on the part of the corporation.

What makes this balancing act so troublesome? The complexity of the modern corporation clearly plays a role. The functioning of a corporation often has far-reaching consequences that are sometimes difficult to foresee. Claims are often mutually exclusive. Because resources are scarce by definition,[1] the question of conflicting claims arises in almost all cases. Thus defined, it seems that the challenge of addressing the corporate dilemmas is reduced to a problem that differs only marginally from everyday problems in interpersonal relations. Every choice involves limited resources. The corporate dilemmas, however, are of a more fundamental nature. How can a justified claim from a stakeholder, a particular perspective on the corporate objective, or a justified claim on the basis of a role of an employee or manager that conflicts with the corporate interest, at the same time be considered as part of the corporate interest? Is it possible to hold that all stakeholder interests and the different opinions of internal parties constitute the corporate interest? We have seen that the corporation retains a certain degree of independence with respect to those rights and interests. How can a responsible and independent choice between the conflicting claims be made? What does the corporate interest comprise precisely? How can the corporate interest encompass moral obligations?

Stakeholder and corporate interests

The ambiguity presented above marks the corporation's relationships with its stakeholders. In many cases, the interests of stakeholders—certainly in the short term—conflict with those of the corporation. At the same time they are also extensions of each other. It is possible to view the corporation, just as civil society, as a cooperative association for the mutual benefit of stakeholders. In their account of this relationship, Freeman and Gilbert emphasize the meaning of the corporation for stakeholders. The corporation is nothing more than a series of cooperative associations. Consequently, the corporate interest is the result of the demands of these stakeholders. It is thus in the interest of the corporation to ensure that continued stakeholders support. Without this support, the corporation cannot exist.

Corporations are fundamentally cooperative institutions. In our view, if a corporation fails to help person X with project P, then X will search for an alternative and withdraw support from the corporation.[2]

Here, a corporation is viewed as a community within a community. The corporation is a cooperative association of stakeholders. It is presumably this model based on an Aristotelian-Thomistic foundation that Rawls has in mind when he describes society as an association of associations.[3] Society is a community in which the individual does not participate directly but through organized communities. A corporation can be such a community. David Gauthier is also of the opinion that principles at the level of society repeat themselves at the level of the corporation. According to Gauthier:

The firm will want to create an environment in which its employees will be, and want to be, the sort of persons who have internalized principles of decision-making that enhance the overall goals of the corporation. They will want to have employees who do not think directly of the realization of their own particular concerns, their own particular values, but who have incorporated a certain corporate ethos into their decision-making principles, and have done this because they can then expect to do better within the corporate environment. But the corporation itself, in interacting with other corporations in the larger scale co-operative venture of society, will also be concerned to incorporate such principles into its own decision-making procedures.[4]

The corporation as citizen

According to Henk van Luijk,[5] the first professor in business ethics in Europe, the corporation is generally not viewed as voluntarily contributing to achieving a reasonable level of social prosperity. According to van Luijk, this view can be traced back to the theoretical dichotomy between prudence and morality. It is precisely because we view a corporation's pursuit of self-interest as at odds with morally responsible conduct that we are unable to see corporations as normal participants in society who, like all other participants, have to contribute to realizing and maintaining a liveable society.

The withering away, on the theoretical level, of a traditional dichotomy, may help to open the door to practices in which corporations willingly accept specific civil responsibilities, not primarily for profit reasons, but neither refusing the concomitant benefits that may accompany their choices.[6]

A corporation can be seen as the focal point within a network of relationships. Tension can arise in each of these relationships. The corporate interest in profit is sometimes at odds with acting responsibly with respect to other parties. At the same time, these parties benefit from a well-functioning corporation. In the relationship between a corporation and external stakeholders, just as in the relationship between a corporation and its management and employees, and in the relationship between internal functioning units, both conflicting and common interests exist that may result in ambiguity.

The corporate interest may, certainly in the short term, be at variance with the interests of society. In cases where environmental investments are called for, the continuity of an already struggling company is ensured only by postponing or minimizing implementation. In this way, corporations can attempt to minimize costs or even to externalize them. Society can, however, also be seen as a cooperative association with the goal of achieving the mutual interests of the parties involved. Rawls, for instance, considers "a well-ordered society as a scheme of cooperation for reciprocal advantage regulated by principles which persons would choose in an initial situation that is fair."[7] Because it concerns a decision that is taken under specific circumstances, Rawls does not consider the norms for regulating society as the result of an opportunistic *ad hoc* choice by the social parties. That would have been the case if the parties were only prepared to make a contribution to the prosperity of society if it served their own interests. In setting up society, rational and unprejudiced people, according to Rawls, will opt for cooperation. This choice is formulated in certain obligations for regulating how people coexist. Van Luijk draws the same conclusion with respect to the functioning of a corporation. The corporation is also a party in society, which implies that it can be held to the same obligations. An increasing number of important social projects can only be realized through voluntary cooperation of various factions in society: corporations, governments, NGOs, and the media, for example. Civil society demands of participants to contribute their share to the common responsibilities. The concept of civil society is a normative concept, according to van Luijk. Participating in society implies acceptance of the responsibility to contribute to the interests of the whole. For van Luijk, corporations are not excluded from this as "in a participatory market society, civil corporations are almost human."[8]

THE CONTRACT MODEL IN THE BUSINESS CONTEXT

A corporation can be seen as the midpoint in a network of relationships with various types of stakeholders that are characterized by ambiguous internal patterns of interests. On the one hand, there is the question of conflicting interests, while on the other, these interests are interrelated and extensions of one another. The central question is how an acceptable balance can be achieved in this relationship between the corporate interest, internal interpretations thereof, and stakeholder interests.

In the history of modern Western philosophy, two comprehensive solutions[9] have been advanced for resolving the oppositional relation between self-interest, or the corporate interest and the interest of the other, or the general interest. These are the market model and the contract model.[10] In its own way, each of these two approaches denies the fundamental character of the distinction between morality and self-interest or corporate interest. The market model postulates that, provided that a number of conditions are met, a balance between morality and self-interest will ensue by itself.[11] The contract model resolves the tension between morality and self-interest by constructing a situation where parties freely enter into a (fictional) contract in which agreements are made. These covenants curb the unrestrained pursuit of self-interest and are mutually beneficial to all parties.

The first school of thought has become dominant in the modern Western philosophical tradition. If everyone pursues his or her self-interest, an optimal situation for the whole will naturally follow. Everyone must be free to maximize his or her self-interest. Government interference must be kept to a minimum and should be primarily concerned with ensuring fair competition. Cartels and monopolies are prohibited as they impede the efficient functioning of the free market which ensures a morally optimal result. This can be assured by ensuring free access to the market. Furthermore, the market must be transparent so that all market players have optimal opportunities to pursue their self-interest.

As a solution to the tension between (corporate) interest and morality, the market model is marked by a number of insurmountable problems. First, the market has a number of significant imperfections:

1. To the extent that a balance can be achieved, this is only in the short term. In the longer term, we are constantly dealing with imbalance. The model only makes it probable that market forces will effect a balance and, thereby, a moral optimum. Before this balance is achieved, however, a new disturbance introduces a new process of adaptation. A morally optimal situation (i.e. balance) therefore becomes an unattainable ideal. During the adaptation process, all kinds of situations arise that are unacceptable from a moral point of view.

2. Market parties—including corporations to the extent that they allow themselves to be driven by the market model—are inclined not to take account of external effects, and especially where these involve costs, to pass them on to the community.

3. Within the market model, market parties are unable to find optimal solutions through cooperation (also with respect to collective goods). This imperfection is known as the prisoner's dilemma. The "free rider" behavior that is inherent in the egotistical and rational actions of the market parties postpones the socially desired optimum permanently.

A second, more principled, argument against the market model as a solution for the tension between self-interest and morality concerns the paradoxical nature of moral demands. According to this model, no moral demands should be imposed on corporations.[12] From the perspective of the market-model, moral demands are to be resisted if the corporation is to function in a morally responsible manner. It is clear that corporate leaders will find no solace in this ambiguous guideline. Since the market model makes no contribution to responsible decision-making, we can conclude that it fails as a *normative* instrument.

The reasoning behind the contract model is at odds with the market model. The point of departure in this approach is that people willingly limit the pursuit of self-interest to achieve a mutual or superior common interest. Sometimes use is made of a sort of "state of nature," an imaginary basis from which individuals arrive at a contract. For Hobbes, this state of nature is characterized by the unrestrained pursuit of self-interest. Because people perceive this as a situation of permanent insecurity, they enter into a social contract on the grounds that they have more to gain by doing so. In contract theories, the contract is not based on a notion of general interest that comes about "naturally." To promote the general interest, all parties voluntarily restrict the pursuit of self-interest and mutually coordinate their actions.

The contract concept is grounded in two philosophical traditions. One is the legal tradition that can ultimately be traced back to Roman law. The other is the socio-political philosophical tradition as developed by political thinkers such as Thomas Hobbes, John Locke, Jean Jacques Rousseau, and more recently John Rawls and David Gauthier. Great differences exist between these contract theories. The judicial concept of a contract was developed in order to make complex transactions and, by implication, cohesive forms of social cooperation possible. This judicial concept was later used by social contract philosophers to legitimize the existence of the state as the outcome of social cooperation. This theory provides the foundation for the rights and obligations of citizens and the state.

The judicial concept of the contract was developed on the basis of existing practices that needed only fine-tuning. The idea of a contract already existed as formalized in the judicial framework. The concept of a social contract was developed to understand a complex situation in a new way. Nevertheless, the core notion behind the contract is the same in both traditions. A balance is sought between the rights and interests of individuals and that of the collective. It is this feature in particular that makes the contract model relevant for the corporate context. It is, after all, in the relationship with its stakeholders that a certain degree of tension can be located between corporate interest and morality: success of the corporation against acting responsibly toward stakeholders. The contract model depicts these interests in relation to one another.

Contractarian ethics in a business context

One reason for the appeal of the concept of a contract is that it is firmly anchored in the Western philosophical tradition.[13] Another reason why it seems excellently suited to the business context is that many relationships in this domain are already structured by contractual agreements. Managers feel comfortable with thinking in terms of contractual relationships and are quick to develop basic intuitions for evaluating contractual relationships. It is therefore not surprising that scholars in the field of business ethics use the concept. Authors such as Donaldson,[14] Dunfee,[15] Donaldson and Dunfee,[16] Gauthier,[17] Hessen,[18] Keeley,[19] van Luijk,[20] and Velasquez[21] all apply the contract model to the business context.

In a detailed analysis of the corporate social contract literature, Ben Wempe[22] points out the widely divergent ways in which contracts are employed. The authors appear unconcerned with explaining their particular use of the concept. Velasquez uses the concept of a contract in connection with the corporate responsibility for products. He limits his analysis to the relationship between consumers and the corporation and asserts that "the relationship between a business firm and its customers is essentially a contractual relationship."[23] Hessen's contract model states that "a corporation is simply and literally a voluntary association of individuals, united by a network of contracts."[24] In his first publication about a social contract for business in 1982, Donaldson describes a contract "between productive organizations and individual members of society, not between productive organizations and some supra-individual, social entity."[25] This contract forms the moral legitimization of corporations as productive organizations.[26] Keeley is of the opinion that organizations themselves *are* a series of contracts.

What I have argued is that organizations are not metaphysical or moral persons, but are themselves contracts: series of working agreements between natural persons specifying mutual (not necessarily equal or voluntary) rights and obligations.[27]

Donaldson and Dunfee outline a moral contract that "defines the space for communities (societies, companies) to develop their own moral rules."[28] In this way, they indirectly define corporations as a community that comes into being as the result of "microsocial contracts."

These approaches differ with respect to who the individual contracting parties are. They can be the citizens in society, the participants in the corporation, and/or the corporation itself. Nor does agreement exist on the goal that the contract partners are pursuing: to bring about a transaction, to create the corporation, or to create a liveable society (or to achieve all three). Furthermore, there are differences with respect to the character of the contract: hypothetical or actual; discrete or relational; macro, meso, or micro; procedural or substantive; relative or absolute. None the less, the contract theories all attempt to provide insight into the concrete moral obligations of a corporation.

As applied to the business context, three types of contract theories can be distinguished:

1. *Relationships as discrete contracts.* In some theories,[29] the concrete relationship(s) of a corporation are seen as individual contracts. With the aid of the contract model, we are able to formulate the concrete obligations of the corporation with respect to these parties. This contract model provides insight into the concrete obligations that individual relationships imply for the corporation. Velasquez limits himself to corporation's relationship with its clients. Donaldson[30] applies the concept largely to the relationship between a specific corporation, employees, and customers. In a later publication,[31] the same author outlines a contract that implies a number of concrete obligations with respect to employees and consumers. In their book *Ties that Bind*, Donaldson and Dunfee formulate some hypernorms and algorithms (moral rules of thumb) for stakeholder management in general.[32]

2. *The corporation as a result of a contract.* Other theories[33] view the corporation as the result of a social contract entered into by the participants. The corporation is perceived as a social community. The contract gives insight into the obligations of the corporation with respect to the contract partners. A corporation is established by a contract, much in the way society is in Hobbes's contract theory, for example. In general, this concerns a hypothetical contract. The contract partners are the employees. Multiple stakeholders are sometimes involved as well. In this view, the corporation is perceived as a common project of all parties involved. Thanks to their cooperation a higher return is achieved than would be the case if everyone worked for himself. In exchange for their contribution to the continued existence of the corporation, the contract partners receive a share of the returns. These returns should be greater than the returns that each would realize alone. Rawls and in his footsteps Gauthier, consider society a "cooperative venture for mutual advantage."[34] According to Gauthier, this reasoning can also be applied to corporations. A corporation is also a community that can be viewed as a "cooperative venture."[35]

3. *The corporation as a contract partner.* Finally, other theories[36] view the corporation as a contract partner that together with other social parties forms society and assumes a share in the communal project. Here, the use of the

concept of a contract provides insight into the nature of the obligations of corporations as constructive partners. Donaldson and Dunfee outline a global macrosocial contract within which communities have the freedom to establish microsocial contracts. The macrosocial contract limits this freedom and regulates possible conflicts. The community includes not only local societies but also national and multinational corporations. According to Gauthier, the corporation is a social partner that on this basis makes a contribution to the continued existence of society. Van Luijk considers corporations to be "normal" citizens that have a contribution to make to the continued existence of society. He writes:

We, as individuals and as corporations, can largely thank our ability to realize our self-determined objectives to the institutionalized support from many other individuals and organizations, from the justice system through our transport and telecommunication to, where necessary, the police. It is also, therefore, no more than reasonable that that participatory arrangement that makes a real and actual contribution to the representation of the general interest, as a collective responsibility, should rest upon all participants in social intercourse.[37]

The heuristic value of the concept of contracts

Before we can determine whether, and if so which, contract theory is suitable for the corporate context, we first have to pause to discuss a number of methodological aspects.

Just as other theories and concepts, the social contract is a heuristic device. Applying the contract concept does not mean that the relationship between the corporation and its stakeholders should be transformed into contractual relationships. Applying the concept of a contract to these relationships means that we—by understanding the relationships *as if* we are dealing with contractual relationships—are able to understand a number of corporate obligations.

The contract concept can be viewed as a metaphor. By understanding the relationships of a corporation in terms of contracts, we use an available and familiar concept from one context as an instrument in another. By using a computer as metaphor for the human brain, we hope to acquire further insight into the functioning of the brain. The relationship of a multinational corporation with the country where it operates can be understood as a guest–host relationship. By introducing this analogy, it is possible to evaluate morally actions in the context of this relationship. The multinational should behave like a "guest," is not responsible for keeping house, and should not interfere in matters related to housekeeping. In fact, contractarian philosophers such as Hobbes, Locke, and Rousseau also use this technique. People no longer found the medieval model of the state—as part of the divine order—acceptable as legitimization for the authority of the head of state. Employing the contract concept made it possible to understand the state and the role of the monarch as the result of an implicit agreement of its citizens.

The social contract is hypothetical by definition. Because the contract serves as the foundation for the moral obligations of a corporation, it must be hypothetical. An empirical contract has to relate to an existing social arrangement, which requires a moral foundation in turn. A social arrangement can never provide a moral justification.[38] At the same time, however, the social contract is real. Despite the fact that the rights of black South Africans were neither recognized nor protected by South African law until 1991, they still existed. The concept of a social contract is therefore moral in nature.[39]

THE CONCEPT OF A CONTRACT

In order to determine whether a contract model is suitable for framing moral issues in the business context, we must first identify the defining features of a contract. What are the characteristics of contractarianism in general? What are the tell-tale traits of a contract in everyday intercourse? What difference does it make whether an agreement is recognized as a contract? What turns norms into contracts? Furthermore, it is necessary to determine how the functioning of a corporation can be understood and how the contract model relates to it. Once these questions have been answered, we can examine whether a contract can be employed as a means for conceptualizing the moral responsibility of a corporation, given the special nature of the corporate context.

A contract is a binding agreement between two or more parties. Such an agreement can be reached orally or in writing. The need for contracts arose when anonymity became increasingly prevalent in economic exchange relationships. In societies where cooperation is entirely based on family or tribal relationships, contracts are superfluous. In situations where it is purely a question of a straight exchange of goods, contracts are equally unnecessary. This applies to simple transactions where the parties involved are directly able to establish the quality and quantity of the goods offered. For transactions where, for example, the handing over of goods and services takes place at different times, trust is indispensable.[40] That is why customs were created within the later prehistoric societies: to ensure this trust. If an agreement was reached under certain conditions, for example, in the presence of a witness and making use of a set formula ("I hereby declare that ... "), it was binding. In cases of non-compliance, the negligent party could be compelled to fulfill his obligations, if necessary, by means of force. In that way, and in those societies, a primitive form of civil law developed that included procedures and instruments to enforce compliance with agreements (maintenance of law). The invention of writing made further refinement possible whereby the rules for entering into an agreement could be set down. The contract itself could also be set down formally, if necessary through the agency of a civil-law notary. This made agreements possible that are more complex.

Two characteristics of contracts

What is it that makes an agreement binding? What is characteristic of a contract? When can we maintain that no contract exists? There are (at least) two characteristics on which the binding character of a contract rests: *reciprocity between autonomous parties*; and *(confidence in the) effectiveness of the agreement*. In the absence of these attributes, an agreement is not a contract and does not have a binding character.[41] In the following section, we will describe these two characteristics and in Chapter 6, these characteristics are developed into contractual principles and qualities of the contracting parties.

Reciprocity between autonomous parties. Reciprocity or mutuality is a precondition for the existence of contracts. Reciprocity refers to the anticipation of mutual advantage or gain by all contracting parties. The condition of mutuality is met when "*all* participants perceive a possible improvement from their pre-exchange positions."[42] The advantage that can be gained is not restricted to economic gain. Contractual agreements can even be entered into to prevent harm. Reciprocity requires that the mutual obligations created by the agreement in a goal–means relationship are mutually dependent. For example, A and B enter into an agreement where A sells his house to B for the amount of $X. Transfer will take place at time T. A and B have entered into a mutual obligation. A's purpose is to obtain the money. The means is the transfer of the house. For B, the goal is to acquire the house and the amount to be paid is the means to achieve this. Both A and B stand to benefit.

Mutual advantage as such does not necessarily mean people have a contract. Rather, this advantage has to be recognized and agreed to by both parties. Party A cannot impose a contract on party B just because the transaction would benefit both A and B. For all we know, A's neighbor might have an identical house for sale at a better price. Contracts are voluntary agreements between autonomous actors. Therefore, parties must be authorized to enter into an agreement. This authority is crucial. The desire to enter into an agreement in itself is not an adequate precondition. The exchange a robber initiates with the threat "your money or your life" can therefore not be considered an agreement, even though he wants the victim's money and the victim wants to stay alive. The absence of authority over the life of the victim implies that no agreement can be made.[43] Autonomy is a precondition for a contract and both parties are required to acknowledge the autonomy of the other.

(Confidence in the) effectiveness of the agreement. The binding nature of a contract depends on its effectiveness or sustainability—the extent to which contractors comply with the terms of the contract.[44] The actual bindingness depends on the general compliance of the parties they address. Should one party fail to meet the terms of the contract, the other party has grounds to demand compliance, to expect compensation, or to annul the contract. The value of a contract is affirmed not only by parties keeping to it but also, and particularly, when they do not. Moreover, reciprocity is empty without some form of compliance or the intention to comply.

Contractors will not enter into contracts if they think that their contracting partners will not live up to the terms of agreement.[45] This confidence must not be seen as the outcome of an agreement, but indeed, as a precondition for agreement. In the example about the sale of the house, both A and B must be assured that the house will be delivered at time T. Since some elements of the transaction will occur in the future, A and B must both have the ability to enforce the agreement. This entails an enforceable commitment. It becomes equally evident that the binding nature of a contract points to a social framework that offers the parties sufficient security that the agreement can be enforced if necessary. Trust is the result of the more or less reliable operation of the contract body created by society:

The contract mechanism works not because there is justified trust in creating commitments. To the contrary: trust in the creation of commitments is justified because the contract mechanism works.[46]

Tension can arise between the two characteristics. Let us suppose that A, while in a state of emotional instability that is not visible to others, sells his house to B. On the basis of this sale, B has sold his own house in the meantime. At the moment of the transfer, A realizes what he has done and wishes to call everything off. The demands of the economic system require that the faith that B was justified in placing in the agreement be taken into account. Without this trust, society cannot function. Because the institution of contracts can exist only by virtue of this assurance, preference is given to effectiveness above reciprocity. Even where there is no doubt that A's will is not in accordance with the agreement, many national civil codes state that a commitment still exists because B has justified faith in the transaction.[47] B can, therefore, demand fulfillment of the agreement. From the discussion about returning the property of Jews who died in concentration camps during the Second Word War, it appears that confidence in the institution of the contract does not always carry more weight than reciprocity. Even though the current owner of a painting that was stolen or sold under pressure during the war acquired it in a proper manner (at an auction, for example), the social pressure to return the painting to the Jewish heirs is immense. In the eyes of society, the fact that the autonomy of the original owner was violated carries more weight.

A contractual relationship has, in fact, a bilateral structure. If a third party participates explicitly in the contract, a more complicated situation arises. The example of the transaction involving previously Jewish-owned property illustrates this. In actual fact, two transactions are involved. The bindingness of the transaction that the Jewish war victims entered into has consequences for later transactions. To what extent is the one party's failure to fulfill an agreement a justification for another party to back out of his or her obligations as well? The way a contract between two parties affects a third party is a question that plays no role in the contract concept, or not directly. Indirectly, it is emphatically present. The characteristic of trust in the effectiveness of an agreement, in particular, refers to the context within which a contract between two parties is established. Through this, a contract is a social institution. The society the contracting parties are members of has an interest in the proper functioning of this institution. The contract as an institution is one of the instruments that makes coexistence possible. Especially in complex communities, it is a necessary requirement. The enforceability of the agreement embodied in the contract is guaranteed by society—even through the use of sanctions if necessary. Even though a contract is tailored to a relationship between two parties, society functions in a special way as third party. Failure to live up to a contract undermines society. Therefore, on the basis of the agreement they entered into, the negligent party defaults not only on their obligations toward their contractual partner but also on their obligations to society. Indirectly, a contract serves as a cross-reference to the broader social contract.

TOWARD A THEORY OF THE CORPORATION

The corporate social contract theory portrays the corporation as the focal point within a network of contracts on the basis of which moral responsibilities can be ascribed to the corporation as an independent moral entity. The theory itself rests upon a synthesis of three different approaches to the nature of the corporation:

(1) transaction costs theory and agency theory (Coase,[48] Jensen and Meckling,[49] Williamson[50]);
(2) stakeholder theory (Dodd,[51] Brenner and Molander,[52] Brenner and Cochran[53]);
(3) (social) contract theory of corporations (Donaldson,[54] Donaldson and Dunfee,[55] Freeman and Evan,[56] Keeley[57]).

An integration of the first two approaches forms the basis for the social contract theory of the corporation (Hill and Jones[58]). In this section, we argue that a contract theory of the corporation is a logical step in the development of the theories of the corporation since its inception in the early 1930s. This development can be seen as a discovery of new moral dimensions to the concept of the contract. The "transaction costs" approach acknowledges the element of exchange. Stakeholder theory acknowledges the rights of the contracting parties. Social contract theory also acknowledges greater normative principles to which the contracting parties are bound and the requirement of institutionalizing these principles to ensure compliance. The history of applying the notion of the contract to corporations shows a progressive enrichment of this concept.

The transaction costs model of a corporation developed by Coase, the stakeholder theory of the corporation, and the (social) contract theory of the corporation are intended in the first place as instruments to understand how corporations function.

Theories of agency and transaction

The neoclassical theory of the corporation is only a partial theory of the corporation. This approach merely outlines how a corporation functions in the market. In this approach, the corporation is a "black box." The market behavior of a corporation is understood as a function of the input factors described in a production function and driven by profit-maximization. What happens in the "black box" is not subjected to analysis. Since the 1930s, theories have been developed both from an economic[59] and a behavioral perspective[60] to provide insight into precisely what happens inside the "black box." The contract concept plays an important role in these theories.

According to Coase, activities are incorporated and therefore taken off the market if it is more efficient than acquiring the parts and products on the free market. The costs involved in acquiring goods on the open market include searching for products and services, organizational costs, costs related to the uncertainty of having the appropriate resources available at the right time, etc. In establishing a corporation, a number of parties is bound to the corporation and is placed under its authority. In this way the corporation avoids these costs and operates more efficiently. That corporations have an efficiency function suggests that the market does not function quite as smoothly (i.e. perfect competition, market transparency, homogeneous goods) as the neoclassical economics assume. All the market parties, including those who are bound to the corporation, pursue (as does the corporation itself) purely their own interests. They are prepared to accept the authority of the corporation because they stand to gain more by doing so. The fact that wages are paid to an employee does not necessarily distinguish him or her from a "contractor" operating in the free market. The employee offers a product and receives compensation for it. It is characteristic of employees not that they supply a product in exchange for wages but surrender freedom (within limits) and place themselves under the authority of the corporation. The employee is no longer free to carry out work as he or she sees fit. Employees do the job that they are assigned and carry it out in the manner instructed.

The core idea in Coase's theory relates to the "make or buy" decision. Should a corporation carry out a certain activity or acquire it on the market? In this regard, the corporation maintains two types of relationships: one with the parties bound to the confines of the corporation; and another with external parties with whom it does business. Although he does not explicitly use the term "contract," Coase does refer to contract-like relationships. These are contracts in a limited sense of the word: contracts as transactions or exchanges. Exchanges are made both with the employees and the market parties. Coase views the corporation as a spider in a web—as the focal point of a multitude of relationships. It is from this viewpoint that initiatives are developed.

The agency theory of Jensen and Meckling[61] elaborates on Coase's transaction costs theory. Transaction costs theory shows that costs are involved in market transactions. If these are higher than the organizational costs, the entrepreneur will decide to bring the activity in-house. However, Coase does not show exactly what these organizational costs consist of. Agency theory fills this gap. It defines the agency relationship as: " . . . a contract under which one or more persons (the principal(s)) engage another person (the agent) to perform some service on their behalf which involves delegating some decision-making authority to the agent."[62] Because both parties in the relationship are profit-maximizers, the agent does not automatically act completely in accordance with the interests of the principal. Agency costs are the costs of controlling the agent, the costs for hiring the agent, and the loss of prosperity that the principal suffers because the agent serves not only the interests of the principal but also his or her own. The question that lies at the center of agency theory is:

. . . how to structure the contractual relation (including compensation incentives) between the principal and the agent to provide appropriate incentives for the agent to make choices which will maximize the principal's welfare given that uncertainty and imperfect monitoring exist.[63]

According to Jensen and Meckling, contractual relationships form the core of the corporation. Among others, there is a contractual relationship between the owners and management, management and employees, the corporation and its customers, and the corporation and its capital providers. Corporations, just as other types of organizations are seen as "legal fictions, which serve as a nexus for a set of contracting relationships among individuals."[64] In all these relationships, agency costs and control of the agent play a role. The relationships that the corporation creates and maintains can be seen as a market in itself. Drawing a distinction between internal and external (contractual) relationships as Coase does, is therefore futile:

There is in a very real sense only a multitude of complex relationships (i.e. contracts) between the legal fiction (the firm) and the owners of labor, material and capital inputs and the consumers of output.[65]

Every contract involves agency costs—whether it is an internal contract with employees or an external contract with other stakeholders. What must be investigated is how these costs can be kept to a minimum. Jensen and Meckling concentrate primarily on the ownership structure within the corporation. They examine what happens when the entrepreneur (the owner-manager) needs to raise money on capital markets for the development of new activities. They limit themselves to new possibilities: borrowing money or attracting venture capital by issuing stocks. The ownership structure of the corporation is determined by the relationship between internal and external assets, as well as by the relationship between internal corporate assets (stocks presided over by the manager) and external corporate assets (stocks presided over by outside stockholders). A complex situation in which three parties play a role is thus created: the manager (possibly as partial owner), the stockholders, and the creditors. Jensen and Meckling investigate how the agency costs in the relationship(s) between the owner(s) and the management are affected as an increasing proportion of the stocks come into the hands of external stockholders. In addition, they examine how this affects possible opportunistic behavior of managers and the extent to which it comes at the cost of the value of the corporation.

In this theory, relationships are viewed as individual contracts. Whether a relationship with managers, external stockholders, or funds sources is created depends to a great extent on the ownership structure of the corporation and on the conditions of the market. The interdependence among the different partners is expressed in the balance that is created by the participants' interaction. Jensen and Meckling do not elaborate further on this process.

Although Jensen and Meckling concentrate on the ownership structure, their reasoning can be applied to other corporate relationships. Williamson[66] explicitly involves the multiplicity of corporate relationships in his theory and elaborates on this. He specifically investigates the costs of a series of transactions that is carried out over time between a corporation and a partner. The extent to which parties must devise long-term, transaction-specific investments to make the transaction possible largely determines the nature of the contractual relationship. In his opinion, the principles he outlines apply to all corporate relationships: employees, owners, suppliers, customers, the community, and management. When such investments are necessary, both partners have an interest in continuing the relationship and to see to it that a contract is renewed when it expires. Without this assurance, the investment as a whole must be expressed as the price of a transaction. In this way, a bilateral monopoly is established. In such a relationship, it is possible to make adjustments based on changing circumstances. Although the buyer and seller have an interest in the modification of the contract, each party also has an interest in acquiring maximum advantage. However, in order to avoid higher transaction costs, both parties have an interest in creating management structures to prevent opportunism. Repetitive transactions in which no corporate-specific investments are necessary can be acquired on the market. As this type of investment is necessary, the party involved must be offered guarantees so that he or she is prepared to make such an investment. Depending on the nature of the relationship, it could be desirable to include the party in the Board of Directors. According to Williamson, the Board of Directors must be a management body

... whose principal purpose is to safeguard those who face a diffuse but significant risk of expropriation because the assets in question are numerous and ill-defined, and cannot be protected in a well-focused, transaction-specific way.[67]

According to him, including a representative of the owners in the board of directors is the perfect way to prevent opportunism. In the case of employees, it is generally not necessary or desirable to include them in the Board of Directors. That would entail too many costs in the form of instruction, the risk that they will be too occupied with operational issues, and the danger of opportunism. In order to prevent asymmetry in the information between employees and management, it is sometimes desirable to allow employees to attend Board meetings as observers. The theory of the firm, as described above, has a number of implications for the moral status of the corporation.

1. All individuals are motivated by self-interest. It is the corporation, or the management acting on behalf of the owners, who attracts partners to the project and binds them through contracts.
2. There are contracts between the manager and the owner (Jensen and Meckling) and contracts of the manager (on behalf of the owner) with a number of parties that make a contribution to the corporation. The corporation, or the manager on behalf of the owner, finds itself within a network of relationships with presumably equal obligations. These relationships are seen as transactions.
3. The concept of the contract has an extremely limited meaning here. The obligations apply only to the extent that there is a certain level of mutuality. The contracting parties can lay a claim to a share of the benefits generated on the basis of cooperation. Their efforts on behalf of the collective are recognized by means of a share in the proceeds. That is the content of the contract. The focus of concern is mainly the power dynamics (information lead) that hinder fulfillment of the terms of the contract and, thereby, the realization of efficient contracts.
4. This approach provides no insight into how the different contracts affect one another. Williamson does acknowledge the mutual dependence of the different contracts, without further elaborating on it. According to Williamson,

The study of corporate contracting is complicated by interdependencies within and between contracts; changes in one set of terms commonly require realignments in others. It will nevertheless be instructive to examine the contracts of corporate constituencies in a sequential rather than fully interactive way.[68]

Stakeholder theory and the corporation as a focal point in a network of discrete contracts

Until the 1980s, the focus of stakeholder theory was on the empirical/instrumental value of this approach. Stakeholder theory was viewed as contributing to a better description and understanding of the functioning of corporations in the market. It was also regarded as an instrument that contributes to the successful management of a corporation. This does not detract from the fact that normative elements play an implicit role in instrumental stakeholder theory.[69] This normative dimension has been acknowledged since its inception[70] and the theory is now partially employed to define corporate social responsibilities.[71]

The instrumental character of stakeholder theory, as applied until recently, is apparent in the definition of a stakeholder. The Stanford Research Institute defines stakeholders as "those groups without whose support the organization would cease to exist."[72] When stakeholder demands conflict, a choice between mutually exclusive claims has to be made. In a purely opportunistic strategic analysis, everything ultimately centers on power. Which stakeholders does the corporation need or make good use of, and which stakeholders have the capacity to make life difficult for the corporation? For the opportunistic strategist, the world is filled with opportunities and threats and the art is how to maneuver through them.

The normative aspect of stakeholder theory is also present in different ways. It is expressed in the description of a stakeholder as every group that has a stake in the corporation. Not only the parties internal to the corporation are important but all the parties who have an interest in the corporation. Important in this regard is that the corporation has a moral obligation to honor the legitimate expectations of stakeholders.

The insight that normative elements are inherent to stakeholder theory is based on two flaws in the narrow instrumental approach. First, the instrumental approach is not entirely consistent. It is terribly risky and therefore strategically (instrumentally) unwise to evaluate the expectations of stakeholders purely in terms of the corporate interest. Insignificant and powerless stakeholders can unexpectedly, through coalitions with other stakeholders, form a power factor. In this context, environmental groups capable of influencing consumers form a good example.

Second, it was realized that normative elements are inherent to the stakeholder concept because fundamental questions within the instrumental approach remained unanswerable. What ends should the corporate interest serve? And what, precisely, is the corporate interest? Every answer to these related questions is normative by nature.[73] The stakeholder concept is used in a broad sense:[74] "All persons or groups with legitimate interests in procedural and/or substantive aspects of corporate activity."[75] With the acknowledgement of its normative aspects, stakeholder theory has grown into a theory for corporate governance[76] and corporate social responsibility.[77]

Hill and Jones have integrated the stakeholder concept with agency theory. They expand the principal–agent paradigm—which is limited to the relationship of the owner/stockholders with management—to a "generalized theory of agency."[78] Corporate management should be seen as an agent of all stakeholders. Stakeholders differ in terms of their interest or "stake" in the corporation and the degree of power they exercise over management. The negotiation process between stakeholder and agent is always marked by a degree of friction and it is erroneous to assume that a natural balance will develop. An analysis of the stakeholder–agent relationship must thus focus on what kind of relationship this is and how it can be managed.

When the corporation is seen as the result of a series of individual transactions, the corporation is a junction within a network of exchange relationships where transactions can be effected. These relationships can in a certain sense be viewed as contracts. The idea that a corporation can be viewed as a focal point within a network of contracts clarifies the position of the stakeholders. On the basis of the transaction-relationship, stakeholders create the corporation. If these transaction-relationships are viewed as contracts, stakeholders also become contracting parties. In two senses, one can even speak of a partnership role. The stakeholder is a corporate partner who not only forms part of the corporation but also a contract partner with whom the corporation conducts a transaction.

The relationships a corporation maintains with its stakeholders, who in fact make the corporation possible, can be seen as contractual relationships. Each contract defines the obligations the corporation has to meet with respect to the stakeholder in question. Among other rights, a bank that lends money has the right to be repaid at the agreed rate of interest. If the bank is a large creditor, it has the right to all the relevant information concerning corporate policy. The same holds true for shareholders. They take risks and therefore have the right to know how the corporation manages their money. An employee has a right to just remuneration for services rendered. In addition, employees have a right to the information that is necessary to understand how their own actions relate to the corporate goals. A customer has a right to accurate information about the product that he or she buys. It also includes information about, for example, the service that the corporation provides. These are clear obligations. The corporation accepts these obligations in order to secure the commitment and support of its stakeholders. Obligations differ depending on the kinds of stakeholders and types of relationships. Consequently, the agreements that corporations and stakeholders enter into differ and involve different responsibilities. The explicit or implicit contracts or agreements that are entered into with stakeholders determine the obligations of a corporation. By seeing the corporation as the focal point within a network of relationships with its stakeholders, the concept of a contract can be applied as an instrument for moral analysis.

THE (SOCIAL) CONTRACT THEORY OF CORPORATIONS

According to transaction costs theory, the corporate institution was created in order to generate greater prosperity through more efficient production. The obligations of the corporation do not extend beyond the obligations involved in the individual transactions conducted by the representatives of the corporation. Stakeholder theory shows that stakeholders have rights that must be acknowledged and respected by the corporation. The integration of transaction costs and agency theory into stakeholder theory and the acknowledgement of the normative element in both theories lead to a contract model of the corporation. In this model, the corporation is the focal point within a network of relationships with individual stakeholders that can be understood as contractual relationships. A social contract is, however, essential to ensure coherence between the different contracts with individual stakeholders. Thus, the contract becomes more than simply a transaction and a richer concept of the contract ensues. The contractual relations of a corporation are related to one another. We have seen it is better to refer to the corporation as a multiparty contract than a multitude of lateral contracts. Precisely this characteristic of a corporation calls for a broader framework. This framework can be seen as a corporate social contract. The participants are the internal and external stakeholders, who, through this social contract, bring the corporation into being as a social entity. Just as Rousseau held that the state comes into being as an expression of the collective will of the people, so, too, does a corporation come into being as a result of the consent of its stakeholders.[79] Entering into a contract confirms individual stakeholder trust in the social framework that is created by the collective stakeholders.

An important function of a corporate social contract is to provide a framework for embedding individual contracts. To be able to view the relationships of responsibility within a corporation as contractual accountability, the social contract must establish that the conditions for entering into a contract are possible. To that end, the social contract must, for example, formulate rules for setting priorities and limits that need to be considered in individual contracts and their termination.

The existence of corporate obligations can result in mutually conflicting demands being placed on the corporation. The balancing act between the various obligations cannot be mastered in the individual contracts. This issue can only be "resolved" by viewing the corporation as the effect of a contract with all the stakeholders. The corporation as a social contract brings institutions into the world that all parties are considered to be in agreement with and which regulate the distribution of scarce resources among the various stakeholders. These regulatory measures must offer the individual stakeholders sufficient grounds to consider the corporation a trustworthy partner.

A corporation acquires its identity through the corporate social contract. It contributes to coordinating the efforts of different stakeholders. It also provides a cooperative structure for internal parties. In addition, it binds activities over the course of time. In this way, the corporate social contract creates unity in a multiplicity of activities. The corporate social contract also provides an identity in the sense that it serves to distinguish the one corporation from the next. Examples include setting objectives for actions that are distinct from those of individual members and formulating a unique set of obligations. By understanding the corporation as the result of a social contract with its stakeholders, we can view the corporation as an independent collective entity. This is in keeping with our tendency to see an individual's actions as cohesive. We also employ the concept "identity" as a way to qualify that cohesion. In the same way, we can see the multiplicity of activities developed by a number of people as a cohesive whole. This unified framework or group identity drives the cooperation. Due to the existence of such an identity, it is possible to distinguish the corporation from its individual members as well as from other collectives. The corporate objective plays a crucial role in a corporation's identity. These are the instruments by means of which cohesion is assured. They make it possible to understand the actions of every employee as those of the corporation and to distinguish the corporation from its competitors.

The corporation as social contract comes into being through stakeholders granting their trust and being prepared to enter into relationships within an organizational framework. Internally, the social contract provides a structure to the parties and functionaries who are to give shape to the corporation. In this, society as a collective is an indirect, albeit crucial, party. Here, we can think of those living in the surrounding area, the region the corporation is located in, the developing world, future generations, the different authorities, and the media. A corporation often has an indirect relationship with all these parties. As a result, the corporation partakes in the broader social contract. The notion of the contract can be employed on four levels to bring the corporation's responsibility into focus:

1. The relations with individual stakeholders can be conceived as individual contracts and are directed at the reciprocal advantage of individual stakeholders and the corporation.
2. The internal relation of cooperation between subsidiaries, subdivisions, departments, and functionaries can be conceived as contracts. The objective is to align actions so as to effectively and efficiently meet responsibilities toward stakeholders.
3. By entering into individual contracts, stakeholders indirectly establish the corporation as social contract. Partly implicitly, the corporation as social contract sets boundaries on the individual contracts and creates the corporation as a distinct identity.
4. Through the corporation's active participation in society, an indirect contribution is made to the broader social contract. The social contract enables society's existence and determines the possibilities and limits of

corporate functioning. The social contract provides social parties with the basis for making agreements with a corporation.

Integrity and the corporation as social contract

In Chapter 2, we gave an exposition of the characteristics of the concept of integrity. Integrity requires that wholeness or alignment is strived for in three areas: between different values, norms, and ideals that motivate action; between words and deeds; and finally, with the environment. In Chapter 3, it was argued that the corporation can be conceived as a moral subject and that the concept of integrity can consequently be employed in connection with corporations.

The notion of the contract attempts to comprehend the relationship between conflicting values, norms, and ideals. The concept of the contract aims at resolving the tension between the ends (utilitarianism) and the means (rights). A contract translates these values into concrete requirements with respect to the behavior of a corporation (behavioral principles) and the characteristics of an organization (corporate qualities), thus working toward alignment of words and deeds. The individual contracts with stakeholders presuppose the social contract corporation and, furthermore, the corporation's participation in the social contract. In this way, the contract contributes to an alignment of individual agreements and the demands of society. The notion of the contract thus contributes to the realization of the three forms of wholeness or alignment that integrity requires.

Avebe

In January 1986, it looked like the time had come for Avebe, the Dutch cooperative potato company, to close down. The National Investment Bank (NIB) was not prepared to write off a 100 per cent government-guaranteed loan of $90 million, and further financing was also rejected. Some 2,200 people were on the brink of losing their jobs, and about 5,000 farmers connected with the cooperative were about to lose their sales outlet. Moreover, it seemed that the last in a series of environmental investments that the firm had committed to in the 1970s would be impossible to complete. What were the reasons behind these problems?

The processing of potatoes produces a lot of wastewater. At the end of the 1960s, Avebe produced as much wastewater as 14 million people do in a year— more than the entire Dutch population at the time. For years, the water had simply been discharged into the open ground. The proteins this water contained posed a serious problem. The rotting process generally killed off all aquatic organisms in its vicinity and smelled foul. For years, though, it was considered perfectly normal. It was seen as the price that had to be paid for the sake of securing jobs. However, at the end of the 1960s and the beginning of the 1970s this attitude changed. The public pressure on Avebe to do something about the stench became so great that the company presented an action plan in 1976. The plan to lay a pipe that would pump the water directly into the sea was rejected by the provincial authorities. People preferred purification at the source. However, that meant that several locations had to be closed down, while the few that remained operational had to run for longer periods a time. Eventually it was decided to build purification installations at the remaining locations. According to the plan, Avebe would be "clean" by 1981.

It quickly became apparent that this time schedule was unrealistic. The financial position of Avebe simply would not allow it. Since 1978, the company had recorded significant losses. It was the national government in particular that had to jump in several times to keep Avebe from going under. Due to these support operations, Avebe became the recipient of a large number of environmental investments. In 1986, only the site at Ter Apelkanaal needed to be rebuilt. The cost of the project was estimated at $35 million. Avebe's financial position was simply too weak for this.

Passing the buck

The adage "the polluter pays" raises a number of fundamental questions. For instance, what to do if the polluter is unable to pay? And if the polluter is a company, should it be closed down? Would that be fair to its employees and suppliers? Such measures would give the competition abroad a good chuckle since they are not faced with such tough environmental standards. Other questions pertain to who or what is the polluter. Where exactly does the responsibility lie? Who has to bear the costs of investment?

Classical economists would not hesitate to point at the owners or stockholders as the responsible party. In this case, the owners are the members of the cooperative: the suppliers/farmers. Thus, the farmers are responsible for paying for the required environmental investments. But these are special kinds of owners. Given the cooperative structure, the members can be asked to make good the losses suffered at the end of each year. Over the years, the farmers at Avebe contributed in this way to make good the loss of up to $70 million. This obligation pushed several of them into bankruptcy. To be sure, the farmers were in no hurry to contribute once again to investments that would not be directly profitable.

High interest rates exacerbated the problem. Avebe had almost no capital of its own. In order to pay for its environmental investments, Avebe had to borrow large sums of money. At a time marked by high interest rates, Avebe (with a government guarantee) ended up with heavy debts to the banks. In 1986, the company had $300 million in debt against a capital base of $15 million. It owed between $25 million and $30 million in interest. Without those interest rates, the company would have operated at a profit instead of a loss during the previous years. Leniency on the part of the banks would have been enough to save the corporation. The NIB, however, refused to cancel the debt of $90 million or to provide new financing. Avebe was seen as a bottomless pit.

The employees, too, felt that they had given up more than enough in the past. According to a Dutch labor organization,[80] a structural wage sacrifice of $7 million had been made in the 1982–5 period. In addition, about 1,000 jobs had been lost since 1980. According to the unions, if the employees were held accountable for this obligation, they would once again have to shoulder the costs of mismanagement that arose prior to 1984.

Local government was equally reluctant to help. Up to that time, Avebe had received preferential treatment. The usual environmental taxes had been waived since 1973 due to the precarious financial position of the firm. According to the province of Groningen, however, the environmental investments in question were normal business investments. Moreover, the province was not a lending institution, they said.

A special commission chaired by former Unilever CEO Goudswaard was instated to establish whether Avebe could be saved from bankruptcy. To secure the continuity of the company the cooperation of everyone was required. A lack of support from a single stakeholder group would have been tantamount to terminating the collective project.

Avebe's situation is a good example of the Dirty Hands Dilemma. Significant interests were at stake regarding its survival: employment for its members/ farmers; work for its employees (and indirect employment for the community); the return on investment for its creditors; and sales for its suppliers. The obligation to secure Avebe's future ensued from the rights of the *collective* stakeholders. For Avebe, these obligations implied that painful decisions had to be taken. If the interests and rights of *individual* stakeholders were a threat to the future of the corporation, the individual rights and interests would have to give way.

In this model, the individual stakeholders are all individuals or groups of individuals who had a right to be heard.

1. The cooperative was set up by and for the members/farmers, who collectively suffered hardships for years in the hope that Avebe would survive the setbacks. That was not out of altruism. The farmers thought they were serving their long-term interests as best they could. However, more was at stake than cold figures alone. The farmers felt obliged to contribute toward Avebe's survival despite the uncertainty of their future. The members/ farmers demanded fair compensation for their products. They had a right to expect Avebe to make an effort in this regard.

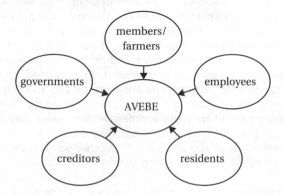

Fig. 5.1. Stakeholder model: Avebe.

2. The employees, too, had a right to be heard. They generally worked hard for the company for many years. They acquired knowledge and expertise that were tailored to Avebe and, therefore, of little worth to other companies. That meant that finding a new job would not be easy. In addition, their families were settled in the area and could not simply pick up and move. To ensure Avebe's survival, they took a cut in pay and collectively accepted the lay-off of co-workers during earlier reorganizations. Among other requirements, the employees also demanded a healthy working environment, reasonable pay, and a guaranteed future income. They too, were justified in expecting Avebe to work toward achieving these goals.

3. The nearby residents tolerated the stench for years. While this was originally seen as a sort of "natural phenomenon" and accepted, technological developments made a less-odorous production method possible. The nearby residents demanded that Avebe make an effort to help to create a liveable environment.

4. Time after time the creditors (banks and the government) made the continuity of the corporation possible by extending extra credit. However, they too had stakeholders to whom they were accountable. They required Avebe to handle the available capital with care, so that the amount lent could be paid back within the agreed time limit and at the agreed rate of interest.

5. Local and national government were constructively involved in the corporation for many years. The government itself represented a collection of rights and interests of stakeholders. The government required Avebe, as a corporate citizen, to take the livability of the environment of the nearby residents into account.

All of Avebe's stakeholders had legitimate expectations of the corporation that were based on implicit or explicit agreements. Its managers were therefore under constant pressure. It was their responsibility to serve the corporate interest as well as possible and, as an extension thereof, to honor the corporation's obligations toward its stakeholders. This responsibility conflicted—at least according to the managers who were trying to secure the continuity of the corporation with the above rights and interests in mind—with other requirements such as meeting tougher environmental standards. The environment, too, was a fundamental interest at stake. The toll the corporation was taking on the natural environment could be seen as a "sacrifice" (costs) made for the sake of the corporation's future. In this sense, the environment qualified as a special interest that could not be viewed as the "stake" of any one group or individual. For some people, though, the environment was a very concrete interest. This applied especially to the nearby residents. However, the environmental interest was also of a special nature in that damage to the environment would have far-reaching consequences for groups who could not yet be identified and whose voices may not always be heard. Future generations, for example, can neither be seen nor heard. Also in this sense, the environment was (and is) an interested party. In the case of Avebe, it was seen as a key interest: something that merited protection, just as it does today.

The natural environment is increasingly seen as an autonomous party deserving respect as an end in itself. However, here too, its lack of voice plays a role. If it is also regarded as intrinsically valuable, we need to monitor how it is treated. The government is an obvious candidate for fulfilling this function, but this role is not free of difficulties. The government does not represent the natural environment alone. It has to balance the expectations of all its stakeholders.

To keep Avebe afloat, its managers had to make painful decisions. The farmers received compensation below production costs; people were laid off; and the environmental requirements were undermined or postponed for as long as possible in order to keep production costs to a bare minimum. The rights and interests of the individual stakeholders were weighed up against the continuity of the corporation. In order to ensure its future, production had to be kept as efficient and inexpensive as possible while the company tried to overtake the competition. This often meant that the rights and interests of the individual stakeholders were forced to take a backseat. Whenever managers defend their actions with statements such as: "the competition forced me to do it," or "if I don't do it, somebody else will," or "I might as well just close shop," they are usually trying to justify their actions. Avebe, too, pointed out the pressure from abroad. German and French rivals had less stringent environmental requirements to meet, which allowed them to charge less for their products. The necessity of ensuring continuity—that was in the interest of the collective stakeholders—was therefore used to ignore the minimal obligations to individual stakeholders (including the environment).

Aided by the cabinet's Goudswaard commission, Avebe secured the minister's support. He was willing to contribute toward a final rescue operation—on the condition that the other parties pitched in. On the basis of this plan, Avebe succeeded in getting the other parties around the negotiating table and they, too, showed their willingness to contribute toward the rescue operation. In a real show of force, reconstruction of the company began in Ter Apelkanaal. In 1989, a new potato starch factory came on line and in 1990, the largest surface-area water purification plant in Europe became operational. The total cost of Avebe's whole clean-up operation came to an astronomical $350 million. By 1986, Avebe was out of the red. In the 1988/9 fiscal year, it actually recorded profits of some $17 million. For a time, it appeared as if Avebe's technological edge had become a competitive advantage. In the meantime, the environmental standards in Europe were tightened. It started to look like Avebe would be able to earn money with its expertise in this "new" field.

In the 1980s, the basis of trust in the corporation seemed to have disappeared. The activities of the Goudswaard commission focused on building a new basis for trust in Avebe. A new social contract was drawn up with all the parties and a new basis was laid for contracts with the individual stakeholders. Minimum obligations were established with respect to all stakeholders. The maximum obligations were also established with the relevant stakeholders. The environment was recognized as a stakeholder that had to be respected. As such, it became one of the corporation's minimum obligations. With respect to the farmers, the employees, the banks, and the governments, new minimum obligations were defined. By sitting around the table, the individual parties were able to see their relative obligations in mutual cohesion, which led them to adopt the new social contract. With respect to the farmers, Avebe took on an "extra effort" obligation. First and foremost, this meant a maximum effort to ensure the sale of their harvest at the best possible prices.

The Dirty Hands Dilemma is indeed extreme given that it necessitates a choice between at least two moral demands. Usually, it concerns a conflict between an end and the means: is it justified to sacrifice the rights and interests of the individual stakeholders (individual rights) in order to secure the collective good?

By viewing the corporation as a focal point within a network of relationships—and by understanding these relationships as separate contracts—it is possible to resolve the Dirty Hands Dilemma after all. The aim of a contract is to view the collective interests of the contracting parties in relation to the rights of the individual parties. To view the corporation as a collection of contracts, the corporation should also offer a framework for trust on the grounds of which the individual stakeholders will be willing to enter into the contract. The corporation as a social contract is the framework that grounds the individual contracts. By entering into individual contracts, one consents to the corporation as a social contract. This imposes limits on the contracting freedom inherent in the individual contracts while, at the same time, offering a basis for trust in the corporation for all its individual partners.

ETHICS IN BUSINESS

III

ETHICS IN BUSINESS

INTRODUCTION

As intellectually stimulating as they may be, ethical theories devoid of practical applicability have little to offer in terms of resolving concrete dilemmas. At the same time, practical concepts and criteria may be useful but risky to implement if they lack theoretical grounding. In the final part of this book, we employ the theories we have discussed to develop concrete ethical criteria for everyday business practice.

In Part I, we examined the respective classical ethical theories. Although these theories can be applied to corporations, it becomes problematic in circumstances where we are confronted with dilemmas. An important reason for this is that a dilemma is seen as a choice between two mutually exclusive obligations. Resolving a dilemma is always a painful choice. The notion of integrity was introduced to understand the connection between the respective conflicting values, norms, and ideals without negating the tension between them.

In Part II, we argued that it is justified and meaningful to conceive the corporation as a moral subject and that the concept of integrity can be applied to the corporation. In Chapter 4, the three dilemmas, the Dirty Hands Dilemma, the Many Hands Dilemma, and the Entangled Hands Dilemma that typify the functioning of corporations were discussed and analyzed in more detail. These three corporate dilemmas put the integrity of a corporation in question. That is to say, the wholeness of the motives, the coherence between words and deeds, and the relationship with the environment in which a corporation operates.

A closer analysis of the three corporate dilemmas revealed the ever-present conflict between the values, norms, and ideals. The enormous systemic pressure the leader or manager encounters and the problem of representative action also received attention as contributing factors in the difficulty in resolving dilemmas.

We proposed that a "solution" to the three dilemmas can be found in conceiving the corporation's relationships with its stakeholders, the relationships within the corporation, and the relations between the different roles as contractual relations.

Four types of contracts can be identified within an organizational framework. The relationships with stakeholders can be viewed as contractual relations. The internal relations, too, can be seen as contracts. The corporation itself can be viewed as the result of a social contract. Moreover, the corporation participates as corporate citizen in the broader social contract.

In Part III, the respective theoretical frameworks converge to contribute to an overarching corporate integrity model. In Chapter 6, the notion of integrity in relation to corporations is developed in further detail. Following this, the manner in which the notion of the contract can give concrete meaning to corporate integrity is examined. This will be executed by examining how the corporation can overcome the obstacles that stand in the way of establishing a corporate social contract. We will then look into the qualities an organization should possess to formulate successfully a corporate social contract so as to contribute to the resolution of the three corporate dilemmas.

In conclusion, Chapter 7 sets out a framework that corporations can employ to embed integrity into their daily business practices. The objective of this analysis is to offer an instrument to corporations and its representatives who take their moral responsibilities seriously to help them identify what these responsibilities are and how they can be communicated.

6

Ethical Criteria for Corporations

Co-authored with Pursey Heugens and
Hans van Oosterhout[1]

In this chapter, we formulate integrity requirements for corporations. These integrity requirements are grounded in the autonomy approach and corporate social contract theory. The integrity requirements can be applied to the actions of corporations but they also make demands on the organization as such. The integrity requirements that are developed are based on deductive as well as inductive research.

MUTUAL SUSTAINABLE ADVANTAGE

The three corporate dilemmas challenge the integrity of a corporation. A corporation is confronted with a multitude of legitimate stakeholder expectations, a diverse range of internal interpretations of the corporate mission, and varying contributions of the respective departments and employees. At the same time, employees have to combine their role as representative of the organization with additional justified expectations due to other roles that have to be fulfilled. Corporate integrity involves striving for a balance between conflicting values, norms, and ideals, pursuing equilibrium in the corporate ambitions and demands, and taking the social environment into account.

In viewing the corporation as a contract, concrete meaning can be given to the integrity requirements. The two defining characteristics of contracts are mutuality/reciprocity and effectiveness/sustainability. Accordingly, contractual relations have the aim of realizing sustainable mutual advantage for both parties.[2] On the corporate level, where all stakeholder contracts converge, sustainable mutual advantage requires creating a balance where there is tension between contractual obligations. The corporate mission should thus be formulated as realizing sustainable mutual advantage. In addition, a corporation should affirm the conditions that will enable the autonomous contract partners to have confidence that the corporate mission and agreements will actually be realized. When the corporation as social contract meets these requirements, the conflicting demands of the three corporate dilemmas can be reconciled.

In the business literature, the concepts "sustainability" and "sustainable development" are often used in connection with corporate social responsibility. These concepts point to a search for balance between the often mutually conflicting social expectations directed at corporations. In the 1960s and 1970s, the concept of sustainable development was introduced in the public debate about the impact of environmental degradation on the well-being of current and future generations.[3] In the early years, the main focus and concern was the depletion of natural resources such as raw materials and energy resources.[4] In the 1980s, the Brundtland report established the connection between environmental degradation and socio-economic development. Environmental sustainability can only be pursued if poverty and lack of education, for example, are addressed. In the 1990s, John Elkington[5] was among those who reflected on the consequences of sustainable development for corporations. He argues that corporations have environmental, social, and economic impacts on society and could contribute to sustainable development. Moreover, a positive impact in these spheres is a prerequisite for gaining the trust of society and ensures the continuity of the corporation. In this framework, stakeholders can be divided into three categories:

(1) those who have a stake in the economic prosperity the corporation generates;
(2) those who have a stake in the corporation's responsible treatment of the natural environment; and
(3) those who have a stake in the social progress the corporation promotes.

Corporate sustainability requires companies to perform responsibly in the economic, environmental, and social spheres. Corporations need to satisfy what Elkington calls the "triple bottom line" of profit, planet, and people.[6] In his view, it is possible to measure the value of all social impacts and to determine whether a corporation adds social value. In the final analysis, Elkington employs a utilitarian notion of sustainable development. It is, however, also possible to understand the notion of "sustainable development" in deontological terms. When we speak of a "license to operate" that corporations have to "earn," we invoke the rights of economic stakeholders, the natural environment, and social stakeholders. The notion "sustainability" can also be conceived in terms of justice. Benefits and burdens should be fairly distributed among stakeholders. It is even possible to interpret the concept in virtue-ethical terms. In that case, the emphasis is on the efforts of a corporation to add social value. In our vision, a crucial aspect of the meaning of "sustainability" lies in achieving the correct balance between stakeholder rights and interests and thereby adding value to society.

The ultimate aim of corporate functioning

Corporate integrity ultimately entails weighing the different stakeholder interests. To determine what exactly should be strived for with corporate integrity, we need clarity about which stakeholder demands we can regard as legitimate. On this basis, we can develop principles and virtues that constitute the minimum requirements for carefully weighing the different values, norms, and ideals.

Since stakeholder interests differ from one corporation to the next, giving a detailed, standardized exposition of these interests is not feasible. We therefore find it sufficient to summarize the targeted interests that different companies set down in their own codes. These are experienced as the more concrete obligations they have toward their respective stakeholders. To examine this we have, with the assistance of Friedl Marincowitz, analyzed a hundred codes of the largest (in terms of turnover) corporations in the world.[7]

Each stakeholder category in Table 6.1 depicts the responsibilities that corporations themselves describe in connection with the Dirty Hands Dilemma.[8]

The corporate codes also describe the objectives that are acknowledged in connection with internal cooperation. These are summarized in Table 6.2.

With respect to the tension that is experienced between the different roles that managers and other employees who represent the corporation have to fulfill (the Entangled Hands Dilemma) some concrete aims are also included. Table 6.3 gives an overview of these corporate goals.

Realizing all of the above objectives is possible only under ideal circumstances (free of dilemmas). In the face of conflicting demands, creative solutions should be sought that add value and do justice to these interests. Sometimes the interests are of such importance that they have to be fully realized even if it means that other interests cannot be fully realized as a result. The fundamental question thus becomes to what extent adequate principles are embedded in corporate conduct and what qualities the corporation possesses to guarantee optimal solutions and that justice is done to the interests that cannot be thoroughly realized.

There are two ways that corporations can guarantee integrity. First, focused action can ensure the integration of interests. Second, organizational measures can be taken to stimulate desirable behavior and to prevent undesirable behavior. In the section that follows, we shall propose and examine a set of principles for managing stakeholder relations with integrity. We start with two behavioral assumptions and deduce from them the behavioral principles for corporate integrity. Moreover, we develop a set of corporate qualities that facilitates the realization of optimal solutions for corporate dilemmas.

Table 6.1. Elements of stakeholder benefits regarding the Dirty Hands Dilemma

Stakeholder	Stakeholder advantage
Customers (or: consumers, clients, customers)	Supplying sufficient/good/high/superior/excellent/ reliable quality products and services and offering good value.
	Providing reasonable/competitive prices (and payment conditions) commensurate with quality.
	Providing products and services at the right place and time and in the right amount.
	Providing customized products for minorities.
	Helping customers to make the best possible use of the products and services.
	Preventing misuse/abuse of products.
	Sustaining or enhancing the health and safety of consumers.
Capital providers (or: stockholders, owners, investors)	Achieving a maximum/superior/satisfactory/sound/ competitive/acceptable/above-the-market-average return on the capital in the long term, in fair proportion to the level of risk in the line of business.
	Conserving, protecting and (above-the-market-average/ maximize) increasing the owners'/investors' assets/ capital.
	Repaying loans on time under reasonable conditions.
	Providing stable and secure job opportunities.
Employees (or personnel, staff, human capital, including applicants and temporary workers)	Making the best possible use of each person's skills, abilities, and knowledge.
	Encouraging/challenging/encouraging/optimizing personal development/growth/use of talents.
	Offering good/competitive/excellent terms of employment/compensation (according to employee efforts).
	Offering productive/responsible/challenging/pleasant/ enriching work and working environment.
	Creating/enabling/guaranteeing a balance between work and private life.
	Seeking mutually beneficial/long-term relationships.
Suppliers, joint ventures and contractors	Paying competitive market prices in reasonable time.
	Making reasonable demands.
Society (or community)	Respecting human rights/dignity (of those affected by the activities) and promoting them wherever practicable.
	Recognizing government's legitimate obligation to society (legitimizing government's authority).
	Observing, both directly and indirectly, all relevant local laws and regulations.
	Supporting public policies and practices that promote human development and democracy.

Table 6.1. (*Contd*)

Stakeholder	Stakeholder advantage
	Setting an example in countries where human rights are seriously and systematically violated and abandoning commercial activities in countries where this is made impossible.
	Supporting/participating in local initiatives that promote peace, security, diversity, and social integration. For example, collaborating with community organizations (e.g. government agencies and industry groups) dedicated to raising standards of health, education, product safety, workplace safety, and prosperity.
	Being a good corporate citizen through charitable donations, educational and cultural contributions, and employee participation in community and civic affairs.
	Adopting practices that permit the transfer and rapid diffusion of technologies and know-how.
	Making timely payment of tax liabilities.
	Doing business with stakeholders who do not systematically violate national and international social standards.
Competitors	Refraining from acquiring access to competitors' assets through improper means.
	Refraining from casting competitors in a bad light.
	Preventing incidents.
Natural environment (health, safety and environment)	Offering safe, clean, orderly, and healthy working conditions; eliminating/preventing injuries/incidents.
	Preventing harm to, and helping to optimize, animal welfare.
	Preventing/limiting/reducing/controlling negative environmental impacts such as the direct and indirect pollution of soil, water and air, noise, creation of waste products, and use of hazardous materials.
	Using energy and other natural resources effectively and prudently/efficiently.
	Collecting and having waste processed separately and re-using or recycling it where possible.
	Preventing/preserving natural environment or treating the environment with due care.
	Refraining from directly or indirectly appropriating natural resources if it would irreversibly damage the natural environment and/or threaten the livelihood of the community.
	Restoring and improving the safety and liveability of the natural environment.

Table 6.2. Elements of corporate benefits and indirect stakeholder benefits regarding the Many Hands Dilemma

Elements	Examples
Efficiency	Cost-awareness; proper execution of tasks; employee input; no duplication of tasks; efficient use of corporate means.
Cooperation	Proper use of corporate means for internal ends; teamwork; no counter-productive competition; mutual support; complementing each other; participation; communication.
Flexibility	Prevention of mistakes and timely correction of mistakes; making adequate use of opportunities.
Unity	Shared purpose; shared vision; complementary strategy of sub-units; consistent and unequivocal public image.
Effectiveness	Realizing collective objectives; improving output, improving quality.

Table 6.3. Elements of corporate benefits and indirect stakeholder benefits regarding the Entangled Hands Dilemma

Careful use of	Examples
Finances	No misuse of funds for personal gain; no diversion of funds (embezzlement); no unjustified billing of hours; correct handling of funds received; correct handling of expense returns.
Equipment and goods	Proper use of equipment and goods; safe use of equipment and goods; protection and conservation of equipment and goods; no neglect of maintenance; no reckless use of corporate vehicles; no misuse of corporate means of communication; no theft of equipment and goods; no taking home business equipment and goods for private use.
Information	No leakage of confidential/secret information; no unauthorized use of corporate information; no use of insider information when trading shares or other securities.
Staff	Careful treatment of personal information; good employee relations and a collegial work environment, no violation of personal integrity.
Authorities	No non-performance of tasks in return for money or favors from stakeholders; no acceptance of gifts from stakeholders; no favoring of friends and family; no conflicting sideline activities.
Working time	Sufficient effort; use of drugs and alcohol prohibited; no private activities during working hours; no unjustified calling in sick.

BEHAVIORAL PRINCIPLES FOR CORPORATIONS

The binding character of the different types of corporate contracts lies in the reciprocal character of the confidence that respective partners have that their agreements will be realized. In this section, we will examine the obstacles a corporation and the respective parties have to overcome to ensure the "bindingness" of contracts. On this basis, the behavioral principles can be deduced that should steer a corporation so as to function with integrity.

According to Oliver Williamson, two behavioral assumptions characterize contracting individuals: bounded rationality and opportunism. The first acknowledges limits to cognitive competencies. The second "substitutes subtle for simple self-interest seeking."[9] Since the corporation can be conceived as a multiparty contract, these behavioral principles bring into focus a number of obstacles to assuring the binding character of corporate contracts.

Bounded rationality

Modern institutional economics rejects the assumption that economic actors are capable of maximizing their utility. Instead, it holds that they are "*intendedly*" rational but only "limitedly" so. Decision-making takes place under the condition that is commonly referred to as bounded rationality. According to Herbert Simon,[10] three reasons can be advanced why actual behavior falls short of objective rationality. First, rationality requires complete knowledge and anticipation of the consequences following each choice. In practice, decision-makers always have fragmentary knowledge and a limited capacity to foresee all the consequences of their decision to enter into or decline a contract. Second, since the consequences of contractual decisions lie in the future, the imagination must take over the role of direct experience to attach value to these consequences. Imagination is, however, limited in its accuracy and consistency. Decision-makers often misjudge the significance of a particular decision. As a result, potential contracting parties often weigh their alternatives incorrectly. Third, rationality requires a selection from all of the choices open to a decision-maker. These choices usually include a selection from all potential contracting parties and from all possible contractual terms. Furthermore, rational contracting parties must consider all the governance modes that can be used to enforce the potential contract.

Within the corporate context, this bounded rationality is intensified by the fact that the corporation has to be seen as a multiparty contract. Viewed as a multitude of parallel contracts, the corporation has to make a choice if stakeholder demands conflict. Such friction will be the rule rather than the exception. After all, meeting expectations involves costs, in most cases at least in the short term. Every demand met means a reduction in the number of opportunities to satisfy others. This means that management has to employ the right criteria to weigh all these different demands. What should be considered as the corporate interest depends on the interpretations of the parties involved and cannot be determined in advance in most cases. Every agreement a stakeholder makes with the corporation has consequences for the other contracting parties. A corporation does not enter into a series of individual contracts with an equal number of stakeholders but into a system of mutually related contracts. Each stakeholder has expectations on the basis of each contract. The dynamics that follow make it impossible to predict the result.

Opportunism

The behavioral premiss of opportunism refers to a strong self-interest-seeking tendency.[11] Opportunism can take on particularly blatant forms such as lying, stealing, and cheating but, generally, more subtle forms are observed. In the context of contracts, opportunism refers to "calculated efforts to mislead, distort, disguise, obfuscate, or otherwise confuse,"[12] as well as to the tendency to renege on previous commitments in the light of new opportunities. Opportunism is a significant source of behavioral uncertainty in economic transactions, the latter being the "ultimate cause for the failure of markets and for the existence of organizations."[13] To assume that human agents are opportunistic is not to suggest that they will act opportunistically in every context. The assumption is rather that some individuals will be opportunistic some of the time. Moreover, opportunistic motives do not necessarily have to lead to opportunistic behavior. Opportunistic tendencies can be suppressed by establishing properly designed institutions that change the incentive structure of potential defectors in such a way that cheating and obfuscation are discouraged.

   Opportunism plays an important role in the corporate context. The very reason for the existence and the future of a corporation depends on stakeholders that are prepared to make a commitment to the corporation for something in return. As soon as the benefits no longer weigh favorably against the costs, a stakeholder can withdraw his or her support for the corporation.[14] If a crucial stakeholder takes such action, it could mean the demise of the corporation. This can be a major source of insecurity for other stakeholders and one that can stand in the way of long-term participation. This is particularly true if investments are made. An example of this is the employee who specializes in his field by taking extra courses. In doing so, he misses out on other opportunities for professional development that makes him less attractive to other potential employers. He is willing to make this investment only if the framework offered by the corporation guarantees the profitability of his investment.

The corporation can be seen as a cooperative association created by means of a social contract entered into by all interested parties. A cooperative association such as this is conceivable only if its purpose extends beyond the self-interest of the individual stakeholders at any time. A long-term cooperative association is possible only if its external objectives go beyond the self-interest of the stakeholders. In fact, all corporations aspire to certain ideals whether they are aware of it or not. If a corporation exists for a long time, there must be something that keeps stakeholders interested in taking part in the venture. This can be called "relational contracting" (as opposed to discrete contracting). Parties engaged in relational contracting are expected to place the value of their ongoing cooperative ventures at the same level or even above that of immediate economic gain.[15] It is not the discrete contract, but the relationship between the contracting parties that is primary.[16]

Contracting barriers

To examine the problems a corporation has to overcome to ensure the bindingness of the different (types of) contracts, we analyze two behavioral assumptions characteristic of the corporate context in relation to two key features of the general contractarian framework. This leads to a matrix of four perspectives on contracting, each combining a primary feature of the contract with a behavioral assumption characteristic of the corporate context (see Figure 6.1). On the one hand, these issues pose a threat to contracting: they are latent undermining factors. On the other hand, these four issues form the basis for developing moral criteria for binding contracts and handles for dealing with the fundamental corporate ethical dilemmas.

Desolation. The characteristic of mutuality means that contracts are not binding and will not come into being unless all parties envision a future benefit that can be derived from it. The behavioral assumption of bounded rationality, however, may interfere with the anticipation of such advantages by potential contractors. Bounded rationality can hamper the acknowledgement of reciprocity in a number of ways. Corporations may fail to acknowledge certain parties as potential stakeholders. It can be the result of a delay in acknowledging some

	Bounded Rationality	Opportunism
Mutual advantage	Desolation	Deception
Sustainability	Defeasance	Defection

Fig. 6.1. Contracting barriers.[17]

stakeholders or of overestimating certain stakeholder interests. This failure can manifest in side effects or unforeseen effects of corporate activities. Another possible cause is that the impact of corporate actions is underestimated, with the result that certain stakeholders are unintentionally excluded from a decision. Another possibility is that the effects manifest only in the long term and that these are simply not visible yet. This problem arises especially with regard to future generations. Bounded rationality poses an obstacle to reciprocity also in another sense. Corporations can misunderstand their stakeholders. This often occurs in the case of powerless or inexperienced stakeholders. One reason for this is that it is the powerful stakeholders who first and foremost set the corporate agenda. Bounded rationality with respect to mutuality may therefore lead to desolation. That is, neither the stakeholders nor the corporation can translate mutual interests into contracts. Corporations and stakeholders are isolated from each other through failure to link up with the contract that holds the business community together. Since contracts are the foundation and cement holding together corporations and stakeholders, potential contracting parties may ultimately fail to identify corporations as such. The reverse is also true. Because of similar cognitive problems, corporations may fail to acknowledge certain parties as potential stakeholders. Either way, the requirement of reciprocity may lead to desolation in the presence of bounded rationality.

Deception. Desolation is not the only obstacle to the requirement of mutuality. Not only is the mutual nature of contracts threatened by the lack of cognitive abilities among their potential parties, it is also negatively impacted by the presence of opportunistic tendencies in at least some of these potential contracting parties. Because of opportunism, contracting may be seriously impeded by calculated efforts to mislead or confuse contracting parties in constructing a mutually binding contract. An example of a well-known problem caused by opportunism in the context of contracting is that of "adverse selection."[18] This follows from the general unwillingness of contracting parties to reveal their true intentions or their intentional distortion of information that might reveal their inability to comply with the terms of the contract. Disrespect or arrogance also precludes acknowledging stakeholders as full contracting partners. Opportunism then leads to choosing in favor of the interests of the most powerful stakeholders and neglecting those of others. The obstacle of deception summarizes the problems associated with mutuality in the face of opportunism.

Defeasance. The second characteristic of the general contracting framework concerns the requirement of sustainability or effectiveness. This characteristic refers to the general condition that a contract's bindingness depends emphatically on complying with its terms. Again, the condition of bounded rationality can seriously frustrate the practice of contracting. Because of the limited anticipatory capacities of agents in the business context, contracting parties may end up being bound to a contract that they cannot—through no fault of their own—reasonably honor. Such is the case, for example, when the conditions under which parties have entered into a contract have changed dramatically while the contract itself provides no provisions for such contingencies. It must be noted, though, that all contracts are incomplete in this sense for no contract can cope with all future contingencies.[19] Ultimately then, the central question becomes whether a contract can still be considered binding under drastically changed circumstances. This question pertains to the problem of defeasance; the possibility of a contract becoming null and void owing to unforeseen circumstances.

Defection. Defection stems from a confrontation between the effectiveness of the agreement and opportunism. Straightforward examples from a game-theoretical perspective—such as the well-known prisoner's dilemma—demonstrate that it is often worth while for actors to defect on the extant commitments while all other parties remain faithful to them.[20] Combined with the fact that all contracts offer room for fraud and deceit because of their inevitable incompleteness, any contractual context provides a vast array of stimuli to renege on obligations. *Ex-post* or post-contracting opportunism is often referred to in the literature as a "moral hazard."[21] This refers to the tendency of a contracting party to fail to comply with the terms of the contract even though everyone has agreed to them. Given the propensity towards opportunistic behavior of at least some of the contracting parties, the problem of defection is always real and present.

The basic principles for regulating corporate stakeholder contracts

How can a corporation give concrete meaning to its responsibilities in anticipation of these obstacles? Put differently, which shortcomings will stakeholders blame corporations for if their interests are not satisfied? Or, under what circumstances can stakeholders reasonably be expected to consent to the corporation's conduct even if their own interests are pushed aside? In short, what are the basic principles or minimum obligations that should govern stakeholder relationships?

The behavioral principles we present here were distilled by means of inductive research (which principles at the root of contractual relationships are actually experienced in real life?)[22] combined with a deductive approach (which principles can we logically deduce by interpreting stakeholder relationships as contracts?). These inductive and deductive analyses enabled us to develop criteria for corporate behavior that form the preconditions for resolving the corporate dilemmas responsibly. The goal is to establish the principles that apply to *all* stakeholder contracts within the corporate context.[23]

On the basis of our research, we differentiate five principles that can be used to address the four contracting problems discussed above.[24] Four principles (empathy, fairness, solidarity, and reliability) correspond respectively with the

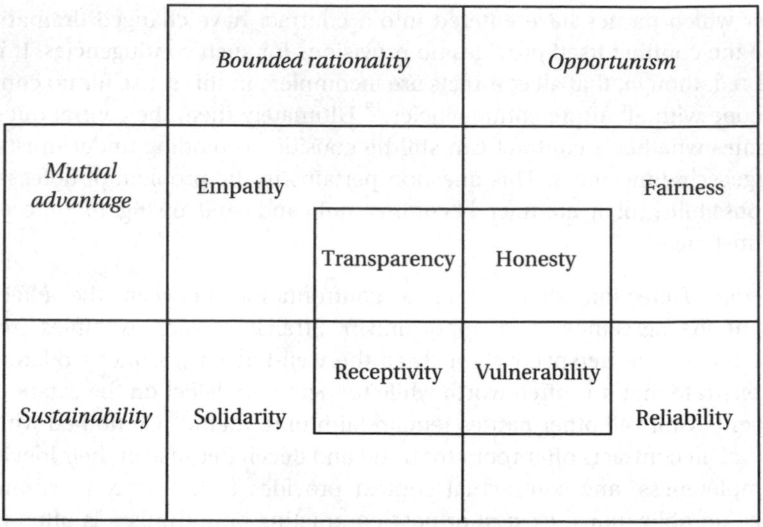

	Bounded rationality		Opportunism
Mutual advantage	Empathy		Fairness
		Transparency	Honesty
		Receptivity	Vulnerability
Sustainability	Solidarity		Reliability

Fig. 6.2. Behavioral principles.[25]

four contracting problems defined. The principle of openness applies to all four contracting barriers but its meaning differs with respect to each. It is accordingly translated as transparency, honesty, receptivity, and vulnerability. The behavioral principles and their significance to the practice of contracting are illustrated in Figure 6.2.

If a corporation violates one or more of these principles the contracts in question can be considered void, as these principles are the essential components of a binding contract. Safeguarding the principles in the relationship between company and stakeholders is a mutual endeavor. They also enable us to develop principles for the conduct of employees and other stakeholders who have access to corporate assets (i.e. the Entangled Hands Dilemma). By viewing job-related relationships between co-workers, departments, and business units as contracts, we can also develop principles for conduct regarding the Many Hands Dilemma. Solving the internal dilemmas of entangled hands, and many hands (i.e. guaranteeing unity) can enhance, for example, the reliability of the corporation in its relation with external stakeholders. In this sense, resolving the Entangled Hands and Many Hands Dilemmas is a precondition for getting the core of the problem of dirty hands.

The principle of openness

Openness is a key principle and a necessary condition for securing mutuality and sustainability in the face of both bounded rationality and opportunism. Each contracting barrier requires a different kind of openness. Openness

Table 6.4. Behavioral principles in the literature[26]

Behavioral principles	Based on general (political) contract theory: general contracting principles	Based on economic or corporate contract theory: contracting principles for business	Based on other theories: stakeholder principles
Openness	Kant (1785); Rawls (1971)	Freeman (1994); Gauthier (1986); Phillips (1997); Velasquez (1998)	Bird (1996); Blok (1978); Cameron (2000); Gassenheimer et al. (1998); Nash (1990); Preston (1999); Sharma & Vredenburg (1998)
Empathy		Brock (1998)	Bird (1996); Gassenheimer et al. (1998); Tone Hosmer (1998)
Fairness	MacNeil (1980); Rawls (1971)	Brock (1998); Dees (1992); Donaldson (1989); Gauthier (1986); Keeley (1988); Saldu (1995); Freeman (1994); Freeman & Evan (1990); Phillips (1997); Velasquez (1998)	Beugré (1998); Deutsch (1975); Etzioni (1988); Gassenheimer et al. (1998); Nash (1990); Preston (1999); Shankman (1999)
Solidarity	MacNeil (1980)	Bucklin (1973); Calton & Lad (1995); Donaldson & Dunfee (1999); Hirschman (1970); Keeley (1988)	Gassenheimer et al. (1998)
Reliability	MacNeil (1980)	Freeman (1994); Gauthier (1986)	Calton & Lad (1995); Das & Teng (1998); Nash (1990); Preston (1999); Shankman (1999)

can take on four different forms: transparency, honesty, receptivity, and vulnerability.

The sub-principle transparency. To address the barrier of desolation, parties that envisage at least some shared interest in cooperative arrangements must have sufficient knowledge of the interests and capacities of other potential contractors (i.e. parties to the contract). This enables potential contractors to recognize each other as genuine partners and makes the realization of contracts possible. Even if contracting parties succeed in recognizing each other as agents with common interests, they might still have reservations if they do not know with whom they are dealing. The principle of authentic transparency therefore requires that potential contractors provide potential contracting partners with sufficient and relevant information with respect to their goals, behavioral standards, and intentions. Particularly relevant is information that is likely to affect the interests and subsequent decisions of co-contractors. If fellow contractors are insufficiently informed (for example, a consumer who is incapable of understanding the dangers of a certain product) the contract is no longer binding.[27]

A free choice is an informed choice. Contractual relationships must thus be based on the free exchange of information and a clear understanding of what the contract purports to be. In this regard, a contract would lose its bindingness if, for instance, consumers purchased a particular product that later turned out to be different from what they were promised. Stakeholders are entitled to know what is expected of them and what they themselves can expect. For example, a company that requires employees to spend at least five years working abroad to qualify for a top position should inform prospective employees of this well in advance. When a corporation abuses the ignorance of a stakeholder, he or she is reduced to nothing but a means to realizing the corporate ends. In that case, the "other" is not treated as an autonomous party to the contract. Although revealing information may make potential contractors vulnerable to several kinds of exploitative behavior, desolation is a far worse fate. Transparency and opening up to provide relevant information is not only important in the pre-contractual phase. It continues to be of critical importance also after concluding the contract, especially if contractors change their policies or when unforeseen changes in the terms of the contract need to be made. Stakeholders and internal actors have the right to information that is relevant to their position as contractor. Especially with respect to fundamental issues, it is imperative that the corporation presents stakeholders with a clear vision of its integrity.

The sub-principle of honesty. To address the problem of deception, the mere disclosure of information is not enough. Contractors must also be able to rely on its truthfulness, particularly given the propensity toward opportunistic behavior in the economic sphere. Disclosure must therefore be complemented with honesty. As Donaldson puts it, "productive organizations must avoid deception or fraud."[28] In negotiating a contract, both parties must refrain from intentionally misrepresenting the facts of the situation. From a Kantian perspective, misrepresentation of information cannot be universalized because lying is a parasitic activity. It is only worth while to lie when others are likely to assume that we are telling the truth and when others are likely to tell the truth. Rawls argues that if misrepresentation were not prohibited, fear of deception would inhibit the freedom to enter into contracts. According to Velasquez, misrepresentation is also coercive: people who are intentionally misled act like the deceiver wants them to and not as they would have freely chosen to act had they known the truth.[29] As Bird puts it:

[I]t is wrong to lie, to deceive knowingly and intentionally because lying is a form of hypocrisy: organizations speak as if they attempt to comply with the elements of the contract at the same time as they knowingly act to ignore or contravene the elements they overtly embrace. In many settings, not disclosing amounts to the same thing as lying. When one holds in silence information that others would consider vital if they knew about it, then not disclosing can be as intentionally misleading as if one uttered a direct lie.[30]

Accurate information should not only be disseminated among stakeholders. Communication between departments, employees, and managers should also be open and honest. With respect to the Entangled Hands Dilemma, employees should, for example, not only be expected to use corporate assets in a transparent way, they may also be expected to reliably report on possibly conflicting activities.

The sub-principle of receptivity. The disclosure of relevant information is necessary but not sufficient to address the barrier of defeasance. Bounded rationality requires the firm to be open to the opinions of its stakeholders and that departments, employees, and managers are open to the opinions of one another. It also requires employees to be open to opinions of their employer regarding the Entangled Hands Dilemma. The principle of receptivity refers to the ability of contractors to listen to and acknowledge the problems, questions, and suggestions of fellow contractors. For a binding contract, the parties need to be given the opportunity to raise relevant issues. According to Dunfee et al.,[31] an individual should be able to exercise voice: the right to present your side of the case. A general unwillingness to be open to stakeholders is certainly blameworthy. "Even though others do not inherently possess rights to our sympathy, consent or even empathy, they do possess a right to receive from us a minimal hearing if and when they address us with legitimate moral concerns."[32] When contractors refuse to listen to the claims, demands, and concerns voiced by fellow contractors, their grasp of the pay-off structure of a given contract diminishes. Contractors are then more likely to misrepresent the interests of contracting partners by projecting their own isolated beliefs upon them. This obstructs the possibility of mutual learning by the parties to a contract, which reduces the potential organizational benefits a contract produces.[33]

The sub-principle of vulnerability. A precondition for entering into a contract with a stakeholder is a social framework that imposes sanctions on the failure to fulfill mutual obligations. A contract that can be concluded completely free of consequences is worthless. Vulnerability is the guise of openness that addresses the contracting problem of reneging. In short, this principle refers to the willingness of a contractor to be corrected by other parties or institutions, either by constructive criticism or by an appropriate set of sanctions. Such sanctions need not be financial—they can just as well entail an obligation to permit public scrutiny. This renders vulnerability more encompassing than receptivity. Contractors that are vulnerable to sanctioning by other contractors are generally perceived to be more trustworthy because of the stake they have in realizing the terms of the contract they are a party to. A high degree of accountability serves reliability. If contractors can be held accountable to conform to the terms of the contract, they will be considered more reliable than if they cannot.[34] Passing on accountability by hiding behind other stakeholders (with excuses like "the competition made me do it," "I have to abide by laws of the country where I operate," and "I just follow orders") undermines the vulnerability and with it, the integrity of the contractor. Moreover, just like the principle of receptivity, vulnerability stimulates processes of contractor-driven learning by using information, ideas, and suggestions from contracting partners.[35]

The principle of empathy

The contracting barrier of desolation is partly addressed by the principle of empathy, which requires contractors to put themselves in the position of their potential partners. The resulting change in perspective enables potential contractors to anticipate the mutual advantages that a contract will bring. This imaginary act of trading places does not necessarily lead to either positive (i.e. sympathy) or negative (i.e. antipathy) feelings for the other party. Hosmer[36] emphasizes the importance of imagination in this respect; in particular the ability to see and acknowledge the full mixture of potential benefits and harms that may ensue from the action or inaction of potential contractors. When contractors are unwilling to put themselves in the position of other parties to the contract we may speak of "moral blindness."[37] It is clear that such blindness lowers the probability of developing lasting contractual relationships. Moreover, moral blindness diminishes an actor's foresight with respect to the advantages and disadvantages of a potential contract. Moral blindness decreases the chance of a good contractual relationship between the corporation and its stakeholders and of good internal relationships.

The contractor should therefore also consider the full range of intended and unintended effects of the decisions and choices that are made. It means more than just mapping the consequences for the contracting partners prior to making a decision. It also implies keeping careful track of the effects of policy implementation and ensuring that the preconditions of a fair contract remain intact. For example, if a company states the risks of its product in its instructions, we should be able to expect that company to have checked the actual effects of such instructions. In some countries, for instance, many people misinterpret the toothbrush symbol on candy packaging as proof of dental safety, while it actually means exactly the opposite. If it were really the company's intention to warn consumers about the risk of cavities, it should have come up with a more effective symbol. However, if it simply wishes to wash its hands in innocence, no research into a more appropriate symbol will be conducted. Empathy regarding the Dirty Hands Dilemma has to do with the organization's ability to keep looking out for issues and problems, foresee and envision the consequences of current activities, and interpret or appreciate issues and problems adequately. With regard to the Many Hands Dilemma, the principle of empathy entails among others that functionaries and departments make the effort to gain insight into the responsibilities and objectives of other actors in the corporation. Empathy regarding the Entangled Hands Dilemma implies, for example, that employees are able to assume the corporate interest and take in a representative stance. It also means that employees should be capable of seeing or foreseeing the consequences of their conduct for the corporation.

The principle of fairness

Fairness is the primary principle for solving the problem of deception. Fairness of a contract demands that contractors voluntarily consent to its terms. Especially when power relations are asymmetrical, a corporation must ensure that stakeholders consciously and willingly agree to the terms of the contract. No contracting party ought to be forced to enter a contract under duress or coercion.[38] If the other party is compelled to accept the terms of the contract, the contract cannot be binding. An employee who is unable to avoid the dangers of certain types of hazardous work due to an oversupply of labor does not freely and consciously accept the "conditions" of the contract. A manager who uses intimidation, aggression, or blackmail to spur an employee to improper behavior abuses his position of power. A contract is a free agreement whereas coercion and consent are mutually exclusive. A contractor must refrain from exploiting a situation where a contracting partner is induced to act irrationally, that is, disregarding his own interest. To extract consent to an agreement that the stakeholder would not make if he or she were thinking rationally, the corporation is exerting undue pressure to coerce.

The principle of fairness is fundamental when differences in wealth and power among potential contractors are prominent. In the presence of inevitable inequalities, fairness requires that equal cases be treated equally and unequal cases unequally in proportion to their inequality (Aristotle's principle of equality[39] or what Etzioni calls "symmetry.")[40] Everyone must therefore have equal opportunities for entering into a relationship with the corporation. This requires the corporation as well as internal actors to be unbiased, independent, and objective. Restraint in accepting business gifts is therefore in order given that it can erode objectivity and independence (i.e. steadfastness) in a relationship *and* keep better suppliers from getting their fair chance. Such practices that tamper with competition can undermine the very system that makes contracting possible. Fairness in contractual relationships demands the conscientious avoidance of unjustifiable discriminatory treatment of other members of a microsocial community.[41] Fairness demands a contribution to realizing the terms of the contract and sustaining contractual relations that is in proportion to the benefits that are reaped from the contract.

Fairness also encompasses reversibility.[42] Regarding the Dirty Hands Dilemma, reversibility implies that the organization applies its expectations of others also to itself. The same standards apply to both parties. Inconsistencies arise, for instance when the restrictions on accepting business gifts are much greater than on giving them. Here, the corporation's buyers are expected to shy away from situations where their clear thinking might be clouded by accepting business gifts. At the same time, the corporation itself puts its customers' buyers in the very same position, thereby spurring them on to make market-inefficient decisions. To take another example, any company that checks to make sure that its suppliers do not use child labor but that fails to undergo such an audit itself is inconsistent. Double standards can sabotage the fairness of the relation in that the company places higher requirements on its suppliers than on itself. Reversibility with respect to the Entangled Hands Dilemma means that employees should treat the corporate assets as they would treat their own.

The principle of solidarity

It has already been argued that a contract is only fair when the terms of the contract are consciously and voluntarily consented to by all parties involved. Calton and Lad[43] argue that contracts can only be considered voluntary on the condition that the option to exit the contractual relationship is included in the contract. Contracts are always incomplete because no contractor can foresee all possible future contingencies. An explicit clause in the contract guaranteeing the option to exit the contract safeguards the principle of conscious and voluntary consent.[44] Unforeseen contingencies may alter the benefits of a contractual relationship to one or several of the parties involved. If these changes are fundamental, contractors ought to have the right to leave.[45] Most importantly, as MacNeil[46] points out, the right to exit assumes contractual solidarity on behalf of the contracting parties. Contractors should therefore refrain from seeing a slight change in the contract's pay-off structure as a reason to exercise that right. Although contractual relations entail the right to re-evaluate the contract in the light of new circumstances, the parties concerned should at the same time respect the value the contract represents to other contract partners and resist opting out too readily. Loyalty involves the decision to withstand the relationship under adverse conditions.[47] For example, it is not acceptable for a powerful corporation to point a finger at a stakeholder not fulfilling obligations if it does not do so itself. The same applies to internal relations of cooperation. Likewise, an employer may legitimately expect a certain degree of flexibility from his or her employees, for instance to be willing to work overtime or even to change functions or location if required. The freedom of an individual stakeholder unilaterally to terminate a contact with the corporation must be constrained. If the withdrawal of a stakeholder has drastic consequences for others' ability to fulfill their contracts, conditions need to be established to limit the use of the exit clause. According to Freeman,[48] a contract between A and B that imposes costs on C should give C the option to become a party to the contract under renegotiated terms. The rationale behind this is that each stakeholder will want assurance of the possibility to renegotiate in the event that it becomes C.

The principle of reliability

The principle of reliability best counteracts the problem of reneging. This principle requires that contractors align their words and actions—that they do what they have promised or committed themselves to. Not only does the corporation say what it does—it also does what it says. According to Dunfee *et al.*, promises should be kept.[49] Ethical behavior implies fulfilling consciously and freely made promises, both of an implicit and an explicit kind. According to Kant, the failure to keep a promise undermines its very value. It goes further than merely keeping those agreements that have been made explicitly. Implicit agreements also have to be honored. An employer spying on his employees in order to increase productivity or to prevent employee idleness or theft does not necessarily infringe upon any explicit agreements of the labor contract. This act is, nevertheless, in conflict with the implicit agreement to respect the privacy of employees. In the context of contractual compliance, the value of reliability can be broken down into a number of components.

Reliability requires sufficient coherence and uniformity in the behavior of the different constituencies (internal stakeholders) comprising the corporation as a contracting party. Reliability is clearly in jeopardy if one part of a corporation complies with the terms of a contract while another part blatantly disregards it. The same applies when an employee agrees to a request from another department without notifying his manager, or when an organization's communication with employees and stockholders about a particular issue is inconsistent. The principle of corporate reliability requires that the internal problems of many and entangled hands are adequately managed. The corporation must function as a team and form an independent entity (i.e. the Many Hands Dilemma) and the employees must represent the interests of the corporation (i.e. the Entangled Hands Dilemma). Employees that leak confidential information, perform conflicting sideline activities, and spread gossip about colleagues or managers undermine the coherence and unity both of stakeholder and internal contracts. Reliability refers to the independent stance of corporations amid multitude stakeholder expectations and demands. Functioning as an independent entity in the matrix of stakeholder forces requires steadfastness of corporations. In this regard, it is a corporation's duty to capitalize on its opportunities. It should aim for the best possible deal every time it sits down to negotiate. For example, a purchasing department that does not try to achieve the best price/quality ratio will fail to perform properly. Steadfastness also means that painful choices sometimes have to be made that can clash with the rights and interests of certain stakeholders. It requires courage to dirty one's hands and to stand one's ground under compromising circumstances. Reliability also demands that contractors display relatively predictable behavior over the course of time. Parties that are predisposed to changing their behavior at random are likely to renege on their contractual obligations.

Reliability also requires the corporation to take heed of the entirety of its contractual obligations. Whenever a corporation is viewed as a social contract, this perspective is tied to a certain point in time. Shortsightedness can pose great risks for both management and stakeholders who fail to take into account the expectations of future stakeholders. Since most relationships with individual stakeholders involve a series of contracts linked together in time, a contract with an individual stakeholder can have consequences for the corporations' relationship with future stakeholders. Each single contract should therefore be seen within the context of the broader picture. Agreeing to all demands and expectations without being able to realize them undermines the reliability and, by implication, the integrity of the contractor. Corporations should therefore take relevant stakeholders into account in other contracts. For example, when party B inflicts damage on organization A, also indirectly damaging stakeholder C of A, A should, out of solidarity with C, call B to account and, if possible, claim damages (sanctions). C places its trust in A to treat the interests of C with care in the relation A has with B. Reliability also means that employees should call one another to account for abusing corporate assets and neglecting responsibilities. Finally, reliability means that the contract partner is not automatically led by the most powerful partner.[50]

The principles in practice

The behavioral principles should form the foundation of all contracts. The corporation that fails structurally to embed these principles is morally incompetent. Stakeholders have a right to blame a corporation for such ineptitude and to take counter measures or even dissolve the contract if necessary. Not only does this put the effectiveness of the specific stakeholder contract in danger but it also jeopardizes the corporate social contract. After all, failure to satisfy the conditions of a contract with one stakeholder can affect the contracts with the others. Moreover, these behavioral principles are the moral preconditions

Table 6.5. Contracting principles

Contracting Principles	Aspects
Openness	Transparency The contractor provides sufficient, authentic, and relevant information on who and what it is (its values). The contractor provides sufficient, authentic, and relevant information on what it stands for (the dos and don'ts). The contractor provides sufficient, authentic, and relevant information on its aims/ideals. Honesty The information provided by the contractor on who it is reflects reality. The information provided by the contractor on what it stands for reflects reality. The information provided by the contractor on its aims reflects reality. Receptivity The contractor listens to criticism, questions, and suggestions from its contracting partners. The contractor acknowledges just criticism from its contracting partners. The contractor facilitates contracting partners to give criticism and suggestions and to pose questions. Vulnerability The contractor accepts blame on the basis of just criticism of its contracting partners. The contractor changes its conduct on the basis of just criticism of its contracting partners. The contractor compensates contracting partners for breaching the contract.
Empathy	The contractor shows serious awareness of its (potential) contracting partners' interests and corresponding expectations. The contractor shows serious awareness of the autonomy of the contracting partner and the other potentially conflicting contracts the contractor and the contracting partner each may have. The contractor shows serious awareness of the main and side effects that its actions will have on its contracting partners. The contractor shows serious awareness of the extent to which the contracting partners' interests are actually realized.
Fairness	The contractor ensures that its (potential) contracting partners are not pressured into giving consent to the contract. The contractor treats all current and potential contracting partners equally. The contractor distributes the benefits and burdens of the relationship with the contracting partners in proportion. The contractor applies its own expectations of its contracting partners to itself.

Table 6.5. (*Contd*)

Contracting principles	Aspects
Solidarity	The contractor offers its contracting partners adequate opportunities to terminate the contract in the event of material, unforeseen changes in the conditions of the relationship.
	The contractor refrains from terminating the contract in the event of minor changes.
	The contractor ensures that its contracting partners refrain from terminating the contract in the event of minor changes by helping contracting partners.
	The contractor involves those contracting partners who are affected by the consequences of changes in the contractor's relationship with other contracting partners.
Reliability	The contractor respects explicit and implicit promises.
	The contractor acts in a coherent, uniform, and predicable manner.
	The contractor takes heed of each contract in other contractual relations.
	The contractor calls contracting partners to account (or others that infringe upon the contract) and sanctions them.

for the effectiveness of any social contracting system in the corporate context. A systematic failure to fulfill any one or more of these principles therefore undermines the reliability of the economic system. There are thus both (long-term) instrumental and normative reasons for honoring these principles.[51] The most basic reason for corporations to honor these principles is that it legitimizes business.

As long-term and complex stakeholder relationships imply constant re-contracting, the pre-contractual principles (i.e. empathy and fairness) should also be in force in the contracting phase. The principle of openness facilitates the re-contracting process. If unforeseen changes occur during the contractual phase, the corporation should be able to adapt the contract on the condition that it is transparent and honest and that it adopts a position of vulnerability.

These behavioral principles are minimum obligations. On the one hand, they are the necessary, generally applicable requirements for governing stakeholder relations. On the other hand, they are requirements that do not place excessive demands on the corporation, on internal actors, or on managers and employees as individuals. The degree to which a contractor can be expected to keep to these principles depends on the extent to which the other contracting party respects them. Whether these principles become embedded in the relationship depends on the efforts of both parties. If one of the contractors fails to stick to these principles, the other party has reason also to pay less attention to honoring the principles. For example, a corporation cannot be expected to show receptivity if a stakeholder is unwilling to build a constructive relationship. As the code of IHC Caland asserts: "Everybody who addresses us on the basis of actual involvement and understanding of our activities and position, can expect an open attitude from us." In other words: a stakeholder who shows no interest in engagement can count on much the same attitude from the company.

A crucial question that arises is how to determine whether a relationship qualifies as a contract, which in turn indicates when these principles apply. A corporation that fails to observe the principles can always claim that no contract was in place with the party in question and that the principles were thus not applicable. The pre-contractual principles (i.e. empathy, fairness, transparency, and honesty) apply to all stakeholders who have the potential of being contract partners (i.e. parties that have something to offer the corporation and that are willing to do something in return). The principles of solidarity, reliability, receptivity, and vulnerability apply solely to contracts entered into on the basis of mutual agreement. These contracts can be dissolved with the consent of both parties (taking into account the other stakeholders who could experience negative consequences as a result). Annulment is also possible if any one of the parties fails to fulfill the terms of agreement or contradicts one of the principles (in so far as the others still observe the principle of solidarity). Stakeholders who at first glance may appear to have only demands (i.e. stakeholders who only want something from the corporation but have nothing to offer in return) may, on closer inspection form sub-parties of the corporation's contract with society.[52] Society's representatives can therefore require the corporation to honor the contractual principles in its relationship with these parties as well. The remaining question—who qualifies as representative—will not be addressed in this book.[53]

Examples of principles in practice

A number of examples that cover the embeddedness and absence of the behavioral principles can be distilled from the cases that have so far been discussed. IHC Caland can be praised for its firm, open, and authentic stand on the limited role of corporations in relation to host country governments. Likewise, it can be praised for frankness on its opinion that the human rights situation alone of any one country is no reason to stop doing business there (transparency: +). By refusing to back down, IHC did not withdraw from the contracts it had entered into with its customers (reliability: +). At the same time, IHC Caland was severely censored by social groupings such as politicians, pension funds, and trade unions because it failed to show the slightest sensitivity to the issue in its communication with the public. NGOs expected more understanding from the corporation than was conveyed by a statement of the irate chairman of the Management Board: "What are you getting steamed up about, our platform lies 160 miles off the coast" (empathy: −). It was only when IHC finally sat down with NGOs to discuss the recently published code that they could appreciate the corporation's reasoning. After this the public storm died down (transparency and vulnerability: +).

In the KPN case, several other principles came to the fore. For example, following a press report on a deal with the Chinese government, who at that time was accused of violating human rights, KPN was unable to indicate whether and, if so, which ethical norms it applied in selecting its business partners (transparency: −). The code project KPN launched in 1998 and that culminated in its roll out in 2000 focused on matters such as improving its authenticity. It aimed at articulating an unambiguous position on the most poignant dilemmas it faced and conveying a clear message to the public (transparency: +). The fairness of KPN's relations with consumers was questioned as the corporation was accused of misusing its monopoly position to inflate rates (fairness: −). KPN was also reproached for erecting higher than acceptable exit barriers by charging customers exorbitant fees for switching to other providers (solidarity: −). At the same time, however, KPN demonstrated its commitment to the disabled. Blind and visually impaired consumers can purchase a special telephone at sharply reduced prices, while people who are deaf or hard of hearing have access to speech recognition equipment (empathy: +).

After the sinking of the *Herald of Free Enterprise*, the owner of the ship, P&O, was reticent in cooperating in reconstructing the disaster while it undertook major efforts to clear its name (vulnerability: −). With regard to the Brent Spar and Nigeria issues, Shell was severely blamed for social reticence (openness: −). Four years later Shell is cited as an example of corporate transparency (openness: +).[54] Shell did not hesitate to admit its reticence and sought opportunities to right its wrongs and improve the organization. It was in this context that it set down its accounting and reporting process (see Chapter 7) to enhance openness toward the outside world. And in the Avebe case, stakeholders were given the opportunity to pull out of the business, while they were encouraged to stay on at the same time (solidarity: +). The final result was a reasonable compromise that was found acceptable by one and all (fairness: +). Having discussed the principles for governing stakeholder relations, we will now turn our attention to the ethical qualities against which corporate intentions can be judged.

CORPORATE QUALITIES

Corporate qualities are those characteristics embedded in the corporate structure and culture that encourage employees to engage responsibly with the three fundamental ethical dilemmas. By examining the extent to which these qualities are embedded we can judge the moral character of the organization. Which ethical qualities can corporations possess or acquire?[55]

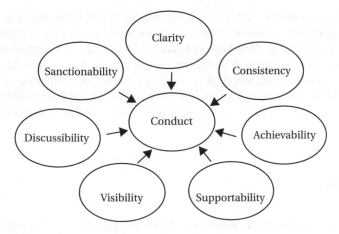

Fig. 6.3. Corporate ethical qualities.

In order to obtain a systematic overview of the factors that comprise corporate intentions, we[56] studied a large number of real-life cases where the organizational context led to the negation of stakeholder expectations and the violation of the contractual principles.[57] On the basis of the conduct displayed in these cases, we developed criteria for intentions of a contractor, that is, a corporation. The categorization of these corporate deficiencies has led to the identification of seven corporate qualities, each of which relates to the three fundamental dilemmas. These qualities address the shortcomings identified.[58] The qualities we identified are depicted in Figure 6.3 and will be discussed in the following section.

Clarity

Corporate clarity about employee contractual responsibilities is the first criterion that delineates the ethical quality of the organizational context. Clarity refers to how accurate, concrete, and complete the organization's expectations are of the moral conduct of its employees. Applied to the Entangled Hands Dilemma, this quality refers to the level of organizational clarity about how employees should handle corporate assets. The likelihood of an imbalance in this area is greatest where employees act at their own discretion with no guiding frame of reference. A lack of clarity regarding the acceptance of gifts, for instance, can lead to uncertainty among employees, the idea that "anything goes" and the inflation of ethics, and an ever-widening gap between practice and the desired norm. By the same token, vagueness regarding their tasks and job-related responsibilities can prompt everyone to think that someone else is taking care of certain matters while nothing is in fact being done. It can also produce situations where responsibilities are easily passed on to another level and where employees hide behind a lack of knowledge and purposefully keep themselves blind to the facts (the dimension of the many hands). With regard to the Dirty Hands Dilemma, clarity refers to employee awareness about the responsibilities that the corporation acknowledges toward its stakeholders. It is, after all, necessary to be aware of stakeholder responsibilities in order to satisfy them.[59]

Consistency

Consistency concerns the extent to which the organization's expectations of employee conduct are coherent, univocal, unambiguous, and compatible. Employees emulate the behavior of superiors. This referent behavior can work quite subtly, even without the referent being aware of it. Management is an important reference group in this regard. A popular, yet no less truthful, expression is that ethics starts at the top.[60] Sincere leaders set the example for sincere followers, just as ill-disposed leaders set the standard for ill-disposed followers. The organization may very well stipulate clear responsibilities to guide employee conduct, but if the behavior of referents undermines these standards, employees receive inconsistent signals. Adequate guidance requires the desired norms and values to be exhibited by the referents at all times. The example set by management is probably the most frequently cited factor behind ethical and unethical behavior.[61]

Achievability

Not only is it important that the corporate culture and structure meet the requirements outlined above, ethical expectations should also be practicable. The quality of achievability concerns the degree to which the corporation enables employees to meet the expectations regarding the three fundamental corporate dilemmas. No expectation can be fulfilled unless it is feasible. Although dilemmas by definition contain expectations that cannot be satisfied simultaneously, it certainly does not mean that these cannot be properly balanced. The corporation should therefore refrain from saddling its employees with unrealistically high expectations and provide them with realistic handles for balancing dilemmas. It must, for example, see to it that employees have access to the resources necessary for realizing legitimate expectations. As to the coordination required in the case of the many hands dimension, specific responsibilities might be impossible to achieve due to insufficient authority, lack of time and means, inadequate knowledge and skills, or lack of information.[62] Achievability in the dirty hands dimension has to do with whether the corporation refrains from creating unrealistically high expectations on the part of external stake-holders and leaving them to employees to fulfill.[63] Achievability in relation to the entangled hands issue means that employees are capable of realizing expect-ations in connection with the organization's assets. For example, zero tolerance regarding the private use of corporate assets (such as the personal use of office supplies) is generally untenable within this context. In short, the organizational context must be focused on resolving dilemmas instead of unnecessarily creating further dilemmas.

Supportability

Supportability pertains to whether employees endorse the proper use of cor-porate assets (entangled hands), close coordination with their immediate col-leagues and supervisors (many hands), and the active realization of the interests of stakeholders (dirty hands). The corporate context either stimulates or hinders employee commitment. If employees feel that they are not taken seriously or are not treated fairly, it may be at the cost of their loyalty toward the corporation along with the care they usually take in their use of the organization's assets. They might even try to balance the scales of justice[64] by engaging in unethical conduct (entangled hands). If a corporation's employees cannot trust their co-workers or immediate supervisors, the whole organization could suffer a breakdown in coordination and cooperation (many hands). An inability to endorse the corporation's policy toward its stakeholders indicates inadequate support for corporate activities. As a result, the entire corporation stands to lose face (dirty hands). The embeddedness of the quality of supportability refers to the capacity of employees to integrate the interests of the corporation, their co-workers, and external stakeholders. The central question with regard to this organizational quality is to what extent the organization encourages its employ-ees to recognize and realize the legitimate expectations concerning the three fundamental dilemmas.[65]

Visibility

Visibility concerns the extent to which employee conduct and the effects thereof are manifest. Where clarity refers to the ethical expectations regarding employee behavior (input), visibility concerns the consequences of their actions (output). Visibility breaks down horizontally and vertically. Vertical visibility refers, for example, to the degree of manager awareness of unethical employee behavior (top-down) or vice versa (bottom-up). Horizontal visibility concerns the degree to which employees are aware that a colleague has acted unethically. In a context of high visibility, employees generally succeed in modifying or correcting their own behavior or that of their co-workers, supervisors, or sub-ordinates.[66] Research suggests that ethical behavior is influenced by the individual's perception of the likelihood of getting caught as this dark prospect is preceded by its own shadow.[67] Visibility fosters a balance with regard to the three fundamental dilemmas. As to the entangled hands issue, visibility discourages fraudulent behavior and facilitates a proper response in the event that an employee has indeed overstepped the line. Visibility regarding the many hands issue promotes good teamwork so that the employees can function as a unit. By ensuring a bridgeable distance between employees and stakeholders, the likelihood that Dirty Hands Dilemmas will defy an ethical resolution is reduced.

Discussibility

According to Solomon and Hanson:[68] "Ethics becomes a problem in most companies not because of ethical indifferences of ignorance but rather because it is just not part of the conversations." Discussibility refers to the degree to which employees can talk about the Dirty Hands, Many Hands, and Entangled Hands Dilemmas. Just as with the ethical quality of visibility, discussibility can be divided into horizontal and vertical components. A context with a high degree of discussibility means, for example, that lack of clarity on certain expectations is open to discussion, that unethical behavior can be discussed, and that employees must account for their conduct. A closed organizational context is marked by the fact that criticism is neither encouraged nor accepted. In such an environment, employees are never called to account for their actions and they are encouraged to keep their mouths and ears shut. Bad news is not appreciated: the culture is characterized by an attitude of killing the bearer of bad tidings, screening bad news, paying lip-service, and blocking out negative information.[69]

Sanctionability

A corporation that embodies the above qualities remains vulnerable if it tolerates incidental cases of unethical behavior as opposed to punishing people for them. In failing to punish unethical behavior, the corporation spreads ambivalence regarding the proper balancing of dilemmas. It conveys the message to employees that upholding norms and values is not a priority. In this regard, Treviño *et al.* assert that "Discipline for rule violators serves an important symbolic role in organizations—it reinforces standards, upholds the value of conformity to shared norms and maintains the perception that the organization is a just place

Table 6.6. Ethics qualities of corporations

Ethics qualities	Organizational dimensions		
	Entangled hands— responsibilities with regards to the organization.	Many hands— responsibilities within the organization.	Dirty hands— responsibilities on behalf of the organization.
Clarity	Employees have clarity about how they should treat the assets of the organization.	Employees have clarity about their job-related responsibilities.	Employees have clarity about what stakeholders expect of them.
Consistency	Referents make enough effort to treat the assets of the organization with care.	Referents make enough effort to fulfill their functional responsibilities.	Referents make enough effort to satisfy stakeholder expectations.
Achievability	Expectations on how the corporate assets should be treated are feasible.	Employees have the means to fulfill their job-related responsibilities.	Created stakeholder expectations can be satisfied.
Supportability	The organization fosters support for the careful treatment of the corporate assets.	The organization fosters support for adequate coordination between employees.	The organization fosters support for satisfying stakeholder interests.
Visibility	Consequences of how the corporate assets are treated are visible.	Consequences of how job-related responsibilities are fulfilled are visible.	Consequences of how stakeholder expectations are satisfied are visible.
Discussibility	Dilemmas, problems, and criticism regarding how the corporate assets are treated can be discussed.	Dilemmas, problems, and criticism regarding how job-related responsibilities are fulfilled can be discussed.	Dilemmas, problems, and criticism regarding how stakeholder expectations are satisfied can be discussed.
Sanctionability	Staff is sanctioned if assets are deliberately mishandled.	Staff is sanctioned if functional responsibilities are deliberately neglected.	Staff is sanctioned if stakeholder expectations are deliberately ignored.

where wrongdoers are held accountable for their actions."[70] The corporation as a social contract offers mechanisms to ensure that employees and managers comply with the contracts. Thus, the seventh and last ethical organizational quality is sanctionability. Sanctionability refers to the degree to which people can be punished for irresponsible conduct and rewarded for responsible behavior. Such punishments or rewards can be either formal (for example, an extra bonus) or informal (for example, a pat on the shoulder, a wink, or a compliment). Sanctions constitute important behavioral stimuli and are therefore a relevant aspect of the organizational context.[71]

These qualities are often interrelated. Visibility is a necessary precondition for revealing and discussing unethical behavior, and subsequently sanctioning it. Furthermore, a supervisor will in most cases talk to an employee about his unethical behavior only if the supervisor himself behaves ethically (consistency). By describing the extent to which these qualities are embedded in corporate practices, we are able to judge the ethical intentions or efforts of the corporation. These qualities unambiguously encourage employees to take proper care in their treatment of stakeholders (the Dilemma of the Dirty Hands), corporate assets (the Dilemma of the Entangled Hands), and one another (the Dilemma of the Many Hands).

Examples of qualities

We have illustrated the application of the corporate qualities of companies elsewhere.[72] Here we will give an example of the insufficient embeddedness of each quality.

Insufficient clarity: Construction workers start retailing the bricks left over from a project they worked on, since management could not decide what to do with the leftover materials. In a very short time, a bustling retail trade develops after unusually large orders are deliberately made on behalf of the company.

Insufficient consistency: The owners of a grocery store set a bad example by frequently taking things out of the warehouse during working hours to give to their family and friends. In reality, only small amounts are involved and it is a question of passing it from one hand to another. Because the warehouse staff is aware of these practices, they have an excuse to take things home themselves. Once started, the practice progresses from bad to worse. By the time these practices finally come out into the open, the wife of one of the employees is selling products from the store at the street market.

Insufficient achievability: Employees at an investment fund are not permitted to trade privately in a particular security over a period of twenty-four hours before or after a transaction by the fund in that security. It is impossible for employees to consistently observe this rule as (a) they are often unable to forecast what the fund will do within the next 24 hours; and (b) they are unable to reverse private transactions when it becomes clear that the fund has traded in the same securities. The result is a lack of employee support for both the letter and the spirit of the rule. It subsequently becomes common practice for employees to privately trade in securities of which it is internally known that the fund will shortly be buying or selling a large package.

Insufficient supportability: The employees of a large production company treat company vehicles recklessly and carelessly. During working hours, employees regularly hold rally contests with the company vehicles on the company site. It is also common practice for employees to urinate in the company vehicles, to stick sandwiches into the radio fascias, and to disregard the traffic rules on site. If the oil light comes on showing that the oil needs to be topped up the general reaction is "no need to do anything, the light will go out of its own accord." Among other things, the employees blame their behavior on the lack of any sense of company pride. Employees feel little if any involvement in the company as they feel that management never displays any appreciation of their efforts.

Insufficient visibility: A bank employee who controls the validity of customer signatures and whether accounts can cover the requested transfers also checks fund transfers that are made by the bank's internal employees. The checked transfer slips are placed in an internal mail pouch that is not sealed until the end of the day. This gap in the processing process leads to several cases of internal fraud (employees putting unchecked transfer slips directly into the pouch when the controller goes to lunch or the washroom) before the internal audit department becomes aware of this organizational failure.

Insufficient discussibility: An employee becomes aware of the sideline activities of one of his co-workers. When he tries to discuss it with fellow employees, he is roundly attacked. He then approaches management but the incident is ignored. Before he can take his complaint to the CEO, the powerless employee is fired for dubious reasons.

Insufficient sanctionability: A partner at a large law firm has been harassing his female secretaries on a regular basis for several years. Such sexual harassment varies from questionable comments on the clothing of the secretaries to sexual advances and mandatory dates after work. Two secretaries claim to have been forced to kiss the partner. The victims of his advances assumed that they would be fired if they lodged a formal complaint. When the Board of Directors and the Director of Personnel are finally informed of their partner's behavior, they refuse to take action against the accused. The reason for their apathy is the director's contribution to the success of the firm. He is good for winning more than ten new major clients a year.

THE CORPORATE INTEGRITY MODEL

The criteria discussed are depicted in Figure 6.4. Corporate integrity is expressed in the extent to which a corporation is equipped to realize mutual

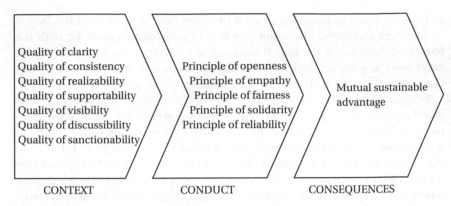

Quality of clarity
Quality of consistency
Quality of realizability
Quality of supportability
Quality of visibility
Quality of discussibility
Quality of sanctionability

Principle of openness
Principle of empathy
Principle of fairness
Principle of solidarity
Principle of reliability

Mutual sustainable
advantage

CONTEXT   CONDUCT   CONSEQUENCES

Fig. 6.4. The Corporate Integrity Model.

sustainable advantage through balancing conflicting values, norms, and ideals. Corporate integrity requires that the ethical qualities are embedded in the corporate context so as to manage employees in an adequate manner and so that stakeholders are acted toward in a fashion that is in keeping with the distilled principles. Where qualities function as criteria that can be employed to evaluate the corporate culture and structure, behavioral principles function as criteria to assess the corporation's relationships and behavior. Because the context stimulates conduct and conduct builds the context, principles and qualities are interrelated. For example, the principle of openness is stimulated by the qualities of visibility and discussibility. Although the organizational qualities and behavioral principles are connected, the one cannot be translated into or replaced by the other.

Can the corporation be blamed for each violation of these integrity criteria? The developed criteria constitute the integrity of the corporation, with the implication that an inadequate realization of the criteria impairs the integrity of the corporation. The extent to which a company is blameworthy or acts in a blameworthy fashion depends on the degree to which the criteria are disregarded. The greater the violation of the criteria, the greater the blame. The degree of blame depends also on the achievements of other corporations. For example, if only 75 per cent of employees feel that their dilemmas are discussible, the corporation is lacking and can be held accountable. However, should it turn out that the percentage in many other organizations in the region or sector is only 50 per cent, then the first organization is faring quite well. Finally, the blameworthiness of a corporation depends on the mutual relation between the integrity requirements that are realized or violated. A company that disregards stakeholder interests will be blameworthy in relation to the extent to which the principles and qualities are properly embedded. But when the principles and qualities are not imbedded, the blameworthiness will decrease in accordance with the decrease in damage a corporation inflicts on stakeholders.

How can we apply the Corporate Integrity Model to the bribery case discussed at the end of Chapter 4? In the case of bribery, the question is not simply whether bribes are actually paid and accepted. What is also at stake is what the organization does to prevent offers of bribes and what steps are taken in the event that bribes are made. Moreover, in making a moral judgment, the effects of bribery on stakeholders should be taken into account. Even if no bribes have been paid, the corporation does not necessarily deserve to be judged as moral. Less praise is in order if it proves that the organization has not taken a single precautionary measure while employees continue to do business that is prone to corruption (for example, in developing countries, involving major orders or complex negotiation constructions). However, to criticize heavily a corporation that is completely free of misconduct for its lack of a formal policy would generally be taking things too far. After all, any corporation can explain the absence of a clear policy by referring to the strength of its culture to fill in the gaps. Nevertheless, even if a lack of policy gives no cause to criticize a corporation, an inadequately developed policy does give reason to call the corporation to account.[73] If an incident occurred, the corporation would win little praise for waiting to develop a policy until after the proverbial horse has bolted. That is why it is wise for corporations to set out to implement structural procedures, even if the culture is up to standard.

A corporation that fires employees for accepting bribes can still be worthy of our praise if its culture and structure contain maximum measures to discourage employees from accepting bribes. Moreover, the visibility of such cases highlights how well the organization manages its dilemmas. Some organizations pay bribes not only to secure the interests of their primary stakeholders (a big order can safeguard employment at the local level) but also to make a positive contribution to the local community. Their line of reasoning is often as follows: "Everything considered, the objections against paying bribes are outweighed by the social benefits if we win the order. Our rival is after all also willing to pay bribes but this company shows less respect for local human rights than we do." Therefore, even if the corporation pays bribes, it could still be acceptable when seen from the perspective of its overall effect. However, should it prove that the qualities are not embedded in the organization's culture and the payment of bribes affects the autonomy of the recipient, then matters cannot be viewed in such a positive light.

There are two reasons why it is important to align the three perspectives that converge in the corporate integrity model. First of all, good intentions have to be converted into good deeds, which have to have the desired results. The corporate qualities create a context in which principles can be honored. And it is in those relations where these principles can be discerned that the desired effects can be achieved. Qualities therefore need to relate positively to principles, which, in turn, need to be related to sustainable mutual and balanced advantage. On the other hand, this means that we need to work in reverse by first outlining and judging the desired output and then relating this back to the desired conduct and input. Conduct enjoys moral value only if it adds something to the output. By the same token, input is devoid of moral value unless it contributes to conduct and thus indirectly to the corporate output. In short, input, conduct, and output are the three lines of approach relevant in determining the coherence of a corporation's ethics. In the next chapter, we shall show how the resulting Corporate Integrity Model can be applied and implemented in practice.

KPN

KPN distributed its business code two years after the internal project *Ethical and Socially Responsible Business* was launched in 1998. This undertaking had the aim of developing policy so as to secure its "license to operate" as well as better to define its identity. The team in charge of the project was led by the CEO and consisted of ten high-ranking line managers and ten representatives of functional departments. As part of their research for developing the code, the supporting project team conducted interviews with almost a hundred key figures at all levels of the organization. They also organized eight meetings to give employees throughout the organization an opportunity to articulate their own dilemmas and to analyze stakeholder expectations and issues. Almost 250 actual dilemmas were gathered. Just over half exhibited the dirty hands structure, almost 30 percent contained a many hands component, and almost 35 percent had an entangled hands dimension.

After ample deliberation, KPN chose not to formulate a too detailed code of conduct. The idea was not for it to become a compliance guidebook that would enable employees to determine exactly what to do under which circumstances. The content was formulated in general terms to stimulate employees to translate its meaning in practice themselves and to open up dilemmas for discussion. The code is therefore concise and the wording is personal. Also, rather than stating desirable and undesirable behavior in detail, it was decided to articulate stakeholder responsibilities (the desired output) and the effort required from the organization (the desired input) in general terms. The code makes explicit what KPN stands for. It formulates the core values that ground the company and that characterize the conduct of KPN representatives. It also articulates what they aim for—the key responsibilities towards stakeholders. As such, the code represents the identity of the company and the image of the organization as a whole.

Eight stakeholder groups were named in connection with the responsibilities of the organization. They are: customers (excellent service), employees (a stimulating and sociable work environment), shareholders (satisfactory growth in value), business partners (joint growth), competitors (vigorous and fair competition), the environment (protection), society (socially engaged), and NGOs (measuring conduct against international standards). The effort of the organization was captured in four core values: professionalism, innovation, commitment, and respect. The three dilemmas surface repeatedly in these core values. Professionalism, for example, is described as "Customers and business partners are able to build on what we do for them" (dirty hands dimension); "We all have clear responsibilities toward each other, as well as expectations" (many hands dimension); and "We treat the company's resources with care. We apply high standards when using modern means of communication such as the Internet and e-mail" (entangled hands dimension).

The title of the code, *What Unites Us*, alludes to the content of the code: that which binds employees and stakeholders to KPN. Defining the collective responsibilities of employees stimulates cooperation and partly addresses the question of many hands. As employees identify with the organization, support for a careful resolution of the question of entangled hands should grow.

The code describes the terms of the corporate social contract. It presents a clear vision of the responsibilities KPN is willing to take on, but also of what cannot be expected of the organization. The principle of openness is the golden thread that runs through the description of stakeholder responsibilities. This is reflected in its commitment to timely and adequate communication with shareholders, open relations with suppliers, dialogue with NGOs, and disclosing information to employees concerning relevant corporate developments. Discussibility is a central ethical quality in the KPN code. The corporate culture should create the conditions where dilemmas and behavior can be discussed. "Managers are committed to creating an open climate in which employees and their superiors hold each other accountable for observance of the code."

Some assertions clearly indicate that the code articulates ambitions or aspirations. For example, the KPN code asserts that the quality of products is excellent, that the law is observed, that the work environment is pleasant, and that employees are aware of societal expectations of the company. The possibility does exist that employees will not take the code seriously, especially if they cannot relate it to their experiences. As observed in Chapter 2, it is the identifying commitments that are characteristic of integrity. In this regard, the CEO asserts in the code: "The Company Code is an ambitious one and some of the things it describes have not yet been achieved. It is therefore essential that we continually encourage each other to put the code into practice. This is precisely the kind of commitment that unites us."

In the foreword of the code, it is stated that the document applies to employees, business partners, and the companies in which KPN has a controlling interest or management control. In signing their employment contract, new employees also bind themselves to the code. Also of importance is the manner in which compliance to the code takes place. The last paragraph of the code emphasizes the individual responsibility of employees to address each other on conduct. Employees are also encouraged to address their immediate superiors should he or she display questionable behavior. In the event that a desired response is not forthcoming, employees can direct queries and reports to the *KPN Security &*

Integrity Helpdesk, a kind of ethics hotline. With this, transparency is aimed at within the organization (incidents are made visible) and sanctionability is increased (unacceptable behavior is not tolerated).

KPN started a large-scale implementation phase in the summer of 2000. All subdivisions were expected not only to communicate the code within one year but also to embed it in the culture and structure of the company. As from summer 2001, the company monitors the compliance with the code of all subdivisions.

After accepting the draft version of the code in September 1999, the Board of Management was still haunted with problems. They were confronted with the question of how this new foundation could be truly integrated into daily life and into the business model. They also wanted to avoid the whole process becoming just another one of those cultural programs employees were fed up with. KPN found a solution close to its heart. At the end of 2000, KPN started with the translation of the code into an integrative business model. The business model had to place the different organizational activities (like plans, processes, projects, functions, and departments) in relation with one another. The eventual model, *The Connector*, reflects the relation between the input (the four core values) and output (the eight core responsibilities). In the right part of the model, the output, each area reflects a stakeholder responsibilty (the added value). The left part consists of areas which reflect the organization itself, the input, like leadership, strategy and policy, culture and technology. The code offers the basis for the model to be filled in. Each sentence in the code is translated as a target in at least one of the areas in the model. The integrity of the model is defined by the coherence within and between the areas.

Since May 2001, *The Connector*—the "dashboard" of the organization—is accessible via the KPN Intranet. At the push of a single key, all employees can examine real-time information on *The Connector* and, depending on individual authority, access specific information about different departments. Each area reflects the norms and indicators relevant to it and the current state of affairs in the area along with historical data. The real-time information that is made available on complying with the code makes for adequate management supervision. In the next chapter, we will see how companies can develop integrity and which good indicators for measuring integrity can be identified.

7

Incorporating Corporate Ethics

The criteria developed in Chapter 6 can be used as guidelines for moral leadership and for formulating a code of ethics. These criteria also serve as a framework for embedding a code in the corporation, managing stakeholder relationships, and auditing and reporting on corporate integrity. These applications correspond to four phases of developing integrity that are discussed in this last chapter. As the Corporate Integrity Model is integrated into these phases, the true form and content of the balanced company will finally emerge. We shall see that each of these phases logically flows from the definition of (corporate) integrity as it is defined in Chapters 2 and 6.

SETTING UP AN INTEGRITY MANAGEMENT PROCESS

This chapter sets out how the integrity management process can unfold. Managing integrity is an iterative process and the choice of activities and the order in which they are undertaken depend greatly on the particular position of the corporation in question and on the activities already completed. In this discussion, we focus on four successive stages that structure the process and provide a solid basis for further development. We discuss the importance of management commitment, the development of a code of ethics, implementing the code, and auditing its effectiveness in practice. It is essential that senior management demonstrate commitment to improve and guarantee corporate integrity. Although the pressure to improve corporate integrity might come from the outside world or from middle management or even one's employees, it is ultimately senior management that has the final say on how and to what extent the corporation should improve its integrity. Given that management fulfills the function of role model, its unequivocal support for the undertaking is imperative for successful implementation. The phase that follows is the development of a code of ethics. This entails defining and specifying the corporation's responsibilities, principles, and virtues. It requires reflection on the desired integrity as a point of departure for boosting the commitment of the parties

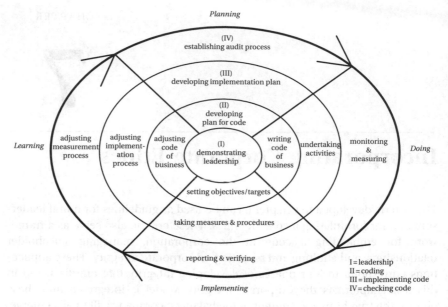

Fig. 7.1. The Integrity Management Process.

involved (management included). From a communication and auditing perspective, it is sensible for a company to put its targeted integrity in writing in the form of a code. To activate the code in the corporation's actual business practices it must be properly implemented. This means bringing the corporate culture and structure in line with the code. The fourth phase, the auditing process, includes checking whether the code is honored in practice, communicating the auditing results, and making adjustments if necessary. Finally, each of the four phases (management commitment, code formulation, code implementation, and auditing), breaks down into the basic steps of "plan, do, implement, and learn."

The integrity management process consists of the following steps that are discussed in more detail in the following sections:[1]

(1) Leadership:
Senior management makes a visible and lasting commitment to corporate integrity and toward employees and their external stakeholders. Leadership permeates the entire process.

(2) The code formulation process:
The company determines, in so far as it is possible, how the code of integrity will be developed.
The company inventorizes the dilemmas employees are confronted with and the legitimate expectations of (internal and/or external) stakeholders with the aim of defining the corporate values, norms, and responsibilities. It then decides what to include in the written code of business. Both

internal and external stakeholders may be consulted in the discussion about dilemmas, expectations, and what to include in the code.

The code provides the basis for formulating specific objectives and outcomes to be pursued on the operational level. The code's feasibility may also be considered at this stage.

The code may be revised in the light of operational experiences.

(3) The implementation process:

The specific objectives are used as the basis for drawing up an implementation plan, i.e. how these objectives and results can be achieved.

The corporation engages internal and/or external stakeholders to discuss the code and arrangements are made to guarantee compliance.

On the basis of suggestions from employees, additional procedures and measures may be established to encourage employees to implement the code and to strengthen the engagement process with the relevant external stakeholders. To keep these to a minimum, management can identify and remedy significant shortcomings in the procedures and measures in advance of implementation.

Adjustments are made to the implementation plan on the basis of experience gained during this process.

(4) The auditing process:

An audit plan is drawn up on the basis of the implementation plan and the content of the code. This includes establishing the crucial processes and the key integrity indicators to be used for monitoring those processes.

The key integrity indicators are used as the basis for measuring and monitoring of the code's implementation on central and local level.

The results are verified and reported internally and/or externally.

Adjustments are made to the audit process or other processes on the basis of insights gained during the monitoring and reporting processes.

The pivotal role of stakeholder dialogue

As already noted in the discussion of the principle of openness and the virtue of discussibility in Chapter 6, stakeholder dialogue forms an important component of any corporation's integrity. From a strategic point of view, stakeholder dialogue can serve a number of purposes:

(1) to acknowledge stakeholders as serious sparring partners;
(2) to influence positively stakeholder perceptions concerning corporate intentions or certain negative events;
(3) to influence positively stakeholder expectations about corporate behavior;
(4) to illuminate the background to ethical issues by explaining the relevant dilemma and the potential benefits to be gained versus the stakeholder interests that will have to be sacrificed;

(5) to develop operational standards and indicators through sharing dilemmas with stakeholders;

(6) to create awareness of stakeholder expectations at all levels of the corporation; and

(7) to account for the corporation's integrity so as to secure stakeholder support and to obtain suggestions for improvement.

In principle, stakeholder dialogue should permeate the entire process. However, it is mostly conducted only at certain key steps of the process (i.e. step 1.2: developing a code of business and phase 4: checking the code). Also, the targeted results and content of the dialogue will depend on the particular stage in the process. Generally speaking, it is possible to distinguish three different forms of stakeholder dialogue. In stakeholder *consultation*, the corporation gathers information from stakeholders related to its planned activities such as the code of business and the reporting indicators to be employed. In the stakeholder *engagement* stage, the stakeholders follow the company's performance to respond with constructive criticism. Finally, during stakeholder *feedback*, stakeholders present the corporation with an evaluation of completed activities, for example on the quality of the code. Figure 7.2 illustrates these types of stakeholder dialogues step by step.

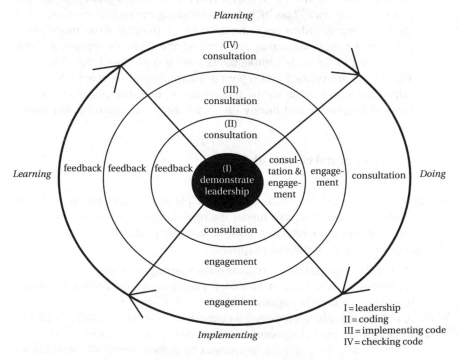

Fig. 7.2. Stakeholder dialogue in relation to the Integrity Management Process.

Generally, it is not necessary to sit down at the table with each and every stakeholder. The idea is to give them sufficient assurance that dilemmas are being balanced and that their fundamental rights and interests are treated with adequate consideration. A good stakeholder dialogue takes account of every relevant stakeholder perspective. A working definition of a "relevant perspective"—which varies from company to company—provides a basis for inviting representatives to partake in the dialogue. Stakeholder participation in thinking through the issues the corporation faces can also be viewed as a way of extending accountability. In this way, all the contracting parties strive toward achieving an optimum result. In the process, stakeholders will most likely have to accept that compromises have to be made.

That said, including stakeholders in the process of thinking through dilemmas certainly does not diminish the corporation's accountability. Stakeholder dialogue must not be confused with some kind of representational democracy. It merely provides the basis for better decisions, thereby enhancing the company's integration with its stakeholders.

LEADERSHIP WITH INTEGRITY[2]

Albeit a truism that verges on triviality "leadership with integrity" is essential in any corporate context. In the discussion of the ethical quality of consistency (Chapter 6), we pointed out how important it is for managers to set a good example in creating an ethical climate. Good examples encourage people to join in; bad examples do not. Even though employees nowadays are less obedient and more emancipated, they tend to remember bad examples that create negative expectations. Good examples are easily taken for granted. Leadership involves expressing explicit support for the norms and values for which the organization stands.[3] That means more than just complying with, or "living" with them. Leaders need to motivate, encourage, and inspire their employees to act according to these values. In this sense, leadership goes beyond mere management. Good management enhances order and consistency through planning, implementation, comparing behavior with the code, and taking corrective action.[4] Leadership, by contrast, concerns not only the extent to which managers should be guided by adopted values in making strategic decisions. It also concerns the extent to which they should give meaning and a shared sense of purpose to those strategies and policies they decide to implement. Furthermore, leadership is the ability to help employees to discover for themselves the meaning and content of integrity in a manner that corresponds with the corporate virtues, principles, and objectives. Leadership also refers to the ability to inspire and secure employee commitment to act with integrity.[5] Given the intermediary function of senior managers, they bear a major responsibility in representing the corporate interests to stakeholders and in representing stakeholder interests to the corporation. Because of their overview of all the separate business units, it is senior management that aligns the organization and takes action when irreconcilable norms and values are identified among units.

Leadership is more than a necessary condition for advancing through the integrity management process. It is no less than a constituent element of corporate integrity. This gives way to a certain paradox. On the one hand, management commitment is a condition for enhancing the corporation's integrity. On the other, corporate integrity fosters enhanced leadership.[6] The corporate integrity requirements formulated in Chapter 6 can be used to distill specific integrity requirements for managers. Managers play various roles in this respect: demonstrative (their own conduct in line with the requirements), facilitative or conditioning (making it possible for their employees to act with integrity), and monitoring (ensuring that the principles and qualities are properly embedded). The quality of clarity requires managers to communicate clearly what is expected of employees in their daily conduct. To establish a consistent corporate context, managers' signals to employees have to be unambiguous. The quality of realizability is promoted by providing employees with realistic targets. At the same time, inspiring and encouraging employees to demonstrate integrity helps to secure the virtue of supportability. Keeping in mind the visibility of the context, managers in particular should monitor their employees to make sure that they conduct themselves with integrity. By demonstrating transparency in their own actions, managers can improve their employees' understanding of how they function. By the same token, the virtue of discussibility requires managers to take a vulnerable stance and to remain receptive to criticism from employees. This can also take the form of regularly broaching the topic of current dilemmas within a given department. Similarly, sanctionability requires that managers take a clear stand when their employees violate the standards.

Managers are not only context-builders. They are also ambassadors of stakeholder principles. The principle of openness demands that managers accept constructive criticism from stakeholders. Empathy requires that managers not only think in terms of the short-term and long-term corporate effects for stakeholders (whether intentional or not) but also recognize what stakeholders can do for the corporation. The ability to distribute the costs and benefits equally over stakeholders brings us to the principle of fairness. Similarly, solidarity refers to the ability of managers to refrain from misusing their position of power to chain stakeholders to the corporation. Given their decision-making authority, managers are the most suitable candidates for keeping an eye on the exit options of contracting parties. Finally, reliability implies that managers safeguard the cohesion and harmony of the various stakeholder contracts.

To ensure management commitment, it is essential to clarify the purpose and need of integrity for companies in general, and for the corporation in particular. This can be done by giving negative and positive examples of other corporations, presenting the available data on the corporation's present level of integrity in relation to it, letting various stakeholders express their criticism of the corporation, and confronting management with their own actions. Insight into the need to work on integrity can often be obtained by means of a quick scan (whether based on extant information, or not) of discrepancies, risks, and opportunities of a corporation.

Issues in leadership

Table 7.1 shows several specific issues that can arise in the first phase.[7]

(1) An explicit management commitment to integrity certainly has its risks. The more explicit and visible the commitment, the greater the expectations of others regarding the ethical quality of leaders' conduct, and the greater the damage if management falls short in satisfying them. The harder one beats the drum (no matter how good one's intentions may be) the greater people's disappointment if performance does not match the expectations created. Nevertheless, this explicit commitment is vital to fostering support for corporate integrity among employees.

(2) The next related issue concerns the emphasis on the role of management. Over-emphasizing the importance of leadership could (albeit unintentionally)

Table 7.1. Issues in leadership

Issue	Continuum		
1. Level of leadership visibility	Implicit	|------------------|	Explicit
2. Degree of emphasis on the special role of management	No emphasis	|------------------|	Great emphasis
3. Level of requirements on manager conduct in the past	New code is retroactively applicable	|------------------|	The past is a closed book
4. How change takes place	Gradual change	|------------------|	Single turning-point
5. Rate of difference in project participation between management and employees	Management first	|------------------|	Management and employees simultaneously

have a negative impact on employees. To grant management special status creates an impression of employees as followers, which can instill the perception that success is simply a matter of obeying orders. This could deprive them of their sense of responsibility. However, if the role of management is underplayed, it risks instilling diffidence in employees. Needless to say, the consequences of a "wait-and-see" attitude are highly undesirable. So is the perception that integrity is desirable only in the lower echelons, where the code serves solely as the proverbial stick that managers beat their employees with.[8]

(3) It is important that past conduct of the corporation's managers is not disputed. Alleged past improprieties not only damage the credibility of managers, the entire process is negatively affected by it. It is generally unreasonable to want to investigate each and every possible past misdemeanor. To be sure, the deeper one delves, the more it will become apparent that almost everyone is flawed. Moreover, backbiting and gossip can impair management credibility. It is often difficult to determine how much value to attach to workplace chat because such stories are often so far removed from the truth that it would be risky or even unfair to be swayed by them. Managers who have been involved in unethical practices can, however, contribute to boosting integrity within the organization. For instance, imagine the positive effect of managers who are known for ignoring the mores eventually expressing their commitment to make amends for their conduct in future. The crucial point is to determine which past practices can be tolerated and in which areas those practices threaten the credibility of the commitment to manage integrity.

(4) Timing the targeted change in management integrity can be difficult as well. Making a fundamental change to behavior overnight can lead to a deluge of skeptical reactions. People generally see integrity as a pattern of actions or behavior. Overnight transformation is impossible and claims to such radical changes would damage the credibility of the managers in question. Only the future can tell whether these commitments are genuine. A process of gradual improvement is therefore preferable, although care should be taken that the steps that are to follow are not put on hold for too long. It is thus crucial to determine how much commitment (the bare minimum) would be necessary to begin phase two.

(5) The final leadership issue concerns the extent to which the moral quality of managers can be taken into account without involving the individuals they manage. As stated above, effective leadership requires a delicate balance between taking the lead and stimulaing the independence of the team and its members. If a manager gets too far ahead of his team, they run the risk of "losing" each other—with the manager burning out and the team giving up on the race. An improvement process centered on interaction between both sides is desirable even if—in the case of habitual patterns—one of the parties has to take the first step to initiate change. Under such circumstances all eyes would be on the manager responsible—and rightly so.

A BUSINESS CODE OF INTEGRITY

The concept "code" has its origin in the Latin *codex* (or from the Old Latin *caudex*). In ancient Rome, a code referred to a wooden table with a wax veneer (or a set of such tables) that could be written on, or a book of bound and folded sheets of papyrus or parchment. In common usage, the concept of a code usually has two meanings. The first refers to a system that gives meaning to a series of symbols, signs, or signals such as Morse code, the binary code, and barcodes. In this regard, there is also a theory of codes. This is the division of mathematics that focuses on the design, decoding, and analysis of codes in the conveyance of information. The second meaning of a code refers to statutes: collections of rules and regulations. The term "codex" is mainly used in the field of law. A few well-known collections of laws are the *Code of Hammurabi*, the *Codex Theodosianus*, and the *Codex Juris Canonici*.[9] Derived from French, the concept gained worldwide notoriety in the *Napoleonic Code*, or the "civil code."

Nowadays, a code generally signifies a set of rules of conduct set down in writing that apply to multiple persons or groups. The *New Encyclopaedia Britannica*[10] defines a code as a more or less systematic and comprehensive written statement of rules on a given subject. These codes may or may not be authoritatively proclaimed, and the subject may be broad or narrow and range in importance from school dress codes to elaborate civil law codes. A moral code addresses fundamental issues that are at stake. Dress codes and rules of etiquette are irrelevant to morality.

A code of business ethics is often viewed as a document that expresses what a corporation considers as its moral norms and values.[11] However, a set of moral norms and values can also be considered a code without necessarily committing them to writing. The code is in that sense the real practices an organization develops. Consequently, all organizations have a code.[12] This is evident from assertions such as "that's simply how we see things," "that's just how things work here," and "that's the way we are." The *Concise Oxford Dictionary*[13] gives a similar, yet broader, definition. It calls a code the "prevalent morality of a society or class" and refers to it as "people's standard of moral behaviour." Whereas a code as an explicit document has to be interpreted from the written word, the second, broader definition bases a code on people's behavior. Codification therefore needs to cover the development of both implicit and explicit norms and values. By the same token, decodification refers to the process of unraveling a code. Codes have a regulative function. They regulate people's actions and preserve regularity—a pattern or structure—in people's actions. Acting according to a code is to act in accordance with an integrated system (i.e. integrity). A code is also constructive in nature. It lends meaning to individual experiences regarding both one's own actions and those of others. In that sense, a code can also be seen as a secret code: to reveal the meaning of a code everyone involved must present his or her own interpretation.

Here we shall limit the definition of a code to those written and adopted norms and values of choice that apply to managers and their employees for solving ethical dilemmas. A corporate code can therefore be seen as a document that indicates the basic corporate responsibilities toward stakeholders, and that formulates virtues and principles applicable to the entire corporation. A primary characteristic of a code is that it is unique to each corporation in that it expresses the mission and what the corporation stands for.[14] The elements of a corporate code are given in Figure 7.3.

A business code of integrity focuses on all of these elements. It coordinates corporate efforts, conduct, and consequences. Corporate codes are often limited to the corporate mission and responsibilities toward stakeholders (mission and/or responsibilities statements), or to principles, norms, or rules of conduct (codes of conduct or statements of principles), or to corporate values (values or virtues statements). A virtues statement offers employees a great degree of flexibility in translating values in the context of a given dilemma. A code of conduct, especially when it articulates well-defined norms, is much more concrete and coercive. In formulating the corporation's responsibilities, a mission statement generates dilemmas rather than offering any guidance for resolving them. Only when it prioritizes stakeholders does it ever succeed in offering guidelines for decision-making. The integrity of these sub-codes (pertaining to input, conduct, and impact) can be judged by observing the mutual integration of their elements and the degree to which they relate to one another. Sub-codes can also be detailed according to particular jobs, corporate assets, stakeholders, or regions.

A business code of integrity can be seen as a description of the social contract between corporations and their stakeholders. Such a code shows how the rights of stakeholders should be respected and how representatives should give shape to the corporation's responsibilities. A code not only sets down the integrity requirements, it also details them while highlighting the relation between the virtues, principles, and responsibilities (input, conduct, and impact). For example, the KPN code emphasizes that the core values should always be upheld even if some responsibilities cannot be met. Some codes also set down

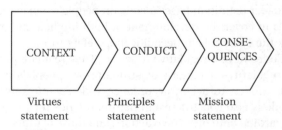

Fig. 7.3. Elements of business codes of integrity.

the corporation's expectations of its stakeholders. A code can also offer the grounds (motivation, trust, and shared views) and/or the framework (rules, conditions) for more concrete contracts with stakeholders. The term *business* code underscores the autonomy of the corporation and addresses not only individual responsibilities but also what the corporation as independent moral entity can be held accountable for.

In Chapter 1, we noted how many corporations nowadays use a code of ethics. Despite a number of studies on the effectiveness of corporate codes of ethics, strong empirical evidence either for or against the effectiveness of codes is still lacking.[15] Nevertheless, a number of observations can be made about codes. The power of a code lies in the process of thinking through what it should cover. It is a process of personal and collective reflection on one's dilemmas, responsibilities, principles, and virtues and those of the greater whole one is a part of. On the one hand, it is a process of exploring what it is that sets the corporation apart from the rest of the world. On the other, it is a quest for what it is that the corporation has in common with others. The formulation of a code is an irreversible process that creates expectations that are either difficult or impossible to temper. Refraining from publishing such a code at the last minute or scrapping an existing code without replacing it with something else are sure-fire ways to elicit criticism from stakeholders. Once a code has been communicated, stakeholders will hold the corporation to account. A code is also an instrument for both internal and external dialogue. It becomes easier to exchange thoughts when there is something tangible that can be discussed. In the development of a code, putting it in writing is decisive as it forces people to make choices.

A corporate code is an instrument for achieving cohesion in daily operations. It stimulates managers and employees to see the interconnectedness of the different responsibilities. A code offers a tool for getting functionaries from various departments within the company to sit down together to discuss matters. It is also a stepping-stone for formulating sub-codes for specific issues. On the one hand, a code is fairly static (once it is set down in writing it is not be likely to change soon), and on the other, it is spirited (it encourages people to live and breathe it—to experience it to the full). The corporation that establishes a code takes a proactive stance. The company without a code relinquishes control to its critics and is left to wait for them to make the first move. As Preston observes: "Companies allow their critics to shape the agenda in ways that put business in a perpetually defensive mode, talking about 'what they may have done wrong' instead of 'what they are doing right.' "[16]

Code-related issues

The following issues generally arise during the formulation of a business code of integrity.[17]

Table 7.2. Code-related issues

Issue	Continuum
Process	
1. Number of people involved in drawing it up	One person |------------------| Every manager and employee
2. Scope of each person's commitment to the drafting process	Zero (expressed in hours) |------------------| Very intensive (expressed in hours)
3. Number of external stakeholders involved in drawing it up	No external stakeholder |------------------| All external stakeholders
4. Scope of each stakeholder's commitment to the drafting process	Zero (expressed in hours) |------------------| Very intensive (expressed in hours)
5. Moment in the process that the code is made explicit	Code as input for reflection process |------------------| Code as output from reflection process
Content	
6. Code's target group	Employees only |------------------| All stakeholders
7. Variance between code and current practice	Description of current practice only |------------------| Description of most desired practice
8. Type of code	Conduct requirements

Input requirements — Output requirements

Issue	Continuum
9. Types of statements	Negative statements |------------------| Positive statements
10. Number of items to include in code	One item |------------------| All items
11. Level of detail for each item	General description of items |------------------| Concrete details of items
12. Direction of standards	One-way standards only |------------------| Two-way standards only
13. Level of compliance	Non-binding |------------------| Compulsory
14. Number of codes	One all-encompassing code |------------------| Multiple sub-codes as well
15. Reference to external codes	None |------------------| Exhaustive

Five issues can be identified in the code development process. (1 and 2) The more employees are involved in drawing up the code, the more visible their dilemmas and intuitions and the greater the support for the code when it is ready.[18] An intensive, organization-wide debate can, however, easily lead to endless and inconclusive ruminations. Moreover, consulting everyone is likely to create the impression that they can expect to see their ideas reflected in the final result. If the code does not meet this expectation, support for the code could suffer. (3 and 4) Similar issues are pertinent when external stakeholders are involved in the development of the code. The more vulnerable the stance of the corporation, the greater the expectations, which could lead to disappointment with the final result. On the other hand, the involvement of these stakeholders can enhance both the code's quality and external support for the code. (5) A related issue is deciding when to commit the code to paper. Some corporations do so after a relatively brief preliminary process and put the draft up for discussion inside and outside the organization. Others prefer to begin by submitting the whole matter to intense discussion both internally and externally before setting it down in writing. In the case of the former, the code serves as input for discussion, whereas in the case of the latter it constitutes the output. In the case of the former, it is more difficult to formulate a good code and adjust it later and in the case of the latter, it is more difficult to streamline the discussion.

The following issues are relevant to drafting the content of a code. (6) First of all, there is the question of whose conduct the code aims to address. Will the code apply to the employees only or also to all external stakeholders? If the content of a code is seen as (partly) formulating the contract with stakeholders, it has to move beyond simply setting down employee responsibilities toward the corporation. Similarly, an internal code is more likely to express matters more directly than an external code. An external code is also a public relations tool and care must be taken not to create the impression that everything it sets down is based on actual violations of integrity in the history of the corporation. (7) Formulating ideals brings the future in focus and may motivate employees to work toward those ideals. If ideals are too far removed from reality, they will lose their motivating and stimulating force. Slogans in a business code can make people see corporate integrity as a collection of empty promises and false pretenses that can lead to resistance and criticism. On the other hand, formulating realistic targets has the drawback that new ones must be formulated every time that the old ones are met. In addition, if other corporations do happen to formulate idealistic aims (that are not altogether achievable), a realistic code may be interpreted in the same way. By the same measure, people may assume that reality falls short of that code even if it is not the case. (8) As noted, a code can be worked out on the basis of input, conduct, or effects, or any combination of the three. Using only one of the three approaches can help to keep the code uncomplicated. However, using all three at once offers ground for clarifying how the three spheres interrelate. Moreover, this approach provides more handles for finding good solutions to the corporation's dilemmas. (9) Negative statements are those that set down what the employees and stakeholders should not do. Positive statements set down what has to be done. The objection to negative statements is that employees are quick to see them as threats. The disadvantage of positive statements, however, is that they are more difficult to verify. This makes the application of sanctions less tenable. (10) Setting down rules and regulations for virtually all the dilemmas that employees might encounter is one way to capitalize on what the code has to offer. A major disadvantage is that it can create the impression that no other issue matters. Moreover, the myriad of issues (at stake in any organization) can jeopardize the code's message, its flexibility, and employees' sense of responsibility. (11) The more an item is worked out in concrete terms, the clearer and less ambiguous the code becomes. However, any code that goes into every gray area in minute detail runs the risk of becoming too long and unwieldy for practical usage. (12) By setting down expectations of external stakeholders, the corporation can come across as being critical of its business partners. The wrong dosage of this can easily lead to accusations of moral arrogance. A probable response is indignation at being dictated to. Moreover, the greater the corporation's demands on its stakeholders, the more they will expect from the corporation in turn. (13 and 14) The aim toward clarity and cohesion between the various items and themes that can be codified makes it useful to incorporate each sub-code under one all-encompassing code. The disadvantage of a "blanket" code is that it can quickly grow into an inaccessible and pedantic handbook. Moreover, some rules and regulations might be so specific to certain jobs that they are meaningless to anyone else.

(15) There are two ways to formulate norms for a business operation. An existing set of external standards[19] can be adapted to the requirements of the company's operations or a unique set of standards can be developed exclusively for the company. The use of an accepted set of standards has a number of advantages. Firstly, established standards have often been formulated in a dialogue with society and are often endorsed by an independent institution. Secondly, an independent complaints procedure is sometimes already in place. Thirdly, the implications of this general set of standards for the management system have usually already been thought through. Using an accepted set of standards also has a number of drawbacks. It can never be a substitute for proper corporate policy. An external standard is usually a document that reflects the operation of the business from a particular perspective. The objective of achieving a balance between conflicting stakeholder expectations often falls beyond its scope. Given that each company is unique, a set of external standards will need to be modified or supplemented in order to arrive at set of norms that is appropriate to the corporation. Developing an appropriate code for the specific company will increase the chance of the set of norms becoming fully integrated into the corporate practices. Moreover, once external (international) standards have been adopted, it is often difficult to tailor them to the actual

situation. They therefore tend to lag behind what is needed in practice. Companies that adopt external standards run the risk of failing to incorporate new issues and new stakeholder needs into their codes. Adopting one's own set of standards forces the company to be alert. Furthermore, an appropriate set of standards offers an opportunity for a company to be positively distinguished from competitors.

The dilemma approach

In developing a business-specific code, it is important to first map the dilemmas that employees, and possibly external stakeholders, might encounter. A code provides handles for resolving those frequent and/or risky dilemmas that the target group may actually encounter. Evident norms (for example, "you should not murder your colleague") usually need not be included, since these add nothing to what we already know. The quality of a code lies precisely in its incorporation of those norms that lie beyond the realm of common sense and those that are not automatically realized. Making these moral intuitions more explicit makes comparisons possible that reflect the gap between the desired and actual situation.

Dilemmas can be identified during special sessions where participants are invited to formulate (anonymously if so desired) their own work-related dilemmas. A representative pallet of dilemmas can be compiled by taking samples from a cross-section of employees. A variety of methodologies is available for formulating dilemmas. For example, by first giving employees some examples of possible dilemmas, they can learn how to recognize and formulate their own. During dilemma-analyzing sessions, a discussion panel of employees can analyze the range of actual dilemmas that they have come up with. In this way, they can determine which norms and values are in conflict, which risks are related to the alternative courses of action, which moral standards should be given precedence, and what elements to include in the code. The aim of these decoding and coding sessions is to reveal the similarities and differences between moral intuitions and to open them up for discussion while searching for areas of possible agreement. As soon as this is achieved, the panel has to search for other dilemmas that challenge the newly formulated position.

In correspondence with the Kolb Learning Cycle,[20] such dilemma debates are marked by four phases.

1. Every participant expresses his or her own moral dilemmas.
2. Through a process of critical reflection, the unique characteristics of the dilemmas crystallize. The participants also discover what it is that made the specific situation a dilemma situation, which norms and values played a role in the related decision-making process, and why one alternative

instead of another was opted for. During this phase, various experiences can be compared and contrasted.

3. This reflection process produces a standard (a specific value, norm, principle, rule, or goal) for generalizing the alternatives in phase two.

4. The standard can furthermore be applied to other situations as a basis for new experiences, after which it can be modified or more sharply delineated. At the same time, employees can teach themselves to translate abstract notions into difficult real-life situations. By means of this iterative process (the process of decoding and recoding), they can bring their intuitions into better focus, which ultimately leads to the targeted corporate code. In general, case discussions can create space for generating standards (from phase 1 through 2 to 3: the inductive side of the cycle). Thereafter, the standards can be translated into practice (from phase 3 through 4 to 1: the deductive aspect).

This way of working helps to group the individual dilemmas by subject (what does the dilemma revolve around?) and by solution (what is needed to resolve the dilemma?). Both the content and the structure most suitable to the code slowly emerge in this approach. If employees do not identify any dilemmas for a certain area, it may mean that corporate, stakeholder, and private expectations are already concrete enough or that certain legitimate expectations still need to be acknowledged. It can, therefore be a good idea to involve external stakeholders or consultants in order to cover all areas. In addition, conferring with external parties is often a better way to determine which dilemmas to expect in the near future and how the corporation can respond to these in its code in advance.

The outcome of inventorizing dilemmas in this way can give management valuable insight into the nature and frequency of real dilemmas and their causes. This exercise becomes even more valuable where such dilemmas prove to be the result of ambiguous signals from management itself.

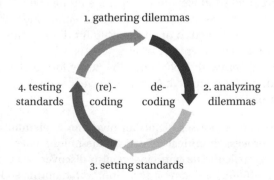

Fig. 7.4. Code of conduct development process.

As to the content of a code, it is important that it provides clarity. It has to be authentic and should express what the corporation considers important. A good code must be functional. Its standards need to serve as the basis for identifying indicators and gauges that can be used to evaluate how well the code is observed. Moreover, in a good code all these standards display a certain degree of coherence. A good code lays the basis for good implementation, and then, the next phase can commence.

IMPLEMENTATION

The way a code is implemented depends largely on the involved parties' opinions on implementation. Several important guidelines are illustrated in Figure 7.5.[21]

(1) First of all, integrity management comes down to creating a framework that imbues all parties with confidence instead of waving an incriminating finger at them. The point is not so much to track down abuses and their perpetrators but to work on building a healthy organization and stakeholder relationships. In this regard, Linda Paine asserts that a values-based approach could be more effective than the compliance-based approach. The former is rooted in personal self-governance and more likely to motivate employees to behave in accordance with shared values.[22] Although compliance and values-based approaches are complementary, the most effective approach is primarily value-orientated (based upon empirical research by Treviño *et al.*). Employees judge the motives of senior management in implementing integrity. It is therefore important that they perceive it to be a sincere attempt to have all employees do what is right instead of an attempt to create a back door for executives in case of a legal mishap.[23] An important consideration (that also

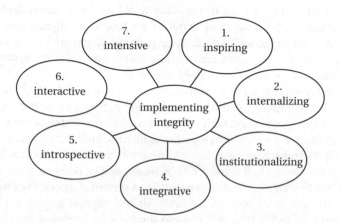

Fig. 7.5. Guidelines for implementing integrity.

applies to the other phases of the process) is the conception of humans that is employed and the kind of self-affirmation it generates. In this regard, McGregor[24] asserts that if managers assume that employees are opportunistic, they will most probably act accordingly. When employees sense they are not trusted, they will act accordingly and reinforce the assumptions of managers. That opportunism is a central theme in Chapters 5 and 6 is not to suggest that all contract parties are opportunists. The objective is precisely to prevent opportunistic behavior and the contractual problems it generates.

(2) The code's roll out involves converting the code's words into actual behavior in order for it to be fully internalized by employees. The implementation of a code always entails interpretation by those who use it. It is therefore necessary systematically to think through the true meaning of the code.

(3) The code's implementation also entails its proper institutionalization: setting down adequate procedures, structures, and systems to encourage people to follow the code and monitoring them in this process.[25] One such example is to create a database of stakeholders with information on the relationship, content, and conditions of the contract, and to include the relevant contact persons within the organization. Paine mentions the examples of using information systems designed to provide timely and accurate information, structuring reporting relationships with built-in checks and balances to promote objective judgment, and using performance appraisals that are sensitive to means as well as ends.[26]

(4) Implementing integrity, as the term already suggests, should also be integrative. The planned activities and procedures should fit the corporation's extant culture and structure as much as possible. Moreover, the measures and activities need to be linked together as far as possible.

(5) Each employee should be able to translate the code's meaning for his or her own concrete situation. They can ask themselves various questions in this regard. What does the code really mean for me? How should I translate the code into what I do and how I act in my daily work? To what extent do I already satisfy the code? Which areas of behavior do I need to change and to what extent? How am I supposed to do that? Implementing integrity is therefore also an introspective process where each employee must work out the discrepancies between the code and his or her daily practices.

(6) At the same time, integrity is more than just a personal matter. After all, it has to be visibly implemented in the interaction between employees and managers and in their interaction with external stakeholders. Implementing integrity entails, for example, sitting down together to discuss, understand, and internalize its meaning by mirroring each other's behavior, ascertaining where improvements in relationships and context can be made, and working on these together.

(7) Corporate integrity is far removed from a system of quick fixes that cause more harm than good and that creates absurd expectations. Treviño *et al.* observe that a quick-fix approach conveys the message to employees that senior management is simply trying to protect itself in the event that the company is

Table 7.3. Implementation issues

Issue		Continuum	
1. Treatment of unethical practices from the past	General pardon	|-----------------|	Retroactive effect
2. Time investment per employee	Zero	|-----------------|	Very intense
3. Spread of activities over time	Concentrated in time	|-----------------|	Spread over time
4. Degree to which explicit attention is paid to integrity	Implicit	|-----------------|	Explicit
5. Implementation direction	Top-down	|-----------------|	Bottom-up
6. Level of standardization in roll out per employee/ department	Ready-made	|-----------------|	Customized
7. Spread of employee focus on the code over time	Simultaneous implementation	|-----------------|	Many different phases
8. Degree of obligation to implement the code	Noncommittal	|-----------------|	Compulsory
9. Composition of the groups taking part in the activities	Per department	|-----------------|	A-select
10. Point in time for adjusting structure	Prior to the code's dissemination	|-----------------|	After the code has been brought up in the corporation
11. Training form	Manager as trainer	|-----------------|	External trainer
12. External stakeholder participation in roll out	Direct	|-----------------|	Indirect
13. Reasons for mobilizing people to focus on integrity	Repressive approach	|-----------------|	Preventative approach
14. Employee endorsement of the code	No one	|-----------------|	The entire code is signed by everyone
15. External stakeholder endorsement of the code	None at all	|-----------------|	Signed by every external stakeholder

taken to court.[27] Keeping corporate integrity up to standard requires intensive maintenance from the entire staff. They also need to stay constantly alert in order to reinterpret and reformulate various elements of the code as the contracting conditions between the corporation and stakeholder change.

Implementation issues

The following issues can arise during the implementation phase.

(1) A new or revised code usually heralds a fresh start. The old habits that are now prohibited by the code no longer serve as justification for certain actions or behavior. This, however, is no reason to gloss over past abuses. Improper conduct from the pre-code period remains relevant and can still be brought up for discussion. At the same time, the code generally refines and sharpens existing norms and values. Employees cannot, however, retroactively be called to account on this basis. The advantage of a general pardon is that it closes the past without negating the past. It creates the space to learn as much as possible from past unethical practices—including those yet to be revealed. (2) Another issue concerns how much time employees are expected to spend on the code. This naturally comes down to weighing up the importance of the integrity project against that of other projects and activities. (3) Some companies opt for conducting the activities around the code within a short time frame, which can give them the necessary momentum to take that big step forward. Conversely, others take the time to make sure that the code is properly integrated into their operations. By spreading out the time that people are required to spend thinking about the code, they begin to see the code as a normal part of their work. (4) A related issue concerns how explicitly the code should be opened up for discussion. The more explicit the focus, the more the code will come to be seen as an independent instrument. The more implicit the focus, the more the code will be regarded as part of people's ordinary work. (5) Some organizations implement the code in a top-down fashion. Such a "cascading" approach starts at the highest echelons and trickles down level by level to the rest. Yet, other organizations opt for a bottom-up approach, where employees at the lowest echelons develop their views and pass these on to the next echelon that gets to work on the results in turn. Finally, senior management receives suggestions from every part of the company on how to bring everyone's daily practice in line with the code.

(6) The sixth issue has to do with whether to opt for a ready-made or a customized implementation process for each department. Some corporations dictate a standard approach that departments are required to follow. The aim of this approach is to ensure that everyone is treated the same. This keeps those departments that are opposed to the project from shirking their responsibilities via a different (read: easier) route. Moreover, standardization makes it possible to compare different departments. At the same time, other companies offer

their departments a kind of menu from which they can choose their own means and instruments. Such menus aim to reflect the specific needs of each department without having to reinvent the wheel each time. Finally, there are also companies that let their departments work on the code as they see fit on the condition that they actually do spend time on it. (7) The issue of to what extent the process should be standardized concerns not only the way that the code is rolled out but also its phasing. Some companies require all departments to take part in certain activities simultaneously or set deadlines for them to work on the code (regardless of the individual methodologies). Other corporations give their departments free reign because senior management does not want to tamper with the departments' autonomy. (8) Companies may decide either to force their departments and employees to spend time on the code or to give them complete freedom. On the one hand, most corporations would generally like to be able to rely on their employees' integrity. On the other, they would also like to oblige everyone to take part in the activities. Those people with a lax attitude toward the process are generally the ones who could do with a good dose of "vitamin I" ("I" for Integrity). One must also consider whether units should be punished for their passivity or rewarded for taking an active stand. Many companies wrestle with the fact that integrity cannot be instantly imposed. The only way to bring about lasting improvement is voluntarily and through the inner drive of its people. The voluntary character of implementing the code, however, must not lapse into a lack of commitment where organizational entities simply ignore the matter without having to account to anyone.

(9) By rolling out the process within each department, the focus is on people's regular work relations so that agreements can be made. However, some companies opt for training their employees "a-select" instead. In this approach, employees are taken out of their normal work environment and given an opportunity to reflect. Moreover, the participants get the opportunity to learn from the experiences of those in other departments. (10) Sometimes, it is necessary to make changes to the organizational structure before presenting the code to employees to reduce the possibility of resistance. A code is doomed to failure if the corporation's structure makes it impossible—from the perspective of the employees—for people to adapt their conduct to the code. Changes to the organizational structure prior to the code's distribution make it clear to employees that the code has consequences for the organization's policy, which makes it serious business. Other organizations let their employees make suggestions during the course of the project as to which conditions in the organization's structure need to be modified to increase support for the changes to come. (11) Management, internal advisors (such as members of an integrity project group), or external consultants can lead these departmental and management team meetings. Having managers lead these sessions is a good way to capitalize on their ability to set a good example. The disadvantage is that the managers themselves might be part of the problem at hand, which will prevent it from being properly formulated or addressed. The advantage of a good external

consultant is that he or she generally has a good deal of expertise and skills and the neutrality necessary for opening integrity up for discussion in a proper manner.

(12) Companies have various strategies at their disposal for involving their external stakeholders in the code's roll out. Sometimes, companies opt explicitly for anchoring the code within the organization, before giving it external backing. This helps to prevent situations where employees are at a loss for words when faced with critical questions from outside parties with regard to the code. Moreover, most employees tend to see any code that is first communicated to the outside world as a public relations stunt. In that case, they would not feel obliged to pay any real attention to it. Furthermore, if the discrepancy between the code and its actual use is too great, the outside world is likely to see it as nothing but a collection of empty words, which can damage the corporation's image. The longer the internal start-up time, the longer the outside world will have to be patient until the code is revealed. Nevertheless, publicizing the code can put pressure on management to pay attention to ethics and integrity. Some companies do not disseminate their code externally at all since they hold the opinion that the best way to communicate the code is through the (changed) conduct of their employees.

(13) A project-based focus on integrity can be the result of painful incidents that cost the corporation either money or its image. Should this be the case, it is important to prevent such incidents from occurring again. Such easily recognizable incidents usually work as powerful levers for setting the organization in motion. The more concrete the incident, the more convincing the importance of working on it and the greater the chance, unfortunately, of integrity being addressed from a compliance perspective only. (14 and 15) The final two issues concern the degree to which managers and employees or external stakeholders should commit themselves to the code in writing. Compulsory endorsement of the code is one way to get people to study it. A code that has been signed is also easier to enforce by law. At the same time, this can also give people the impression that integrity is nothing but a legal formality.[28] Moreover, before any of the employees can justifiably be expected to adhere to the code, the corporation itself needs to be relatively flawless.[29] The risk of having the code signed by managers and employees is that it might unleash a legal witch-hunt against those who refuse to endorse it. At the same time, if there are no consequences for refusal, no one will feel encouraged to sign the code. The general disadvantage of having the entire code endorsed by external stakeholders is that it loses its power to address stakeholders individually. A code will, after all, contain several passages that are not relevant to the specific stakeholder. This problem can be remedied by requesting external parties to consent only to those passages of the code that affect them personally or even developing sub-codes (for example, a code for suppliers).

The different means available for opening up the corporate code for discussion both internally and externally are discussed elsewhere.[30] Kaptein also identifies and discusses more than thirty instruments for embedding one or more of the ethical qualities in organizations as they relate to each of the three dilemmas.[31]

THE INTEGRITY AUDIT

A business ethics or integrity audit can be viewed as a systematic approach to describing, analyzing, and evaluating the efforts, conduct, and/or impact of a corporation and/or of those who represent it now or in the future.[32] Measuring corporate integrity promotes transparency (the quality of visibility) and reflects involvement with stakeholders (the principle of empathy). In more concrete terms, audits are conducted for the following purposes:[33]

(1) to communicate an appreciation of the importance of integrity;
(2) to enhance the awareness of the people whose practices are audited;
(3) to communicate the corporation's receptiveness to employee and external stakeholder experiences and concerns;
(4) to know and understand what is expected from the corporation and to identify discrepancies in practice;
(5) to benchmark departments, business units, and stakeholders and compare them with each other and other companies;
(6) to identify and improve the weak areas of the organization's integrity;
(7) to improve decision-making. The audit provides information on imbalances in the internal and external stakeholder relationships and sets the direction for improvement;
(8) to stimulate further steps in the implementation of the code. Measuring performance is an irreversible process that creates expectations. If these expectations are not realized, senior management will attract criticism;
(9) to see the progress and effectiveness of integrity management with reference to multiple measurements;
(10) to prevent discussions with stakeholders on the basis of inaccuracies.

In the book *Ethics Management*,[34] six kinds of audits are discussed and it is shown how to conduct them, what their results mean, and which measures to take on the basis of the audit results. Two separate audits can be conducted for examining corporate intentions. The *Qualities Monitor* examines the corporate culture and the *Integrity Measures Scan* examines the organizational structure. The *Individual Integrity Assessment* audits the intentions, intuitions, and circumstances of present employees and applicants. The *Conduct Detector* is used to audit present or past employee conduct and possibly even that of other stakeholders. The *Stakeholder Reflector* describes (i.e. reflects on) stakeholder expectations and the extent to which these are realized. The stakeholder reflector can also be used to record stakeholder perceptions of the extent to which the principles are embedded in the relationship with the corporation. Finally, the

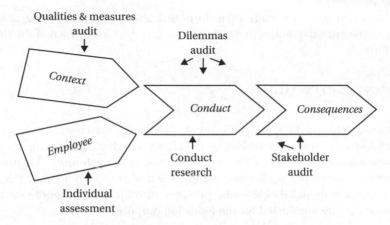

Fig. 7.6. Types of audits.

Dilemma Decoder is a procedure for reconstructing and analyzing dilemmas as explained in the previous section (i.e. decoding dilemmas).[35]

Identifying Key Integrity Indicators

Indicators translate values, norms, and objectives into measurable units and are used to measure performance and progress. The fewer the indicators needed to reach the same accurate and meaningful conclusion, the better the audit. The selection of indicators depends on the key business processes that anchor integrity. What are our most fundamental dilemmas? On which issues do we lose or attract stakeholder support? Where exactly lies our integrity? The proper development of indicators coupled with short-term and long-term targets should be based on broad internal consultation. The aim is to create maximum support and to establish what is crucial and what is achievable. Stakeholder dialogue can also produce indicators of interest to stakeholders. For the purpose of benchmarking, it is useful to draw on indicators that are used by other companies. Two important requirements for an indicator are that the data it generates are accurate and meaningful for the intended audience.[36] "Accurate" refers to valid, reliable, comparable, measurable, and verifiable information. "Meaningful" refers to the relevance of indicators for stakeholders who want to see their concerns reflected in, and addressed by, the indicators. Indicators should not only be developed to measure results but also to measure input and behavior, with attention to the totality of complex causal relations between the indicators. Such an approach is consistent with the *Balanced Scorecard* as developed by Robert Kaplan and David Norton.[37] The balanced scorecard translates the desired achievements into operative and coherent terms, and the measurements represent a balance sheet of respectively internal and external results. They advance four perspectives (the financial perspective, supplier perspective, internal processes perspective, and the learning and growth perspective). From an integrity perspective, it is often more desirable to involve a broader range of stakeholder perspectives. Finally, it should be possible to relate the indicators back to the code. Indicators that cannot be distilled from the code as a result of new themes or expectations give cause for adjusting the code accordingly. By taking the code as point of departure in the development of indicators, it is placed at the heart of the management philosophy of an organization (see also the KPN case at the end of Chapter 6).

Appendix 1 presents several examples of "soft" indicators that are based on internal and external stakeholder perceptions, and "hard" indicators that can be measured more objectively. Indicators can generally be expressed in average or maximum and minimum scores, in their spread, how they change through time, in absolute and relative scores by unit or department, and as divided by personal details (such as age or gender). Ratio indicators express the balance between different aspects (for example, environmental investments as percentage of total investments or the number of surplus employees made redundant as percentage of profits). The integrity criteria in Chapter 6 were developed by deducing from the corporate mission the behavioral principles required for realizing the mission, and identifying those corporate qualities that are required to support the principles. In this way, the chain of causal relations between input, conduct, and consequences is construed. Organizations can further apply this method with a view to developing specific key integrity indicators.

The importance of reporting[38]

An ethics or integrity report (often called a sustainability report)[39] can be viewed as a report on the degree to which a corporation has honored the terms of its contract with stakeholders. We have already noted the desirability of corporate reporting as input for stakeholder dialogues and as output from stakeholder dialogues.

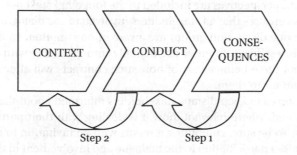

Step 2   Step 1

Fig. 7.7. Development of key integrity indicators.

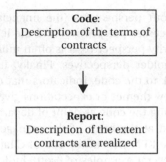

Fig. 7.8. Relationship between the code and the report.

The most important reason for setting up an internal reporting structure is to institutionalize adherence to and improvement of the code. Subsidiaries and business units or departments within an organization can account for their performance through an internal reporting system that enables the holding company to monitor the embeddedness of integrity. The external effect of an integrity report is important as well. An annual or biennial report can stimulate or strengthen trust in a corporation by reducing the bounded rationality of stakeholders. To report on its progress and performance signifies a corporation's willingness to reveal its vulnerability, which in turn encourages stakeholders to make constructive contributions. Integrity reporting also limits the scope for opportunistic behavior in that it counters an unbalanced or selective account of corporate performance and makes the corporation accountable for its integrity.[40]

An integrity report lends structure to the accountability process. Reporting promotes regular statements of progress to date. What are the effects of the company's policy? What is its impact on stakeholders? What issues are of significance now or likely to become relevant in the future? What points of view have been taken into account? What differences of opinion are at play? What objectives have been formulated? What results have been achieved? Regular reporting renders a company's approach to addressing its responsibilities transparent and easily understandable. Reporting also provides a way of checking that all relevant perspectives are included in the (ongoing) stakeholder dialogue. Reporting also ensures that all stakeholders involved in the dialogue (consisting of more than one discussion group) are aware of one another. In this way, the corporation is less likely to enter accidentally into contracts with stakeholder groups without them being aware of how such contracts will affect other areas that are important to them.

Reporting serves to keep distant stakeholders informed about the company's performance and, where relevant, how it is dealing with their particular rights and interests. To be sure, combining a report with an invitation to respond can boost stakeholder participation in the dialogue and involvement in the company itself. Integrity reporting does carry certain risks. Weak spots that are published in the report may come across in exaggerated form to an outsider. Such reports can also lead to higher stakeholder expectations and supply competitors with sensitive information. Moreover, the possibility also exists that management might manipulate the information in such reports. Lastly, it is often unpleasant to explain setbacks in certain areas, especially when it is the result of reduced efforts on the part of the corporation. Failing to report, however, also has its risks. It is therefore better to ascertain how the risks of reporting can be managed. Taking careful steps is one way to avoid raising over-ambitious expectations. It is also important to give stakeholders the opportunity to think along with the company every step of the way. This allows them to take on certain responsibilities and makes them more willing to accept decisions that conflict with their short-term interests.

If a company has various reports (financial, environmental, and social), it is important for them to be harmonized and integrated as much as possible. If it is to account successfully for its integrity performance and facilitate dialogue on issues that transcend any of the three spheres, an integrated reporting structure is imperative. Figure 7.9 depicts this integrated structure.

An integrity report highlights:

(1) The items contained in the various, more specific reports;
(2) The corporate efforts, conduct, and outcomes;
(3) The dilemmas in and between the different areas and how the company addresses them; and
(4) the values and norms that have been developed in stakeholder dilemma discussions.

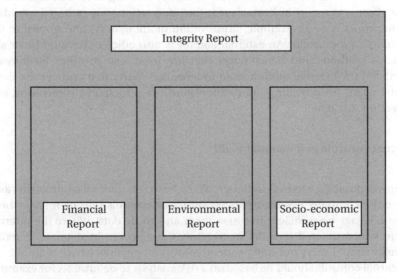

Fig. 7.9. Integrated structure of different reports.

Alongside the triple bottom line layout, a report can use the same structure as the code. A good corporate code should after all have a structure capable of report.

The role of the auditor

An independent and objective expert auditor can be employed to verify the corporate integrity reports. An auditor can check the data on the input, throughput, and output of the corporate stakeholder contracts. In this way, he or she facilitates the contracting process. Verifying information is desirable for a number of reasons. If audit results are used to review managers of departments or business units, the validity of this information must be without doubt. An auditor could check whether the reporting process provides an accurate view of the state of affairs. Stakeholders also want assurance that the information they have access to is reliable. For example, stakeholders partaking in the dialogue want to be kept informed about the discussions that are taking place with other stakeholders. They specifically want clarity about the nature of the agreements the company has with other parties and how these affect them. An external auditor could evaluate the quality of each dialogue and assess the coherence among the respective dialogues. Stakeholders who want to follow the dialogue, but who do not wish (or are unable) to participate, want to be sure that the dialogue is being accurately reflected in the report. Verification by an auditor guarantees accuracy and completeness also in this regard. In some cases, it is desirable for the auditor to assist in organizing and conducting the stakeholder dialogue, for example in the event that a survey is being used. The function of the auditor is to assure individuals that the information thus gathered would be put to proper use (for example, preservation of anonymity) and to ensure the reliability of the results. An external auditor is also efficient because he or she employs methods and benchmarks that are used also in other businesses. Moreover, the external auditor is an independent party that reduces the costs for the agent (in providing information) and the principals (in receiving and correcting this data).

Internal controls and external audit

Wherever possible, external audits should be based on internal controls. In cases where the company has incorporated sufficient controls into its management system, it may be sufficient to assess them and verify data. Where the internal controls incorporated into the management system are inadequate, external auditors should carry out independent control procedures where required.

Internal controls should be based on a risk analysis to determine, for example, what could go wrong or keep the company staff from acting in accordance with the norms and values. The external audit should also be based on a risk analysis, for example to establish what problems with the gathering of information could lead to false statements in the company's integrity report.

It is useful to keep unverifiable statements to a minimum in the reporting process. They would not convince a critical reader anyway. Auditing procedures (for testing controls and substance) include actual examinations, confirmations, documentation, observations, interviews with the management and/or stakeholder representatives, surveys, re-performance, and analytical procedures.

From an auditing perspective, materiality is very important. The omission of any item or group of items is material if stakeholders require knowledge of the item/s for forming an opinion on a given issue. Several areas in which the verification process is limited include:

1. The *non-actions* of employees are usually impossible to report on, let alone verify. For example, most companies would find it nearly impossible to declare that none of their employees ever accepts any bribes. Only one example to the contrary is needed to invalidate that claim, and even if such verification were possible, it is usually extremely labor-intensive.
2. *Plans* for the future can also be difficult to verify. It is virtually impossible for an auditor to ascertain their feasibility. Nor would it be wise to attempt to do so. Only the future will tell. In the event that such plans could have implications for the present situation, verification may be desirable and possible.
3. *Abstract assertions* defy verification. No one will verify a statement such as "The company respects human rights." Nor is the translation of principles into standards verifiable. An example of this is: "The company respects human rights. This is evident from the fact that we make no use of child labor." As long as there is insufficient or no expertise available for determining the set of standards that adequately supports such principles, no auditor will be able to certify such claims.
4. Risky claims are those that include *absolute words* such as "all," "every," and "always" (for example, "All employees are treated equally") and those that use active verbs in connection with certain standards (for example, "Our relationships with suppliers attest to our respect").
5. Claims that are difficult to verify contain *subjective* quantifiers such as "regularly," "sometimes," "very serious," "several," and "usually," or vague formulations such as "we have training programs" and "we meet with our stakeholders."

Issues that arise in the auditing process

Table 7.4 shows some issues that have to be addressed when embarking on auditing and reporting.

Table 7.4. Issues in the design of a reporting system

Issue		Continuum	
1. Manner of reporting	Verbal	|------------------|	Written
2. Reporting period	Continuous	|------------------|	Once every 5 years
3. Level of external disclosure	None/ silence	|------------------|	All/ full disclosure
4. Type of reporting	One integrated report	|------------------|	Reporting per item
5. Scope of stakeholders report is directed at	One stakeholder	|------------------|	All stakeholders
6. Scope of items reported upon	One item	|------------------|	All items
7. Level of assertions	Total value added	|------------------|	Specific norms
8. Rate of change of assertions per period	Standard assertions	|------------------|	Different assertions each period
9. Kinds of standards adopted	All own standards	|------------------|	All external standards
10. Object of standards		Conduct standards	
	Input standards		Output standards
11. Types of indicators	'Hard'	|------------------|	'Soft'
12. Monitoring methods	One method	|------------------|	Great variety
13. Extent of verification	None	|------------------|	Every assertion
14. Dialogue with stake-holders	No stake- holders	|------------------|	Every stakeholder

Various items (such as 2, 3, 5, 6, 7, and 12) depend on how complete and extensive the report needs to be. The more data, the greater the chance that the report gives its readers the information that they want. At the same time, this can make the report less readable and inaccessible. The more detailed the report, the more time is necessary to collect and verify information. Such considerations also apply to items 13 and 14. In general, most stakeholders will appreciate more verification along with a stakeholder dialogue while the available financial resources can place limits on this. (1) It is important that the report does not come across as a one-way communication channel; the idea is rather for it to facilitate feedback. The openness of the company in this regard should come across in how much it accounts for its activities on a daily basis. After all, not all information can wait for the publication of an annual report. (8) The first reports frequently contain a great diversity of assertions. In the course of time a more stable and coherent set of assertions develop. Whereas some companies will have experimented with different assertions in order to present a relatively constant set, others may opt for highlighting new items each year depending on the latest trends. (11) "Hard" indicators are usually easier to verify than "soft" ones. However, information on the latter is usually easier to gather.

The results of the audit will, as a rule, provide information that can be used to improve moral leadership, the business code, supporting systems and procedures, and the auditing methods used. By continually rethinking and running through the described integrity cycle, the company can anchor its integrity in a lasting manner.

EPILOGUE

In this chapter, we discussed four phases of integrity management that flow from the definition of integrity advanced in this book. As integrity means—among other things—internal consistency, integrity management refers to bringing the organization into alignment with objectives, principles, and qualities. A crucial phase of integrity management is thus attending to leadership. The structure and culture should also be aligned with the desired integrity. For this purpose, a code is a suitable instrument to establish and communicate the desired integrity of a corporation and to integrate different approaches. Particularly since the integrity of an organization is related to the greater whole of which it is a part, accounting for one's responsibilities follows automatically. In this regard, monitoring and reporting are important components of integrity management.

This book

In this book, we developed an integrity approach for corporations. A balanced company will carefully deal with the dilemmas it is confronted with. With this goal in mind, the internal organizational culture and structure will possess the necessary ethical qualities, and in the relations with contracting parties, some basic behavioral principles will also be embedded. In this book, we developed a conceptual model that integrates corporate contract theory in particular with virtue ethical theory. We also developed an approach to how these virtues and principles can be managed, monitored, and verified. Having formulated realistic criteria for corporate practices, we hope to bring business ethics theory into greater alignment with the corporate context and to provide corporations with a more integrated perspective on how to balance conflicting ethical expectations. In conclusion, we hope to have made clear that a *balanced company* needs to be grounded in a balanced ethical theory and sustained by people in business who have an open and balanced mind.

Toward the "New Shell"

Shell's code

In 1976, Shell presented its general policy under leadership of former senior officer, Gerrit Wagner. At that time, people were primarily concerned about the power of multinationals. This was partly because of the immense power the largest of these multinational corporations exerted over the Third World. It was perceived as the perpetuation of colonialism under a new name. The OECD code of conduct was developed in response to this issue. Shell came up with its own code at the same time. Sometime thereafter, Wagner would say: "A lot of those things aren't really ethics, you know, they're just part of careful operations. You have to watch out with ethics. A lot of things simply coincide with the kind of intelligent, careful management necessary for staying in business."[41]

The 1976 code set down the aims of the corporation. The objectives of Shell companies were to engage efficiently, responsibly, and profitably in oil, gas, chemicals, and other selected businesses, and to participate in the search for and development of other sources of energy. Shell companies sought a high standard of environmental and social performance without compromising its competitiveness. Several stakeholders were also mentioned (shareholders, employees, customers, and society) along with Shell's responsibilities toward them. These areas of responsibility were seen as inseparable. The basic policy formulated the following concrete principles:

1. Shell sees profit as a condition for all of its economic activities.
2. Shell policy follows the OECD guidelines for multinational corporations and the ILO's Tripartite Statement of Principles.
3. All transactions will be completed with integrity and honesty.
4. Employees must avoid conflicts of interest.
5. Shell will stay out of political activities and refrain from making donations to political parties and politicians.
6. Employees may engage in community activities including running for election to public office.

7. The utmost care will be exercised with regard to safety, security, and the environment.
8. Shell is part of the society in which it functions. It will lend a helping hand with social issues that are not necessarily directly connected to the corporation as such.
9. Shell will communicate openly with its stakeholders.

Partly as a result of the major public pressure that Shell had to cope with after the Brent Spar affair and its presence and practices in Nigeria, Shell decided to modify its code after having subjected it to intense internal and external discussion.

The code that was adopted in 1997 made special mention of human rights. Shell's new responsibility toward society included its duty "to express support for fundamental human rights in line with the legitimate role of business." The company also took a stand on the contribution corporations can make to sustainable development. Shell's task is "to give proper regard to health, safety and the environment consistent with their commitment to contribute to sustainable development."

It is interesting to note what the new code discarded. The code of 1976 held that Shell was barely in the position to exert any influence at all on its social, political, and economic environment. That was its reason for keeping out of political issues. This passage was omitted from the revised code, which signaled that Shell implicitly accepts that it bears a certain level of political responsibility.

The references to the code of the International Labour Organization and the OECD guidelines were also scrapped. Shell can no longer risk referring to other codes, like the UN Declaration of Human Rights, for fear of eliciting (too) high a set of expectations from the outside world. Neither does Shell want to commit itself (or be committed) too strongly. Instead, the new code endorses certain principles that indirectly subscribe to other codes of conduct.

Shell also supplemented its list of stakeholders with a "business partners" category. It now targets mutual advantage in its relationships with contractors and suppliers and in joint ventures. In addition, the code now asserts that Shell's business partners are required to honor Shell policy. This is seen as a key criterion for any new or continuing partnerships. Shell thus accepts some degree of responsibility for the way that its business partners discharge their obligations.

In the year 2000, the code was available in 51 languages, covering the local tongues of 99.9 per cent of Shell employees. Moreover, it has been adopted in all the countries where Shell operates, as well as by each of its joint ventures in 43 countries. Shell companies in 135 countries also have a procedure in place to ensure that new employees receive the code and 109 countries boast a new employee training program to facilitate embedding the business code.

Report

When the revised code was presented at the shareholder meeting in 1997, many demanded an explanation from Shell as it contained several lofty aims. Questions were raised as to how they could be achieved, what was being done to operationalize the code, and what was actually being accomplished.

Although the shareholders did not accept a proposal for code-based reporting, the Committee of Managing Directors concluded that sooner or later such a reporting system would have to be institutionalized. An annual report was seen to be an important tool for setting the dialogue with society in motion and sustaining it. As a result, it was decided to produce an annual report without any further ado. The Social Accountability Team was installed in October 1997 and tasked with supporting the internal and external stakeholder dialogue by publishing an annual social report.

With the aid of instruments such as a survey of its 130 operating companies, Shell could get a centralized overview of all the activities that were undertaken to realize the business principles. The CEOs of the various operating companies were asked to write a letter to declare what activities they had undertaken over the past year to operationalize the business principles (known as the Shell Business Principles letters). The 1998 report entitled *Profits and Principles—Does There Have to be a Choice?* gives an account of the results. It reports on how the company has given shape to each of the business principles. In addition, it also discusses issues Shell faces and all that can or has gone wrong. A significant amount of attention is paid to the dilemmas the corporation faces. Human rights, climate change, globalization, and Shell's operations in politically sensitive regions are some of the areas highlighted. The annual report also includes the auditors' report. External auditors verified several parts of the report. Their report states that the accuracy of Shell's assertions has been verified. Finally, the report also provides information on how Shell will continue to report on its social, economic, and environmental responsibilities in future. The report expresses the aim to integrate the economic, environmental, and social dimensions within five years on the basis of data generated by its information systems. It also asserts that external auditors will verify this information as well.

The 1999 Shell Report[42] entitled *People, Planet & Profits: An Act of Commitment* gives an account of the progress the corporation has made. This report communicates a firm commitment to make a contribution to sustainable development. It also classifies Shell's various business principles according to the three dimensions of sustainable development and reports on the corporation's performance in each of them. Shell's dilemmas are brought into focus once again and the whole report is certified with the auditors' report. The scope of this 1999 report is broader and discloses more information than the first report.

According to the report, Shell has the intention to report to the public in due course on the basis of the information systems that are in place. In order to set up a new information system, Shell first needs to know what kind of information is required. To meet this challenge, various stakeholder representatives and groups representing society have been working together to identify key indicators and how they could be measured. For Shell, it is important that the indicators measure its sustainability performance and that they provide information to sustain the dialogue between the company and its stakeholders. At the same time, the company also needs to find a way to make this information available at an acceptable cost. Moreover, this information has to be verifiable and comparable with the data of other companies.

The Shell Report 2000, entitled *How Do We Stand?*, presents the latest progress. It reminds its readers that the reporting process is still in its infancy. Especially the development of indicators and the related verification process still have a long way to go. Only a few items (like *The Shell People Survey* and the outcomes of the Shell Business Principles letters) were verified—yet only marginally. The report contains the following passages and assertions that articulate Shells' normative views:

1. "We are totally committed to a business strategy that generates profits while contributing to the well-being of the planet and its people. We see no alternative."
2. "Cost cutting does not mean cutting corners."
3. "A real dialogue must be a two-way conversation. We must listen, engage and respond to our stakeholders."
4. "Transparency is important to building trust and credibility."
5. "We believe more than ever that sustainable development is the right approach because values and principles are important to us, and it makes good business sense."
6. "Reducing emissions to air, water and land is critical to our contribution to sustainable development."
7. "We strive to be a responsible member of society and contribute to the welfare of our staff and the communities in which we operate. We support fundamental human rights and continue our battle to improve safety... Please help us learn what we do well and what we can do better. We value your views."
8. "People have become increasingly concerned about the potential effects of chemicals on health and the environment. We want to listen and understand these concerns and to anticipate and respond openly to questions from consumers and regulators... We are actively seeking to gain a better understanding of the effects..."

In its quest to contribute to sustainable development, Shell aims at integrating ethical principles into its stakeholder relationships and ethical qualities in its culture and structure. Spearheads in this regard are to increase its internal and external openness (i.e. discussibility and visibility). The former can heighten the clarity and consistency of its actions while avoiding setting unrealistic targets. The latter directly boosts its authenticity and indirectly augments the other contracting principles.

Shell has also developed the so-called Sustainable Development Management Framework, a description of diverse phases to embed its principles in its decision-making and conduct. This framework is also supported by an extensive toolkit of best practice and procedures to help users to apply it in their own activities. There are also sub-codes in place on, for example, corruption and bribery, and collecting information. The framework has been distributed to the management teams of almost all countries where Shell is active. Besides the publication of the report, Shell runs a global advertising campaign to communicate to the public what it is doing in the face of the dilemmas it and society faces. The campaign is also designed to stimulate the debate on Shell's approach and to include as many stakeholders in the dialogue as possible. Those wanting to engage Shell are invited to do so by using the speed and interactivity of the World Wide Web. Engagement in this sense is slowly becoming a routine part of the way Shell does business. Despite the fact that, as Shell itself emphasizes, there is still a long way to go, the signs so far have certainly been encouraging.

APPENDIX: EXAMPLES OF INTEGRITY INDICATORS

This appendix gives an overview of possible integrity indicators. The indicators are classified after the three corporate dilemmas and a distinction is drawn between "hard" and "soft" indicators (Chapter 7). In accordance with the proposed method in Chapter 7, key integrity indicators can be distilled and placed in a causal relationship with one another.

Table A.1. Examples of *soft* indicators for Dirty Hands Dilemmas regarding customers

Stakeholder	Soft indicators for input	Soft indicators for conduct	Soft indicators for output
Customers	The degree to which the corporation makes clear to employees what their responsibilities are toward customers.	The corporation provides sufficient, authentic and relevant information to customers on who it is, what it stands for, and what it aims to accomplish.	The organization supplies high quality products and services.
	The degree to which direct managers set a good example for employees in treating customers responsibly.	Information the organization provides to customers reflects reality.	The organization asks reasonable prices commensurate with quality.
	Employees can realize the norms pertaining to customers.	The corporation is open to customer criticism, suggestions, and questions.	Its products are available at the right place and time and in the right amount.
	The corporation stimulates employees to identify with consumers.	The organization takes proper note of customer criticism.	The organization has reasonable sale and payment conditions.
		The organization shows a good understanding of the extent and way in which the interests of customers are realized.	The organization produces sufficient products and services tailored to indigenous consumers.

Table A.1. (*Contd*)

Stakeholder	Soft indicators for input	Soft indicators for conduct	Soft indicators for output
	The degree to which an employee cannot get away with irresponsible conduct toward customers.	The mutual benefits and responsibilities are reasonably divided between the organization and customers.	The organization helps customers to make the best possible use of products and services.
	The extent to which an employee who mistreats a customer appreciates having his conduct discussed.	If the organization fails to keep its promises, there are enough ways for customers to end the relationship with the corporation without too much cost.	The products and services that customers purchase do not put their health or safety at risk.
	The extent to which an employee who mistreats customers on a regular basis is reprimanded and, if necessary, punished.	The organization and its representatives show their willingness to realize the corporate responsibilities toward customers.	The products and services that customers purchase are healthy and safe.

Table A.2. Examples of *hard* indicators for Dirty Hands Dilemmas

Stakeholder	Hard indicators for input	Hard indicators for conduct	Hard indicators for output
Customers	Formal policy regarding responsibilities toward customers (e.g. complaints, marketing, and advertising, improvement programs).	Service and price uniformity per customer group.	Degree to which product adds to consumers' well-being.
	Instruments available (budgets, percentage of working time) to give substance to consumer policy.	Investments in product improvement programs as a proportion of budget or turnover.	Product innovation rate.
		Scope and type of communication with customers as a proportion of total communications (e.g. on finished products, ingredients/ components).	Number and nature of complaints from consumers.
	Training programs to improve customer orientation.		Number of consumer boycotts and protests.
			Customer retention rate.

Table A.2. (*Contd*)

Stakeholder	Hard indicators for input	Hard indicators for conduct	Hard indicators for output
	Information systems for tracing customers' interests and expectations (e.g. number of studies on customer trends).	Number and intensity of consultations with customers' representatives.	Product price/quality ratio.
	Systems and mechanisms for rapid and credible communication with customers.	Speed of response to customer complaints.	Length of time that products remain sold out.
		Customer complaints not observed by the corporation.	Percentage of product range offered to indigenous consumers under the market price.
	Screening procedures (e.g. new product and services, new customers).	Number of customer policy and consumer law transgressions.	Number and gravity of accidents owing to product use.
	Monitoring and documentation systems on external standards, complaints, product failures, legal precedents (e.g. number of inspections and audits).	Number and nature of contract cancellations.	Frequency and intensity of negative publicity.
		Number and nature of product recalls.	Number of quality awards.
		Reporting of near product failures expressed as proportion of time worked, units of production, output, people employed.	
	Sanction systems (procedures on customer-unfriendly conduct).	Damages paid to customers as proportion of total transactions.	
	Protection systems for customers (e.g. privacy).	Number of transgressions and scope of repercussions for employees guilty of irresponsible conduct towards customers.	
		Height of exit barriers (e.g. terms of notice for contracts and ease or difficulty of substituting product parts).	
Stockholders	Formal policy regarding responsibilities toward stockholders	Efficiency of business processes.	Turnover.
		Frequency of board meetings.	Net profit.

Table A.2. (*Contd*)

Stakeholder	Hard indicators for input	Hard indicators for conduct	Hard indicators for output
	(directors' remuneration, dividends, mergers and acquisitions).	Transparency about salaries, bonuses, pension plans, stock options, and long-term incentives.	Rate of return on assets (ROA).
	Screening procedures for new directors and executives.	Scope and type of communication toward stockholders.	Rate of return on equity (ROE) or total shareholder return.
	Formal decision-making procedures in Board.	Compliance with financial reporting standards.	Rate of return on investment (ROI).
	Explicit job descriptions for directors and executives.	Spread of ownership (value and percentage of options and actual ownership by executives and employees).	Stock price movements.
	Information systems for tracing stockholders' interests and expectations (e.g. number of studies on stockholder trends).	Whether or not stocks are freely negotiable.	Solvency and liquidity.
			Reserves.
			Length of period to repay loans.
			Stock price.
	Systems for rapid and credible communication with stockholders.	Number of failures to comply with financial regulations and policy.	Dividend paid per share in stock.
	Documentation of important investment decisions.	Number of employees fired because of fraud and embezzlement.	Brand value.
	Checks and balances in the board structure.	Ratio between profits paid and retained.	Measures of intangible financial value like intellectual property, new patents, education, and training.
	Measures against hostile takeovers.	Number of tax audits.	Number of proposals rejected and amendments adopted at stockholder meetings.
	Procedures to prevent insider trading (i.e. appointment of compliance officer, record of activities, lock-up periods).	Research intensity (percentage R&D Investment/ revenue).	Included in ethical mutual funds.
	Sanction systems for fraud and embezzlement by managers and employees.		Qualified auditors' report
	Monitoring and documentation		

Table A.2. (*Contd*)

Stakeholder	Hard indicators for input	Hard indicators for conduct	Hard indicators for output
	systems on external standards, complaints, and legal precedents.		
Employees	Policy and documentation regarding responsibilities toward employees (e.g. remuneration, career development, grievances, equal opportunity, diversity, flexible working, representation, health and safety, whistle blowing procedures, leave arrangements, employee commitment).	Wage differential from top to bottom (ratio of top salary to lowest salary; ratio of top 10% to lowest 10%).	Number of employees in permanent and temporary service.
	Protection procedures against unemployment, harassment, security incidents, and the violation of privacy.	Percentage of women and minorities in management positions.	Number of employees dismissed.
		Average salary of women and minorities compared with general average.	Personnel turnover and average length of employment.
	Information systems toward employees.	Age structure.	Ratio of jobs accepted to jobs offered.
	Fair grievance and disciplinary procedures.	Percentage of employees belonging to a trade union.	Average working hours.
	Systems of independent representation.	Frequency of meetings between Board and staff council.	Salary/wages.
	Proper employee files.	Anomalies addressed allowing for negotiation and appeal.	Ratio of lowest wage to local cost of living.
		Facilities for daycare.	Illness or absentee rates.
		Facilites for special personal leave.	Number of trade union conflicts.
		Training and education programs and budgets.	Number of legitimate sexual harassment complaints.
		Investment in illness and injury prevention.	Number of visits to company counselor or physician.
		Costs of providing daycare and other pro-diversity benefits.	Number of whistle blowing incidents and the related consequences for employees.
		Cost of severance pay per employee.	Number of employees who contest their dismissal in court.
			Training intensity per employee.

Stakeholder	Hard indicators for input	Hard indicators for conduct	Hard indicators for output
		Proportion of job performance reviews and exit interviews.	Total employee/stock option volume.
		Term of notice for employees to terminate their employment.	Paid leave for mothers/fathers.
		Communication about pricing and margins.	Frequency of time loss due to safety matters (lack of safety).
			Number of safety incidents.
			Number of cases won/lost in court relating to employee dismissal.
Suppliers	Formal policy regarding responsibilities toward society (gifts, bribery, segregation of duties).	Communication about pricing and margins.	Number of complaints from suppliers.
	Reference to ethical standards in contracts.	Trade with marginalized groups.	Number of contracts cancelled by suppliers before end of term.
	Tracking the speed of payment.	Activities that are undertaken to increase suppliers' ethical content of operations.	Duration of relationship.
	Documentation on contracts and their selection.	Confirmation that the suppliers conform to ethical standards.	Duration of contracts.
	Formal decision-making procedures for selecting suppliers.	Number of contracts terminated because suppliers did not conform to supplier code.	Number of suppliers who have gone bankrupt because of corporation's policy.
	Information systems toward suppliers.	Degree to which suppliers are selected on the basis of community and environmental performance, too.	Ratio between price paid/quality delivered.
	Monitoring and auditing system.		Actual payment terms applied.
	Supply chain management systems.	Number of cases won/lost when taken to court by suppliers.	
	Systems to protect confidential supplier information.		
Society	Formal policy regarding responsibilities toward society (volunteer work, donations, human rights).	Number and content of consultations with NGOs and governmental bodies.	Financial contributions to charities and community as percentage of total sales.
		Frequency of informational	Percentage of pre-tax profits

Stakeholder	Hard indicators for input	Hard indicators for conduct	Hard indicators for output
	Records on, for example, donations, employee community involvement. Information and feedback systems for representatives of society. Training and education programs for employees and suppliers on human rights. Community relations program. Monitoring systems regarding social developments (e.g. budget for studies). Procedures to review social acceptability of decisions. Number of employees who have completed human rights training program.	meetings for media and press releases. Number of visits received by the company. Participation in and support of community bodies. Activities for promoting human rights. Investments in underdeveloped regions. Activities to resolve social issues. Participation in community activities. Number of statutory violations, lawsuits and damages paid as a result. Percentage of local employees. Distribution of tax paid in each country. Number of social impact studies conducted as the basis for investment decisions. Percentage investment proposals rejected because of poor social standards in targeted country.	contributed to philanthropic organizations. Total amount of taxes paid to central and local government. Number and nature of complaints from neighbors. Multiplier effect of presence in communities (generation of business). Value of technology and skills transfer. Degree to which products and services boost society's prosperity and well-being. Percentage of sales made in socially illegitimate and questionable markets. Contribution to political parties.
Competitors	Policy for anti-bribery and management detection systems.	Number of employees dismissed for accepting bribes.	Number of cases lost after being taken to court by rivals.
Natural environment	Formal policy regarding environmental responsibilities. Environmental management system, including annual plans for improvements.	Number and intensity of discussions with environmental groups. Investment in the environment as percentage of total investments.	Total emissions. Damage due to fatal industrial accidents. Material intensity per unit of activity. Material intensity/ energy

Table A.2. (*Contd*)

Stakeholder	Hard indicators for input	Hard indicators for conduct	Hard indicators for output
	Risk management system on both production and product levels.	Number of fatal industrial accidents. Use of hazardous chemicals/materials.	consumption per dollar stockholder value added. Clean up.
	Formal and hierarchical integration of the environmental management system.	Waste and waste treatment (re-use/recycling). Number of failures to comply with permits or regulations in the environmental area.	Energy consumption (percentage renewable, water consumption, raw material use.) Greenhouse emissions.
	Explicit competence and responsibility at executive management level.	Number of inspections and audits.	Output harmful to ozone (CFC, VOC).
	Time and money allocated to environmental training.	Human resources devoted to environmental concerns.	Insurance premium (as proxy for effectiveness risk management).
		Dollars spent in response to major incidents.	Impact on bio-diversity. Number and content of complaints.

Table A.3. Examples of *soft* indicators for Many Hands Dilemmas

Indicators for input	Indicators for conduct	Indicators for output
Extent to which job description is clear to employees.	Number of unfair accusations for mistakes made by others.	Extent to which external stakeholders are sent from pillar to post.
Extent to which employees feel that their superiors take proper care with their tasks and authority.	Number of times that others went unpunished for blameworthy behavior.	Degree to which internal responsibilities get lost. Degree of employee solidarity.
Extent to which employees feel that tasks assigned can be executed.	Extent to which the same people are assigned onerous tasks.	Degree to which employees feel that their activities contribute to the achievement of corporate objectives.
Degree to which employees are stimulated to identify with the organization and internal partners.	Extent to which some functions are ignored. Extent to which some functions are discredited.	Degree of employee frustration about joint projects.

Table A.3. (*Contd*)

Indicators for input	Indicators for conduct	Indicators for output
Degree to which job-related problems can be discussed.	Extent to which appreciation is received for good work.	Degree of employee confidence in setting up new joint projects.
Degree of employee awareness of colleagues fulfilling their responsibilities.	Degree to which employees help colleagues with problems.	Degree of decisiveness at internal consultations.
Degree to which employees feel that fulfilling responsibilities is rewarded and neglecting responsibilities is punished.	Degree of awareness of functions in other departments.	
	Extent to which important information is shared internally.	
	Extent of vulnerability in joint projects.	
	Degree to which unscrupulous colleagues seize opportunities.	
	Degree to which internal agreements are kept.	

Table A.4. Examples of *hard* indicators for Many Hands Dilemmas

Indicators for input	Indicators for conduct	Indicators for output
Frequency of job training.	Percentage of time spent on consultation.	Duration of time that problems remain unsolved.
Codes of conduct.	Percentage of time spent on activities beyond job description.	Speed at which new recruits reach required performance levels.
Sanctioning mechanisms regarding job responsibilities.	Number of joint projects between departments.	
Recruitment and selection procedures.	Number of conflicts between departments and functionaries.	Degree to which mistakes are reported.
Meetings within departments.		Time lapse after mistakes are reported.
Meetings between departments.	Number of (successful/failed) internal conflict mediation sessions.	Extent of individual target achievement.
Minutes of meetings.		

Table A.4. (*Contd*)

Indicators for input	Indicators for conduct	Indicators for output
Description of responsibilities and job description.	Number of unsuccessful projects due to internal friction.	Extent of group target achievement.
Replacement procedures.	Attendance of internal meetings.	Percentage of agreements kept.
Extent of job rotation.		Number of unassigned mistakes.
Number and details of explicit contracts.	Employee awareness of generally relevant information.	Dismissal of employees for poor performance.
Information channels (bottom-up and top-down).	Time spent supporting new recruits.	Number of new products and services developed in interdepartmental projects.
Systems for protecting/ guaranteeing agreements.	Time spent on under-achieving employees.	
Mistakes register.	Time spent on vulnerable employees (illness, etc.).	Number of stakeholder requests followed up.
Complaints system.		
Performance feedback system.	Difference between highest and lowest output per employee.	
Reverse policing.		
Personalized products and actions (product labeling).	Extent of employee shares in joint proceeds (e.g. profit-sharing).	
Multiple decision-making procedures (the four eyes principle).	Degree to which organizational policy is actually adopted in subdivisions.	
Orientation program for new recruits.	Compatibility of systems.	

Table A.5. Examples of *soft* indicators for Entangled Hands Dilemmas

Indicators for input	Indicators for conduct	Indicators for output
Extent to which organization makes clear to employees what their responsibilities are regarding corporate assets.	Improper use of budgets.	Level of job satisfaction.
	Personnel fraud.	Stress level and overly stressful work situation.
	Unjustified billing of working hours.	
Extent to which manager sets a good example	Incorrect handling of funds received.	Degree of frustration among employees regarding defective corporate assets due

Indicators for input	Indicators for conduct	Indicators for output
in responsible treatment of corporate assets.	Incorrect handling of expenses returns.	to colleagues' carelessness.
Extent to which employees can realize norms regarding corporate assets.	Embezzlement of funds.	Unusually high employee expenditure patterns.
	Reckless use of company vehicles.	Extent of internal cooperation.
Extent to which corporation stimulates employees to treat corporate assets with care.	Misuse of means of communication.	
	Neglect of maintenance.	Extent to which suppliers prefer doing business with specific buyers.
	Theft of business equipment.	
Degree to which employee cannot get away with irresponsible conduct regarding corporate assets; the others always find out.	Taking home business equipment for private use.	Frequency of whistle blowing.
	Leaking of confidential information.	
	Unauthorized use of access codes.	
The extent to which irresponsible treatment of corporate assets can be discussed with the (alleged) perpetrator.	Use of insider information when trading shares or other securities.	
	Insufficient effort.	
The extent to which employees that treat corporate assets irresponsibly on a regular basis are reprimanded and, if necessary, punished.	Employees fail to observe stipulated working hours.	
	Alcohol and drug use.	
	Private surfing on the internet during working hours.	
	Falsely calling in sick.	
	Non-performance of tasks in return for money or favors from stakeholders.	
	Acceptance of gifts from stakeholders.	
	Favoring of friends and family.	
	Conflicting sideline activities.	
	Misuse of personal information.	
	Verbal abuse.	
	Bullying	

Table A.6. Examples of *hard* indicators for Entangled Hands Dilemmas

Indicators for input	Indicators for conduct	Indicators for output
Ethics hotline for misuse of corporate assets.	Number of media reports on employee leakage of confidential information.	Halt to production due to sabotage and obstruction.
Training in use of corporate assets.		Halt to production due to neglect of maintenance.
Codes of conduct for careful use of corporate assets.	Unaccountable inventory discrepancies.	Damage to reputation due to improper employee conduct.
Sanction mechanism for misuse of corporate assets.	Employee expenses improperly billed to the company.	Amount of fines paid due to improper employee conduct.
Recruitment and selection procedures.	Damage to company property.	Amount of damages paid for improper employee conduct.
Security system for minutes and agreements.	Incongruous leave of absence due to illness.	
Degree of job rotation.	Supervisors' awareness of sideline activities of colleagues.	Competitors' use of leaked confidential information.
Information channels (bottom-up and top-down).		Number of hours spent on repairing company property due to improper employee conduct.
Register of misuse of corporate assets.		
Complaints system.		
Performance feedback system.		The actual technical life span of company property compared to average life span.
Personification products and actions.		
Multiple decision-making procedures.		Total lost income due to improper employee conduct.
Conflict of interests register.		
Administration.		Costs incurred due to improper employee conduct.
Orientation program for new recruits.		

NOTES

CHAPTER 1

1. See, e.g., L. S. Paine, 1994. "Managing for organizational integrity." *Harvard Business Review*, 72: 107–17.
2. See also D. M. Messick, & M. H. Bazerman, 1996. "Ethical leadership and the psychology of decision-making." *Sloan Management Review*, Winter: 9–22.
3. See also L. S. Paine, 1994. "Managing for organizational integrity." *Harvard Business Review*, 72: 107–17.
4. L. K. Treviño, & S. A. Youngblood, 1990. "Bad apples in bad barrels: a causal analysis of ethical decision-making behavior." *Journal of Applied Psychology*, 75(4): 378–85.
5. Ibid.
6. Cited in J. E. Post, A. T. Lawrence, & J. Weber, 1999. *Business and Society: Corporate Strategy, Public Policy, Ethics*. McGraw-Hill. 9th edn.: pp. 111 and 378.
7. D. Chappell, & V. DiMartino, 1998. *Violence at Work*. International Labour Organization.
8. National Council on Alcoholism and Drug Dependencies 1998. *Alcohol and Other Drugs in the Workplace*.
9. See, e.g., J. Lambsdorff, 1999. "Corruption in empirical research: a review." *Transparency International: Working Paper*. See also the Transparency International Corruption Index on: www.transparency.
10. KPMG Integrity Management Services November 1999. *2000 Organizational Integrity Survey*. Washington, DC.
11. M. Punch, 1996. *Dirty Business: Exploring Corporate Misconduct*. London: Sage Publications.
12. J. Elkington, 1997. *Cannibals with Forks: The Triple Bottom Line of 21st Century Business*. Oxford: Capstone.
13. Like, for example, the title of the article "Corporate Angels" suggests. (In *Global Finance*. December 1999: 24–5.)
14. See also DeGeorge's exposé on the amoral myth of business, where he departs from the assumption that ethics and business are two separate worlds. R. T. DeGeorge, 1990. *Business Ethics*. New York: Macmillan.
15. See, e.g., C. D. Stone, 1975. *Where the Law Ends: The Social Control of Corporate Behavior*. New York: Waveland Press.
16. M. Weber, 1948. *From Max Weber: Essays in Sociology*. Trans. by H. H. Gerth, & C. Wright Mills, 1991. London: Routledge; M. Weber, 1980 (1920). *Wirtschaft und Gesellschaft: Grundrisse der verstehende Sociolgie*. J. Tübingen: Winkelmann. 5th edn.
17. B. DeMandeville, 1714. *The Fable of the Bees*. P. Hart (ed.). Harmondsworth: Penguin: p. 24.
18. Ibid.
19. A. Smith, 1910. *The Wealth of Nations*. London: Everyman's Library. repr. in 1975: p. 13.
20. Ibid., 400.
21. See also the discussion of Hayek and Friedman in Ch. 3.

22. i.e. 2.5 billion pounds. *The Ethical Investor*. EIRIS, July/August 1999: 1.
23. A. L. Domini, & P. D. Kinder, 1984. *Ethical Investing*. Reading, MA: Addison-Wesley.
24. M. Alperson, A. T. Marlin, J. Schorsch, & R. Will, 1991. *The Better World Investment Guide*. New York: Prentice Hall.
25. EIRIS, London.
26. Council on Economic Priorities 1998. *The Corporate Report Card: Rating 250 of America's Corporations for the Socially Responsible Investor*. A Dutton Book.
27. Domini Social Investments 1999. New York.
28. R. Levering, M. Moskowitz & M. Katz, 1984. *The 100 Best Companies to Work for in America*. New York: New American Library.
29. *The 100 Best Companies for Gay Men and Lesbians*. Pocket Books.
30. Council on Economic Priorities 1994. *Shopping for a Better World*. New York: Sierra Club Books.
31. J. Elkington, & J. Hailes, 1989. *The Green Consumer Guide*. London: Gollanz.
32. Ethical Consumer Research Association 1993. *The Ethical Consumer Guide to Everyday Shopping*. Manchester.
33. H. Van Luijk, 1997. "Business ethics in Europe." In P. Werhane, & R. E. Freeman (eds.). *Encyclopedic Dictionary of Business Ethics*. Blackwell: p. 75.
34. G. R. Weaver, L. K. Treviño, & P. L. Cochran, 1999. "Corporate ethics practices in the mid-1990s: an empirical study of Fortune 1000." *Journal of Business Ethics*, 18: 283–94.
35. KPMG Canada 1999. *Business Ethics Survey: Managing for Ethical Practice*. Toronto.
36. KPMG Business Ethics & Integrity Services India 1999. *1999 Business Ethics Survey Report India*.
37. KPMG Germany & Universität Erlangen-Nürnberg 1999. *Unternehmensleitbilder in Deutschen Unternehmen*. Frankfurt.
38. B. Farrell, & D. Cobbin, 1996. "Mainstreaming ethics in Australian enterprises." *Journal of Management Development*, 15(1): 37–50.
39. M. Kaptein, H. Klamer, & J. Ter Linden, 1999. *De Integere Organisatie: Het nut van bedrijfscodes*, KPMG, NCW, & Stichting Beroepsmoraal en Misdaadpreventie. The Hague.
40. J. Mahoney, 1997. "Business ethics in Great Britain." In P. Werhane, & R. E. Freeman (eds.). *Encyclopedic Dictionary of Business Ethics*. Blackwell: p. 78. Research in the summer of 1999 concludes that 78% of the top companies in the UK have a code of ethics, but the low response rate of 12% is not enough evidence to substantiate this claim. London Business School & Arthur Andersen 2000. *Ethical Concerns and Reputation Risk Management: A Study of Leading UK Companies*.
41. G. R. Weaver, L. K. Treviño, & P. L. Cochran, 1999. "Corporate ethics practices in the mid-1990s: an empirical study of Fortune 1000." *Journal of Business Ethics*, 18: 283–94.
42. KPMG 1999. *Business Ethics Survey: Managing for Ethical Practice*. Toronto.
43. See www.eoa.com.
44. G. R. Weaver, L. K. Treviño, & P. L. Cochran, 1999. "Corporate ethics practices in the mid-1990s: an empirical study of Fortune 1000." *Journal of Business Ethics*, 18: 283–94.
45. F. Fukuyama, 1999. *The Great Disruption: Human Nature and the Reconstruction of Social Order*. London: Profile Books: p. 3.
46. See, e.g., Dan Schiller, 1999. *Digital Capitalism: Networking the Global Market System*. Cambridge: The MIT Press.
47. A. Toffler, 1980. *The Third Wave*. New York: William Morrow.
48. M. Weber, 1978. *Economy and Society*. Berkeley: University of California Press.
49. F. Fukuyama, 1999. *The Great Disruption: Human Nature and the Reconstruction of Social Order*. London: Profile Books: p. 4.
50. Ibid., 7.
51. K. Kelly, 1998. *New Rules for the New Economy: Ten Ways the Network Economy is Changing Everything*. London: Fourth Estate.
52. Union of International Associations. *Yearbook of International Organizations*. Brussels: UAI.
53. L. K. Treviño, & K. A. Nelson, 1999. *Managing Business Ethics: Straight Talk about How To Do it Right*. New York: John Wiley & Sons.

54. Union of International Associations 1999. *Yearbook of International Organizations*. Brussels: UIA; R. van Tulder (ed.). 1999. *Redrawing Organizational Boundaries*. Department of Public Management. Rotterdam School of Management.

55. See also: T. Donaldson, 1989. *The Ethics of International Business*. New York: Oxford University Press; R. T. DeGeorge, 1993. *Competing with Integrity in International Business*. New York: Oxford University Press.

56. See also R. T. De George, 1999. *Business Ethics and the Information Age*. Washington: Bentley College.

57. R. B. Shaw, 1997. *Trust in Balance: Building Successful Organizations on Results, Integrity and Concern*. Jossey-Bass Publishers: p. 209.

58. Ibid.

59. See, e.g., J. Elkington, 1997. *Cannibals with Forks: The Triple Bottom Line of 21st-Century Business*. Oxford: Capstone.

60. Ibid.

61. See, e.g., the establishment of the Global Reporting Initiative in late 1997 with the mission of designing globally applicable guidelines for preparing enterprise-level sustainability reports.

62. See also M. Kaptein, & J. Wempe, 1998. "The ethics report: a means of sharing responsibility." *Business Ethics: A European Review*, 7(3): 131–9.

63. For example, a strong majority of people in the USA says they refuse to work for a company with a history of environmental incidents, insider trading, or worker accidents. See R. Sandroff, 1990. "How ethical is American business?" *Working Woman Magazine*, September: 113–16.

64. D. B. Turban, & D. W. Greening, 1997. "Corporate social performance and organizational attractiveness to prospective employees." *Academy of Management Journal*, 40: 658–72. See also J. Frooman, 1997. "Socially irresponsible and illegal behavior and stockholder wealth." *Business & Society*, 36: 221–49.

65. See, e.g., PriceWaterhouseCoopers, 2001. "Fraud Survey." www.pwc.com.

66. F. Fukuyama, 1999. *The Great Disruption: Human Nature and the Reconstruction of Social Order*. London: Profile Books: p. 6.

67. C. S. McCoy, 1985. *Management of Values: The Ethical Difference in Corporate Policy and Performance*. Marshfield, MA: Pitman Publishing Inc.: p. 34.

68. See M. Kaptein, 1998. *Ethics Management: Developing and Auditing the Ethical Content of Organizations*. Dordrecht: Kluwer Academic Publishers, especially section 2.3.

69. See J. Collier, 1998. "Theorizing the ethical organization." *Business Ethics Quarterly*, 8(4): 621–54.

70. See also M. G. Velasquez, 1992. *Business Ethics: Concepts and Cases*. New Jersey: Prentice Hall.

71. Sometimes, however, one's relationship with one's self (the care for one's body) or with God is also included in the domain of morality.

72. See also W. K. Frankena, 1973. *Ethics*. New York: Prentice Hall. 2nd edn.

73. See T. Donaldson, & T. Dunfee, 1999. *Ties that Bind: A Social Contracts Approach to Business Ethics*. Boston: Harvard Business School Press.

74. Ibid., 46.

75. T. van Willigenburg, 2000. Paper presented at the workshop "Integrity in Theory and Practice", Ethics Research School, Free University, Amsterdam, 8 November 2000.

76. See also M. Benjamin, 1990. *Splitting the Difference: Compromising and Integrity in Ethics and Politics*. University Press of Kansas.

77. T. van Willigenburg, 2000. Paper presented at the workshop "Integrity in Theory and Practice", Ethics Research School, Free University, Amsterdam, 8 November 2000.

78. We are thinking here especially of the theories of moral obligations, the deontological and the teleological (utilitarian) approaches. See also G. E. M. Anscombe, 1958. "Modern moral philosophy." *Philosophy*, 33: 1–19.

79. See H. J. L. van Luijk, 1985. *In het Belang van de Onderneming: Aantekeningen voor een bedrijfsethiek*. Delft: Eburon. Van Luijk describes the "regionalization" of ethics in this

context as "designing ethics from a completely critical involvement with specific areas of conduct" thereby referring also to Michael Walzer 1989. *Spheres of Justice: A Defense of Pluralism and Equality*. Oxford: Basil Blackwell.

80. We believe that better insight into the moral issues that arise in the business context can contribute to the development of ethics for "everyday life." Common ethical approaches usually deal with everyday issues abstractly and in isolation from the contexts in which they arise.

81. J. Collier, 1998. "Theorizing the ethical organization." *Business Ethics Quarterly*, 8(4): 622.

82. See also M. Bovens, 1998. *The Quest for Responsibility: Accountability and Citizenship in Complex Organizations*. Cambridge: Cambridge University Press: p. 4.

CHAPTER 2

1. See, e.g., M. W. Baron, P. Pettit, & M. Slote, 1997. *Three Methods in Ethics*. Malden: Blackwell Publishers Inc.

2. Consequentialists also regard the nature of an action and the intentions as morally relevant. A moral judgment is, however, ultimately based on the consequences of an action.

3. In practice, the difference is not as sharp as is suggested here. Many deontologists regard intentions as morally relevant.

4. For an extensive discussion of consequentialist ethics, see S. Scheffler, 1997. *Consequentialism and its Critics*, Oxford Readings in Philosophy.

5. J. Bentham, 1789. "The Principles of Morals and Legislation." In A. Ryan (ed.), 1987. *Utilitarianism and Other Essays*. Penguin Books: p. 65.

6. Ibid., 88.

7. See chs. 13 and 14 of Bentham's *Introduction to the Principles of Morals and Legislation*.

8. See M. G. Velasquez, 1992. *Business Ethics: Concepts and Cases*. New Jersey: Prentice Hall. 3rd edn., pp. 62–3.

9. See also Velasquez, who identifies several similar problems. Ibid.

10. For another exposition of deontological or Kantian ethics, see M. W. Baron, P. Pettit, & M. Slote, 1997. *Three Methods of Ethics*. Blackwell Publishers.

11. W. D. Ross, 1930. *The Right and the Good*. London: Oxford University Press.

12. I. Kant, 1785. *Groundwork of the Metaphysics of Morals: 421*. Ed. by M. Gregor, 1997. Cambridge: Cambridge University Press: p. 31.

13. Ibid., 421.

14. Ibid., 422.

15. Ibid., 422.

16. Ibid., 422.

17. Ibid., 423.

18. Ibid., 429.

19. J. Rawls, 1971. *A Theory of Justice*. Cambridge, MA: Harvard University Press.

20. Velasquez discusses three lines of critique against Kant's theory. A first problem is that Kant's theory is not exact enough to be consistently useful. Secondly, some critics claim that there is substantial disagreement concerning what the limits of the moral rights are and how conflicting rights should be balanced. Thirdly, there are counter-examples that show that the theory sometimes goes wrong, for example, with regard to the criteria of universalizability and reversibility. M. G. Velasquez, 1992. *Business Ethics: Concepts and Cases*. New Jersey: Prentice Hall. 3rd edn., pp. 84–6.

21. For an extensive account of virtue ethics, see, e.g., R. Crisp, & M. Slote (eds.), 1997. "Virtue Ethics." *Oxford Readings in: Philosophy*. Oxford University Press.

22. Aristotle. *Ethica Nicomachea*. Edition of R. McKeon, 1941. New York: Random House: p. 935.

23. Ibid., 942.

24. Ibid., 952.

25. Ibid., 957.

26. See A. MacIntyre, 1981. *After Virtue: A Study in Moral Theory*. London: Duckworth.
27. Plato, *Meno*, 110b.
28. Aristotle. *Ethica Nicomachea*. Edition of R. McKeon, 1941. New York: Random House: pp. 956–7.
29. Ibid., 957.
30. D. Hume, 1739. *A Treatise of Human Nature*. Edition Dolphin Books 1961. New York: Doubleday & Company: p. 512.
31. A. MacIntyre, 1981. *After Virtue. A Study in Moral Theory*. London: Duckworth: p. 178.
32. See also, H. B. Veatch, 1974. *Aristotle: A Contemporary Appreciation*. Bloomington/London: Indiana University Press.
33. Luke 6: 43.
34. Aristotle. *Ethica Nicomachea*. Edition of R. McKeon, 1941. New York: Random House: p. 943.
35. J. Dewey, 1972. "Reconstruction in philosophy." In J. de Graaf, 1976. *Elementair Begrip van de Ethiek*. Haarlem: Callenbach, p. 46.
36. See, e.g., G. J. Warnock, 1976. *The Object of Morality*. London: Methuen.
37. W. K. Frankena, 1973. *Ethics*. New York: Prentice Hall. 2nd edn., Ch. 4.
38. Ibid., 76.
39. H. A. Prichard, 1912. "Does moral philosophy rest on a mistake?" *Mind*, 21: 121–52; H. A. Prichard, 1949. *Moral Obligation*. Oxford: Oxford University Press. P. Foot, 1978. *Virtues and Vices*. Berkeley, Calif.: University of California Press.
40. G. E. M. Anscombe, 1958. "Modern moral philosophy." *Philosophy*, 33: 1–19.
41. Thomas Nagel distinguishes five categories: personal commitment, obligations, rights, utility, and perfectionist ideals. T. Nagel, 1979. *Moral Questions*. Cambridge: Cambridge University Press.
42. See also T. C. McConnel, 1987. "Moral dilemmas and consistency in ethics." In C. W. Gowans (ed.). *Moral Dilemmas*. New York: Oxford University Press.
43. B. Williams, 1981. "Ethical consistency." In *Moral Luck*. New York: Cambridge University Press.
44. See T. C. McConnel, 1996. "Moral residue and dilemmas." In H. E. Mason (ed.). *Moral Dilemmas and Moral Theory*. New York, Oxford: Oxford University Press. See also N O. Dahl, "Morality, moral dilemmas, and moral requirements." In H. E. Mason (ed.). *Moral Dilemmas and Moral Theory*. New York, Oxford: Oxford University Press.
45. T. C. McConnel, 1996. "Moral residue and dilemmas." In H. E. Mason (ed.). *Moral Dilemmas and Moral Theory*. New York, Oxford: Oxford University Press, p. 37.
46. See also M. Bovens, 1998. *The Quest for Responsibility: Accountability and Citizenship in Complex Organizations*. Cambridge: Cambridge University Press.
47. L. S. Paine, 1947. "Integrity." In P. Wurhane, & R. E. Freeman (eds.). *Encyclopedic Dictionary of Business Ethics*. Blackwell, p. 336.
48. See, e.g., G. Taylor, 1981. "Integrity." *Aristotelian Society*, supplementary vol. 55: 143–59; M. Benjamin, 1990. *Splitting the Difference: Compromising and Integrity in Ethics and Politics*. University Press of Kansas: 52; A. Montefiore, & D. Vines (eds.), 1999. *Integrity: In the Public and Private Domains*. London: Routledge. The Oxford English Dictionary describes integrity as: "1. The condition of having no part or element wanting; unbroken state; material wholeness, completeness, entirety. 2. Unimpaired or uncorrupted state; original perfect condition; soundness. 3.a. Innocence, sinlessness. b. Soundness of moral principle; the character of uncorrupted virtue, honesty, sincerity."
49. See M. Benjamin, 1990. *Splitting the Difference: Compromising and Integrity in Ethics and Politics*. University Press of Kansas: p. 46.
50. As held by Solomon, e.g., B. Solomon, 1999. *A Better Way to Think about Business: How Personal Integrity Leads to Corporate Success*. New York: Oxford University Press.
51. M. Benjamin, 1990. *Splitting the Difference: Compromising and Integrity in Ethics and Politics*. University Press of Kansas: p. 47.
52. Benjamin distinguishes six prototypes that fall short of integrity: the moral chameleon, the opportunist, the hypocrite, the weak-willed person, the sef-deceiver, and the alienated victim of external coercion.

53. G. Taylor, 1981. "Integrity." *Aristotelian Society*, supplementary vol. 55: p. 144.

54. See L. S. Paine, 1997. In P. Werhane, & R. E. Freeman (eds.). *Encyclopedic Dictionary of Business Ethics*. Blackwell: pp. 335–6.

55. M. Philip, 1999. "Citizenship and integrity." In A. Montefiore, & D. Vines (eds.). *Integrity: In the Public and Private Domains*. London: Routledge: pp. 19–47.

56. See L. S. Paine, 1997. "Integrity." In P. Werhane, & R. E. Freeman (eds.). *Encyclopedic Dictionary of Business Ethics*. Blackwell: p. 335.

57. E. H. Erikson, 1950. *Childhood and Society*. New York: W. W. Norton.

58. T. E. Becker, 1998. "Integrity in organizations: beyond honesty and conscientiousness." *Academy of Management Review*, 23: 157.

59. See also C. I. Barnard, 1938. *The Functions of the Executive*. Cambridge, MA: Harvard University Press: p. 267. Barnard holds that responsibility is the property that makes internal morality effective in conduct.

60. B. Williams, 1981. *Philosophical Papers 1973–1980*.

61. L. S. Paine, 1997. "Integrity." In P. Werhane, & R. E. Freeman (eds.). *Encyclopedic Dictionary of Business Ethics*. Blackwell: pp. 335–6.

62. As Bob Solomon eloquently formulates: "Before we can *do*, we must *be*, even if what we become, surprisingly, is the accumulation and outcome of, among other things, our actions. But that means that among the consequences of our actions, indeed, foremost among them or prior to them, we must keep in mind who we are and what we are making of ourselves, our own ideals, and how we see ourselves and how others see us, too." B. Solomon, 1999. *A Better Way to Think about Business: How Personal Integrity Leads to Corporate Success*. New York: Oxford University Press: p. 63.

63. Ibid., 40.

64. A. Montefiore, 1999. "A philosopher's introduction." In A. Montefiore, & D. Vines (eds.). *Integrity: In the Public and Private Domains*. London: Routledge: p. 10.

65. D. Vines, 1999. "Integrity and the economy." In A. Montefiore, & D. Vines (eds.). *Integrity: In the Public and Private Domains*. London: Routledge: p. 66.

66. A. MacIntyre, 1981. *After Virtue. A Study in Moral Theory*. London: Duckworth: p. 191.

67. B. Solomon, 1999. *A Better Way to Think about Business: How Personal Integrity Leads to Corporate Success*. New York: Oxford University Press: p. 39.

68. See also ibid.

69. H. J. L. van Luijk, 2000. *Integer en Verantwoord in Beroep en Bedrijf*. Amsterdam: Boom, p. 153.

70. Ibid.

71. See, e.g., L. McFall, 1987. "Integrity." *Ethics*, 98: 5–20; R. C. Mayer, J. H. Davis, & F. D. Schoorman, 1995. "An integrative model of organizational trust." *Academy of Management Review*, 20: 709–34.

72. See also B. Solomon, 1999. *A Better way to Think About Business: How Personal Integrity Leads to Corporate Success*. New York: Oxford University Press, p. 39; M. Kaptein, 1999. "Integrity Management." *European Management Journal*, 17(6): 625–33.

73. T. van Willigenburg, 2000. "Bedreigen morele compromissen onze integriteit?" Paper presented at the workshop "Integrity in Theory and Practice", Ethics Research School, Free University, Amsterdam, 8 November 2000.

74. Ibid.

75. C. Hampden-Turner, & F. Trompenaars, 2000. *Building Cross-Cultural Competence: How to Create Wealth from Conflicting Values*. John Wiley & Sons.

76. Ibid., 8.

77. Ibid., 9.

78. See M. Benjamin, 1990. *Splitting the Difference: Compromising and Integrity in Ethics and Politics*. Lawrence, Kan: University Press of Kansas.

79. See also ibid.

80. See also C. Calhoun, 1995. "Standing for Something." *Journal of Philosophy*, 92: 235–61.

81. Benjamin defines integrity as a reasonably coherent and relatively stable set of highly cherished values and principles; verbal behavior expressing these values and principles; and

conduct embodying one's values and principles that is consistent with what one says. M. Benjamin, 1990. *Splitting the Difference: Compromising and Integrity in Ethics and Politics*. Lawrence, Kan: University Press of Kansas: p. 51.

82. See also A. W. Musschenga, A. W. van Haaften, M. Slors, & B. Spiecker (eds.), 2001. *Personal and Moral Identity*.
83. "IHC Caland will stay in Burma." *Algemeen Dagblad*, 5 June 1999.
84. The information in this section is based in part on the *Burma\Myanmar Annual Report 1998*, Burma Center Netherlands, 1998.
85. The information in this section is based in part on the *Burma\Myanmar Annual Report 1998*, Burma Center Netherlands, 1998.
86. "IHC Caland komt critici maar nauwelijks tegemoet." *Telegraaf*, 5 June 1999.
87. Ibid.
88. "ABP geeft IHC respijt bij gedragscode." *Trouw*, 5 June 1999.
89. Ibid.
90. "Botsing IHC en ABP dreigt." *Limburger*, 2 June 1999.
91. "ABP wacht nog op gedragscode van IHC Caland." *Het Parool*, 5 June 1999.
92. "Botsing IHC en ABP dreigt." *Limburger*, 2 June 1999.
93. The *Burma\Myanmar Annual Report 1998*, Burma Center Netherlands, 1998; "Oil companies Investing in Burma under fire in Europe." *The Irrawaddy*. June 1999: pp. 14–15; Burma Center Netherlands, 1999. *Questions for IHC Stockholders Meeting*.
94. L. de Waal, 1999. "Investors also guilty of situation in Burma." *Trouw*, 1 June.

CHAPTER 3

1. F. A. Hayek von, 1967. "The moral element in free enterprise." *Studies in Philosophy, Politics and Economics*. London: Routledge: 229–36.
2. Ibid., 303.
3. Hayek is also inconsistent. What applies for employees can also be said of the stockholders. They are no more bound to the corporation. They can simply withdraw their money from the corporation by selling their stocks and invest it in another company. That is even desirable to achieve an optimal allocation of production resources. Nevertheless, the corporate objective can be equated with the interest of the stockholders. The fact remains that it is usually more important that employees remain with a company than for stockholders to do so. According to Hayek, a corporation may not pursue social objectives because the corporation goes beyond its bounds in doing so and it creates a justification for government control. The same argument, the prevention of government control, can however be used to argue for a broader notion of corporate responsibility. If a corporation limits itself solely to the maximization of profit in order to serve the interests of the shareholders, correcting measures on the part of the government will follow eventually. To prevent this, corporations should consider enlightened self-regulation and recognize their social responsibilities.
4. W. Dekker, 1989. "The responsible corporation and the subversive side of business ethics." In G. Enderle, B. Almond, & A. Argandona (eds.). *People in Corporations: Ethical Responsibilities and Corporate Effectiveness*. Dordrecht: Kluwer Academic Publishers: p. 17.
5. M. Friedman, 1962. *Capitalism and Freedom*. Chicago: University of Chicago Press. See also, M. Friedman, 1970. "The social responsibility of business is to increase its profits." *The New York Times Magazine*. 13 September. Also included in W. M. Hoffman, & J. Mills Moore, 1984. *Business Ethics: Readings and Cases in Corporate Morality*. New York: McGraw-Hill Book Company.
6. As does Hayek, Friedman acknowledges that there are moral rules in force in the market. However, he does not consider these norms to be moral. He equates corporate responsibility with the pursuit of social ideals. If morality, as it relates to corporations, can be equated with the achievement of all sorts of idealistic objectives and allowing yourself to be led by

all sorts of altruistic motives, Friedman is right. A corporation, however, is no Florence Nightingale. At the same time, it does have a number of moral obligations.

7. M. Friedman, 1970. "The social responsibility of business is to increase its profits." *The New York Times Magazine.* 13 September.

8. J. K. Galbraith, 1977. *The Age of Uncertainty.* Boston: Houghton Mifflin: p. 274.

9. Ibid., 277.

10. Ibid., 278.

11. Werhane uses the term "aggregation model" here. See P. H. Werhane, 1985. *Persons, Rights and Corporations.* New York: Prentice Hall, Englewood Cliffs: p. 40. This specification suggests a relatively arbitrary way of bringing together a number of entities. If a corporation is perceived in this manner, this is usually from an outsider's perspective. In our opinion, the term "job-related responsibility" expresses more accurately the intentional character of the cooperative association different individuals decide to enter into and make a contribution to by fulfilling a given function.

12. R. Hessen, 1979. *In Defence of the Corporation.* Stanford: Hoover Institution press, XV. Cited in P. H. Werhane, 1985. *Persons, Rights and Corporations.* New York: Prentice Hall, Englewood Cliffs: p. 40.

13. M. G. Velasquez, 1983. "Why corporations are not morally responsible for anything they do." *Journal of Business and Professional Ethics,* 3: 1–18.

14. M. G. Velasquez, 1998. *Business Ethics: Concepts and Cases.* New York: Prentice Hall, Englewood Cliffs: 3rd edn.

15. M. J. H. Cobbenhagen, 1927. *De Verantwoordelijkheid in de Onderneming.* Roermond: Romen.

16. Cobbenhagen is not alone in this. In 1932, Berle and Means recognized the consequences of the separation of ownership and management. The managers of a corporation are not only employees who direct the company on behalf of the owners. They also assume the moral responsibilities of the director owner. A. A. Berle, & G. C. Means, 1932. *The Modern Corporation and Private Property.* New York: Macmillan.

17. P. Kuin, *Social Responsibility: There's More to Management.* London: Uniliver.

18. Ibid.

19. G. A. Wagner, 1979. *Beschouwingen van een Ondernemer.* Kampen: Kok: p. 89.

20. H. J. Van Zuthem, 1978. *Macht en Moraal in Arbeidsverhoudingen.* Assen: Van Gorcum: p. 139.

21. F. A. Hayek, 1967. "The moral element in free enterprise." In *Studies in Philosophy, Politics and Economics.* London: Routledge: 229–36.

22. K. E. Goodpaster, & J. B. Matthews Jr, 1982. "Can a corporation have a conscience?" *Harvard Business Review.* Repr. in T. L. Beauchamp, & N. E. Bowie (eds.), 1983. *Ethical Theory and Business.* New York: Prentice Hall; K. E. Goodpaster, 1987. "The principle of moral projection: a reply to professor Ranken." *The Journal of Business Ethics,* 6(4): 329–32.

23. K. E. Goodpaster and J. B. Matthews Jr., "Can a corporation have a conscience." *Harvard Business Review.* Repr. in T. L. Beauchamp, & M. E. Bowie (eds.), 1983. *Ethical Theory and Business.* New York: Prentice Hall: p. 72.

24. Ibid., 76.

25. I. W. M. Spit, 1986. *Multisubjectieve Activiteit en Morele Verantwoordelijkheid.,* Thesis: Utrecht: pp. 43–4.

26. D. Copp, 1979. "Collective actions and secondary action." *American Philosophical Quarterly,* 16(3): 177.

27. I. W. M. Spit, 1986. *Multisubjectieve Activiteit en Morele Verantwoordelijkheid.* Thesis: Utrecht: p. 46.

28. P. H. Werhane, 1985. *Persons, Rights, and Corporations.* New York: Prentice Hall, Englewood Cliffs: p. 39.

29. Ibid., 59.

30. Ibid., 52.

31. I. W. M. Spit, 1986. *Multisubjectieve Activiteit en Morele Verantwoordelijkheid.* Thesis: Utrecht: p. 121.

32. See, e.g., P. French (ed.), 1972. *Individual and Collective Responsibility: The Massacre at My Lai*. Cambridge: Schenkman; P. A. French, 1984. *Collective and Corporate Responsibility*. New York: Columbia University Press; P. French (ed.), 1991. *The Spectrum of Responsibility*. New York: St. Martin's Press; P. French, 1992. *Responsibility Matters*. Kansas University Press; P. A. French, 1995. *Corporate Ethics*. Fort Worth: Harcourt Brace & Company.

33. The terms "aggregate" and "conglomerate" are used here in the same sense a geologist would use them.

34. P. A. French, 1984. *Collective and Corporate Responsibility*. New York: Columbia University Press: p. 17.

35. Ibid., 38.

36. Ibid.

37. T. Donaldson, 1982. *Corporations and Morality*. New York: Prentice Hall, Englewood Cliffs: p. 22.

38. K. E. Goodpaster, & J. B. Matthews Jr, 1982. "Can a corporation have a conscience?" *Harvard Business Review*. Repr. in W. M. Hoffman, & J. M. Moore (eds.), 1982. *Business Ethics: Readings and Cases in Corporate Morality*. McGraw-Hill. 2nd edn.: pp. 184–94.

39. K. E. Goodpaster, 1983. "The concept of corporate responsibility." *The Journal of Business Ethics*, 2(1): 1–22; K. E. Goodpaster, 1987. "The principle of moral projection: a reply to professor Ranken." *The Journal of Business Ethics*, 6(4): 329–32.

40. I. W. M. Spit, 1986. *Multisubjectieve Activiteit en Morele Verantwoordelijkheid*. Thesis: Utrecht: p. iii.

41. P. A. French, 1984. *Collective and Corporate Responsibility*. New York: Columbia University Press: p. xi.

42. Ibid., xii.

43. See, among others, I. W. M. Spit, 1986. *Multisubjectieve Activiteit en Morele Verantwoordelijkheid*. Thesis: Utrecht: p. 59.

44. See A. Van den Beld, 1984. *Filosofie van het Menselÿk Handelen*. Assen: Van Gorcum.

45. I. W. M. Spit, 1986. *Multisubjectieve Activiteit en Morele Verantwoordelijkheid*. Thesis: Utrecht: p. 86.

46. Furthermore, abstention by a corporation is problematic if an employee acts on his or her own authority and certainly, the corporation does not incite employees to behave in this manner. We discussed this earlier.

47. *RSV inquiry of the Parliament: The Rise and Fall of Rijn-Schelde-Verolme 1977–1983; 1983–1984*. The Hague. Proceedings in Lower House. 1984–5. Session, 17817, no. 16: p. 301.

48. See H. L. A. Hart, 1968. *Punishment and Responsibility*. New York: Oxford University Press.

49. Ibid., 151–2.

50. The meaning of "corporate practice", as it is used here, deviates from MacIntyre's use of the term. Although he also believes it concerns a manner of doing something, a pattern of action, for him a practice describes an ideal pattern of action. Immoral practice is thus excluded. A practice, according to MacIntyre, is always something positive. Here, the concept is used in a more neutral sense. It relates to all concrete structuring factors, which are expressed in the joint action of people. This meaning matches the common usage of the concept.

51. Compare also Wittgenstein's "family resemblances."

52. See, e.g., S. P. Robbins, 1987. *Organization Theory: Structure, Design, and Applications*. Prentice Hall. 2nd edn.

53. See, e.g., J. C. Collin, & J. I. Porras, 1994. *Built to Last: Successful Habits of Visionary Companies*. London: Century.

54. For example, the reward structure has an influence on the culture. If the income of employees is partly based on performance, this will have radical consequences for the behavior of the employees involved. The perception that managers have of employees' motivations is clear. The employees are, to a large extent, motivated by money and to a lesser extent by bearing responsibility and a congenial working atmosphere. As soon as they can earn more elsewhere, they will opt for a new employer. Employees who work within such a reward system will usually act according to such an expectation pattern.

55. C. Argyris, & D. A. Schön, 1978. *Organizational Learning: A Theory of Action Perspective.* Reading: Addison-Wesley Publishing Company.

56. See, e.g., L. S. Paine, 1994. "Managing for organizational integrity." *Harvard Business Review,* 72: 107–17; J. A. Patrick, & J. F. Quinn, 1997. *Management Ethics: Integrity at Work.* Thousands Oaks: Sage Publications; L. W. J. C. Huberts & J. H. J. van den Heuvel (eds.), 1999. *Integrity at the Public-Private Interface.* Maastricht: Shaker Publishing; M. Kaptein, 1999. "Integrity management." *European Management Journal,* 17(6): 625–33.

57. J. L. Badaracco, 1997. *Defining Moments: When Managers Must Choose Between Right and Wrong.* Boston: Harvard Business School Press.

58. M. V. *Herald of Free Enterprise,* Report of the (Sheen) Court, No. 8074, Department of Transport, July 1987, section 14.1.

CHAPTER 4

1. In his article, *The Parable of the Sadhu,* McCoy describes a similar incident during a climb in the Himalayas. During the climb the expedition met an Indian acetic, a Sadhu, who was barely clothed and quite ill. If he did not get help soon, he would die. The expedition decided to leave the man behind and to continue their climb. A lot of effort went into setting up this unique expedition. McCoy noted that the circumstances during the climb had much in common with the business context: great stress, a lot of adrenaline, an all-encompassing goal, and the feeling of having a unique opportunity. C. S. McCoy, 1983. "The parable of the Sadhu." *Harvard Business Review,* 61: September–October.

2. R. H. Coase, 1937. "The nature of the firm." *Economica,* 4. Repr. in J. B. Barney, & W. G. Ouchi (eds.), 1986. *Organizational Economics.* San Francisco: Jossey-Bass Publishers: p. 85.

3. Ibid.

4. See also the analysis by Mark Bovens of the concept of passive responsibility. M. Bovens, 1998. *The Quest for Responsibility: Accountability and Citizenship in Complex Organizations.* Cambridge: Cambridge University Press.

5. The distinction between personal responsibility, on the one hand, and functional responsibility, on the other, gives rise to a number of problems. If something is expected of someone on the basis of the role he or she fulfills or because someone works for a corporation where moral lines are clearly crossed, it is understandable (and perhaps even a personal duty of those involved) to call attention to this. This is referred to in the literature as "whistleblowing." Depending on the seriousness of the situation, one can be justified in expressing this criticism externally as well. In extreme situations, it is even acceptable to do this anonymously. This issue is not discussed here. M. Bovens, 1998. *The Quest for Responsibility: Accountability and Citizenship in Complex Organizations.* Cambridge: Cambridge University Press.

6. Ibid.

7. Deuteronomy 21: 6–7.

8. Matthew 27: 24.

9. See M. Walzer, 1973. "Political action: the problem of dirty hands." *Philosophy and Public Affairs,* 2, Winter: 161; S. Benn, 1983. "Private and public morality: clean living and dirty hands." In S. Benn, & G. F. Gauss (eds.). *Public and Private in Social Life.* New York: St. Martin's Press: 155–81.

10. See also J. L. Badaracco, 1992. "Business ethics: four spheres of executive responsibility." *California Management Review,* 34: 64–79.

11. Genesis 3: 15.

12. 1 Tim. 6: 10.

13. R. Mees, 1952. *De Moraal in het Handelsleven.* Amsterdam/Antwerp: World Library: p. 15.

14. Ibid., 17.

15. Ibid., 46.

16. Ibid., 47.

17. This does not mean however, that he, described the Dirty Hands Dilemma as a conflict of conscience.
18. N. Machiavelli, 1961 (1981). *The Prince*. Harmondsworth: Penguin Books: Ch. XV, p. 92.
19. J. P. Sartre, 1948. *Les Mains Sales*. Paris: Gallimard. See also: *Dirty Hands and Three Other Plays*. Trans. by L. Abel, 1989. New York: p. 218.
20. M. Walzer, 1973. "Political action: the problem of dirty hands." *Philosophy and Public Affairs*, 2, Winter: 161.
21. D. P. Thompson, 1987. *Political Ethics and Public Office*. Cambridge/Massachusetts/London: Harvard University Press.
22. See also B. Groce, 1918. "Per un detto del Machiavelli." *La Critica*, 28: 193. See furthermore, the analysis of I. Berlin, 1981. *Against the Current: Essays in the History of Ideas*. New York: Oxford University Press.
23. I. Berlin, 1981. *Against the Current: Essays in the History of Ideas*. New York: Oxford University Press.
24. Ibid., 50.
25. N. Machiavelli, 1961 (1981). *The Prince*. Harmondsworth: Penguin Books. Chapter XV, p. 91.
26. I. Berlin, 1981. "The originality of Machiavelli." In *Against the Current: Essays in the History of Ideas*. New York: Oxford University Press: p. 64.
27. Ibid., 53.
28. Ibid., 57.
29. M. Walzer, 1973. "Political action: the problem of dirty hands." *Philosophy and Public Affairs*, 2, Winter: 161.
30. See, e.g., S. Hook (ed.), 1961. *Determinism and Freedom in the Age of Modern Science*. New York: Collier Books; T. Honderich, 1988. *A Theory of Determinism: The Mind, Neuroscience, and Life Hopes*. New York: Oxford University Press.
31. J. Gray, 1984. "Introduction." In Z. Pelczynski, & J. Gray (eds.). *Conceptions of Liberty in Political Philosophy*. London: Athlone.
32. Ibid.
33. D. P. Thompson, 1987. *Political Ethics and Public Office*. Cambridge/Massachusetts/London: Harvard University Press.
34. Ibid., 22.

CHAPTER 5

1. This is scarcity in the economic sense of the term: sacrifices must be made to obtain resources. Scarcity implies, therefore, that choices must be made.
2. R. E. Freeman, & D. R. Gilbert Jr, 1988. *Corporate Strategy and the Search for Ethics*. Englewood Cliffs, New York: Prestice Hall: p. 164.
3. J. Rawls, 1972. *A Theory of Justice*. London/Oxford/New York: Oxford University Press: 79.
4. D. Gauthier, 1991. "Morality and markets: the implications for business." In B. Harvey, H. J. L. van Luijk, & G. Corbetta (eds.). *Market Morality and Company Size*. Dordrecht: Kluwer Academic Publishers: pp. 60–1.
5. H. J. L. van Luijk, 1994. "Rights and interests in a participatory market society." *Business Ethics Quarterly*, 3(3): 79–97.
6. Ibid.
7. J. Rawls, 1972. *A Theory of Justice*. London/Oxford/New York: Oxford University Press: 33.
8. H. J. L. van Luijk, 1994. "Rights and interests in a participatory market society." *Business Ethics Quarterly* 3(3): 79–97.
9. We consider the socialist model, in which the government acts as guardian of the general interest, as an example of the contract model. The legitimization of the government's (monarch's) role relies on the implicit support of the citizens.

10. Here we are referring to a moral contract. The moral concept "contract" must be distinguished from the legal meaning of that concept. Rather than the term "contract," one could use the term "covenant" or "treaty."

11. This opinion is held by both Adam Smith and other classical economists and by most adherents of a free-market theory.

12. Milton Friedman considers it a (moral) duty of corporations not to get involved with moral norms. See Ch. 3 of this book for an elaborate discussion.

13. See also D. Gauthier, 1977. "The social contract as ideology." *Philosophy and Public Affairs*, 6: 130–64.

14. T. Donaldson, 1982. *Corporations and Morality*. New York: Prentice Hall, Englewood Cliffs; T. Donaldson, 1989. *The Ethics of International Business*. New York: Oxford University Press: Ch. 4.

15. T. W. Dunfee, 1991. "Business ethics and extant social contracts." *Business Ethics Quarterly*, 1(1): 23–52.

16. T. Donaldson, & T. W. Dunfee, 1991. "A theory of social contracts." Paper presented during the "Conference on Interdisciplinary Approaches to the Study of Economic Problems." The Stockholm School of Economics; T. Donaldson, & T. W. Dunfee, 1994. "Toward a unified conception of business ethics: integrative social contracts theory." *Academy of Management Review*, 19: 252–84; T. Donaldson, & T. W. Dunfee, 1995. "Integrative social contracts theory: a communitarian conception of economic ethics." *Economics and Philosophy*, 1: 85–112; T. Donaldson, & T. W. Dunfee, 1999. *Ties that Bind: A Social Contracts Approach to Business Ethics*. Boston: Harvard Business School Press.

17. D. Gauthier, 1991. "Morality and markets: the implications for business." In B. Harvey, H. J. L. van Luijk, & G. Corbetta (eds.), 1991. *Market Morality and Company Size*. Dordrecht/Boston/London: Kluwer Academic Publishers, 57–65; D. Gauthier, 1977. "The social contract as ideology." *Philosophy and Public Affairs*, 6: 130–64; D. Gauthier, 1986. *Morals by Agreement*. Oxford: Clarendon Press.

18. R. Hessen, 1979. *In Defence of the Corporation*. Stanford: Hoover Institution; R. Hessen, 1979. "A new concept of corporations: a contractual and private property model." *Hastings Law Journal*, 30: 1327–50.

19. M. Keeley, 1988. *A Social-Contract Theory of Organizations*. Indiana: University of Notre Dame Press.

20. H. J. L. van Luijk, 1995. "Rights and interests in a participatory market society." *Business Ethics Quarterly*, 3(3): 79–97. Van Luijk uses the term transaction ethics. This concept is more limited than that of the contract.

21. M. G. Velasquez, 1992. *Business Ethics: Concepts and Cases*. New York: Prentice Hall, Englewood Cliffs. Here the concept of contract is limited to the corporation–consumer relationship.

22. B. Wempe, 2001. "Taking Social Contracts Seriously." Paper presented at the conference of the "International Association of Business and Society" in Sedona.

23. M. G. Velasquez, 1998. *Business Ethics: Concepts and Cases*. New York: Prentice Hall, Englewood Cliffs, New York: pp. 270–3.

24. R. Hessen, 1979. "A new concept of corporations: a contractual and private property model." *Hastings Law Journal*, 30: 1330.

25. T. Donaldson, 1982. *Corporations and Morality*. New York: Prentice Hall, Englewood Cliffs: p. 42.

26. Ibid.

27. M. Keeley, 1988. *A Social-Contract Theory of Organizations*. Indiana: University of Notre Dame Press: p. 226.

28. T. Donaldson, & T. Dunfee, 1991. "A theory of social contracts." Paper presented during the "Conference on Interdisciplinary Approaches to the Study of Economic Problems." The Stockholm School of Economics.

29. See M. G. Velasquez, 1992. *Business Ethics: Concepts and Cases*. New York: Prentice Hall, Englewood Cliffs: 270–3. See also: T. Donaldson, 1982. *Corporations and Morality*. Englewood Cliffs; New York: Prentice Hall. T. Donaldson, 1989. *The Ethics of International Business*. Oxford University Press: Ch. 4.

30. T. Donaldson, 1982. *Corporations and Morality*. New York: Prentice Hall, Englewood Cliffs.
31. T. Donaldson, 1989. *The Ethics of International Business*. New York, Oxford: Oxford University Press.
32. T. Donaldson, & T. Dunfee, 1999. *Ties that Bind: A Social Contracts Approach to Business Ethics*. Boston: Harvard Business School Press.
33. See, among others: M. Keeley, 1988. *A Social-Contract Theory of Organizations*. Indiana: University of Notre Dame Press: p. 226. See also R. Hessen, 1979. "A new concept of corporations: a contractual and private property model." *Hastings Law Journal*, 30: 1330. See furthermore D. Gauthier, 1986. *Morals by Agreement*. Oxford: Clarendon Press: p. 315.
34. D. Gauthier, 1986. *Morals by Agreement*. Oxford: Clarendon Press: p. 315.
35. D. Gauthier, 1991. "Morality and markets: the implications for business." In B. Harvey, H. J. L. van Luijk, & G. Corbetta (eds.), 1991. *Market, Morality and Company Size*. Dordrecht: Kluwer Academic Publishers.
36. See, among others: T. Donaldson, & T. Dunfee, 1991. "A theory of social contracts." Paper presented during the "Conference on Interdisciplinary Approaches to the Study of Economic Problems." The Stockholm School of Economics; T. Donaldson, & T. Dunfee, 1994. "Toward a unified conception of business ethics: integrative social contracts theory." *Academy of Management Review*, 19(2): 252–84; T. Donaldson, & T. Dunfee, 1995. "Integrative Social Contracts Theory: a communitarian conception of economic ethics." *Economics and Philosophy*, 11: 85–112. See also D. Gauthier, 1991. "Morality and markets: the implications for business." In B. Harvey, H. J. L. van Luijk, & G. Corbetta (eds.), 1991. *Market, Morality and Company Size*. Dordrecht: Kluwer Academic Publishers.
37. H. J. L. van Luijk, 1993. *Om Redelijk Gewin: Oefeningen in bedrijfsethiek*. Amsterdam: Boom Meppel: p. 214.
38. See T. Donaldson, 1989. *The Ethics of International Business*. New York: Oxford University Press: p. 57.
39. Ibid., 59.
40. See M. Kaptein, 1998. *Ethics Management: Auditing and Developing the Ethical Content of Organizations*. Dordrecht: Kluwer Academic Publishers: Ch. 2.
41. See also P. Heugens, M. Kaptein, & H. van Oosterhout, 2000. "Normative principles for the governance of stakeholder relations." Paper presented at the "Academy of Management Conference" in Toronto. Van Oosterhout elaborates on effectiveness as a necessary condition for normativity in general. See J. Van Oosterhout, 2002. *The Quest for Legitimacy: On Authority and Responsibility in Governance*. ERIM Ph.D. Series. Rotterdam: Erasmus University Rotterdam.
42. I. R. MacNeil, 1980. *The New Social Contract: An Inquiry into Modern Contractual Relations*. New Haven, London: Yale University Press: p. 44.
43. J. H. Nieuwenhuis, 1979. *Drie Beginselen van Contractrecht*. Deventer: Kluwer: p. 14.
44. As Heugens *et al.* write: "Even Thomas Hobbes, arguably the most radical contractarianist in political thought because of his view that individuals ought to relinquish everything to the sovereign by means of the social contract in return for the sovereign's protection of their lives, explicitly made a provision for the effectiveness of that contract. In his view, the social contract loses its bindingness on the stairs to the scaffold, or when a neighbor is feared more than the sovereign." P. Heugens, M. Kaptein, & H. Van Oosterhout, 2000. "Normative principles for the governance of stakeholder relations." Paper presented at the "Academy of Management Conference" in Toronto: pp. 11–12.
45. F. Fukuyama, 1995. *Trust: The Social Virtues and the Creation of Prosperity*. New York: Free Press.
46. J. H. Nieuwenhuis, 1979. *Drie Beginselen van Contractrecht*. Deventer: Kluwer: p. 17. See also J. Van Oosterhout, P. P. M. A. R. Heugens, and S. P. Kaptein, 2000. 'Normative documents, the contract model, and stakeholder management'. Paper presented at the annual IABS Meeting, ESSEX-JCT, Vermont, March 2000.
47. Ibid., 64.
48. R. H. Coase, 1937. "The nature of the firm." *Economica*, 4. Repr. in J. B. Barney, & W. G. Ouchi (eds.), 1986. *Organizational Economics*. San Francisco: Jossey-Bass Publishers.

49. M. Jensen, & W. Meckling, 1976. "Theory of the firm: managerial behavior, agency costs and capital structure." *Journal of Financial Economics*, 3(4): 305–60.
50. O. E. Williamson, 1975. "*Market and Hierarchies: Analysis and Antitrust Implications.*" New York: Free Press; O. E. Williamson, 1979. "Transaction cost economics: the governance of contractual relations." *Journal of Law and Economics*, 22: 233–61; O. E. Williamson, 1983. "Credible commitments: using hostages to support exchange." *American Economic Review*, 73: 519–40; O. E. Williamson, 1985. *The Economic Institutions of Capitalism*, New York: Free Press; O. E. Williamson, 1984. "Corporate governance." *The Yale Journal*, 93: 1197–1231; O. E. Williamson, 1996. *The Mechanisms of Governance*. New York: Oxford University Press.
51. E. M. Dodd, 1932. "For whom are corporate managers trustees?" *Harvard Law Review*, 1145–63.
52. S. N. Brenner, & E. A. Molander, 1977. "Is the ethics of business changing?" *Harvard Business Review*, 55: 54–65.
53. S. N. Brenner, & P. Cochran, 1991. "The stakeholder theory of the firm: implications for business and society theory and research." Paper presented at the annual meeting of the "International Association for Business and Society," Sundance.
54. T. Donaldson, 1982. *Corporations and Morality*. New York: Prentice Hall, Englewood Cliffs.
55. T. Donaldson, & T. Dunfee, 1999. *Ties that Bind: A Social Contracts Approach to Business Ethics*. Boston: Harvard Business School Press.
56. R. E. Freeman, & W. M. Evan, 1990. "Corporate governance: a stakeholder interpretation." *The Journal of Behavioral Economics*, 4: 337–59; W. M. Evan, & R. E. Freeman, 1993. "A stakeholder theory of the modern corporation: Kantian capitalism." In T. Beauchamp, & N. Bowie (eds.). *Ethical Theory and Business*. New York: Prentice Hall, Englewood Cliffs: pp. 75–93.
57. M. Keeley, 1988. *A Social-Contract Theory of Organizations*. Indiana: University of Notre Dame Press.
58. C. W. L. Hill, & T. M. Jones, 1992. "Stakeholder-agency theory." *Journal of Management Studies*, 2: 131–54.
59. This relates to the transaction costs theory and the agency theory.
60. See also R. M. Cyert, & J. G. March, 1963. *A Behavioral Theory of the Firm*. New York: Prentice Hall, Englewood Cliffs.
61. M. Jensen, & W. Meckling, 1976. "Theory of the firm: managerial behavior, agency costs, and capital structure." *Journal of Financial Economics*, 3(4): 305–60.
62. Ibid., 308.
63. Ibid., 309–10.
64. Ibid., 310.
65. Ibid., 311.
66. O. E. Williamson, 1975. *Market and Hierarchies: Analysis and Antitrust Implications*. New York: Free Press; O. E. Williamson, 1979. "Transaction cost economics: the governance of contractual relations." *Journal of Law and Economics*, 22: 233–61; O. E. Williamson, 1983. "Credible commitments: using hostages to support exchange." *American Economic Review*, 73: 519–40; O. E. Williamson, 1985. *The Economic Institutions of Capitalism*, New York: Free Press; O. E. Williamson, 1984. "Corporate governance." *The Yale Journal*, 93: 1197–231.
67. O. E. Williamson, 1984. "Corporate governance." *The Yale Journal*, 93: 1210.
68. Ibid., 1201.
69. T. Donaldson, & L. E. Preston, 1995. "The stakeholder theory of the corporation: concepts, evidence and implications." *Academy of Management Review*, 20(1): 65–91.
70. R. E. Freeman, 1984. *Strategic Management*. Boston: Pitman Publishing Inc.
71. See, e.g., M. T. Jones, & A. D. Wicks, 1999. "Convergent stakeholder theory." *Academy of Management Review*, 24(2): 206–21.
72. Cited in R. E. Freeman, 1984. *Strategic Management*. Boston: Pitman Publishing Inc.: p. 31.
73. See, e.g., R. E. Freeman, & D. R. Gilbert Jr, 1988. *Corporate Strategy and the Search for Ethics*. Englewood Cliffs, New York: Prentice Hall.
74. See R. E. Freeman, 1984. *Strategic Management*. Boston: Pitman Publishing Inc.

75. T. Donaldson, & L. E. Preston, 1995. "The stakeholder theory of the corporation: concepts, evidence and implications." *Academy of Management Review*, 20(1): 65–91.

76. See R. E. Freeman, & D. L. Reed, 1983. "Stockholders and stakeholders: a new perspective on corporate governance." *California Management Review*, 25(3): 88–106. See also A. F. Alkhafaji, 1989. *A Stakeholder Approach to Corporate Governance: Managing in a Dynamic Environment.* New York: Quorum Books.

77. See A. B. Caroll, 1989. *Business and Society: Ethics and Stakeholder Management.* Cincinnati: South-Western Publishing Company. See also D. J. Wood, 1991. "Corporate social performance revisited." *Academy of Management Review*, 16(4): 691–718. See also M. W. Evan, & R. E. Freeman, 1993. "A stakeholder theory of the modern corporation: Kantian capitalism." In T. Beauchamp, & N. Bowie (eds.). *Ethical Theory and Business.* New York: Prentice Hall, Englewood Cliffs: 75–93.

78. C. W. L. Hill, & T. M. Jones, 1992. "Stakeholder-agency theory." *Journal of Management Studies*, 2: 132.

79. See also P. A. French, 1984. *Collective and Corporate Responsibility.* New York: Columbia University Press: Ch. 7; M. Kaptein, 1998. *Ethics Management: Auditing and Developing the Ethical Content of Organizations.* Dordrecht: Kluwer Academic Publishers.

80. That is the FNB.

CHAPTER 6

1. Pursey Heugens is Assistant Professor of Strategic Management at the Department of Management at the John Molson School of Business, Concordia University, Montreal. Hans van Oosterhout is Assistant Professor of Institutions and Institutional Design at the Department of Business-Society Management at the Rotterdam School of Management, Erasmus University, Rotterdam.

2. M. Kaptein, 1998. *Ethics Management: Auditing and Developing the Ethics Content of Organizations.* Dordrecht: Kluwer Academic Publishers, Ch. 1.

3. Among others, Herman Daly and Barbara Ward focused on environmental responsibilities for future generations. See P. Hawken, 1993. *The Ecology of Commerce: A Declaration of Sustainability.* New York: Harper Business.

4. This issue came to the fore following the publication of the report of the Club of Rome and the oil crisis of 1973. In this context, the resolution of economic and social issues is seen as a prior condition for environmental sustainability. In 1987, the World Commission on Environment and Development (the Brundtland Commission) described sustainable development as: "meeting the needs of the present without compromising the ability of the future generations to meet their own needs." In 1992, the United Nations Earth Summit advanced proposals for giving practical substance to the concept of sustainable development. The proposals of the UN Earth Summit provide the basis for the business view of sustainable development and the associated shift in focus to the continuity and survival of the company's business activities.

5. See also J. Elkington, 1997. *Cannibals with Forks: The Triple Bottom Line of 21st Century Business.* Capstone.

6. Ibid.

7. See M. Kaptein, F. Marincowitz, & I. Sloekers, "Codes of Conduct of Global Corporations." *Erasmus Report Series*, 2002. This research project is part of a broader study on the effectiveness of corporate codes in cooperation with Ans Kolk and Rob van Tulder.

8. The list shows direct responsibilities in so far as they can be traced back to the relevant stakeholders. For instance, ethical investment is not included in the list under the heading "stockholders" since it is indirectly addressed via other stakeholders.

9. O. E. Williamson, 1985. *The Economic Institutions of Capitalism.* New York: Free Press: p. 44.

10. H. Simon, 1957. *Administrative Behavior.* New York: Macmillan. 2nd edn.: p. xxiv.

11. P. R. Milgrom, & J. Roberts, 1992. *Economics, Organization and Management*. New York: Prentice Hall, Englewood Cliffs.

12. O. E. Williamson, 1985. *The Economic Institutions of Capitalism*. New York: Free Press: p. 47.

13. O. E. Williamson, 1993. "Calculativeness, trust, and economic organization." *Journal of Law and Economics*, 36, April: 453–86.

14. Organizations that offer their constituents sufficient compensation to reward them for their contributions are therefore said to be in equilibrium. This phenomenon is known in the literature on organization theory as the Barnard–Simon equilibrium. H. A. Simon, 1976. *Administrative Behavior*. New York: Macmillan. 3rd edn.; C. J. Barnard, 1938. *The Functions of the Executive*. Cambridge, MA: Harvard University Press.

15. O. E. Williamson, 1985. *The Economic Institutions of Capitalism*. New York: Free Press.

16. When this happens, the relation becomes a mini-society or mini-state with an array of norms that far exceed immediate exchange and its connected processes. Discrete contracts are focused exclusively on efficient economic exchange. In the discrete contracting approach contractors are expected not to value anything in their mutual relationships outside the stake they have in realizing the terms of the contract. Relational contracting holds that the relation between individuals is the fundamental unit of analysis of contracts. (I. R. MacNeil, 1980. *The New Social Contract: An Inquiry into Modern Contractual Relations*. New Haven, London: Yale University Press).

17. P. Heugens, M. Kaptein, & H. Van Oosterhout, 2000. "Six normative principles for the governance of stakeholder relations." Paper presented at the "Academy of Management Conference" in Toronto.

18. See, e.g., J. Pratt, & R. Zeckhauser (eds.). *Principals and Agents: The Structure of Business*. Boston: Harvard Business School Press.

19. O. E. Williamson, 1990. "The firm as a nexus of treaties: an introduction." In M. Aoki, B. Gustafsson, & O. E. Williamson (eds.). *The Firm as a Nexus of Treaties*. London: Sage: 1–25.

20. See, e.g., R. M. Axelrod, 1984. *The Evolution of Cooperation*. New York: Basic Books; R. Hardin, 1982. *Collective Action*. Baltimore: Johns Hopkins University Press.

21. P. Milgrom, & J. Roberts, 1992. *Economics: Organization and Management*. New York: Prentice Hall, Englewood Cliffs.

22. We have made an inventory of the dilemmas faced by the employees of nine international corporations during 1994–9. A total of 37 meetings was held with a total of 648 people, who were asked to record their own dilemmas after having played an ethics dilemma game. This resulted in 992 dilemmas, most of which were then presented to a panel of employees at each company. In composing these panels, the aim was to reflect the full range of job-related backgrounds and attitudes towards the organization and the outside world. During the 24 panel meetings that were held, we continued to inquire into the minimum preconditions that should exist in the relationship to make it possible to resolve the relevant dilemmas. The panel members were asked to put themselves into the shoes of the various stakeholders who were involved in the relevant dilemmas and to indicate which criteria they themselves used for judging the integrity of their stakeholders. Which rights do stakeholders have, and how do those relate to the integrity of the corporate relationship with its stakeholders? The resulting list of 28 criteria was then examined in more detail to identify their interconnectedness and to classify them in groups. This made it possible to link the criteria to the 4 contracting problems and to give these groups of criteria a general term per problem. These groups ultimately resulted in the 5 principles. The concrete criteria can be discussed in terms of each principle. In addition, they can also be used as questions in surveys of stakeholders regarding the integrity of the corporation in their relationship.

23. These meso-principles can be used as criteria for evaluating any corporate social contract or contracting stakeholder. In this sense, they transcend the corporation and form part of the social contract for business.

24. P. Heugens, M. Kaptein, & H. Van Oosterhout, 2000. "Normative principles for the governance of stakeholder relations." Paper presented at the "Academy of Management Conference" in Toronto.

25. Ibid.
26. C. D. Beugré, 1998. *Managing Fairness in Organizations*. Westport: Quorum Books; F. B. Bird, 1996. *The Muted Conscience: Moral Silence and the Practice of Ethics in Business*. Westport: Quorum Books; S. Blok, 1978. *Lying: Moral Choice in Public and Private Life*. New York: Pantheon Books; G. Brock, 1998. "Are corporations morally defensible?" *Business Ethics Quarterly*, 8(4): 703–21; G. D. Cameron, 2000. "Ethics and equity: enforcing ethical standards in commercial relationships." *Journal of Business Ethics*, 23: 161–72; T. K. Das, & B. S. Teng, 1998. "Between trust and control: developing confidence in partner cooperation in alliances." *Academy of Management Review*, 23(3): 491–512; J. G. Dees, 1992. "Principals, agents and ethics." In N. E. Bowie, & R. E. Freeman (eds.). *Ethics and Agency Theory: An Introduction*. New York: Oxford University Press; E. Deutsch, 1975. "Equity, equality and need: what determines which value will be used as the basis for distribution justice." *Journal of Social Issues*, 31(3): 137–49; T. Donaldson, & T. W. Dunfee, 1999. *Ties that Bind: A Social Contracts Approach to Business Ethics*. Boston: Harvard Business School Press; A. Etzioni, 1988. *The Moral Dimension: Toward a New Economies*. New York: Free Press. E. Freeman, & W. Evan, 1990. "Corporate governance: a stakeholder interpretation." *Journal of Behavioral Economics*, 19(4): 337–59; R. E. Freeman, 1994. "The politics of stakeholder theory: some future directions." *Business Ethics Quarterly*, 4(4): 409–21; J. B. Gassenheimer, F. S. Houston, & J. C. Davis, 1998. "The role of economic value, social value, and perceptions of fairness in inter-organizational relationship retention decisions." *Journal of Academy of Marketing Science*, 26(4): 322–37; D. Gauthier, 1986. *Morals by Agreement*. Oxford: Clarendon Press; A. O. Hirschman, 1970. *Exit, Voice and Loyalty*. Cambridge, MA: Harvard University Press; M. Keeley, 1988. *A Social-Contract Theory of Organizations*. Indiana: University of Notre Dame Press; J. M. Calton, & L. J. Lad, 1995. "Social contracting as a trust-building process of network governance." *Business Ethics Quarterly*, 5(2): 271–96; I. R. MacNeil, 1980. *The New Social Contract: An Inquiry into Modern Contractual Relations*. New Haven and London: Yale University Press; L. L. Nash, 1990. *Good Intentions Aside: A Manager's Guide to Resolving Ethical Problems*. Boston, MA: Harvard Business School Press; R. A. Philips, 1997. "Stakeholder theory and a principle of fairness." *Business Ethics Quarterly*, 7(1): 51–66; D. Preston (ed.), Clarkson Center for Business Ethics 1999. *Principles of Stakeholder Management*. University of Toronto; J. Rawls, 1971. *A Theory of Justice*. Cambridge, MA: Harvard University Press; D. Reed, 1999. "Stakeholder management theory: a critical theory perspective." *Business Ethics Quarterly*, 9(3): 453–83. D. C. Robertson, & W. T. Ross Jr, 1995. "Decision-making on ethical issues: the impact of a social contract perspective." *Business Ethics Quarterly*, 5(2): 213–40; S. R. Saldu, 1995. "Insider trading and the social contract." *Business Ethics Quarterly*, 5(2): 313–28; G. Sartori, 1970. "Concept misformation." *American Political Science Review*, 64(4): 1033–57; S. P. Shapiro, 1987. "The social control of impersonal trust." *American Journal of Sociology*, 93: 623–58; N. A. Shankman, 1999. "Reframing the debate between agency and stakeholder theories of the firm." *Journal of Business Ethics*, 19: 319–34; S. Sharma, & H. Vredenburg, 1998. "Proactive corporate environmental strategy and the development of competitively valuable organizational capabilities." *Strategic Management Journal*, 19(8): 729–53; C. Taylor, 1992: *The Ethics of Authenticity*. Cambridge, MA: Harvard University Press; M. G. Velasquez, 1998. *Business Ethics: Concepts and Cases*. New York: Prentice Hall, Englewood Cliffs. 3rd edn.; S. Waddock, & N. Smith, 2000. "Relationships: the real challenge of corporate global citizenship." *Business & Society Review*, 105(1): 47–62.
27. M. G. Velasquez, 1998. *Business Ethics: Concepts and Cases*. New York: Prentice Hall, Englewood Cliffs, 3rd edn.
28. T. Donaldson, 1982. *Corporations and Morality*. New York: Prentice Hall, Englewood Cliffs, p. 53.
29. M. G. Velasquez, 1998. *Business Ethics: Concepts and Cases*. New York: Prentice Hall, Englewood Cliffs. 3rd edn.
30. F. B. Bird, 1996. *The Muted Conscience: Moral Silence and the Practice of Ethics in Business*. Westport: Quorum Books, p. 50.
31. T. W. Dunfee, N. C. Smith, & W. T. Ross Jr, 1999. "Marketing ethics." *Journal of Marketing*, July: 14–32.

32. F. B. Bird, 1996. *The Muted Conscience: Moral Silence and the Practice of Ethics in Business.* Westport: Quorum Books, p. 82.
33. T. Donaldson, & T. W. Dunfee, 1999. *Ties that Bind: A Social Contracts Approach to Business Ethics.* Boston: Harvard Business School Press.
34. A crucial variable in this respect is the availability of significant information to all contractors. In case of sufficient disclosure, the building of trust between contractors will be greatly facilitated.
35. S. Sharma, & H. Vredenburg, 1998. "Proactive corporate environmental strategy and the development of competitively valuable organizational capabilities." *Strategic Management Journal*, 19(8): 729–53.
36. L. T. Hosmer, 1998. "Lessons from the wreck of the Exxon Valdez." *Business Ethics Quarterly*, 8(1): 109–22.
37. F. B. Bird, 1996. *The Muted Conscience: Moral Silence and the Practice of Ethics in Business.* Westport: Quorum Books.
38. M. G. Velasquez, 1998. *Business Ethics: Concepts and Cases.* New York: Prentice Hall, Englewood Cliffs, 3rd edn.
39. R. A. Philips, 1997. "Stakeholder Theory and a Principle of Fairness." *Business Ethics Quarterly*, 7(1): 51–66.
40. Etzioni defines symmetry as "a willingness to accord other comparable people, under comparable circumstances, the same standing or right." A. Etzioni, 1988. *The Moral Dimension: Toward a New Economics.* New York: The Free Press: p. 43.
41. T. Donaldson, 1989. *The Ethics of International Business.* New York: Oxford University Press.
42. See, e.g., I. R. MacNeil, 1980. *The New Social Contract: An Inquiry into Modern Contractual Relations.* New Haven and London: Yale University Press.
43. J. M. Calton, & L. J. Lad, 1995. "Social contracting as a trust-building process of network governance." *Business Ethics Quarterly*, 5(2): p. 284.
44. A. O. Hirschman, 1970. *Exit, Voice and Loyalty.* Cambridge, MA: Harvard University Press.
45. As Donaldson and Dunfee have put it in the context of ISCT: a "dissenting member of a community who is distressed about a particular authentic norm may elect to leave the community." T. Donaldson, & T. W. Dunfee, 1999. *Ties that Bind: A Social Contracts Approach to Business Ethics.* Boston: Harvard Business School Press: p. 19.
46. I. R. MacNeil, 1980. *The New Social Contract: An Inquiry into Modern Contractual Relations.* New Haven and London: Yale University Press.
47. A. O. Hirschman, 1970. *Exit, Voice and Loyalty.* Cambridge, MA: Harvard University Press.
48. Freeman states this condition as "the principle of externalities." R. E. Freeman, 1994. "The politics of stakeholder theory: some future directions." *Business Ethics Quarterly*, 4(4): 409–21.
49. T. W. Dunfee, N. C. Smith, & W. T. Ross Jr, 1999. "Marketing ethics." *Journal of Marketing*, July: 30.
50. R. C. Solomon, 1992. *Ethics and Excellence: Cooperation and Integrity in Business.* New York: Oxford University Press, p. 171.
51. See T. M. Jones, & A. C. Wick, 1999. "Convergent stakeholder theory." *Academy of Management Journal*, 24(2): 206–21.
52. See M. Kaptein, 1998. *Ethics Management: Auditing and Developing the Ethics Content of Organizations.* Dordrecht: Kluwer Academic Publishers, Ch. 1 and 2.1.
53. See P. M. A. R. Heugens, M. Kaptein, & J. van Oosterhout, 2001. "Ties that grind: an empirical test of a typology of social contracting problems." Paper presented at the annual meeting of the "Academy of Management," Washington, DC, 3–8 August.
54. See P. Schwartz, & B. Gibb, 1999. *When Good Companies do Bad Things: Responsibility and Risk in an Age of Globalization.* New York: John Wiley & Sons.
55. According to Bob Solomon, virtually all Aristotelian virtues can also be seen as corporate virtues. He considers "honesty, fairness, trust and toughness" as basic corporate virtues. Other corporate virtues that Solomon recognizes are "friendliness, honor, loyalty, shame, competition, caring and compassion." He considers justice "the ultimate virtue of corporate life." He derives the tableau of virtues from specific characteristics of corporate

functioning. Still, it seems to be an arbitrary selection because a number of coincidental characteristics are named. See: R. C. Solomon, 1992. *Ethics and Excellence: Cooperation and Integrity in Business*. New York: Oxford University Press.

56. M. Kaptein, 1998. *Ethics Management: Auditing and Developing the Ethics Content of Organizations*. Dordrecht: Kluwer Academic Publishers.

57. Well-known examples include the explosion of *The Challenger*, the gas leak at Union Carbide in Bhopal, the sinking of the *Herald of Free Enterprise*, the downfall of Barings, and the *Exxon Valdez* oil disaster. Other types of case concern, e.g., the violation of human rights, legal transgressions, pay-offs, business espionage, internal fraud, corruption, the abuse of power, and incompatible sideline activities.

58. The difference between the qualities study and the research into contractual principles is that the aim of the latter study was to examine the principles required to govern contractual relationships. In this qualities study, the focus is on the structural or cultural shortcomings of corporations. The core difference is that the qualities study is internally orientated (what the corporation is), instead of externally orientated (what the corporation does), without forgetting that the former (organizational qualities) is always connected to the latter (relational principles).

59. See, for the organizational risks of unclear norms and values, R. A. Cooke, 1991. "Danger signs of unethical behavior: how to determine if your firm is at ethical risk." *Journal of Business Ethics*, 10: 249–53; J. A. Waters, & F. Bird, 1989. "Attending to ethics in management." *Journal of Business Ethics*, 8: 493–7.

60. R. C. Ford, & W. D. Richardson, 1994. "Ethical decision making: a review of the empirical literature." *Journal of Business Ethics*, 13: 205–21.

61. See, e.g., R. C. Baumhart, 1961. "How ethical are businesses?" *Harvard Business Review*, 39: June–August: 6; S. N. Brenner, & E. A. Molander, 1977. "Is the ethics of business changing?" *Harvard Business Review*, 55, January–February: 57–71; J. B. Ciulla (ed.), 1998. *Ethics: The Heart of Leadership*. Westport: Preager; R. C. Ford, & W. D. Richardson, 1994. "Ethical decision making: a review of the empirical literature." *Journal of Business Ethics*, 13: 205–21; W. H. Hegarty, & H. P Sims, 1978. "Some determinants of unethical decision behavior: an experiment." *Journal of Applied Behavior*, 63: 451–7; R. Jackhall, 1988. *Moral Mazes: The World of Corporate Managers*. New York: Oxford University Press; G. R. Laczniak, & P. E. Murphy, 1991. "Fostering ethical marketing decisions." *Journal of Business Ethics*, 10: 259–71; J. A. Patrick, & J. F. Quinn, 1997. *Management Ethics: Integrity at Work*. Thousands Oaks: Sage Publications; W. E. Stead, D. L. Worrell & J. G. Stead, 1990. "An integrative model for understanding and managing ethical behavior in business organizations." *Journal of Business Ethics*, 9: 233–42; L. K. Treviño, G. R. Weaver, D. G. Gibson, & B. L. Toffler, 1999. "Managing ethics and legal compliance: what works and what hurts?" *California Management Review*, 41(2): 142; J. C. Wimbush, & J. M. Shepard, 1994. "Towards an understanding of ethical climate: its relationship to ethical behavior and supervisory influence." *Journal of Business Ethics*, 13: 637–47; M. Zey-Ferrell, & O. C. Ferrell, 1982. "Role-set configuration and opportunity as predictors of unethical behavior in organizations." *Human Relations*, 35(7): 587–604.

62. See, e.g., M. Bovens, 1998. *The Quest for Responsibility: Accountability and Citizenship in Complex Organizations*. Cambridge: Cambridge University Press; L. K. Treviño, 1986. "Ethical decision making in organizations: a person-situation interactionist model." *Academy of Management Review*, 11: 601–17.

63. See, among others, P. Shrivastava, 1994. "Technological and organizational roots of industrial crisis: lessons from Exxon Valdez and Bhopal." *Technological Forecasting and Social Science*, 45: 237–53.

64. See L. K. Treviño, G. R. Weaver, D. G. Gibson, & B. L. Toffler, 1999. "Managing ethics and legal compliance: what works and what hurts?" *California Management Review*, 41(2): 142.

65. Examples are provided by K. Blanchard, & N. V. Peale, 1988. *The Power of Ethical Management: Why the Ethical Way is the Profitable Way in your Life and in your Business*. New York: Morrow; M. W. Boy, & J. W. Jones, 1997. "Organizational culture and employee counterproductivity." In R. A. Giacalone, & J. Greenberg (eds.). *Antisocial Behavior in*

Organizations. Sage Publications: 172–84; S. Carmichael, 1992. "Countering employee crime." *Business Ethics: A European Review,* 1, July: 180–4; R. A. Cooke, 1991. "Danger signs of unethical behavior: how to determine if your firm is at ethical risk." *Journal of Business Ethics,* 10: 249–53; R. C. Solomon, & K. Hanson, 1985. *It's Good Business.* New York: Atheneum.

66. See, e.g., M. Bovens, 1998. *The Quest for Responsibility: Accountability and Citizenship in Complex Organizations.* Cambridge: Cambridge University Press; T. Donaldson, 1982. *Corporations and Morality.* New York: Prentice Hall, Englewood Cliffs; D. L. Carter, 1990. "Drug-related corruption of police officers: a contemporary typology." *Journal of Criminal Justice,* 18: 85–98.

67. D. L. McCabe, & L. K. Treviño, 1993. "Academic dishonesty: honor codes and other contextual influences." *Journal of Higher Education,* 64(5): 522–38.

68. R. C. Solomon, & K. Hanson, 1985. *It's Good Business.* New York: Atheneum: p. 149.

69. See, e.g., F. B. Bird, 1996. *The Muted Conscience: Moral Silence and the Practice of Business Ethics.* Westport: Quorum Books; L. K. Treviño, & K. A. Nelson, 1999. "Managing business ethics: straight talk about how to do it right." New York: John Wiley & Sons; E. W. Morrison, & F. J. Milkes, 2000. "Organizational silence: a barrier to change and development in a pluralistic world." *Academy of Management Review,* 25(4): 706–25.

70. L. K. Treviño, G. R. Weaver, D. G. Gibson, & B. L. Toffler, 1999. "Managing ethics and legal compliance: what works and what hurts?" *California Management Review,* 41(2): 139.

71. Examples are given by I. P. Akaah, & E. A. Riordan, 1989. "Judgments of marketing professionals about ethical issues in marketing research: a replication and extension." *Journal of Marketing Research,* 26(1): 112–20; L. Falkenberg, & I. Herrenans, 1995. "Ethical behaviors in organizations directed by the formal or informal systems." *Journal of Business Ethics,* 14: 133–43; R. C. Ford, & W. D. Richardson, 1994. "Ethical decision making: a review of the empirical literature." *Journal of Business Ethics,* 13: 205–21; D. J. Fritzsche, & H. Becker, 1983. "Ethical behavior of marketing managers." *Journal of Business Ethics,* 2: 291–9; W. H. Hegarty, & H. P. Sims, 1978. "Some determinants of unethical decision behavior: an experiment." *Journal of Applied Behavior,* 63: 451–7; G. R. Laczniak, & E. J. Interrieden, 1987. "The influence of stated organizational concern upon ethical decision making." *Journal of Business Ethics,* 6: 297–307; L. K. Treviño, & K. A. Nelson, 1999. *Managing Business Ethics: Straight Talk about How to Do it Right.* John Wiley & Sons.

72. M. Kaptein, 1998. *Ethics Management: Auditing and Developing the Ethics Content of Organizations.* Dordrecht: Kluwer Academic Publishers.

73. M. Kaptein, 1998. *Ethics Management: Auditing and Developing the Ethics Content of Organizations.* Dordrecht: Kluwer Academic Publishers. Ch. 3.

CHAPTER 7

1. For a description of a number of requirements that a sustainability management process should satisfy, see: M. Kaptein, & J. Wempe, 1998. "The ethics report: a means of sharing responsibility." *Business Ethics: A European review,* 7(3): 132.

2. See also J. B. Ciulla (ed.), 1998. *Ethics: The Heart of Leadership.* Westport: Preager.

3. See, e.g., L. K. Treviño, L. P. Hartman, & M. B. Brown, 2000. "Moral person and moral manager: how executives develop a reputation for ethical leadership." *California Management Review,* 42(4): 128–42.

4. See J. Weber, 1997. "Leadership." In P. Werhane, & R. E. Freeman (eds.). *Encyclopedic Dictionary of Business Ethics.* Blackwell: p. 363.

5. See also what Burns calls "transformational leadership." J. M. Burns, 1978. *Leadership.* New York: Harper & Row.

6. One factor that complicates this matter is that to improve the organizational culture, change is required from precisely those managers who achieved success in the culture as it was and still is (i.e. in its less-than-optimal form).

7. Securing management commitment (phase 1) sets the process of implementation (phase 3 of the process illustrated in Figure 7.1) in motion. In phase 1 a number of implementation issues can arise that will be discussed later in this chapter.

8. Treviño *et al.* point out the risks of such an approach. L. K. Treviño, G. R. Weaver, D. G. Gibson, & B. L. Toffler, 1999. "Managing ethics and legal compliance: what works and what hurts." *California Management Review*, 41(2): 131–51.

9. The Hammurabi Code dates back to about 1700 BC and was long recognized as the earliest systematic collection of laws in writing with regard to the conduct and fees of surgeons. The Codex Theodosianus appeared between AD 435 and AD 437 and was the first collection of constitutions of the Roman emperors. The Codex Juris Canonici originated in 1582 and has prevailed since 1918 as the official canon law of the Roman Catholic Church.

10. *New Encyclopaedia Britannica* 1974/2: p. 1034.

11. S. Weller, 1988. "The effectiveness of corporate codes of ethics." *Journal of Business Ethics*, 7(5): 389–95; J. Brooks, 1989. "Corporate codes of ethics." *Journal of Business Ethics*, 8(2): 117–29.

12. With regard to business gifts, for instance, a wide variety of implicit codes is in use: no gifts may be accepted; a limit varying from $10 to $1000; acceptable as long as it is reported; acceptable, as long as it can be consumed within 24 hours; acceptable, as long as its value does not exceed the value of the business gifts of the company itself; any goods received are shared or raffled off among the staff; goods received of any significant value are displayed in a glass case or stored in the office basement; any goods received are donated to charity; and anything of value is welcome.

13. The *Concise Oxford Dictionary* 1982: p. 180.

14. A mere summary of legal obligations cannot therefore be considered a business code of integrity.

15. See, e.g., S. N. Brenner, & E. A. Molander, 1977. "Is the ethics of business changing?" *Harvard Business Review*, 55: 57–71; M. Mathews Cash, 1987. "Codes of ethics: organizational behavior and misbehavior." *Research in Corporate Social Performance and Policy*. JAI Press Inc., 9: 107–30; S. Weller, 1988. "The effectiveness of corporate codes of ethics." *Journal of Business Ethics*, 7(5): 389–95; Touche Ross, 1988. *Ethics in American Business*. New York: The Ethics Resource Center 1994. *Ethics in American Business: Policies, Programs and Perceptions. Report of a Landmark Survey of US Employees*, Washington, DC. In their empirical research, Treviño *et al.*, review only those companies that already have codes. To our mind, conducting a longitudinal survey is the only way to establish anything about the effective of codes. L. K. Treviño, G. R. Weaver, D. G. Gibson, & B. L. Toffler, 1999. "Managing ethics and legal compliance: what works and what hurts." *California Management Review*, 41(2): 131–51.

16. S. P. Sethi, 1999. "Challenges of conduct for global business: prospects and challenges of implementation." In D. Preston (ed.). *Principles of Stakeholder Management*. Clarkson Centre for Business Ethics: 9–23.

17. For a detailed discussion of several of these issues, see M. Kaptein, & J. Wempe, 1998. "Twelve Gordian Knots when developing a code of conduct." *Journal of Business Ethics*, 17: 853–69.

18. See M. Kaptein, & J. Wempe, 1998. "The ethics report: a means of sharing responsibility." *Business Ethics: A European Review*, 7(3): 131–9.

19. In the environmental area the European Eco-Management and Audit Scheme (EMAS) or ISO 14001 could be used as a basis. These documents comprise relatively well-crystallized norms, which in theory should be applicable to all businesses. In the area of employee relations, several standards have now been developed. One set of norms, SA 8000, focuses primarily on employees' rights and working conditions. SA 8000 is particularly suitable for companies with offices or branches in developing countries or that purchase from developing countries.

20. See, e.g., D. A. Kolb, 1974. "On management and the learning process." In D. Kolb, I. Rubin, & J. McIntyre (eds). *Organizational Psychology: A Book of Readings*. Englewood Cliffs, NJ: Prentice Hall. 2nd edn.

21. For an in-depth discussion of the basic steps of the ethics process, see M. Kaptein, 1998. *Ethics Management: Auditing and Developing the Ethical Content of Organizations.* Dordrecht: Kluwer Academic Publishers; M. Kaptein, & J. Wempe, 1998. "Twelve Gordian Knots when developing a code of conduct." *Journal of Business Ethics,* 17: 853–69. See also G. Pearson, 1995. *Integrity in Organizations: An Alternative Business Ethic.* London: McGraw-Hill Book Company; L. S. Paine, 1994. "Managing for organizational integrity." *Harvard Business Review,* 72: 107–17; P. MacLagan, 1998. *Management and Morality: A Developmental Perspective.* London: Sage Publications.

22. L. S. Paine, 1994. "Managing for organizational integrity." *Harvard Business Review,* 72: 107–17.

23. L. K. Treviño, G. R. Weaver, D. G. Gibson, & B. L. Toffler, 1999. "Managing ethics and legal compliance: what works and what hurts." *California Management Review,* 41(2): 131–51.

24. D. McGregor, 1960. *The Human Side of Enterprise.* New York: McGraw-Hill.

25. See, e.g., J. A. Petrick & J. F. Quinn, 1997. *Management Ethics: Integrity at Work.* Sage; D. T. LeClair, O. C. Ferrell, & J. P. Freadrich, 1998. *Integrity Management: A Guide to Managing Legal and Ethical issues in the Workplace.* Florida: University of Tampa Press.

26. L. S. Paine, 1994. "Managing for organizational integrity." *Harvard Business Review,* 72: 112.

27. L. K. Treviño, G. R. Weaver, D. G. Gibson, & B. L. Toffler, 1999. "Managing ethics and legal compliance: what works and what hurts." *California Management Review,* 41(2): 131–51.

28. For the risks of the compliance approach, see: L. S. Paine, 1994. "Managing for organizational integrity." *Harvard Business Review,* 72: 107–17.

29. Moreover, any organization that is involved in a law suit that concerns the dismissal of one or more employees does not stand much of a chance if these individuals can cite circumstances such as "no one ever told me," "everyone does it (especially management)," "I was put under pressure," and "the code is being undermined from every angle."

30. See M. Kaptein, & J. Wempe, 1998. "Twelve Gordian Knots when developing a code of conduct." *Journal of Business Ethics,* 17: 853–69. See also, e.g., R. E. Berenbeim, 1999. *Global Corporate Ethics Practices: A Developing Consensus.* The Conference Board.

31. M. Kaptein, 1998. *Ethics Management: Auditing and Developing the Ethical Content of Organizations.* Dordrecht: Kluwer Academic Publishers, Ch. 7.

32. For the way that ethics audits are conducted, see M. Kaptein, 1998. *Ethics Management: Auditing and Developing the Ethical Content of Organizations.* Dordrecht: Kluwer Academic Publishers.

33. See also S. Zadek, 1998. "Balancing performance, ethics, and accountability." *Journal of Business Ethics,* 17: 1421–41; C. Gonella, A. Pilling, & S. Zadek, 1998. *Making Values Count: Contemporary Experience in Social and Ethical Accounting, Auditing, and Reporting.* London: The Association of Chartered Certified Accountants, Research Report 57; M. McIntosh, D. Leipziger, K. Jones, & G. Coleman, 1998. *Corporate Citizenship: Successful Strategies for Responsible Companies.* London: Financial Times/Pitman Publishing.

34. M. Kaptein, 1998. *Ethics Management: Auditing and Developing the Ethical Content of Organizations.* Dordrecht: Kluwer Academic Publishers.

35. It is often useful during the roll out of a code to have departments give an account of the activities they have initiated to operationalize the code. Such an audit encourages people to focus on the code and furnishes management with information on the progress of implementation. Moreover, such a roll out audit can promote the internal discussion and exchange of information with respect to embedding the code in everyday business practice.

36. See also Global Reporting Initiative, 2000. *Sustainability Reporting Guidelines on Economic, Environmental and Social Performance.* www.globalreporting.org.

37. R. S. Kaplan, & D. P. Norton, 1996. *The Balanced Scorecard.* Harvard Business School Press.

38. See also: R. Gray, D. Owen, & C. Adams, 1996. *Accounting and Accountability: Changes and Challenges in Corporate Social and Environmental Reporting.* New York: Prentice Hall; D. Wheeler, & M. Sillanpää, 1997. *The Stakeholder Corporation: A Blueprint for Maximizing Stakeholder Value.* London: Pitman Publishing; S. Zadek, P. Pruzan, & R. Evans, 1997. *Building Corporate Accountability: Emerging Practices in Social and Ethical Accounting, Auditing and Reporting.* London: Earthscan Publications Ltd.; Global Reporting Initiative

2000. *Sustainability Reporting Guidelines on Economic, Environmental, and Social Performance.* Boston.

39. See, e.g., S. Waddock, & N. Smith, 2000. "Corporate responsibility audits: doing well by doing good." *Sloan Management Review,* Winter: 75–83.

40. This also is the basic assumption of financial reporting. See, e.g., R. Watts, & J. Zimmerman, 1986. *Positive Accounting Theory.* New York: Prentice Hall. See for a description of theoretical frameworks used to analyze corporate social reporting: R. Gray, D. Owen, & C. Adams, 1996. *Accounting and Accountability: Changes and Challenges in Corporate Social and Environmental Reporting.* New York: Prentice Hall.

41. B. Greif, & T. Westerwoudt, 13 June 1990. "Dikke vrienden; de vervlechting van belangen tussen Nederland en Shell." ["*Close friends, the interwoven interests of the Netherlands and Shell*"] the *NRC.*

42. For up-to-date information on the Shell Report, please read further at www.shell.com.

SUBJECT INDEX

NAME INDEX